Great Powers and Outlaw States

The presence of Great Powers and outlaw states is a central but under-explored feature of international society. In this book, Gerry Simpson describes the ways in which an international legal order based on 'sovereign equality' has, since the beginning of the nineteenth century, accommodated the Great Powers and regulated outlaw states. In doing so, the author offers a fresh understanding of sovereignty, which he terms juridical sovereignty, to show how international law has managed the interplay of three languages: the language of Great Power prerogative, the language of outlawry (or anti-pluralism) and the language of sovereign equality. The co-existence and interaction of these three languages is traced through a number of moments of institutional transformation in the global order from the Congress of Vienna to the 'war on terrorism'. The author offers a way of understanding recent transformations in the global political order by recalling the lessons of the past, in particular in relation to the recent conflicts in Kosovo and Afghanistan.

GERRY SIMPSON is a Senior Lecturer in the Law Department at the London School of Economics where he teaches Public International Law and International Criminal Law. He has been a Legal Adviser to the Australian Government on international criminal law and was part of the Australian delegation at the Rome Conference in 1998 to establish an international criminal court. He has also worked for several non-governmental organisations and appears regularly in the media discussing the law of war crimes and the law on the use of force in international law. Previous publications include *The Law of War Crimes* (1997) with Tim McCormack and *The Nature of International Law* (2001).

CAMBRIDGE STUDIES IN INTERNATIONAL AND COMPARATIVE LAW

Established in 1946, this series produces high quality scholarship in the fields of public and private international law and comparative law. Although these are distinct legal sub-disciplines, developments since 1946 confirm their interrelation.

Comparative law is increasingly used as a tool in the making of law at national, regional and international levels. Private international law is now often affected by international conventions, and the issues faced by classical conflicts rules are frequently dealt with by substantive harmonisation of law under international auspices. Mixed international arbitrations, especially those involving state economic activity, raise mixed questions of public and private international law, while in many fields (such as the protection of human rights and democratic standards, investment guarantees and international criminal law) international and national systems interact. National constitutional arrangements relating to 'foreign affairs', and to the implementation of international norms, are a focus of attention.

Professor Sir Robert Jennings edited the series from 1981. Following his retirement as General Editor, an editorial board has been created and Cambridge University Press has recommitted itself to the series, affirming its broad scope.

The Board welcomes works of a theoretical or interdisciplinary character, and those focusing on new approaches to international or comparative law or conflicts of law. Studies of particular institutions or problems are equally welcome, as are translations of the best work published in other languages.

A list of books in the series can be found at the end of this volume

Great Powers and Outlaw States

Unequal Sovereigns in the International Legal Order

Gerry Simpson

PUBLISHED BY THE PRESS SYNDICATE OF THE UNIVERSITY OF CAMBRIDGE
The Pitt Building, Trumpington Street, Cambridge, United Kingdom

CAMBRIDGE UNIVERSITY PRESS
The Edinburgh Building, Cambridge, CB2 2RU, UK
40 West 20th Street, New York, NY 10011–4211, USA
477 Williamstown Road, Port Melbourne, VIC 3207, Australia
Ruiz de Alarcón 13, 28014 Madrid, Spain
Dock House, The Waterfront, Cape Town 8001, South Africa

http://www.cambridge.org

First published 2004

Printed in the United Kingdom at the University Press, Cambridge

Typeface Swift 10/13 pt.   *System* LaTeX 2$_\varepsilon$ [TB]

A catalogue record for this book is available from the British Library

Library of Congress Cataloguing in Publication data
Simpson, Gerry J.
Great powers and outlaw states: unequal sovereigns in the international
legal order / Gerry Simpson.
    p.   cm. – (Cambridge studies in international and comparative law)
Includes bibliographical references and index.
ISBN 0 521 82761 2 – ISBN 0 521 53490 9 (pbk.)
1. Equality of states.   2. Great powers.   3. State-sponsored terrorism.   I. Title.
II. Cambridge studies in international and comparative law (Cambridge, England: 1996)
KZ4012.S57   2003
341.26 – dc21   2003048908

ISBN 0 521 82761 2 hardback
ISBN 0 521 53490 9 paperback

Contents

Foreword

International lawyers have become used to living with the tension between such formal rules as state equality or state sovereignty (it is rarely noted that sovereignty is a *formal* rule), on the one hand, and the pervasive facts of inequality and power differentials among states, on the other. The usual response is to relegate inequality to the realm of the political and contingent, and to take comfort in the positive values of formal equality, which after all allows for changes in hierarchies of power over time: just as everyone is free to dine at the Ritz, so everyone may aspire to permanent membership of the Security Council, one of international law's few concessions to formal hierarchy.

Dr Simpson's approach is different and strikingly original. No formalist, he sees in the interplay between equality and inequality, between great power and outlaw status, 'the essence of international law since at least 1815'. International law is a dialogue of power, and its uneven application to different states is fundamental, not accidental. The powerful we will always have with us, and even changes in the cast, or caste, of the powerful will be fewer than we might imagine. And this is not a contingency: formal equality is a device established by the powerful in order to underwrite and prolong their power. At the same time they can engage in the various forms of ostracism – particularly crude these days – which has over time relegated now China, now Vietnam, now Iraq, now Iran, to the outer reaches.

As a descriptive sociology of the international legal system, Dr Simpson's vision is of compelling interest, combining wit, lucidity and breadth of reference. But he does not put this work forward merely as a form of descriptive sociology; it is somehow prescriptive – a vision not only of an 'is' but an 'ought', based on the various imperatives of power. Unless this form of realism is integrated into our understanding of the subject we will continue – Simpson implies – to be trapped in a sterile formalism, an international law of small places.

I hope that is not true. It seems to me that the struggle for equality – equality of a kind, even in the very different conditions of the international system – has a constraining value, and that we should struggle against the idea that, for example, France may use force where Monaco or Andorra may not, just as we should struggle against the view that 'civilisation' (and 'Western civilisation' at that) ever could be, or could have been, a criterion for legal personality. And yet Dr Simpson's long historical account has, among its many values, the special value of the shaking of a stereotype, of making us think whether our own visions of the subject can remain the same. It is thoroughly to be recommended.

JAMES CRAWFORD
LAUTERPACHT RESEARCH CENTRE FOR INTERNATIONAL LAW
UNIVERSITY OF CAMBRIDGE
JUNE 2003

Preface

International law had barely escaped its 'ontological' phase when it was promptly declared dead.[1] The coroner, Slavoj Žižek, declared that the 'war on terrorism' has delivered the *coup de grâce* to an international order based on sovereign equality and capable of constraining power.[2] The global political order was now composed of enemies and friends, not sovereign equals. Others, of a less morbid persuasion, have argued instead that there is a new constitution afoot. On this view, international law has been not fatally wounded by the events of 2001 but transformed by them. The Great Powers are certainly 'impatient with the diplomatic niceties of international law enforcement' but international law, ever adaptable and endlessly pragmatic, will accommodate the new imperatives.[3]

These arguments are not absurd but they do reflect two common vanities in discussions of public international law and its role in international affairs: a tendency to accept the terminal impotence of the discipline and a belief in the novelty of 'new world orders' (a collective obsession since the Twin Towers fell).

In contrast, the image of international legal order presented in this book is of a system marked, since 1815 by a certain continuity of structure. Juridical sovereignty underpins this structure but this sovereignty

---

[1] See Thomas Franck, *Fairness in International Law and Institutions* (1995), 6 (heralding international law's post-ontological phase).

[2] Slavoj Žižek, 'Are we in a war? Do we have an enemy?', *London Review of Books* 24:10 (23 May 2002), 3 ('the new configuration [post-11 September 2001] entails the end of international law which, at least from the onset of modernity, regulated relations between states').

[3] T. Mills-Allen, 'US plans anti-terror raids', *Sunday Times*, 4 August 2002, 1 (paraphrasing Washington 'insiders'). For work along these lines see Michael Glennon, *The Limits of Law, Prerogatives of Power: Interventionism after Kosovo* (2001).

is protean and flexible and is marked through the interplay of three languages: the languages of Great Power prerogative, outlawry (or anti-pluralism) and sovereign equality. In other words, the categories of Great Powers, friends and enemies (or outlaws), and sovereign equals are each important to our understanding of the international legal order. In early 2003, as I wrote this preface, the Great Powers were once again preparing for war with an outlaw state. In the public pronouncements of world leaders at this time, these three languages and categories co-existed, sometimes uncomfortably.

The Great Powers, emboldened by the easy projection of authority in Kosovo and Afghanistan, geared up for a new intervention. In speeches and official statements, the United States and the United Kingdom governments have spoken of the need to apply power, sometimes in the absence of explicit UN Security Council authorisation.[4] This is often characterised as 'unilateralism' but I want to read this behaviour as part of a particular tradition of Great Power prerogative and privilege instituted in 1815. It is important that the Great Powers see themselves as acting in the shadow of international law. But, often, the shadow they see is their own. They make and remake (but rarely break) international law. In this tradition, the Great Powers are loath simply to step outside the law and use brute force. Instead, there has been a practice of willing into existence new legal regimes in moments of constitutional crisis in the international system. These new regimes are characterised by the presence of a phenomenon I want to call *legalised hegemony*: the realisation through legal forms of Great Power prerogatives. In this book I describe this tradition, its internal struggles, its external projections and legitimation through law, and its awkward relationship with law's egalitarian face.

At the same time, the public pronouncements of key officials are careful to invoke the international community at every turn. The Great Powers act not in the name of narrow self-interest but on behalf of a community of interests or, better still, of humanity itself, credentialising their mission with reference to common values. A necessary adjunct to this rhetorical and legal tradition is the presence of states and groups operating outside the universal community, acting in the cause

---

[4] E.g. Julian Borger, 'Straw threat to bypass UN over attack on Iraq', *The Guardian*, 19 October 2002, 1 (quoting UK Foreign Secretary Jack Straw stating: 'We are completely committed to the United Nations route, if that is successful. If, for example, we end up being vetoed . . . then of course we are in a different situation').

of inhumanity.[5] Wars are fought not between adversaries but between the international community and international renegades or between the universal and the particular, e.g. 'human rights' and 'Islamic terrorism'. This language has become more transparent in recent years. The word 'Manichean' has become a cliché of political commentary as observers struggle to come to terms with this idea. The central figure in all this is the outlaw state: a figure whose estrangement from the community of nations and demonisation by that community has long been required as part of the project of creating and enforcing international 'society'.

International law is important in the constitution and regulation of outlaw states. These states are mad, bad or dangerous, or all three. Some are incapable of forming the correct attitude towards the international legal order. They lack 'a reciprocating will' (mad). Some are serial violators of the dominant mores of the international legal order (bad). Others are a threat to the international legal order because of some internal malfunction or propensity to disorder (dangerous). In each case, law supervises the relationship between the community and the outlaw. James Lorimer wrote in 1888 of the need to respond to terror with 'the terrors of the law'. These 'terrors' have been regularly applied to those outside the 'family of nations'. As I indicate in this book, outlaw states are outside the law in one sense but thoroughly entwined in its terrors in another. This dual aspect to the position of outlaw states will be emphasised in some of the later chapters where a link will be drawn between the nineteenth-century practices of demarcation and the contemporary manifestations of it in the designation of states as 'criminal' or 'rogue'. Sometimes this connection is made explicit. Philip Henscher, writing in *The Independent* in early 2001, adopted nineteenth-century language in discussing the then-incumbent Taliban regime in Afghanistan when he remarked: 'Of course, the horrors perpetrated by the regime place it beyond the pale of any standard of civilisation.'[6] In 2002, the US National Security Council celebrated the fact that (in Afghanistan) 'our enemies have seen the results of what civilized nations can, and will, do against regimes that harbor, support, and use terrorism'.[7]

---

[5] Carl Schmitt, *The Concept of the Political*, trans. and ed. George Schwab, 54.
[6] Philip Henscher, 'We should still talk to the Taliban', *The Independent*, Monday Review, 5 March 2001, 5.
[7] *US National Security Strategy*, September 2002 at http://www.whitehouse.gov/nsc/nss3.html.

I describe this tendency as *anti-pluralism*: the practice of making legal distinctions between states on the basis of external behaviour or internal characteristics.[8] This book is also, then, about outlaw states in the international legal order. It describes their encasement in the legal order and separation from it, their role as threat and necessity and the relationship between the idea of outlawry and law's pluralist face.

Finally, international law is also a language of equality. Indeed, one of the most pervasive images of international legal order posits a community of equals engaging in relations through juridical forms. Equality is regarded as integral to sovereignty. In a lecture on the future of international law, in 1920, Lassa Oppenheim called the equality of states 'the indispensable foundation of international society'.[9] More recently Bruno Simma has asserted that 'all states in the world possess suprema potestas and are thus not placed in any kind of hierarchy, international law must proceed from the basis of equal sovereignty of states'.[10] This principle is usually described as *sovereign equality*. To what extent, though, are these articulations of sovereign equality accurate characterisations of the sovereignty order? The idea of sovereign equality does much work in international law but, for my purposes, it has two primary roles. First, it parlays into a commitment to a pluralist international legal order (bluntly, one in which state diversity is tolerated). Or as Vattel put it: 'Nations treat with one another as bodies of men and not as Christians or Mohammedans.'[11] Second, the principle of sovereign equality conveys the idea of an egalitarian international legal order (one in which states are legally equal). There is a tension between the pluralist, egalitarian aspect and the anti-pluralist, hierarchical (or hegemonic) aspect. This interaction establishes the conditions for what I call *juridical sovereignty*.

In this book, then, I offer a fresh understanding of sovereignty grounded in a complex of norms and ideas in which the competing claims of legalised hegemony, anti-pluralism and sovereign equality are arranged and ordered. In doing so, I tell a story about the Great Powers,

---

[8] In a later discussion of the war on Afghanistan and the treatment of the detained prisoners on Guantanamo Bay, I discuss also the way in which the position of outlaw personnel, i.e. Taliban and al-Qa'ida prisoners under US control, reflects the position of the outlaw state in international law: in a lawless space but subject to intense scrutiny and surveillance. See below at pp 343–6.

[9] L. Oppenheim, *The Future of International Law*, Carnegie Endowment for International Peace, Pamphlet No. 39 (1920), 20.

[10] B. Simma, ed., *The Charter of the United Nations: A Commentary* (1994), 87.

[11] Vattel, *The Law of Nations*, ed. J. Chitty (1863), 195.

outlaw states and sovereign equality in the context of the post-1815 international legal order.

. . . .

What is at stake in all this? Every author must face his or her own moments of crisis. Why write? Why write *this*? I suspect there are intellectual and political imperatives (perhaps, even literary values) at work here, as well as serendipity. Intellectually, I wanted to explain a mystery or explore an intuition I had about the international legal order. It seemed to me that the presence of Great Powers and outlaw states was a central but under-explored feature of international society. This, alone, made the project at least plausible. In particular, I have always been frustrated at the mismatch between law's universalist pretensions and its partialities and discriminations. But more than this, the endless debates about humanitarian intervention or anticipatory self-defence or sovereign immunity seemed irresolvable, or at least unfruitful, without a consideration of identity. Much as we disparaged primitive realists for their billiard ball projections in which states were undifferentiated, our commitment to statism was just as remarkable. States were juridically equivalent on the orthodox view and any analysis of, say, sovereign immunity or humanitarian intervention had to proceed from this assumption. And yet, these doctrines seemed to be shaped by the specific identity of the protagonists as much as by a claim to universal application. Immunity was disposable in cases involving outlaws but tenaciously applied to the personnel of the Great Powers themselves. Self-defence expanded to meet the requirements of these powers but was suddenly subject to contraction when outlaws such as Vietnam, in 1979, attempted to justify their actions under the doctrine. This was, it seemed to me, not just international law perverted or applied unfairly. This was the essence of international law since at least 1815. The way international law worked, at least some of the time, was dependent on the identity of the protagonists involved.

At a very basic level, the book also has something to say about some of the most controversial matters in international law and politics. To what extent ought the international community be composed of like-minded states? Is there an advantage to be gained by restricting state diversity in pursuit of the democratic peace? Ought our treatment of 'uncivilised' states in the nineteenth century give us pause when we use the language of democracy, civilisation and decency today? Should international legal rules operate equally as between the Great Powers and the other states or is it unrealistic to expect Russia or the United States or France to be bound by the same restrictions on, say, the use of force as the rest of the international community?

In all this there is the inevitable allure of studying high politics (the Great Powers) and international deviance (outlaw states), each set against the apparent innocence of an international legal order based on sovereign equality. Politically, this book was written as a way of reinterpreting international law's past by rejecting its bogus doctrinal innocence without collapsing it into mere politics. I wanted to understand the Great Powers and outlaw states as legal concepts, as relevant to legality as sovereign equality. The idea was to make a stand for relative autonomy without thereby suggesting that law was emancipation or progress to the brutish materialism of politics or international relations.

More specifically, the writing of this book was motivated by three experiences. First, I had long been drawn to international law theory. The people who interested me were described (though rarely self-described) as 'theorists' and their work simplified complex doctrine and complicated apparently simple propositions about the world. In my own work, I decided to begin tracing the development of an idea across time and study how theories participated in or modified this development. I was interested in the effects of, for example, 'liberalism' on the way people imagined what they were doing.

Second, I had been doing work on 'sovereignty' in international law, e.g. why indigenous peoples did not possess it and how ethnic groups got it. This work seemed unsatisfactory so I shifted from thinking of sovereignty as a given (the problem then being who should acquire it) to conceptualising it as a problem. Here, I became interested in the changes in the form of sovereignty wrought by the adoption of certain legal techniques, e.g. the grading of sovereignty in international organisations and the distinction in theory and practice between good and bad sovereigns.

Third, I had attended two international diplomatic conferences and sat in on various UN and governmental meetings on international criminal law. Here, I had noticed an increasing tendency to distinguish between members of the international community in good standing and dissident states or outlaws, and a long-standing requirement that special privileges be secured for powerful states. As a consequence, at these conferences sovereign equality was quickly displaced by all sorts of hierarchies. Sovereign equality operated in the plenaries but there were small groups of powerful states in meetings euphemistically called 'informal informals', good citizen middle-ranking states in 'like-minded groups' and representatives from 'outlaw' states like Iran and Iraq exiled in coffee shops, ruminating under puffs of smoke. I became interested in explaining or understanding these hierarchies as part of a larger system of equality and hierarchy.

This book then combines these interests. It is a book about sovereignty (but understood in broader terms than my work on self-determination had permitted and in narrower terms than those used by many political scientists), a book that would satisfy my theoretical inclinations (understood here as an interest in the development of ideas across time) and a book that would help explain the puzzle of international law and organisations (being hierarchical and egalitarian, pluralist and anti-pluralist at the same time).

. . . .

Acknowledgements

This book is the product, and I hope a reflection, of a lengthy period of study. I would like to thank José Alvarez for his encouragement at the beginning of this process, his forthright criticism and urgings throughout the writing of the thesis and forbearance at its conclusion. The other members of my doctoral committee, Brian Simpson and James Hathaway, each read drafts of several chapters and offered generous (in both senses of that word) written comments on them. They each prompted me to rethink the substance and presentation of the thesis. Virginia Gordan has provided helpful advice throughout and I benefited greatly from courses taught by Don Regan, Thomas Green, Joseph Raz and José Alvarez in Ann Arbor, John Rankin at Aberdeen, Maurice Copithorne at the University of British Columbia and David Kennedy at Harvard as well as from conversations in Ann Arbor with Vladimir Djeric, Gunnar O'Neill and Christian Tietje.

The University of Melbourne and the Australian National University each supported me during sabbaticals in 1995 and 1999 (during which some parts of the thesis were written). I would like to thank the Dean at Melbourne, Michael Crommelin and the two Deans who supported me in Canberra, Tom Campbell and Michael Coper. My sabbatical in 1999 was spent at Harvard Law School where I was a Visiting Scholar. The London School of Economics has proved a congenial home for me since I joined the Faculty there in 2000 and I completed this book while working at that institution. The thesis was presented in some form or other to responsive audiences in Helsinki, Glasgow, Boston, Edinburgh, Washington DC and Melbourne. Catriona Drew and Susan Marks tolerated, with good grace, my views on the subject of outlaws. Expert research assistance was provided by Ruth Tomlinson, Sonya Sceats, Gus Van-Harten, Jennifer Welch, Neville Sorab and Hannah Ashton-Suissa. I would like to thank, too, Finola O'Sullivan, Jackie Warren and Sara Adhikari at Cambridge University Press for their diligent work on this book. I have been blessed with an unusually lively and intimate group of international law colleagues over the years. In Melbourne: Kris Walker, Pene Mathew, Hilary Charlesworth, Ian Malkin, Di Otto and Tim McCormack. In Canberra: Don Greig, Robert McCorquodale, J. P. Fonteyne, Martin Phillipson and Anne Orford. In London: Chaloka Beyani, Christine Chinkin, Chris Greenwood, Declan Roche, Max du Plessis and Fabricio Guariglia.

Catriona Drew, Nick Wheeler and Deborah Cass each read a number of chapters and made telling contributions to the development of the ideas in the book.

Two parts of this book have been published previously. Chapter 6, 'The Great Powers, Sovereign Equality and the Making of the UN Charter' appeared in a Festschrift for Don Greig in the *Australian Yearbook of International Law* and an early version of Chapter 9 appeared under the title, 'Two Liberalisms' in the *European Journal of International Law*.

I am unable to offer one of those unconvincing apologies for time spent away from children since my daughters frequently interrupted the writing of the book. But perhaps Hannah and Rosa should be thanked. Because, as my Grandmother would have said, when they were born, they brought their love with them, and because, but for them, the book would be much longer.

This book is for Deborah.

Abbreviations

AJIL	*American Journal of International Law*
ASIL	American Society of International Law
BFSP	*British and Foreign State Papers*
BYIL	*British Yearbook of International Law*
CWILJ	*California Western International Law Journal*
DO	Dumbarton Oaks
EC	European Community
EJIL	*European Journal of International Law*
EJIR	*European Journal of International Relations*
EU	European Union
FRY	Federal Republic of Yugoslavia
GA	(United Nations) General Assembly
GATT	General Agreement on Tariffs and Trade
ICLQ	*International and Comparative Law Quarterly*
ICJ	International Court of Justice
ICJ Rep.	*International Court of Justice, Reports of Judgments, Advisory Opinions and Orders*
ICTY	International Criminal Tribunal for the Former Yugoslavia
ILC	International Law Commission
ILM	*International Legal Materials*
ILR	*International Law Reports*
IMF	International Monetary Fund
IO	International Organisation
IR	International Relations
ISAF	International Security Assistance Force
KB	King's Bench
KFOR	Kosovo Force
LNTS	League of Nations Treaty Series

Nato	North Atlantic Treaty Organisation
NIEO	New International Economic Order
NILR	*Netherlands International Law Review*
NLR	*National Law Review*
NYUJILP	*New York University Journal of International Law and Policy*
OECD	Organisation for Economic Cooperation and Development
OPEC	Organisation of the Petroleum Exporting Countries
OSCE	Organisation for Security and Cooperation in Europe
PCAJ	Permanent Court of Arbitral Justice
PCIJ	Permanent Court of International Justice
RDILC	*Revue de droit international et de législation comparée*
Res.	Resolution
RIAA	Reports of International Arbitral Awards
SC	Security Council
SCOR	Security Council Official Records
UKMIL	United Kingdom Materials in International Law
UN	United Nations
UNCIO	United Nations Conference on International Organisation
UNGAOR	United Nations General Assembly Official Records
UNITAR	United Nations Institute for Training and Research
UNTAET	United Nations Transitional Administration in East Timor
UNTS	United Nations Treaty Series
VCLT	Vienna Convention on the Law of Treaties
WTO	World Trade Organisation
YLJ	*Yale Law Journal*

Part I Introduction

1   Great Powers and outlaw states

> The history of the international system is a history of inequality *par excellence*.[1] [T]he sovereignty and equality of states represent the basic constitutional doctrine of the law of nations.[2]

In 1602, Spain and The Netherlands were embroiled in a long running war in Europe and this conflict carried over into hostilities between Dutch trading companies and Portuguese and Spanish maritime interests in East Asia. During one of many engagements on the high seas, an affiliate of the Dutch East Indies Company had captured a Portuguese vessel named 'The Catherine'.[3] On 9 September 1604, a Prize Court in Amsterdam declared the capture lawful and held that the vessel belonged to the Dutch company.[4] The matter probably would have rested there were it not for the fact that among the company shareholders were members of a Mennonite sect who disapproved of war, refused to accept their share of the profits and threatened to establish a competing company in France.[5]

In the same year, Hugo Grotius was about to turn twenty-one. He took a keen interest in the Catherine case and spent the remainder of the year composing his first major work, *De jure praedae* (Commentary on the Law of Prize and Booty), a defence of the Dutch seizure and a sketch of a theory of international law to be fully realised in his classic *De jure*

---

[1] R. Tucker, *The Inequality of States*, 8.

[2] I. Brownlie, *Principles of Public International Law*, 5th edn, 289.

[3] See Martin Wight, 'Western Values in the International System' in H. Butterfield and M. Wight (eds.), *Diplomatic Investigations: Essays in the Theory of International Politics*, 104–5.

[4] See H. Grotius, *De jure praedae commentarius* (1605), *The Classics of International Law* (ed. J. B. Scott), Preface, xiii. The transcript of the proceedings was destroyed by fire shortly after the hearing.

[5] *Ibid.*, xiii, 1, 4–5 and 283–317.

belli et pacis (The Law of War and Peace). *De jure praedae* begins with the words:

A situation has arisen that is truly novel and scarcely credible . . . namely: that those men who have been so long at war with the Spaniards . . . are debating as to whether or not, in a just war and with public authorisation, they can rightfully despoil an exceedingly cruel enemy . . .[6]

This may not be the opening sentence in the literature of international law but it baptises the classical Grotian period.[7] *De jure praedae*, then, inaugurates a particular tradition in international law and does so by characterising certain states as beyond the pale. But *De jure praedae* began the Grotian period in an incongruous manner. This conception of international law that draws legal distinctions among states on the basis of their internal politics or moral characteristics did not become the dominant tradition in the Grotian period following the Peace of Westphalia.

One of the arguments pursued in this book is that the Grotian sensibility seen in the first paragraphs of *De jure praedae* (I describe it as antipluralism) remained in abeyance until the nineteenth century when it again became an explicit part of the international legal structure with the introduction of a distinction between civilised and uncivilised states. This distinction was in turn reflected in the idea that there was a 'Family of Nations' embedded in a wider system of states. Indeed, it was another Grotian principle, that of sovereign equality (or at least that element of it I call existential equality), that informed the practice of states *until* the nineteenth century, was revived by the UN Charter commitment to state equality in the middle of the twentieth century and has remained influential among writers and scholars throughout the periods under discussion.

The *De jure praedae* conception of international law that distinguishes the 'exceedingly cruel', uncivilised or outlaw state from the civilised or democratic state has waxed and waned throughout the modern history of international law. At various times, Turkey, China, Bolshevik Russia and Weimar Germany have been assigned bandit or uncivilised status. With the abolition of the standard of civilisation and the rise of the

---

[6] *Ibid.*, 1.

[7] Martin Wight saw this opening paragraph as a description of 'a dramatic confrontation between the state that is law-abiding and the delinquent state (it is also a confrontation between the state with constitutional processes and the despotic state)'. See Wight, 'Western Values', 104.

Charter conception of pluralism and equality, though, this *De jure praedae*, anti-pluralist tradition seemed to be in permanent recess. However, in recent years, the Charter conception of equality has been undermined by the tendency to characterise some states as 'outlaws'. This motif has (re)surfaced in the practice of international law (in relation to the likes of Afghanistan, Iraq and Serbia) and has become prominent again in some recent international legal theory. Such states are variously characterised as indecent, illiberal and criminal.[8] Liberal confidence in the post-cold war era has produced a flurry of these outlaw states. When the Chancellor of Austria, Wolfgang Schussel, pleaded that Austria was 'not a pariah state' (following the success of far right elements in the 2000 elections there), he was responding to this ascendant tradition.[9] This book, then, partly is concerned with outlaw states and it seeks to understand their role through the interplay of two conceptions of international legal order, an inclusive conception (pluralism) and an exclusive conception (anti-pluralism).

Alongside this distinction between what John Westlake called 'states with good breeding'[10] and delinquent or outlaw states, is another distinction; this one operating to distinguish an elite group of states, commonly referred to as the 'Great Powers', and a large mass of middle and smaller powers who defer to these larger powers in the operation and constitution of international legal order. These Great Powers occupy a position of authority within each of the legal regimes that has arisen since 1815. Sometimes these regimes are constructed around loose affiliations of interested Great Powers (the Vienna Congress), at other times the role of the Great Powers is laid out in the detailed provisions of an originating document (The United Nations Charter). In each instance, these powers have policed the international order from a position of assumed cultural, material and legal superiority. A key prerogative of this position has been a right to intervene in the affairs of other states in order to promote some proclaimed community goal.

[8] J. Rawls, *The Law of Peoples*; A.-M. Slaughter, 'International Law in a World of Liberal States' (1995) 6 *European Journal of International Law*, 503–38 at 510; F. Tesón, 'The Kantian Theory of International Law' (1992) 92:1 *Columbia Law Review*, 53–102. Chapter 10, in particular, takes up the distinction between criminal states and illiberal states in more detail.

[9] *Guardian Weekly* 10 February 2000, Editorial, 'A Question of Principle on Austria', 1. The Foreign Minister, Benito Ferrero-Waldner, went further, insisting 'that Austria is not Naziland', N. Acherson, 'Haider the Pariah Finds an Ally', *Guardian Weekly*, 13 February 2000, 1.

[10] J. Westlake, *Collected Papers*, 6.

These two sets of distinctions are linked (though this is not a primary concern of the book).[11] The Great Powers often identify or define the norms that place certain states in a separate normative universe and there is an identifiable connection between the propensity of the Great Powers to intervene on behalf of the international community and the labelling as outlaws some of those states subject to intervention.[12]

This book, then, is about the idea that states can be differentiated in law according to their moral nature, material and intellectual power, ideological disposition or cultural attributes. The conventional image of international law as a system in which states are at least equal *in law* (we might call this the sovereign equality assumption) is incomplete. Instead, what I want to call *juridical sovereignty* is constructed around an interaction between sovereign equality and two legal forms in which distinctions between states are mandated or authorised. I term these forms *anti-pluralism* and *legalised hegemony*. To take up Grotius's language, some states are placed in the category of 'exceedingly cruel enemies' (outlaws) while others form an elite group of nations acting 'with public authorisation' through legalised hegemony (Great Powers). Each of these categories challenges the image of a system based on equally positioned sovereigns transacting through international legal forms. The international legal order described in this book is composed of unequal sovereigns.[13]

I argue, further, that sovereign equality as a background principle of international law contains three separate ideas. I call these formal equality, legislative equality and existential equality. I suggest that while states are formally equal within the system, their legislative and existential equality has traditionally been compromised by the presence of,

---

[11] The particular ways in which Great Powers construct 'outlaws' could be the subject of another equally large study.

[12] See Chapter 12.

[13] By international legal order I mean the legal system created by states to regulate inter-state affairs. Of course, there are other ways of defining international law. I have adopted a classic textbook definition which (perhaps over-)emphasises the statist roots of international law (see, e.g. M. Dixon, *Textbook on International Law*, 2). International legal order could also be characterised as the law of individuals, states and non-state actors in the international system. I have chosen the conventional definition because the system remains, in important ways, statist. Norms are generated by the activity of states and are attempts to regulate the behaviour of states. The death of the state has been exaggerated by some globalisation theorists in recent years (for an argument along these lines see P. Hirst, 'The Global Economy – Myths and Realities' (1997) 73:3 *International Affairs* 409–27). If anything globalisation is likely to result in some rearrangement of the hierarchy of states rather than their abolition.

respectively, legalised hegemony and anti-pluralism. It is the relationships and structures engendered by these compromises that produce juridical sovereignty.

Let me illustrate all this by reference to the gestation of the recently adopted Statute for a Permanent International Criminal Court. The Statute is an example of the way in which international law is structured around this opposition between equality, on the one hand, and these two forms of hierarchy, on the other. During the drafting process, two problems of organisational design appeared repeatedly. The first concerned the role of the Great Powers in the operation of the proposed Court. The Court is intended to possess jurisdiction over four categories of crimes and acquires it either through a state consent mechanism or by referral of certain matters from the Security Council.[14] In addition, the Council can act to prevent matters from coming before the Court. This power was thought necessary because of the Security Council's special role in and jurisdiction over threats to the peace, breaches of the peace and acts of aggression under the Charter.[15] This rationale, though, did not prevent some states from worrying that the Security Council's powers under the Rome Treaty 'would introduce into the Statute a substantial inequality between States, members of the Security Council and those that were not members, and, as well, between the permanent members of the Security Council and other states'.[16] In its final form the Statute reflects both the requirements of equality (the consent and complementarity mechanisms) and the needs of legalised hegemony (the referral and 'veto' power of the Council).[17]

---

[14] Rome Statute for an International Criminal Court, UN Doc. A/CONF. 183/9; (1998) 37 ILM 998, Articles 5, 12, 13. See, too, the Independent Prosecutor's powers established under Articles 18 and 19.

[15] W. Schabas, *Introduction to the International Criminal Court*; A. Cassese, *The Rome Statute for an International Criminal Court*.

[16] Draft Statute for an International Criminal Court, GAOR. 49th Sess. Supp. No. 10 (A/49/10), 88. See, too, Security Council Resolution 1422 (securing a one-year (renewable) immunity for the peace-keeping forces of non-state parties from the jurisdiction of the ICC) and the 'Article 98 Agreements' concluded between the United States and a number of other states.

[17] This referral power, of course, mirrors an already existing power to bring into existence criminal courts in specific situations. This hegemony was challenged, unsuccessfully, in the two early interlocutory hearings on jurisdiction in *Tadic*. See *Tadic*, Trial Chamber Decision on the Defence Motion on Jurisdiction (10 August 1995) at http://www.un.org/icty/ind-e.htm (decisions); and *Tadic*, Appeals Chamber Decision on Interlocutory Appeal on Jurisdiction, (2 October 1995), Case No. IT-94-1-AR72, reprinted in (1995) 105 ILR 419 at http://www.un.org/icty/ind-e.htm.

A second concern, this time related to the tension between equality and anti-pluralism, arose in debates over the Court's universality. This concern was reflected in discussions at the Sixth Committee over the likely extent of adherence, on the part of states, to the Court's statute. Was the Court to be a truly universal body engaging all of the world's states or was there a risk that the Statute might be ratified by only a small number of like-minded countries, giving, in the International Law Commission's words, 'the impression of a circle of "virtuous" states as between whom, in practice, cases requiring the involvement of the Court would not arise'?[18]

In the end, the Court's statute was adopted by a vast majority of delegates at Rome but these concerns did not disappear. The Statute gives a prominent, though diluted, role to the Security Council, a role some commentators found questionable given the political nature of the Council and the judicial function of the Court. Equally, while the Statute was adopted by a large number of states not all states supported the Court. The United States was a prominent dissenter but among its allies on this matter were the likes of Syria, Iran, China and Iraq. At least some of these states have regularly found themselves, or placed themselves, outside 'the virtuous circle' of states.[19] Commonly, some of them are referred to as outlaws or pariah states. The fear, then, is that the International Criminal Court may become another particularistic institution and part of the deepening constitutionalism of the liberal project; aspiring to universality but remaining relevant only to the good citizens of the international order.

Large parts of this book concern the way in which international organisations such as the International Criminal Court are constructed around these pluralist/anti-pluralist and hegemonic/egalitarian tendencies. Before continuing, though, I want to clear away a possible misconception about the purpose of this book. This is not a book in which I demonstrate that the principle of sovereign equality is a fiction. I am more interested in breaking sovereign equality into its constituent units and re-ordering it than in dismissing it altogether and, in fact,

---

[18] Draft Statute, 47.

[19] The United States' antipathy towards the court can be viewed as a complaint that the ICC is not particularistic enough (see American Servicemen's Act, at http://www.wfa.org/issues/wicc/dodaspatext.html). The preferred American model for international criminal law is one that envisages the application of criminal standards to illiberal regimes and their personnel. The ICTY and the ICTR are more typical of this vision.

I have important points to make about the role of sovereign equality in establishing the originating 'grundnorms' of the international legal order. What I do suggest is that an understanding of sovereignty is incomplete without a full appreciation of the way legalised hierarchies (anti-pluralism and legalised hegemony) structure sovereignty, modify sovereign equality and produce juridical sovereignty. I do not claim that international lawyers lack some instinctive sense of the inadequacies of the sovereign equality principle in explaining the operation of the international legal order. All international law scholars could, no doubt, identify several departures from the strong idea of sovereign equality (which I take to encompass formal, existential and legislative equality). However, there has not been, as far as I am aware, a recent attempt to systematise these departures into a fresh understanding of sovereignty. Indeed, while many international lawyers would be familiar with many of the examples I give of legalised hierarchies (especially the contemporary examples), there is still a tendency to describe sovereign equality in terms of legislative equality, existential equality and formal equality (as if by merely opposing this basket of legal equalities with political inequality, one can capture what sovereign equality means).

One way to view juridical sovereignty (as I have defined it) is to contrast it with the classical view of international law where the state system is organised around a strong principle of sovereign equality. The equality of states, it is argued, has been the defining quality of the system since 1648. This Westphalian era is contrasted with a *pre*-Westphalian period in which hierarchy and centralised authority were the dominant features. I reject this view of the international legal order. In this book, as I have indicated, I argue that the structuring idea of the international system in its modern period (1815–2000) has adopted the form of a 'dialectic' between hierarchical and egalitarian models of inter-state relations.[20] This dialectic has taken two forms. In the first, there is a relationship between hegemonic structures of international governance (the constitutional preponderance of the Great Powers, legalised hegemony) and egalitarian tendencies (the legal equality of states). In the second, a

[20] For descriptions of this shift from equality to hierarchy see, e.g. C. H. Alexandrowicz, *An Introduction to the History of the Law of Nations in the East Indies*; W. A. Phillips, *The Confederation of Europe: A Study of the European Alliance, 1813–1823, as an Experiment in the International Organization of Peace*, chap. 4, fn. 21; E. Dickinson, *The Equality of States in International Law*, chap. 4, fn. 9; chap. 8, fn. 13; I. Clark, *The Hierarchy of States: Reform and Resistance in the International Order*, chap. 4, fn. 68.

tension arises between two modes of identifying legitimate statehood or according full sovereignty in the international community. These are the universalist, pluralist mode (reflected in the UN Charter and classical liberalism) and the homogeneous, anti-pluralist mode (found in recent 'new' liberal scholarship but endemic in international law since 1815).[21]

The relationship between sovereign equality and legalised hegemony is traced through four moments of constitutional design: Vienna in 1815, The Hague in 1907, San Francisco in 1945 and Kosovo in 1999. The discussion of pluralism and anti-pluralism is organised around three periods: the mid-late nineteenth century, Versailles and San Francisco, and, finally, the post-cold war era. In Chapter 11, I consider the operation of juridical sovereignty in relation to the US-led war on Afghanistan following the attack on the United States in September 2001. In this penultimate chapter I elaborate on two aspects of juridical sovereignty. First, I show how an understanding of the way international norms emerge requires an appreciation of the workings of legalised hegemony and anti-pluralism. The opposing arguments of formalists (arguing against the legality of the war in Afghanistan) and pragmatists (arguing for an expanded understanding of self-defence law) are recast as a shared way of thinking about international law based roughly on an implied theory of sovereign equality. This mode of analysis is grounded on an assumption that international legal rules operate in an egalitarian fashion and are universalisable. I argue in the penultimate chapter that juridical sovereignty can result in the establishment of norms that apply to states differentially depending on the position occupied by those states in the legal order. Put bluntly, the Great Powers are subject to a different set of norms from other states in relation to the permissible limits of self-defence. Similarly, outlaw states cannot call on the same juridical resources (territorial integrity and political independence) to constrain acts of force by other states.

---

[21] Compare Martti Koskenniemi, *From Apology to Utopia: The Structure of International Legal Argument*. While it might be possible to see hierarchy (the reality of state power) as apology and equality (legal fiction) as utopia, the picture is more complicated than this. One attribute of sovereign equality, for example, is that states are bound only by those norms to which they consent – this is part of what Koskenniemi calls 'apology'. On the other hand, the attempt to impose norms from above is characterised as utopian i.e. descending norms. Yet, adopting the system described here, norms produced by legalised hegemony are both imposed by the Great Powers on the majority of states from above (utopia) and are concrete (apology).

The second aspect of juridical sovereignty I take up in this final chapter concerns the treatment of outlaw states and outlaw personnel relating to the war in Afghanistan.

· · · · · · · · · ·

In part, this book is a history of the international legal order in the modern era. Certain forms of historical analysis can be seen as a critique of present practices. Yet, as Lassa Oppenheim remarked in his 1907 article, 'The Science of International Law': 'The history of international law is certainly the most neglected province of it.'[22] The purpose of this analysis is to take history seriously by showing how particular arguments (for example those concerning equality and hierarchy) recur in the international law of the modern period and by signalling the ways in which more familiar theoretical accounts of, and debates about, globalisation, nationalism or sovereignty, seen in the light of this history, have a repetitive, derivative quality about them.[23]

This is what John Vasquez called, 'a theoretical intellectual history with a point' i.e. the history of an idea and the role played by that idea in organising the global order.[24] I am not using history to extract some final meaning of 'sovereignty' or 'hierarchy'. If anything, this book will demonstrate why such definitions must inevitably be shallow and ahistorical.[25] The object is to show how sovereignty undergoes ceaseless modification and re-negotiation in the face of material forces in world politics (e.g. war), institution-building, inter-disciplinary struggle and theoretical contestation. The point of all this is to challenge what I take to be various orthodoxies formed around the doctrine of sovereign equality in international law. Typically, these arrange themselves around two versions. In one, the impression is given that sovereign equality

---

[22] L. Oppenheim, 'The Science of International Law' (1908) 2:2 *American Journal of International Law* 313–56 at 316.

[23] David Kennedy's earlier work is important here (e.g. 'A New Stream of International Law Scholarship' (1998) 7:1 *Wisconsin International Law Journal*, 1–49 and 'Theses about International Law Discourse' (1980) 23 *German Yearbook of International Law*, 353–91).

[24] J. Vasquez, *The Power of Power Politics*, 185.

[25] See R. B. J. Walker, *Inside/Outside: International Relations as Political Theory* (1993): 'the very attempt to treat sovereignty as a matter of definition and legal principle encourages a certain amnesia about its historical and culturally specific character' (166). Having said this, I do not follow Walker in adopting an analysis grounded in a wider cultural critique. My focus is on the way international, legal, institutional and diplomatic culture uses and reinterprets the concept of sovereign equality as part of a broader struggle between hierarchy and equality grounded in wider theoretical debates about the nature of international order, the future direction of internationalism and the role of law in creating and maintaining international order.

was invented at Westphalia and has maintained its hold over international law and diplomatic practice since 1648. From Vattel to Marshall CJ in 1825 through Oppenheim in the early twentieth century and onwards to the UN Charter, this story is repeatedly affirmed.[26] A second version tends to convey an impression of progress towards greater equality among nations and a general historical movement in the direction of universality. According to this version, the international system traditionally embraced a very partial view of what constituted equality. States were excluded arbitrarily from the governing structures of the system, sovereignty was partitioned and inequality was rife. The modern period, then, is seen as having introduced a system in which states, for the first time, are treated equally and in which international law aspires to global coverage.[27]

In the next few chapters, I want to sketch an alternative history that challenges the neat linearity of these accounts. My perspective on the relationship between legalised hierarchies and sovereign equality can be seen as cyclical. I argue that sovereign equality has risen and fallen in tune with the imperatives of statecraft, the professional needs of international lawyers and in response to the diversity and particularities of various institutional projects in international law and diplomacy.

I seek to take a long view of this process while maintaining some sort of limits over my subject area. I employ two methods in doing this. First, I have chosen the period beginning in 1815 because it marks the modern period of institutions.[28] In this period, there is the rise of institutionalism, embryonically at Vienna, and more fully at The Hague and Versailles, as well as the introduction of a self-conscious egalitarianism

---

[26] See discussion in Chapter 2.   [27] For a broader assessment, see Chapter 3.
[28] When I use the term 'institutions' I mean a set of phenomena narrower than Hedley Bull's definition of institutions (which can include the machinery of diplomacy and the norms and processes of international law itself (H. Bull, *The Anarchical Society: A Study of Order in World Politics*, 13, 31–2)) but broader than those definitions that equate institutions with organisations. When I describe 1815 as the beginning of the modern period of institutions I mean that, for the first time, at Vienna, a group of states organised themselves, using legal forms, as a directorate with the intention of constitutionalising their dominance and projecting that dominance through treaties and in a series of regular meetings. Institutionalism is closely allied to legalised hegemony on this interpretation. Contrast the Vienna Congress with more ad hoc arrangements growing out of the 1713 Utrecht Conference and the Peace of Westphalia. But see, for a regional institution pre-dating Vienna and envisaging regular meetings of a coalition of states, 'The Peace of Lodi 1454' in M. Wight, *Systems of States*, 111. The pre-1815 history of the idea is recounted in Chapter 2. See, too, Kooijmans, *The Doctrine of Legal Equality of States*, 100.

and constitutional hierarchies in the work of congresses and conventions.[29] The post-Vienna era also represents a time of great expansion for the idea of international law. For the first time, relations between (and, to an extent, within) the European core and the non-European periphery demanded some form of regulation beyond the purely imperial.[30] This expansion was accompanied by an anxiety concerning the validity of alternative civilisations, a universalising project that sought to bring these civilisations into the fold and an exclusionary strategy designed to differentiate Western from non-Western societies. As Holbraad argues, this resulted in a regime that 'introduced divisions in the hierarchy of states more marked than those that had existed before'.[31] If this is accurate then the Concert period must have placed a great deal of pressure on the image of sovereign equality.[32]

Second, 1815 is chosen in preference to, say, 1789 or 1818 because the Vienna settlement was a moment of conscious international regime construction. Of course, all dates are artificial. They suggest that history is capable of being compartmentalised into before and after periods. I do not deny that there were traces of institutionalism in the pre-1815 period (e.g. at Westphalia in 1648 or during the Athenian Confederacy). The year 1815, then, is a point on a continuum rather than a radical break. The Great Power coalition was forming during the Napoleonic Wars and both the idea of equality and the Westphalia settlement were challenged by Napoleon throughout the late eighteenth and early nineteenth centuries.[33] Following Vienna, the Concert system underwent further modifications and refinements. However, 1815 represents a 'constitutional moment' for the international system in which 1815, 1907, 1945 and 1999 are each moments of revolution or reaction. In each case, these revolutionary or reactionary moments encapsulate the developments of

---

[29] E.g. states began to sign treaties in alphabetical order rather than some other political order of precedence. See, generally, A. Nussbaum, *A Concise History of the Law of Nations*, 192. Some writers go further, asserting that 1815 marks the moment when the Great Powers enter into legal, as opposed to political, relations for the first time. See, e.g. H. Wehberg, *The Problem of an International Court of Justice*, trans. C. G. Fenwick.

[30] In this period, relations with independent non-European states became a matter of acute moment. These states included Siam, China, Turkey and the newly created Latin American states (Brazil gaining its independence in 1822). See Nussbaum, *Concise History*, 191.

[31] C. Holbraad, *Middle Powers in International Politics*, 19.

[32] Torbjorn Knutsen, *A History of International Relations Theory*, 133.

[33] A political history of the period could just as well begin with 14 July 1789 (Bastille Day). The revolution begins then and Vienna is a consequence of the revolution.

a previous period and prefigure a set of relatively (or in the case of 1999, potentially) durable developments in the next.

At least three theories of international order are implicated in all of this.[34] Realism purports to explain why hegemony is likely to be a feature of any international order but cannot explain the tenacity of egalitarian norms in that system.[35] Classical liberalism (or legalism) partially is founded on the idea of state equality and universality but cannot fully explain the receptiveness of the international legal order to forms of hegemony and anti-pluralism.[36] A recent form of anti-pluralism I term 'liberal anti-pluralism' has been the intellectual engine behind the shift from universalistic conceptions of international order to more

[34] This book is is not a primer to international legal theory generally. There are numerous philosophies of international law that are mentioned only in passing. These include, most obviously, feminist and critical approaches to world order. It would be a vain and ill-starred project that attempted to describe these contributions to international legal thinking in a single book. It will be apparent, in any event, that the intellectual restlessness and the moral vigour of these approaches generally have been an influence on my thinking here and in my other work.

[35] For a characterisation of realism see Simpson, *The Nature of International Law*, xiv. The realist tradition takes as its focus the idea of international relations as a lawless state of nature in which power is anterior. Realists are dismissive of the promotion of peace through law (naive and misdirected) and hostile towards attempts to create some sort of ideological unity in the world (dangerous). Martin Wight describes this realist view as the 'governing conception' of the United Nations Charter. (For contrasting views see Anne-Marie Slaughter (1994) 4 *Transnational Law and Contemporary Problems* 377–419.) Realists have long argued that sovereign equality is a fiction, that states are hierarchically ordered and that any system which disregarded this fact imperilled its own coherence. Vincent, for example, calls formal equality 'a spurious application of a nominally democratic principle to the unsuitable environment of international relations' (Clark, *Hierarchy*, 219, quoting R. J. Vincent, 'Western Conceptions of a Universal Moral Order', *British Journal of International Studies*, 4 April 1978, 37). Kenneth Waltz famously noted that: 'The inequality of states . . . makes stability possible' ('International Structure, National Force and the Balance of World Power' (1967) 21 *Journal of International Affairs* 224). However, the realist emphasis on anarchy depends on highly contended notions of statehood. Indeed, perhaps, the realist/idealist juxtaposition ought in some ways to be reversed. It is international lawyers and judges who have for years been grappling with the reality of a sovereignty that realists have taken as a given (e.g. *Carl Zeiss Stiftung* v. *Rayner and Keeler Ltd* (No. 2) [1967] 1 AC 853 where the administrative acts of the East German 'state' were under review).

[36] The rationalist tradition, or the classical international law conception, accepts that international affairs occur in a state of nature but one that is capable of generating the sort of minimal social contract upon which an international legal order can be based. The traditions of thought described as positivist, Grotian and statist (despite their differences) belong in this category. These thinkers are committed to the idea of equality among states and believe that states ought not to be distinguished on the basis of their internal characteristics, external politics or ethico-religious commitments.

bifurcated or exclusionary forms but fails to appreciate or recognise either the historical roots of its own project (in standards of civilisation, in commitments to ideological purity, in the labelling of pariah states) or the negative associations of this idea in a heterogeneous world.[37] This thesis and these theories of international order assume the international order to be one in which hierarchy and equality compete within conditions of anarchy. Of course, there are significant utopian and reformist projects within international law that point in the direction of a transformation in the conditions of hierarchy and anarchy themselves. Many internationalist and cosmopolitan theories, influential in the time periods surveyed in the thesis, ultimately seek to move the international order in the direction of central guidance or world government or cosmopolis. Liberal anti-pluralism is related to the reformist or revolutionist projects mentioned above in the sense that some anti-pluralist thought is dedicated to a radical reformation of the international order through the imposition of substantive political preferences on all states within the international system.[38] The book, then, posits juridical sovereignty as a way of thinking about a world of states founded on an opposition between two conceptions of international order while at the same time exploring how these conceptions are anchored to certain theories of international law.

Having established the parameters of the book, it is worth indicating at this stage what this book is *not* about. When I refer to hierarchy and equality, I refer to the way in which a constitutional system

---

[37] Those who emphasise moral solidarity, individual rights or world citizenship, Martin Wight describes as revolutionists because they wish to do away with what is seen as an illegitimate state of affairs operating in international order. See M. Wight, 'An Anatomy of International Thought' (1987) 13 *Review of International Studies* 221–5. For some, the inter-state system (a given for rationalists and realists) is a temporary aberration on the path to enlightened federative unions (Kant), political revolution (Marx), world government or cosmopoli of varying strengths (Zolo, Falk). This anti-pluralism has a darker side when it takes Stalinist or fascist forms. Wight is very sceptical of these forms of anti-pluralism, describing them as 'doctrinal imperialisms' and tracing them from Philip II of Spain to Nikita Khrushchev and including Hitler and Stalin. These illiberal anti-pluralists want to either impose a particular set of credentials on membership of the Family of Nations (for the Soviets it was a command economy combined with professed adherence to some form of updated Leninism) or simply achieve world domination (the Thousand Year Reich). All this can be contrasted with the approach adopted by liberal anti-pluralists; an approach which is more evolutionary than that of the imperial or revisionist powers and which promotes liberal values rather than, say, Islamic ones or Marxist-Leninist ones.

[38] For a general discussion see Simpson, *Nature of International Law*, xi–xxxvii. See, too, Wight, 'Anatomy'.

arranges and orders the status of the legally recognised *actors* within it. So, for example, I am not concerned with the operation of hierarchy as between legal *norms*.[39] The actors in whom I am primarily interested are states themselves and, for want of a better term, state-like groups. By this, I mean those entities in the international order that have been accorded the status of sovereigns. These include sovereigns, semi-sovereigns, half-sovereigns and unequal states but exclude individuals, international organisations and ethnic groups. This is not a book about self-determination. Entities aspiring to sovereignty and statehood are not the subject of the book. Naturally, hierarchies exist between non-state peoples (the Tibetans, the Moluccans) and states (Germany, Thailand) but these are not hierarchies that exist *within* sovereignty.[40] Some entities are, of course, very like states in many respects. One need only think of the Republic of Transkei in the 1980s or the Turkish Republic of Northern Cyprus today. However, these unrecognised territories are not examined in this book because, again, they exist outside the sovereignty system (or sovereignty over them is possessed by another state).[41]

The application of ideas of equality, non-discrimination and equal rights to individuals within the system is of derivative interest to me but this is not a book about human rights or poverty directly.[42] The network of norms and structures and the vast literature on racial discrimination, apartheid and rights to equal treatment are not a focus of this study except inasmuch as each has an impact on the way sovereignty, equality and hierarchy are understood at the inter-state or inter-sovereign level.[43]

---

[39] Of course, the hierarchy of norms has an influence on the status of actors. The operation of Articles 25 and 103 of the UN Charter, for example, ensures that the Security Council can exercise legalised hegemony over other actors in the system and can more readily apply anti-pluralist regimes to outlaw states. See, e.g. *Lockerbie Case (Provisional Measures)* (1992) ICJ Rep. at 3; R. St. J. MacDonald, 'Fundamental Norms in Contemporary International Law' 25 (1987) *Canadian Yearbook of International Law* 115–50; M. Akehurst, 'The Hierarchy of the Sources of International Law' (1977) 47 *British Yearbook of International Law, 1974–75*, 273 (discussing three forms of hierarchy).

[40] It may be that self-determination groups do possess some sort of sovereignty but it is not the juridical sovereignty that I discuss here. See, e.g. the principle of permanent sovereignty over natural resources (e.g. *Case Concerning East Timor*, Portuguese Application Instituting Proceedings, 22 February 1991, para. 27).

[41] This was the reasoning in a number of cases considering the domestic effect of recognition in the United Kingdom. See, e.g. *Hesperides Hotels* [1978] QB 205 at 218, 228–9 and [1979] AC 508 at 537–47; and on the status of the Republic of Ciskei, *Gur Corporation v. Trust Bank of Africa Limited* [1987] QB 599.

[42] See, e.g. C. Chinkin, 'Gender Inequality and International Human Rights Law', in A. Hurrell and N. Woods, *Inequality, Globalization and World Politics*, 95–121.

[43] Sovereign equality does have some bearing on the treatment of individuals. For example, the treatment of aliens is conditioned by the equality existing between

Nor is my focus on the hierarchies that inevitably dominate our think-ing about international relations in the broadest sense. This is not a book about political hierarchy. It is about the translation or 'mistransla-tion' of these political hierarchies into differentiated legal status. So, for example, the distinctions between superpowers, great powers, middle powers and small powers engage me only insofar as these hierarchies have legal or institutional significance.[44] Another preliminary point ought to be emphasised. This book is not concerned with the banal contrast between juridical equalities and material inequalities. It is not an argument against the normative *or* descriptive force of doctrines of legal equality that they co-exist with great physical and intellectual inequalities.

One final point. This book is primarily an analysis of how the inter-national sovereignty order works. I am seeking to expose or uncover the workings of one particular principle within the international legal order over the past two centuries and the role that international lawyers played in developing the principle. I cannot emphasise enough that this is *not* an argument in favour of equality or pluralism (though I can under-stand that these terms often carry positive connotations for people).[45] Nor do I devote attention to whether the legalised hegemony of the Great Powers has had good consequences for the international order (producing stability, for example) or whether some states *ought to be* treated as outlaws.[46] Nonetheless, the latter question, for example, can be informed by an investigation of the historical record. The intellectual and institutional antecedents of contemporary anti-pluralism have an unsavoury aspect to them. Might there not be some sort of ideological

---

states. The laws of State A cannot treat the citizens of State B differently from those of State C. Such treatment would constitute unlawful discrimination. See, e.g. *US and Colombia* (1888) in Moore, *Digest of International Law*, vol. II, 57. See, on the equality before the law enjoyed by individuals, *International Covenant on Civil and Political Rights*, Article 14(1) and (3) and Article 26 GA Res. 2200 (XXI), 16 December 1966, UNGAOR 21st Sess., Suppl. 16 at 52, UN Doc. A/6316 (1966), 999 UNTS 171.

[44] See, e.g. Paul Keal, *Unspoken Rules and Superpower Dominance*; and Julius Goebel, *The Equality of States: A Study in the History of Law*.

[45] For recent arguments against liberal anti-pluralism see J. Alvarez, 'Do Liberal States Behave Better?' (2001) 12:2 EJIL 183; B. Kingsbury, 'Sovereignty and Inequality' (1998) 9:4 EJIL 599. For an argument in favour of hierarchy see P. Cullet, 'Differential Treatment in International Law: Towards a New Paradigm of Inter-State Relations' (1999) 10:3 EJIL 549.

[46] For a jeremiad against the legalised hegemony of at least one Great Power see Peter Gowan, 'Neoliberal Cosmopolitanism' (September–October 2001) 11 *New Left Review* 79–93 and *The Global Gamble*. For an argument that the US is a rogue state see Noam Chomsky, *Rogue States*. For the view that US hegemony fails to adequately explain the operation of the world system see M. Hardt and A. Negri, *Empire*.

disposition on the part of the Great Powers to constitute outlaws out of difference? And might not the contemporary manifestations of this disposition, in retrospect, appear as an expression of an instinctive imperial violence?[47]

. . . .

The rest of this book is structured in the following manner. Chapter 2 re-defines sovereign equality and shows how the term encompasses three quite distinct phenomena. In Chapter 2, I also discuss the relationship between a host of political and material inequalities and legal equality. In Chapter 3, I define more precisely what I mean and do not mean by the term hierarchy and how this term relates to the notion of anarchy. I include here also the different approaches to hierarchy found in work from the International Relations side and from the International Law perspective. These first two chapters then aim at delineating the contours of equality and hierarchy in the construction of juridical sovereignty.

The rest of the book then considers the tension between these two ideas and the conceptions that underlie them through various historical periods. In Chapters 4 to 7 I undertake a closer examination of legalised hegemony. Chapter 4 documents the embryonic legalised hegemony established during the Vienna settlement in 1814 and 1815. This chapter also uses illustrations, drawn from publicists writing in the post-Vienna period, to show how international lawyers managed the relationship between sovereign equality and legalised hegemony in the period following the Congress. One way to view the 1815–1907 period is to see it as one in which the sovereign egalitarianism of international law and institutions competed with the political hierarchy of realist international relations for conceptual acceptance as part of a more traditional pattern of ideological conflict involving power and legality. This, indeed, is an important story. However, this story is complicated by the existence of a tension among international lawyers of the Victorian period about whether to maintain a radical separation of law and politics whereby hierarchy occupied the political domain and equality the legal sphere or whether to adopt a more pragmatic, modern approach to power and law; one that would concede the need for constitutional inequalities.[48]

---

[47] See John Newsinger, 'Elgin in China', (2002) 15 NLR 119–40.

[48] According to the first, formalist, view, the priority of the Great Powers operated within a context of legal equality but did not directly impinge on it. The pragmatists, however, argued that this separation broke down with the rise of institutionalism and the displacement of diplomacy. According to this second view, then, institutions were *about* law and regulation in a way that day-to-day diplomacy was not (see, e.g. I. Clark,

At the beginning of the twentieth century the move to institutions accelerated with the two Hague Conferences (Chapter 5). At the Second Hague Conference a serious fissure emerged in the management of the various contradictions surrounding sovereign equality. Rui Barbosa, the Brazilian delegate, became the advocate for the idea of extreme equality, which was killed off virtually at the moment of its conception in favour of various models of juridical sovereignty able to accommodate institutional hierarchies. In institutional terms, this resulted in the Versailles model where the organs of the League of Nations reflect a compromise between the egalitarian model and the hierarchical model.

Chapter 6 focuses on 1945 when the dual system introduced at Versailles was perfected. Legislative equality became the controlling principle in the design of one chamber, while legalised hegemony dominated the other. This compromise between a hegemonic policing body and an egalitarian assembly was the achievement of Dumbarton Oaks and San Francisco. In Chapter 7, I anticipate future developments in the field of juridical sovereignty but I also return to 1815 by comparing the Kosovo enforcement action with the creation of a new legalised hegemony at Vienna in 1815 where the European Great Powers (this time without the United States) acted in an, initially, extra-constitutional manner to rewrite European boundaries while at the same time announcing a new policy of management and intervention. This new policy was converted from usurpation into legitimacy by the subsequent ratification of the European body politic. I contrast this understanding of the Kosovo intervention with an alternative one based on an evaluation and analysis of the defection by the Holy Alliance from the Vienna settlement in 1822. In this case, a different interventionist policy proved to be transient because insufficiently grounded in the dominant norms of the international legal order.

The story I relate in these chapters is not a history of the Great Powers.[49] Nor is it a history of sovereign equality.[50] Instead, what I have done is select key moments of change or reaction in the history of legalised hegemony. Chapters 4 and 5 describe a trajectory from the

Hierarchy, describing the Concert as the 'formal assertion of the unique privileges and responsibilities of the great powers' (114) and the 'formalisation of hierarchy as an explicit element within the international order' (114)). This latter group of scholars adjusted their conception of international law accordingly.

[49] See, e.g. R. Albrecht-Carrié, A Diplomatic History of Europe Since the Congress of Vienna; and P. Kennedy, The Rise and Fall of the Great Powers: Economic Change and Military Conflict from 1500–2000.

[50] See J. Goebel, Equality of States and P. Kooijmans, The Doctrine of the Legal Equality of States.

imposition of legal hegemony at Vienna to the appearance of a pure theory of sovereign equality in the arguments of the small powers at The Hague. Chapters 6 and 7 then carry over into a dissection of the compromise between hegemony and equality at San Francisco and the apparent revival of regional hegemony in Kosovo.[51]

In the third Part of the book, Chapters 8, 9 and 10, I turn to another form of legalised hierarchy, i.e. *anti-pluralism*. This, too, was a constituting element of juridical sovereignty and, like legalised hegemony, it arose at the beginning of the nineteenth century and was subject to renovation and renewal throughout the modern era before eventually resolving it-self into a specific form of *liberal anti-pluralism* in the twentieth century. I am interested, particularly, in three periods during which the existen-tial equality of states was challenged by the idea that the international system could be based on a demarcation between an inner circle of right-thinking core states and an outer rim of second-class sovereign states. States falling into this second category have tended, themselves, to be divided into two separate groups. I call these criminal states and un-democratic (or uncivilised) states. This categorisation only emerges fully in the final period under study but I attempt to trace its earlier outlines in Chapter 9.[52]

In the first period, beginning in the early nineteenth century and extending through to, at least, the Hague Peace Conferences, the in-ternational legal order was divided into a European-centred Family of Nations and a non-European zone of semi-sovereign, unequal or un-civilised states. This development had a theoretical and a practical com-ponent. In international legal theory, scholars developed a conception of international order in which states were classified according to sta-tus. In international legal practice, a number of doctrines arose that appeared irreconcilable with sovereign equality. These included the unequal treaties regime and the extra-territorial jurisdiction of the European powers expressed through the system of capitulations, as well

---

[51] See D. Ninic, *The Problem of Sovereignty in the Charter and Practice of the United Nations*, describing the United Nations Charter as a sequel to the hegemony of the Great Powers at Vienna (124). I only partly agree with this. True, the Security Council acts as an executive in a manner not dissimilar to the directorate at Vienna. On the other hand, there has been no collective revision of boundaries and no consigning of states into extinction. The Security Council is, in fact, somewhat circumscribed in its latitude for management compared with the European Great Powers in 1815.

[52] The idea that states could be criminal and punished as such was not applied at the Congress of Vienna where the treatment of France was mild compared to more recent peace settlements.

as the exclusion of peripheral states from the constitutional bodies of the international system.[53]

The second period begins at Versailles with the debates over membership of the League of Nations (and the decision to exclude one outlaw, Bolshevik Russia), and the imposition of a highly punitive peace on the criminal state, Germany. Chapter 9 focuses primarily on the San Francisco Conference where a pluralistic view of the new international organisation prevailed over an anti-pluralist position that sought to exclude from the UN states that failed to meet certain democratic standards. After San Francisco the idea of *existential equality* was further reinforced by three institutional developments – in the *Admissions Case*, at Nuremberg and at the General Assembly in 1960. In the *Admissions Case*, the International Court of Justice held that extraneous political criteria were not to be part of the public justification for refusing an entity membership of the United Nations. At Nuremberg, the IMT implicitly rejected the idea of state crime in its focus on individual responsibility and in 1960 the General Assembly passed its famous Declaration on Colonialism in which the idea of civilisation as a condition of statehood was finally abolished.

The third period begins with the fall of the Berlin Wall and features the re-introduction of a number of theories and practices, each of which threatens to revive this practice of demarcation prominent in the nineteenth century. In international legal theory, writing falling under the labels democratic governance, liberal internationalism, neo-Kantianism and republicanism posed a challenge to the dominant pluralist tradition in Charter-based international society (exemplified in the *Admissions Case* and in much of the international law writing of this period).

Meanwhile, the practice of international law has sometimes mirrored and reflected back on these theoretical moves. Paralleling developments in the earlier era, there has been the establishment of new 'outlaw' categories by the Security Council and, hesitantly, the ILC, a more casual approach to Great Power intervention (Iraq, Yugoslavia) and the

---

[53] There is a difference, already alluded to in the text above, between distinctions among sovereignty bearing units and exclusion *from* sovereignty altogether. In contemporary international law, the latter form of inequality results in the distinction between non-state groups (e.g. self-determination movements) and fully fledged states. The same held true in the nineteenth century when large swathes of territory outside the European centres were assigned a status well below sovereignty, e.g. *terra nullius* or protectorates or colonies. This thesis concerns cases where *sovereign* entities are assigned a position of lower status in the system because of some cultural or ideological attributes.

degradation of norms associated with sovereign equality (e.g. the principle of sovereign immunity and the territorial integrity of the likes of Iraq, Yugoslavia, Libya and Afghanistan).[54]

The war against 'terrorism' may provide further support for this trend. The final chapter on Afghanistan suggests that anti-pluralism, if anything, is likely to deepen in its effects. A clash of civilisations combined with the increasingly bellicose attitude of the Great Powers and a more distilled legalised hegemony might well lead to a world former Soviet premier Mikhail Gorbachev warned against, in which there is 'the view that some live on Earth by virtue of divine will while others are here quite by chance'.[55]

---

[54] Though this is, by no means, a one-way process. See, e.g. *Arrest Warrant of 11 April 2000 (Democratic Republic of Congo* v. *Belgium)* at http://www.icj-cij.org/icjwww/idocket/iCOBE/ iCOBEframe.htm, deciding that a Belgian arrest warrant issued against the then-serving Congolese Foreign Minister breached the Democratic Republic of Congo's rights as a sovereign equal.

[55] Address by M. Gorbachev to the UN General Assembly, 43 UNGAOR (72nd mtg) 2, UN Doc. a/343/PV.72 (1988) in B. Weston, R. Falk and A. D'Amato, *International Law and World Order*, 1098.

Part II   Concepts

2   Sovereign equalities

Introduction

This book is about the interaction between sovereign equality and two forms of hierarchy I have labelled anti-pluralism and legalised hegemony. The interplay of these ideas constitutes *juridical sovereignty*, i.e. the particular conception of sovereignty that international lawyers talk and write about.[1] Prior to embarking on this discussion, it is important to be clear about the possible meanings ascribed to sovereign equality. To that end, I want, in this chapter, to unpack or disaggregate the principle of sovereign equality in order to bring out its various meanings.

In Chapter 3, I discuss the different meanings given to the term hierarchy by international lawyers and international relations scholars. I then outline two forms of hierarchy that provide the focus for the book. I term these *anti-pluralism* and *legalised hegemony*.[2] I begin to explore the ways in which these legal hierarchies and some elements of sovereign equality are in tension within the international legal order.

The purpose of this present chapter is fourfold. I begin, in Section 1, by offering an orthodox account of sovereign equality; one that emphasises

---

[1] But see Stephen Krasner, *Sovereignty: Organized Hypocrisy* (distinguishing Westphalian sovereignty and international legal sovereignty), 4.

[2] At least two uses of hegemony, both of which are relevant to this book, should be distinguished. The first refers simply to a form of frontal domination. The second is adapted from Gramsci's reformulation of hegemony to mean a structure of ideas that accompanies this domination and 'naturalises' it. Though it is worth keeping the distinction in mind, it is in fact quite difficult to tease out the separate elements since hegemons usually attempt to legitimise themselves at the level of ideology. See A. Gramsci, *Selections from Prison Notebooks* ed. and trans. Q. Hoare and G. N. Smith, 12–13. For the application of Gramscian thought to international relations see R. Germain and M. Kenny, 'Engaging Gramsci: International Relations Theory and the New Gramscians' (1998) 24:1 *Review of International Studies* 3–21.

its centrality to the legal order, its special status and its doctrinal effects. This orthodox account is then contrasted with the juridical sovereignty presented in the remainder of the thesis. In Section 2, I show how sovereign equality arose and became influential in the post-Westphalia era. Here, I bring out its historical sources in, alternatively, positivism and naturalism, and its contemporary philosophical foundations in the domestic analogy from liberalism. Following this, in Section 3, I indicate that there are three fairly distinct understandings of sovereign equality though these three understandings are often treated as if they were a single principle.[3] I term these understandings: legislative equality, formal equality and existential equality. The combination of these three produces a strong conception of sovereign equality. This strong conception is an ideal type. Juridical sovereignty, then, combines certain elements of the strong version with the existence of legalised hegemony and anti-pluralism. It is juridical sovereignty, I argue, that has defined international law since 1815. Finally, in Section 4, I think about the broader meaning of equality and how the narrow idea of sovereign equality might be located within the field. I begin to think about the forms of substantive or political equality *not* included within the four corners of the legal principle and how these influence our conception of sovereign equality.

Orthodoxies

It is a commonplace in international law that states are equal or, at least, that they possess something called sovereign equality. This form of equality is a foundational principle of the international legal order. There is a mass of support – doctrinal, jurisprudential and scholarly – for at least some variant of the principle.[4] Re-assertions of the doctrine tend to be accompanied by claims for its centrality, its existence in the face of material, cultural, intellectual and military differences, and its long lineage in international law.[5] I will restrict myself here to the modern era and turn to the historical sources of the doctrine in the next section.

---

[3] This is precisely the complaint made by Edwin Dickinson eighty years ago when he decried the inability to distinguish between 'equality of capacity for rights' and 'equal protection of the law'. See Dickinson, *Equality of States*, 133.

[4] See Dickinson, *Equality of States*, 128–232 for examples.

[5] For recent explorations of the principle see P. Cullet, 'Differential Treatment', 549; B. Kingsbury, 'Sovereignty and Inequality', 599; A. D. Efraim, *Sovereign (In)equality in International Organisations*.

In 1825, in the *Antelope Case*, Chief Justice Marshall of the United States Supreme Court remarked that: 'No principle of general law is more universally acknowledged than the perfect equality of nations.'[6] In a classic statement from his treatise, Oppenheim elaborated on this:

The equality before International Law of all member States of the Family of Nations is an invariable equality derived from their international personality. Whatever inequality may exist between states as regards their size, power, degree of civilisation, wealth and other qualities, they are nevertheless equals as international persons.[7]

In 1951, President Basdevant of the International Court of Justice put the matter even more bluntly: 'Before this Court, there are no great or small states . . .'.[8]

The major textbooks are in broad agreement with these dicta.[9] Doctrinally, the significance of sovereign equality is made explicit in the United Nations Charter at Article 2(1) (the Organisation is 'based' on the principle of sovereign equality) and in the 1970 Declaration on Friendly Relations.[10] The Preamble of the United Charter refers to the equality of 'nations large and small'[11] and many writers claim the principle falls within the category of norms of *jus cogens*.[12]

The orthodoxy on sovereign equality assumes that the international system contains a plurality of states and that these states are both similar and different i.e. capable of enjoying equality in some domains but distinct in others.[13] States enjoying sovereign equality are often said to possess internal sovereignty (e.g. a monopoly of legitimate legal authority

---

[6] 10 *Wheat* 66, at 122.

[7] L. Oppenheim, *International Law*, vol I, 3rd edn, 15. See, too, from different eras: The American Institute of International Law, *Declaration of the Rights and Duties of Nations*, ed. Scott: 'Every nation is in law the equal of every other nation'; G. G. Wilson, *Handbook on International Law*, 74; H. Wheaton, *Elements of International Law*, 6th edn, ed. W. B. Lawrence, 58, 118.

[8] ICJ *Yearbook* (1950–1) at 17. See, too, *Prosecutor* v. *Tadic* (Jurisdiction) (Appeals Chamber), at para. 55; 105 ILR at 479.

[9] See, e.g. I. Brownlie, *Principles of Public International Law*, 287.

[10] See also UN Charter Article 74, Article 1(2) and Article 6, *Organisation of American States Charter* ('States are juridically equal, enjoy equal rights and equal capacity to enjoy these rights').

[11] See, too, for precursors, *Moscow Four-Power Declaration* (1943) Article 4, *A Decade of American Foreign Policy: Basic Documents* 1941–9 (1950); and Goodrich, Hambro and Simons: *Charter of the United Nations Commentary and Documents* (3rd edn), 36.

[12] See, e.g. *International Law Commission Report* (1966) 2 ILC *Yearbook* 169, 249; M. Dixon, *Textbook on International Law*, 144.

[13] Bengt Broms, *The Doctrine of Equality of States*, 1.

within a certain territory and jurisdictional primacy in that area) and external sovereignty (e.g. a right to territorial integrity, immunity from suits in the courts of another state).[14] The core idea (of both sovereignty and equality) is that no state is legally superior to another – *par in parem non habet imperium*.[15] The separate opinion of Judge Anzilotti in the *Customs Union Case* is usually viewed as a standard definition of 'independence' but much of the language employed concerns hierarchy and equality.[16] State equality requires the absence of formal superiority and subordination in the legal relations between states.[17] So no state can sit in judgement on another state or sign treaties on behalf of another state.[18] Nor can a state procure the consent of another state to an agreement or treaty through the use of physical coercion.[19] States recognise only one legal superior and that is international law itself.[20] In addition states are said to be bound only by those rules to which they have agreed to be bound. This is the principle of consent.[21]

The principle of sovereign equality also provides the basis for a network of rights and duties found in many substantive areas of

---

[14] For a discussion of the differences between these sovereign powers, see Krasner, *Organised Hypocrisy*.

[15] See, e.g. David Ott, *Public International Law in the Modern World*, 48; Rebecca Wallace, *International Law*, 108.

[16] *Austro-German Customs Union Case* (Advisory Opinion), PCIJ Rep., Series A/B, No 41 (1931).

[17] Arguably, states are in a relationship of subordination to international organisations, especially those organisations with formal collective security roles. Several points ought to be kept in mind here. First, that subordination operates between a state and the particular organ. Second, states in ratifying the UN Charter have consented in advance to be bound by the decrees of the Security Council. Third, and as a corollary to this point, it may be that states are permitted to withdraw from the Charter. But see, on this final point, P. Sands and P. Klein, *Bowett's The Law of International Institutions* (5th edn), 24–5.

[18] *The Schooner Exchange* v. *M'Faddon* 11 US (7 Cranch) 116 L.Ed. 287 (state immunity is based on 'perfect equality and absolute independence of sovereigns' (at 666)).

[19] See Vienna Convention on the Law of Treaties, 1969, Articles 51 and 52, 1155 UNTS 331. See, too, ILC's *Commentary on the Draft Articles on Treaty Law* (1966) 2 ILC *Yearbook* 246–7 (noting that states must take decisions in regard to the maintenance of a treaty, 'in a position of full equality with the other state').

[20] See, e.g. the idea that states are free to resort to a procedure of choice in resolving disputes under Article 33 of the UN Charter. See K. V. Raman (ed.), *Introduction, Dispute Settlement Through the United Nations*, 54, 579.

[21] It was thought that the consent principle generated two further principles: the requirement of unanimity in the creation of legal rules and the principle of non-weighted voting. However, the practice since 1907 has been to approve majority voting in advance under a particular treaty arrangement. Non-weighted voting, meanwhile, is a principle still in operation in universal political organisations (such as the United Nations) but has been abandoned in economic institutions (e.g. the IMF).

international law. In the law on the use of force, both the right to territorial integrity (Article 2(4)) and the right to self-defence (Article 51) are derived from sovereign equality. Even the possession and threatened use of nuclear weapons can be justified as a concomitant of sovereign equality. This, indeed, was a consideration in Judge Fleischhauer's Separate Opinion in *The Legality of Nuclear Weapons*, where he states:

To end the matter with the simple statement that recourse to nuclear weapons would be contrary to international law applicable in armed conflict, and in particular the principles and rules of humanitarian law, would have meant that the law applicable in armed conflict, and in particular the humanitarian law, was given precedence over the inherent right of individual or collective self-defence which every State possesses as a matter of sovereign equality and which is expressly preserved in Article 51 of the Charter.[22]

On the other hand, the prohibition on the use of force (except in self-defence and collective security) secures implementation of the sovereign equality norm. While this norm purports to constrain the application of sovereign authority, it also confirms the importance of state equality by mitigating the effects of superior military force and placing states on a level footing in relation to the unilateral use of force.[23]

At other times, the principle provides a basis for specific treaty or customary rights:

[the] community of interest in a navigable river becomes the basis of a common legal right, the essential features of which are the perfect equality of all riparian States in the use of the whole course of the river and the exclusion of any preferential privilege of any one riparian State in relation to the others.[24]

Finally, as I will go on to discuss in much greater detail, the element of sovereign equality I characterise as *existential equality* encompasses states' rights to organise their communities on any basis they wish. Sovereign equality is a guarantee of state autonomy in the domestic sphere and pluralism and diversity in the international system as a whole.

This, then, is the briefly sketched orthodoxy on sovereign equality. The remainder of the book subjects this orthodoxy to enquiry.

---

[22] Separate Opinion of Judge Fleischhauer in *Legality of the Threat or Use of Nuclear Weapons Case* (Adv. Op. 8 July), (1996) ICJ Rep. at 226.

[23] Ninic, *The Problem of Sovereignty*, 79.

[24] *Territorial Jurisdiction of the International Commission of the River Oder*, Judgment No. 16, 1929, PCIJ, Series A, No. 23, at 27.

Historical and philosophical roots

The idea that states are legally equal has both a political origin and several philosophical sources.[25] The organisation of community on the basis of sovereignty and equality is both cause and effect of two associated processes in international affairs – secularisation and decentralisation.[26] The culmination of these mediaeval processes occurred at Westphalia where there was the rejection of the spiritual dominion of the Catholic Church and the political rule of the Holy Roman Empire as well as an agreement on the secular equality of Catholic and Protestant states (in Germany).[27] So, Westphalia symbolises, for international law, a transition from strict hierarchy to equality or from a vertical ordering, with the Pope and Emperor at the pinnacle, to a horizontal order composed of independent, freely negotiating states.[28]

This transition from authority to consensus occurred as a process rather than in a single transformative moment.[29] States existed, notably on the European periphery, prior to Westphalia and, equally, the vestiges of papal control remained until the Congress of Vienna formally dissolved the Empire.[30] (Ironically, it was the continuing authority of the

[25] A less orthodox (and fascinating) perspective on the history of sovereign equality is found in J. Goebel, *Equality of States*.

[26] This tendency had accelerated with the split between Emperor and Pope in the Middle Ages. The Emperor had power but little universal authority while the Pope had universal authority but little power (Goebel, *Equality of States*, 34). Even the power of the Empire waned well before 1648.

[27] The link between equality and Protestantism can be seen in the work of Martin Luther which features the ideas of secular independence and territorial separation. So, Luther's break with the Emperor and theocrats was also a break with the idea of territorial universalism (see Goebel, *Equality of States*, 76).

[28] As Westlake points out, though, even after Westphalia had supposedly set in place the European state system and legitimated the territorial arrangements within it, 'power was scarcely to be found . . . without a dispute as to its rightfulness or its measure . . .' (*Collected Papers*, 52).

[29] See Harvey Starr, *Anarchy, Order and Integration*, 92; Alexander Murphy, 'The Sovereign State as Political-Territorial Ideal' in T. Biersteker and C. Weber (eds.), *State Sovereignty as Social Construct*, 87. Goebel dates the beginning of this process to 800 AD when the relationship between Charlemagne and the Danes was that between legal equals (36). The earlier Peace of Augsburg (1555), too, recognised the parity of Catholic and Protestant princes. See A. Pearce Higgins, *The Hague Peace Conferences*, 49; H. W. Halleck, *International Law*, 9.

[30] States existed in some cases. But in other cases, the ruler of a particular territory owned it as a fiefdom or as personal property and his religion became that of the territory (the idea of '*cuius regio eius religio*'). The move from feudalism to capitalism mirrors and determines the transition from property to sovereignty. For a provocative argument along these lines see Justin Rosenberg, *The Empire of Civil Society*.

Church and Empire during this period that prevented any other state from establishing universal hegemony for itself. Empire in this sense provided a foundation for sovereign equality.)[31] Nevertheless, Westphalia formalised the acquisition of full sovereignty within a system of ethically and legally equal states. It is at Westphalia that equality, anarchy, sovereignty and independence were fused in the European system.[32] This was not simply a sovereignty of possibility but also a sovereignty of tolerance and constraint. In other words, states were sovereign in the sense that they were at liberty to do as they wished (providing this sovereignty did not interfere with the sovereignty of others) but they were equal, too, in the sense that the interior political order of each sovereign was to be accorded respect and immunity from interference. Mutual recognition of sovereigns was a key element of the Westphalian settlement. Sovereigns were equal in voting power and in the level of protection to be accorded to their internal political practices. It is this strong form of sovereign equality that disappeared after Vienna to be replaced by a juridical sovereignty constituted by the interplay of legalised hierarchies and equality.

The principle of sovereign equality finds its philosophical rationale in the two great theoretical projects of the post-Westphalian period in international law: naturalism and positivism.[33] Commonly, these two theories are thought to be at loggerheads (Eyffinger describes them as 'radical antipoles')[34] with naturalism drawing its source of justification from external, cosmological forces or, in modern versions, a form of rationality embedded in human nature, and positivism emphasising the material, temporal, psychological and human elements of law-making. However, sovereign equality draws sustenance from both these traditions. Appropriately, the classic formulation of the principle from this period comes from Vattel, often regarded as an early positivist, but whose view of equality is replete with naturalistic overtones:

[31] Goebel, *Equality of States*, 46.

[32] A. Eyffinger, 'Europe in the Balance: An Appraisal of the Westphalian System' (1998) 45 NILR 161–87 at 176 and *passim*.

[33] Positivism is a project dedicated to the expulsion of ultimate philosophical rationales (especially naturalist ones) from the legal order in favour of a more agnostic quest for clarity and certainty. Yet, international legal positivism's search for clarity depends on treating states as formal equals for the purpose of providing consent. The preference for (equal) state consent depends on a commitment to some substantive value (the value of sovereignty (states rather than citizens), the value of universality (all states equally rather than a selection of approved states) and the value of equality (all states rather than simply the most powerful)). See Goebel, *Equality of States*, 9.

[34] Eyffinger, 'Europe in the Balance', 172.

Since men are by nature equal, and their individual rights and obligations the same, as coming equally from nature, Nations, which are composed of men and may be regarded as so many free persons living together in a state of nature, are by nature equal and hold from nature the same obligations and the same rights. . . . A dwarf is as much a man as a giant is; a small republic is no less sovereign than the most powerful Kingdom.[35]

For Vattel, equality was a natural right of authentic, pre-existing communities. There are three elements to the natural law argument. One is the idea that states or communities pre-date international law. The legitimacy of these groups is not established by international law but is a presupposition of the international legal system. Second, it is assumed that these entities or communities possess natural rights to liberty and equality that they are unlikely to forswear in the state of society.[36] Third, states are entitled to equality because the men and women of whom they are composed have natural rights to equality.[37]

This idea of naturally existing equality is complicated by the existence of numerous versions of the state of nature. In Rousseau's account, the state of nature is a state of equality and the imposition of law through a social contract represents a degeneration from this Eden. Locke, on the other hand, sees the state of nature as anarchic and the legal order as a civilising system in which equality is perfected.[38] It is in these early writings that we see traces of current theoretical disputes about sovereignty with realists arguing that equality and sovereignty can best be secured through anarchy (Rousseau), and international lawyers believing that

---

[35] E. de Vattel, Le droit des gens, Introduction, Sec. 18 and 19. See also Wolff, Jus gentium methodo scientifica pertractatum, Prolegomena para. 16.

[36] See, generally, Charles Alexandrowicz, An Introduction to the History of the Law of Nations in the East Indies. See F. C. Hicks, The New World Order, 8. Of course, it is not impossible that states would divest their sovereignty. This, indeed, is part of what it means to be sovereign. The question then becomes, can this sovereignty be revived? Two contemporary examples point in different directions. The creation of the United Arab Republic required the combination of two sovereignties (Egypt and Syria) into one. These sovereigns re-established themselves in identical form after the dissolution of the UAR. On the other hand, the merging of sovereignties in the European Union may become (or now be?) irrevocable.

[37] It is a little unclear how the naturalists justify 'equality'. Vattel, Le droit des gens Introduction, Sec. 18 (speaking of states as free persons living in a state of nature because they were composed of free and equal men). Is it the state of nature that generates the right to equality or is it the composition of the state? Are states equal because they are 'like' individuals or are they equal because they are composed of individuals? Naturalists tend to go back and forth between the two conceptions.

[38] J.-J. Rousseau, 'A Discourse on the Origin of Inequality' in The Social Contract and Discourses, 84–117; J. Locke, Two Treatises of Government, 179–201.

only a legal order can provide for the secure enjoyment of sovereignty and a guarantee of equality (Locke). Standing to the side of this debate is Hobbes, for whom the state of nature is the state of perfect, if more or less uninhabitable, equality. Hobbes produced the defining statement on this state of nature and its relationship to equality in *De cive* saying,

> They are equals who can do equal things one against the other; but they who can do the greatest thing, namely, kill, can do equal things. All men therefore among themselves are by nature equal.[39]

Hobbes's answer is neither a legal order composed of equals nor a continuing state of anarchy. For him, only subordination to some superior power can ensure peace (these debates became the foundation for the anarchical conception of international relations as well as numerous game theories and security dilemmas). Hobbes's solution was favoured by many international lawyers in the early twentieth century and became influential in the making of international organisations in the post-First World War era.[40] These lawyers argued for an international order in which, in order to avoid the vices of anarchy, sovereign equality was compromised in centralised international organisations.[41]

Positivist arguments engender similar results to those arising out of the state of nature or the idea of equal rights. Here, the natural law arguments have tended to give way to a doctrine of sovereign equality based more on positive laws and treaty principles.[42] In this version, the primacy of the sovereign state and the requirement that states consent to any international laws applied to their behaviour are each derived from a core notion of sovereign equality. International legal positivism, like its domestic cousin, cherishes certainty and clarity in legal norms. For positivists, these qualities are found in a system where the principal law-generating actors are readily identifiable and where these actors (states) are undifferentiated in their capacity to create law (legislative equality).[43]

Both positivism and naturalism are capable of explaining, justifying and accommodating hierarchy, too. There is an affinity between

---

[39] T. Hobbes, *De cive* vol. I, 3.   [40] See Chapters 4 to 6.

[41] See discussions in Chapters 4 and 5.

[42] But there are still occasional references to natural rights in documents or drafts concerning sovereign equality. See, e.g. Cuban *Draft Declaration of Duties and Rights of States* (1945), UNCIO Doc, vol. 3, 495–9; Panamanian *Draft Declaration of Rights and Duties of States* (1947) quoted in Broms, *Doctrine of Equality*, 71.

[43] See, e.g. J. Watson, 'A Realistic Jurisprudence' (1980) 30 *Yearbook of World Affairs*, 265–86.

arguments based on nature or divine truth and the belief in natural or transcendental inequalities. The division of the world into civilised and uncivilised states was prefigured by Christian principles distinguishing heathen and godly cultures. Positivism, meanwhile, became dominant in an era in which, for the first time, a positive public international law based on European exceptionalism displaced natural law ideas of universality. The treatment of non-European sovereigns under the colour of positivist doctrine attests to the role of inequality in positivist thinking.[44]

To summarise, then, sovereign equality arose over a long period of time in European history.[45] The primary political roots of the principle can be found in the slow dissolution of the Holy Roman Empire and its replacement by a system based on territorial separatism and the state. This process was mirrored by the conflict between the Protestant Kingdoms and the Empire. The stalemate produced by this conflict resulted in the secularisation of territorial politics in Europe. Religion did not disappear as a force in European politics but it became increasingly the case that political conflict no longer tracked religious allegiances (hence the 'unholy alliance').

These political events were, in turn, buttressed by developments in philosophy and law. Bodin's theory of sovereignty, Pufendorf's natural law, Hobbes's state of nature and the renewed influence of Stoic thought, each contributed to the legitimisation of territorial sovereignty and sovereign equality.[46]

The orthodox account of sovereign equality, described in the first section of this chapter, derives much of its authority from this philosophical and historical evolution. International lawyers have tended to see the origins of both their discipline and the modern idea of equal sovereignty in the Westphalian settlement. This has resulted in a relatively uncomplicated conception of sovereignty that emphasises the absence of centralised authority in the international system and a rough legal parity between states within that system. The Holy Roman Empire and,

---

[44] See A. Anghie, 'Finding the Peripheries: Sovereignty and Colonialism in Nineteenth-Century International Law' (1999) 40:1 *Harvard International Law Journal* 1–80.

[45] This is primarily a European story. No doubt some examples of sovereign equality can be found elsewhere but it is the European conception of sovereign equality that has influenced and dominated classical international law.

[46] See J. Bodin, *Six Livres de la Republique* (probably the first theory of sovereignty); S. Pufendorf, *De systematibus civitatum* (according to Martin Wight, the earliest elaboration of the idea of a system of states. See Wight, *Systems of States*); T. Hobbes, *De cive.*

indeed, many of the later imperial projects are viewed as models of hierarchy against which the idea of sovereign equality (independence, anti-
colonialism) could be set. Christian Schreuer offers a variation on this
when he characterises the Vienna Congress as a hierarchical holdover
from the days of Empire. The final blow to hierarchy occurs with the
dissolution of the two central powers' empires.

> The Empire existed until 1806 and the process towards sovereign equality was
> gradual. It culminated with the collapse in the early twentieth century of the
> Austro-Hungarian and Ottoman Empires, and the displacement of the Concert of
> Europe as the most important international arena by an open global community
> of states.[47]

The trajectory traced, in all this, describes a system developing out of
the highly centralised and unequal relations that were the mark of the
pre-Westphalian stage in international affairs to a Westphalian order in
which the sovereign equality of states becomes a defining quality of the
system. The transformation here is one from Empire to anarchy or from
centralised hierarchy to sovereign equality. This is a system that in the
pre-Westphalia phase was dominated by a central religious and legal authority and was composed of a number of entities of differing status
in the system, e.g. principalities and city-states. So, not only was there
a universal order but within it there were enormous heterogeneities of
status and type among the actors. Westphalia, then, emasculated the
Empire, reducing it to one among many sovereigns, and begins a process by which the state becomes a standard item of social organisation
eclipsing the multifarious forms in existence at that time. With the state
comes sovereignty and equality.[48]

The argument presented in the remainder of this book seeks to
modify this image of a transformation from pre-Westphalian hierarchy
to post-Westphalian sovereign equality. It also challenges or, at least,
complicates the orthodox account of sovereign equality presented in
Section 1.

Indeed, 1815 (and not 1648) is the critical moment in the account
offered here. As Bull and Watson say, the pre-1815 period was one in

---

[47] C. Schreuer, 'The Waning of the Sovereign State: Towards A New Paradigm for
International Law?' (1993) 4:4 EJIL 447.
[48] Julius Goebel devotes much of his study, *Equality of States* to refuting this proposition
by arguing that sovereign parity was a feature of the pre-Westphalian landscape from
800 AD: 'Hence it was in the late Middle Ages even the free cities and the
independent dukes were treated as equals by the rulers of states possessing greater
political and economic power' (57). See, e.g. the 1495 Treaty between the King of
Spain, the Duke of Milan and the Pope.

which 'European states sought to deal with Asian states on the basis of moral and legal equality, until in the nineteenth century this gave way to notions of European superiority.'[49] Of course, differences were acknowledged to be significant but the relations between Empires and other civilisations were conducted on the basis of respect and equality.[50] As C. H. Alexandrowicz remarked,

[prior to 1815] The Law of Nations was inherently a universal concept, conditioned by its affiliation with the law of nature and by the highly important and world-wide relations on a footing of equality between the European powers and the East Indian and North African rulers joining in a great trade adventure.

The Concert period beginning in 1815 signalled an era of differentiation and colonisation in counter-point to both the preceding age and, to some extent, the Charter period following it (Chapter 8). 1945 (or better still, 1960) sees a temporary abandonment of this system of anti-pluralism in favour of decolonisation and existential equality between states and a return to the Westphalian ideal.[51]

In the same way, the strong sovereign equality of the 1648–1815 era was displaced by a system that accommodates legalised hegemony. These new hierarchies then permitted the growth of international law and institutions. David Armstrong describes this pattern in the following terms:

From 1815, the Great Powers assumed a privileged status that undermined the formal [sovereign] equality that had prevailed in the previous century and enabled them to set norms and lay down rules for international society as a whole.[52]

The remainder of this book describes and analyses the operation of anti-pluralism and legalised hegemony in the international legal order. However, it is important to be clear at the outset that the special prerogatives of the Great Powers and the constitutional gradation of states on the basis of cultural or ideological traits exist against the background of the continued vitality of different versions of sovereign equality. In the

---

[49] Goebel, *Equality of States*, 5.

[50] See C. H. Alexandrowicz, 'Empirical and Doctrinal Positivisms in International Law' (1977) 47:6 *British Yearbook of International Law, 1974–75* 286, 288. The positivists missed or overlooked all the equal treaties entered into prior to the unequal treaties period.

[51] See, e.g. Werner Levi, *Law and Politics in the International Society*, 122: 'Until the end of WWII, there was a rank order among states based on international comity.'

[52] D. Armstrong, 'Law, Justice and the idea of World Society' (1999) 75:3 *International Affairs* 547–62, 548.

various periods under discussion, and during the institutional projects that defined them, the shape of these legal orders and the institutions within them are characterised by a tension or relationship between the various components of sovereign equality and legalised hegemony/anti-pluralism. This tension or relationship is the very essence of *juridical sovereignty*.

In order to understand precisely what anti-pluralism and legalised hegemony are reacting against, I want to present, in the next section, a re-reading and elaboration of the orthodox view set out in Part 1. In other words, before introducing juridical sovereignty, I want to present a reconceptualisation of sovereign equality itself.

Reconceptualising sovereign equality

The richness of these philosophical and historical rationales for sovereign equality is no guarantee of stable meaning. Meanwhile, modern liberal conceptions of sovereignty have tried to escape this problem by positing states as analogous to individuals in the liberal state. Sovereignty, then, is seen as a form of liberty or immunity from interference, while state equality corresponds to notions of equality found in constitutional orders or in some liberal theory. Here, states become moral persons or collective personalities capable of enjoying the same rights as human beings (within the bounds of reasonableness). This 'domestic analogy' though is unhelpful because there is little agreement on the meaning of equality as it refers to citizens in liberal systems. A central question must always be equality of what? Opportunities? Resources? Income? Respect and Concern?[53] Even juridical equality, an obvious sub-set of general equality, remains susceptible to disagreement over its precise contours. In international society there is another difficulty. To whom does this equality apply? World citizens? Entities? States? Civilisations? All societies have tended to be based on some sort of exclusionary policy. Therefore the question of membership or citizenship precedes any assignment of equality rights. Sovereigns are equal but who is sovereign?

There is the further problem that some of these legal equality rights have the potential to come into conflict. Robert Phillimore, the

[53] See, for a range of views, e.g. A. Sen, *Inequality Reexamined*; J. Rawls, *A Theory of Justice*; F. Hayek, *The Constitution of Liberty*; R. Nozick, *Anarchy, State and Utopia*; C. Mackinnon, 'Sex Equality: On Difference and Dominance' in *Towards a Feminist Theory of the State*, 220–1.

nineteenth-century English jurist, attempted to extract from the general right of equality four specific rights that are separable from rights to independence and sovereignty. These are the right of a state to protect her subjects wherever they are situated, the right to recognition by foreign governments, the right to honour and respect and the right to enter into treaties.[54] Consider two of Phillimore's four equality rights. The right to afford protection to a state's own nationals abroad is in obvious tension with the rights to jurisdictional primacy and territorial integrity of the host state. In the nineteenth century this was resolved, in relations between the core and the periphery, by instituting a system of capitulations whereby Western powers acquired extra-territorial rights in 'less civilised' states.[55] However, these capitulations were regarded as indicators of inequality. Any state forced to permit such invasive legal protections was thought to be not fully equal. Similarly, the right to recognition contradicts the sovereign right to recognise. In both cases, there is a clash between two sovereign rights, each based on equality and respect.

Given the apparent potential for conflict does sovereign equality possess *any* agreed meaning? Two propositions can be safely made. First, only states possess this form of equality. This is not to suggest that the notion of statehood is itself stable. We may not be able to define with exactness what constitutes a state in international law but we know that sovereignty and a right to equality are two essential attributes of statehood.[56] We also know that equality is thought to be applicable to the legal relations between sovereign states.[57]

Second, this equality operates exclusively in the juridical sphere. The standard international law position is one that adopts a realist pose in relation to material capabilities ('of course states are unequal') while stressing the autonomy of the legal zone ('but, at least, they are legally

---

[54] Robert Phillimore, *Commentaries on International Law*, Section 162 (1854) at 149.

[55] Capitulations existed prior to the nineteenth century but they were regarded as acts of hospitality and generosity by the hosts. In addition, there was a level of equivalence in these early cases almost entirely lacking in the nineteenth-century system (e.g. the Ottomans had extra-territorial rights in Amsterdam in the eighteenth century). See Chapter 8.

[56] See Montevideo Convention on Rights and Duties of States (1933) 135 LNTS 19; James Crawford, *The Creation of States* (1979).

[57] But see Simma: 'the reference to sovereign equality could be interpreted as meaning that only sovereign states are entitled to this equality. Such an interpretation appears highly unlikely' (*Commentary*, 79).

equal').[58] It is simple enough to enumerate the various respects in which sovereign states are unequal. States are unequal in territorial size, in economic productivity, in natural advantages, in intellectual resources, in population, in geo-strategic position, in constitutional stability. When international lawyers speak of sovereign equality they refer to a form of juridical equality rather than material or substantive equality. This is not to say that international law is indifferent to these material inequalities or that there are not legal institutions designed to mitigate such inequalities. Indeed, the question of distribution is a pressing one at the international level.[59] However, sovereign equality refers to the distribution of a bundle of immunities, rights and privileges capable of being exercised at the level of law.

But what sort of legal concept is it? The question of whether sovereign equality is a legal right or immunity or a legal principle has been debated by scholars for some time.[60] I have tended to treat it as if it encompassed elements of all three. Sovereign equality is a principle designed to regulate the inter-state system. To that extent it operates to define the relationship between states and their standing in international organisations. However, the principle also forms the backdrop to a series of rights (e.g. the right of self-defence, the right to regulate the behaviour of its own nationals) and immunities (the immunity from exercise of another state's jurisdiction in its territory).

Though these general delimitations and descriptions may be uncontroversial, the precise content of this equality is less determinate. Perhaps, it is worth clarifying what equality adds to our understandings of sovereignty itself. The two words are often conflated and they undoubtedly have close family connections. However, sovereign equality is a particular form of equality and equal sovereigns are a sub-set of the general category of sovereigns.

In order to begin teasing out the meaning of sovereign equality I want to think about what sovereignty would look like in the absence of equality.[61] According to some international lawyers, this may be conceptually illogical. For them, equality is the very essence of sovereignty.

---

[58] 'In particular, the concept of equality among States is to a large extent based on a fiction. The enormous differences between participants in terms of power and wealth have created a constant tension between basic conceptions of international law and reality' (Schreuer, 'The Waning of the Sovereign State', 449).

[59] For a discussion of non-legal equalities and inequalities see Sen, *Inequality*.

[60] See references in Dickinson, *Equality of States*, 130–2.   [61] *Ibid.*, 146.

It makes no sense to claim a state or entity is sovereign if it is in an unequal relationship with another state.

There is, though, a respectable line of thought that would de-couple sovereignty and equality. Alexander Murphy distinguishes sovereignty as a 'territorial ideal' and sovereignty as an 'organising principle' of international relations in his analysis of systemic and anarchic models of sovereignty since Westphalia.[62] Using this distinction, it is possible to view sovereign equality as an organising principle of the post-Westphalia legal order but not a necessary component of the territorial ideal.

The territorial ideal is characterised by sovereign communities organised around territories, unencumbered by duties to those outside these territories. This is a strong, libertarian form of sovereignty which finds its most extreme (admittedly, non-territorial, manifestation) in Hegel.[63] According to this account, states are free to do as they wish. They are at liberty to project power, dominate rivals and annex territory. This version of sovereignty is, in some respects, the antithesis of legality. States are not equal according to this territorial model because equality presupposes at least some rights to exist, participate and make formally equal claims.

This territorial or strong version of sovereign inequality is sometimes referred to as the theory of absolute sovereignty and tends to be associated with nineteenth-century German scholars of the state such as Treitschke and Fichte.[64] It developed as a reaction to Empire, the final confirmation that the Holy Roman Empire had no hold over the sovereign states of Europe. Power is unlimited in this theory and the state is the ultimate expression of power. These states are bound neither to a higher law (natural law) nor to any conception of community with other states in an international legal order. In Ninic's words, sovereignty is 'granted supremacy over international law'.[65]

This idea of absolute sovereignty has fallen into disrepute in recent times, for two principal reasons. First, it has come to be associated with

---

[62] Murphy, 'Sovereign State', 87.

[63] See, e.g. G. W. F. Hegel, *Philosophy of Right* (ed. S. W. Dyde) 257–9, paras. 330–2.

[64] See, too, English versions of this idea found in John Austin, *Lectures on Jurisprudence*, London (1911) vol. I. In fact, some of Fichte's work and, especially, Treitschke's does not really bear this out. See e.g. Fichte, *The Vocation of Man* (ed. and trans. W. Smith); Treitschke, *Politics*, vol. II (trans. A. J. Balfour), 587–8 (attributing the strong Germanic conception of the state to Machiavelli and dismissing it as 'empty of meaning and unmoral'). Treitschke also, however, dismisses liberal theories of sovereignty with their 'good little boy' image of the state (588).

[65] Ninic, *The Problem of Sovereignty*, 8.

Teutonic conceptions of the state at the turn of the century. This, in turn, has linked absolute sovereignty with the Kaiser's ambitions in the Great War and, worse, the authoritarian states of the fascist period. Second, the whole idea of absolute sovereignty came to lack purchase in an era of interdependence. If anything, sovereignty, even in its relativised versions (see below), is undergoing constant modification and re-negotiation. All this is not to deny that traces of the doctrine do still arise. The self-judging reservations attached to a number of declarations accepting jurisdiction of the World Court are reminiscent of the *kompetenz-kompetenz* idea emanating from this conception of statehood.[66]

Sovereign equality, though, as understood by most international lawyers, is an 'organising principle' rather than a 'territorial ideal'. As such, it becomes a doctrine of both liberty and constraint. Equality is the component of sovereign equality that permits co-existence and at least some measure of security. States possess sovereign equality but sovereign equality also operates as a way of structuring their relations. In this sense, it is a relative sovereignty. It is relative in that this form of sovereignty must constantly treat with the sovereignty of other states. In de Visscher's words, 'the theory of relative sovereignty acknowledges the fact that individual states are included in a pattern of relationships which necessarily impose limitations upon their will to be autonomous'.[67] Second, it is constrained by the existence of international law itself and, in stronger versions of the relative sovereignty doctrine, by international law's primacy.[68]

The theory of relative sovereignty is ascendant at present. The sovereignty of states in the present system is thought to be subordinate to international law but equal with that of other states. Relative sovereignty buttresses the sovereign state by offering states in an anarchic system protection from, and equality with, each other. The unmediated exercise of absolute sovereignty will tend to make states both vulnerable and highly unequal.

---

[66] On validity of such reservations see, e.g. *Interhandel Case (Switzerland v. United States)*, *Separate Opinion* of *Judge Klaestad* (1959) ICJ Rep. 6 77–8.

[67] C. de Visscher, *Theory and Practice in International Law*, 30, quoted in Ninic, *The Problem of Sovereignty*, 9.

[68] See, e.g. the Vienna School. For discussion see Symposium 'Hans Kelsen' (1998) 9 EJIL 287–400. In a way, what we have here are two forms of positivism. In the voluntarist version, the consent of states provides the certainty and precision necessary to any positive theory of law. In the legal positivism favoured by Kelsen, the system of international legal rules stands at the apex of the universal system of law, thereby securing certainty.

This doctrine, though distinguishable from the territorial ideal, can still accommodate certain levels of inequality within its overall framework. Here, I want to enlist a number of distinctions with a view to making the ensuing discussion of sovereign equality intelligible. The purpose of this next section, then, is to disassemble and reconstruct the principle of sovereign equality in order to tease out its multiple meanings. I will suggest that the standard account of sovereign equality (even in its relativised forms) appears to encompass at least three distinct forms of equality. These are *formal equality*, *legislative equality* and *existential equality*.[69] It is not uncommon for writers to gather several of these sub-species of sovereign equality together under one rubric. For example, the definition of sovereign equality in the seventh edition of Oppenheim is a combination of equality of representation (*legislative equality*) and immunity (*existential equality*).[70] According to Lauterpacht, every state has a vote but one vote only; the votes of the weakest and strongest carry equal weight; no state can claim jurisdiction over another and the courts of one state do not question the validity of official acts carried out within the sphere of another state's jurisdiction.[71] Similarly, the 1970 Declaration on Friendly Relations, regarded as an authoritative interpretation of the Charter's provisions, combines 'juridical equality' (*formal equality*), and 'internal sovereign equality' (*existential equality*). The two forms of equality I describe as formal equality and legislative equality are combined under the broad heading 'sovereign equality' during the discussions on the establishment of the Court of Arbitral Justice by, among others, the Brazilian delegate Rui Barbosa.

Formal equality

States are formally equal to the extent that they are treated as equals before judicial organs in the international system. This formal equality is the element of sovereign equality that persists unmodified in the face of legalised hegemony and anti-pluralism. If sovereign equality can be reconciled with these hierarchies, then it must do so in this abbreviated form.

---

[69] McNair, for example, distinguishes three different levels of equality which he terms forensic equality (i.e. equality in the assertion and vindication of rights already possessed), equality of capacity and legislative equality (equal voting rights and law-creating potential within the system). McNair, 'Equality in International Law' (1927) 26:2 *Michigan Law Review* 13.

[70] Oppenheim, *International Law: A Treatise* vol. I, 7th edn, (ed. H. Lauterpacht).

[71] *Ibid.*, 793.

As Judge Shahabuddeen said in the *Nauru Case*, restating the principle: 'It seems to me that, whatever the debates relating to its precise content in other respects, the concept of equality of States has always applied as a fundamental principle to the position of states before the Court.'[72] This is what Shahabuddeen calls 'perfect equality'.[73] Indeed, so powerful is this image of perfect equality that the Great Powers themselves have often referred to it in submissions before the Court. In *Mavrommattis Concessions*, for example, the UK counsel pleaded that 'even the Great Powers are entitled to justice at the hands of this Tribunal'.[74]

So, formal equality encompasses the principle that *in judicial settings* states have equality in the vindication and 'exercise of rights'. No state can be barred (on the basis of its status) from bringing a claim in international law that its rights have been violated, and in bringing such a claim the state will be treated equally before law. It is formal equality with which the World Court seemed most concerned in 1946 when it brought to the attention of the Security Council, Article 35(2) of the ICJ Statute:

The conditions under which the Court shall be open to other states shall . . . be laid down by the Security Council, but in no case shall such conditions place the parties in a position of inequality before the Court[75]

It is this basic rule of law notion to which most legal instruments and treatises refer when they speak of equality before the law,[76] equality at law[77] and juridical equality.[78] Formal equality has nothing to say about the substance of these rights or the extent and scope of the rights possessed or the capacity to influence the way rights are distributed. When Oscar Schachter speaks of this juridical version of sovereign equality he distinguishes 'the formal ideal of the equality of states under

---

[72] *Certain Phosphate Lands in Nauru Case* (Preliminary Objections) (1992) ICJ Rep. 240 at 270–1; (1993) 32 ILM 46.

[73] This discussion arises out of concerns expressed by both the Australians and the Nauruans about their relative position (e.g. Gavan Griffith, the Australian Solicitor-General, was keen to ensure that the two parties had equal protection, 'rich or poor, big or small' (CR 91/15, at 42) quoted in Separate Opinion at 270).

[74] PCIJ, Series C, No. 5-I, at 64 quoted in Judge Shahabuddeen, Separate Opinion, *Nauru Case* at 270.

[75] Court Statement of 1 March 1946 (quoted in Karel C. Wellens, *Resolutions and Statements of the United Nations Security Council (1946–1989) – A Thematic Guide*, 622).

[76] Goodrich and Hambro, *Charter of the United Nations*, 37.

[77] Starke distinguishes between 'equality at law' and 'capacity for equal rights and legal duties', J. G. Starke, *Introduction to International Law* (9th edn), 104.

[78] UNCIO Doc. 6 at 457.

law' and the way in which powerful states 'impose limits on the equal application of the law'.[79] Provided these limits do not interfere with judicial processes, they are consistent with the principle of formal equality.[80]

In this way, the distinction between formal equality and equality of rights becomes an important one.[81] All states do not have the same rights (absolute equality or equality of rights) though all states have the *legal* capacity to enjoy the rights they already possess in *judicial* settings (formal equality).[82] The establishment of regional customs or functional customary regimes (e.g. those applying to littoral states as opposed to inland states), for example, results in a system in which differentiated sub-categories of rights and duties must exist.[83] So, there can be significant variance in the actual rights possessed. As Simma puts it, states are able to contract out of equal relations by virtue of the prima facie equality they already possess.[84] Or, to put it another way, states and individuals, equal before the law, can nevertheless create different legal situations.[85] Providing this variance is accounted for by some normative structure and has no effect on the narrow principle of equality before the courts, then formal equality is satisfied. Of course, different rules apply to different states. The point is that rules that do apply to the same states should apply equally.[86] In the words of the British delegation in

---

[79] O. Schachter, *International Law in Theory and Practice*, 9.

[80] The ICJ's lack of compulsory jurisdiction means that not every state can have its day in court. But if a state does have a day in court, the principle of formal equality ensures that it is treated equally there.

[81] This is the distinction made by Lorimer ('If all that was meant was that all states are equally entitled to assert such rights as they have, and that they have an equal interest in the vindication of law, the assertion would be as true of States, as of citizens and individuals', *Institutes*, 171). Lorimer suspected that this is not what was meant at all by the doctrine of equality which instead, he argued, asserted that 'all nations are equal in rights' (quoting Kluber, 73).

[82] There are parallels with the domestic legal system in terms of legal personality, e.g. minors and the insane have equality under the law but they do not possess equal rights in law. Similarly individuals have rights, say under the Canadian Charter, but not all legal persons have rights (e.g. corporations do not possess rights to equality under S.15).

[83] See H. Kelsen, 'The Principle of Sovereign Equality of States as a Basis for International Organisation' (1944) 53 *Yale Law Journal*. See, too, A. Pearce Higgins, *Studies in International Law and Relations*, 26.

[84] Simma, *Commentary*, 87. There are limits. A state may contract away its own sovereignty thereby losing it forever. See, also, *Austro-German Customs Union Case*.

[85] See Hans Kelsen, *Principles of International Law*, 155.

[86] A. Watts, 'The International Rule of Law' (1993) 36 *German Yearbook of International Law* 15–45 at 31.

1945: 'All states enjoy an equality of rights but this does not mean that they have the same rights.'[87]

Sometimes, absolute equality is the term used to refer to the equal capacity for rights or equality of capacity. These phrases suggest that those rights that are possessed by a state are necessarily capable of equal exercise. This, too, has been rejected by the majority of publicists. Lord McNair, for example, rejects the idea that states have what he terms 'equality of capacity' (i.e. equality in the enjoyment of rights) because states are unable to vindicate their rights equally e.g. through the doctrine of self-help.[88]

Before leaving formal equality, I want to discuss its relationship with two other analogous principles: reciprocity and the equal right to self-help.

It might be assumed that reciprocity is an element of formal equality, i.e. the idea that states come before the Court as equals and therefore accept the same set of obligations. However, reciprocity is a principle embedded only in the Optional Clause of the ICJ Statute and is not an essential feature of either jurisdiction generally or the principle of formal equality.

The requirement of reciprocity under the Optional Clause is *derived* from the principle of equality. The Court in *Cameroon* v. *Nigeria* makes explicit the connection between the notion of reciprocity and that of equality, but notes that these 'are not abstract conceptions. They must be related to some provision of the Statute or of the Declarations.'[89] This is what Judge Koroma characterises as reciprocal or jurisdictional equality but it stands somewhat to the side of the formal equality discussed in this section.[90] As Ian Brownlie puts it: 'This condition [the condition

[87] Broms, *Doctrine of Equality*, 72.
[88] McNair, 'Equality in International Law', 131. See, too, Dickinson, *Equality of States*, 3. The term 'capacity' is ambiguous. Legal capacity refers to the formal or theoretical capacity of states to acquire rights as a concomitant of their personality. Political capacity refers to the physical ability of a state to, say, 'perform acts'. It seems obvious that states are unequal in the latter sense.
[89] *Cameroon* v. *Nigeria* (1996) ICJ Rep., at 41 quoting the Court in *Right of Passage over Indian Territory*, Preliminary Objections, Judgment (1957) ICJ Rep. at 145.
[90] Judge Koroma's dissenting judgement in *Cameroon* v. *Nigeria*. Interestingly, in the case of reciprocal formal equality it is only the *substantive* commitments of states that are subject to reciprocity. The *formal* undertakings included in Declarations are not thought to give rise to reciprocal rights: '[t]he notion of reciprocity is concerned with the scope and substance of the commitments entered into, including reservations, and not with the formal conditions of their creation, duration or extinction' (*Military and Paramilitary Activities in and against Nicaragua (Nicaragua v. United States of America)*, Jurisdiction and Admissibility, Judgment (1984) ICJ Rep., at 419, para. 62.

of reciprocity] is a part of the Statute itself and applies to declarations expressed to be made "unconditionally".'[91] Reciprocity is integral, then, to Article 36(2) but is it applicable to all cases before the ICJ?

The Court in *Rights of Passage* held that the principle of reciprocity operated as 'part of the system of the Optional Clause' under 36(2).[92] However, there is no reference to reciprocity in Article 36(1). It would be strange if Article 36(1) included a reference to reciprocity because the treaty and the *compromis* are both highly consensual instruments permitting states to enter into non-reciprocal obligations relating to, *inter alia*, jurisdiction. In this sense, consent overrides equality in the same way that sovereigns must have the right to divest themselves of elements of their own sovereignty.[93]

Hugh Thirlway argues that while reciprocity is an integral part of Article 36(2) it is not a general principle of international jurisdiction. This is not to deny that reciprocity exists in a number of different forms in international law but it is not a mandatory part of every jurisdictional scheme.[94]

The relationship between self-help and formal equality is more complicated. Here, we are considering the vindication of rights in extra-curial settings. Rights are (more) regularly asserted in bilateral inter-state relations than in courts or tribunals. International law departs from its domestic counterpart most obviously in the fact that its enforcement regimes envisage a large element of self-help. Equality before domestic law assumes, in the last resort, that the exercise of rights will be secured by the courts and that individuals will be treated as equals before these courts. International law's enforcement practices have a much less judicial emphasis. Rights will often be vindicated via mechanisms of self-help rather than through court procedures. However, self-help is dependent on the vagaries of power, will and capacity. Larger states have a greater capacity to vindicate their legal claims through the projection of power than do their smaller counterparts. Can formal equality be

---

[91] Ian Brownlie, *Principles*, 727. This is only significant in the sense that Declarations that attach conditions of reciprocity are rendered otiose. See e.g. United Kingdom Declaration Accepting the Compulsory Jurisdiction of the Court, Misc. No 4. (1969), Cmnd 3872. See also *Norwegian Loans Case* (1957) ICJ Rep. at 9; *Anglo-Iranian Oil Co* (1952) ICJ Rep., at 103; Hugh Thirlway, 'Reciprocity' (1983) 15 *Netherlands Yearbook of International Law*.

[92] *Rights of Passage Case* at 125. See, too, Professor Waldock in the Pleadings of this case: 'equality, mutuality and reciprocity are principles which are at the very basis of the Optional Clause system' (*ICJ Pleadings* vol. 4 at 37).

[93] PCIJ A, No. 1, 25.   [94] Thirlway, 'Reciprocity'.

reconciled with this fact? There are two ways to approach this question. One approach would conclude that since self-help is a legal institution, the vindication of rights itself is tainted with inequality. In international law, then, there is no equality before the law or equality under the law but instead a more limited equality before judicial institutions. An alternative approach might argue that, since the law places no barrier before the right of small states to self-help, equality is preserved. The mere fact of incapacity or weakness is a political phenomenon and does not impair the existence of the legal right.

This latter argument is familiar in domestic law where differences in capacity influence the outcome of cases but where legal processes are intended to place the two parties on an equal footing. In international law, it may be more difficult to draw a bright line between legal rights and political power in non-judicial settings. Self-help is a legal institution but the structure of its operation seems wholly dependent on political power. I tend to agree with Fenwick, writing in 1934, when he distinguished substantive rights to equality (existential equality), 'equality with respect to the adoption of new rules of law' (legislative equality) and equal protection.[95] This latter category contained two elements. The first was the idea of equality before the courts (formal equality), a right Fenwick agreed was capable of enjoyment in international law. However, he went on to say that the second element of protection, self-help, operated at the boundaries of the legal and political. Ultimately, the equal right to self-help is problematic. All states possessed the same rights in relation to self-help but the inability of some states to exercise this right empties it of much meaning for those states.[96]

To conclude, formal equality or equality before the law is an integral part of what most lawyers understand as 'sovereign equality'. It is the very essence of what it means to possess legal equality and is compatible with a large range of inequalities. However, this form of equality exists only before judicial organs. It refers to the formal equality of the parties before the Court in relation to their substantive arguments and extends neither to forms of jurisdictional equality nor to equal capacity to vindicate rights outside the judicial context.

In particular, formal equality is consistent with the creation of international organisations in which the Great Powers have commensurately

---

[95] C. G. Fenwick, *International Law* 2nd edn, 152.
[96] Fenwick's solution was to shift enforcement from the bilateral level to the institutional level (*ibid.*, 152).

greater legal status (legalised hegemony). Formal equality also is consistent with international regimes in which certain states are deprived
of sovereign rights on the basis of their 'moral' characteristics (anti-
pluralism) (this is important because, as Jenks notes, stronger forms of
equality based on rights and functions are likely to inhibit the development of effective international organisations).[97] Sovereign equality and
status differentiation thereby are reconciled within this relatively narrow reading of equality. As Goodrich and Hambro note, formal or juridical equality is compatible with 'substantial inequality of participation
and influence in international relations'.[98] However, when lawyers speak
of sovereign equality, they often mean more than simply formal equality.[99] I now want to discuss the two other aspects of equality that are
sometimes thought to be encompassed by the term 'sovereign equality'.

In this book, I argue that states possess an undiluted right to formal
equality. I now want to describe two ideal types of equality: legislative
equality and existential equality. Neither of these two principles has
existed in an unmodified sense since at least 1815. However, the idea
that states have some form of equal right to make and enforce law
and an equal right to full legal personality has remained influential
in international law and in the construction of international regimes
and organisations.

Legislative equality

The principle of legislative equality itself includes at least two different
dimensions of the law-making process in international law and I want
to take care to distinguish these.

First, it describes the idea that states are bound only by those legal
norms to which they have given their consent. Second, and in its
stronger forms, a principle of legislative equality would mandate an
equally weighted vote and equal representation in the decision-making
processes within international bodies, and an equal role in the formation and application of customary law and treaty law. More particularly,
and this is the subject of the next four chapters, a strong commitment
to legislative equality would deprive the Great Powers of any special role
within the international legal order.

---

[97] See W. Jenks, 'The Scope of International Law' (1954) 31 BYIL 12. See, too, M. Sibert,
    Traité de Droit international public, 267 in Broms, *Doctrine of Equality*, 57; International
    Juridical Union, *Declaration of the Rights and Duties of Nations* 1920, Article 3.
[98] Goodrich and Hamro, *Charter of the United Nations*, 37.
[99] See examples in Chapters 1 and 4.

I want to continue by distinguishing these forms of legislative equality from another phenomenon that might be termed '(in)equality of influence'. The first two categories (involving formal rights to equal participation in law-making) and the third, describing equality of influence, are quite different beasts. In the following discussion, I consider the various ways in which the first two principles of equality fail to reflect what actually occurs in law-making at the international level. First, though, I will briefly consider this third category because it needs to be differentiated from the core interest of this book, i.e. *legalised hegemony*.

Inequalities of influence exist in any relatively free political system. Informal applications of raw power can have an enormous impact on the eventual content of legal rules and such influence is impossible to write out of any system of governance including, and, perhaps, especially, international law.[100] This, however, is an acknowledgment of political influence rather than legal hierarchy.[101] Many scholars have pointed out how power differentials operate to affect the emergence of legal norms and the substantive inequalities existing in the international order have given rise to an enormous body of scholarship.[102] As Ngaire Woods has pointed out, the 'Haves' in the international system are not just materially advantaged but have correspondingly greater capacity to influence and shape the content of the rules.[103]

Sometimes this 'influence' translates into legal hierarchies or privileges (e.g. the Security Council, unequal treaties, universal law), at other times it operates solely at the informal, political level discussed in the previous paragraph (virtually any treaty-making conference including those in which participation and representation are on an equal basis). I am interested in inequality only when it takes the first form involving participation at the formal level. I take it as a given that Great Powers are able to exercise more influence in informal settings. The

---

[100] See, e.g. Shaw, *International Law*, 149 (stating, 'it would not be strictly accurate to talk in terms of the equality of states in creating law. The major powers will always have an influence commensurate with their status').

[101] 'The right to contribute to the formation of such obligations and the duty to comply with them when they have been created are the equal attribute and responsibility of all states' (C. Warbrick, 'The Principle of Sovereign Equality' in V. Lowe and C. Warbrick (eds.) *The United Nations and the Principles of International Law: Essays in Memory of Michael Akehurst*, 205).

[102] In international law, see Michael Byers, *Custom, Power and the Power of Rules*. In legal theory, see Marc Galanter, 'Why the "Haves" Come Out Ahead: Speculations on the Limits of Social Change' (1974) 9 *Law and Society Review* 97–114.

[103] N. Woods, 'Order, Globalisation, and Inequality in World Politics' in Hurrell and Woods, *Inequality*, 21.

study of this form of inequality is the professional concern of international relations scholars or those who wish to investigate the sociology of international treaty-making. These are fascinating projects but they are not mine. When I speak of legislative equality or inequality I am more interested in formal reflections of the power differences in the international system.

Unfortunately, these distinctions will not always be obvious. To take a marginal case, Judge Shi, in the *Legality of Nuclear Weapons*, describes what he sees as the difference between inequality of political influence and formally sanctioned legislative inequalities, and links each of them explicitly to sovereign equality:

this 'appreciable section of the international community' adhering to the policy of deterrence is composed of certain nuclear weapon States and those States that accept the protection of the 'nuclear umbrella'. No doubt, these States are important and powerful members of the international community and play an important role on the stage of international politics. However, the Court, as the principal judicial organ of the United Nations, cannot view this 'appreciable section of the international community' in terms of material power. The Court can only have regard to it from the standpoint of international law. Today the international community of States has a membership of over 185 States. The appreciable section of this community to which the Opinion refers by no means constitutes a large proportion of that membership, and the structure of the international community is built on the principle of sovereign equality. Therefore, any undue emphasis on the practice of this 'appreciable section' would not only be contrary to the very principle of sovereign equality of States, but would also make it more difficult to give an accurate and proper view of the existence of a customary rule on the use of the weapon.

The nuclear powers no doubt wield exceptional influence in the development of global nuclear policy. However, according to Judge Shi, this influence is irrelevant in assessments of state practice. Such assessments must be based on sovereign equality rather than differential capacity. In other words, hierarchies of power need not be reflected in judicial reasoning about the creation of customary norms within the system.[104]

However, some inequalities do have legal effects (for example, it may be that the nuclear states do exercise greater power over the law of nuclear weapons *within* the confines of legality through the doctrine of

---

[104] A further complication is introduced when one thinks of the role of judges. If judges 'make' law then the unequal representation of states on the World Court could be said to be a form of legislative inequality (see Chapter 5).

specially affected states discussed below). These legislative inequalities come in two forms. First, legislative inequality operates as a method of imposing norms on non-consenting states. Second, it distinguishes between Great Powers and middle powers in international constitutional law and treaty-making (*legalised hegemony*) and in the creation of custom (the doctrine of specially-affected states) and its application (Chapter 11).[105]

The classic positivist doctrines of law-making insist on some sort of equality of consent in the development of customary international law. This does not mean that every state has the same influence in the creation of custom. It does mean, however, that conformity to the principle of legislative equality requires that states are able to object to the application of customary rules to themselves (the persistent objector doctrine).[106] Treaty law operates in a similar way. States are bound only by those treaties they ratify or those to which they accede.[107] Termination, for example, is possible only in cases of, for example, frustration or change of circumstances (the object of consent having changed).[108]

This principle, though, has been somewhat weakened by claims that the development of universal custom cannot be held hostage to the recalcitrance of a small number of deviant states.[109] As Starke put it, '[F]requently small states were able to hold up important advances in international affairs by selfish obstruction under the shelter of the unanimity rule.'[110] The continued development of universalist, objective norms such as norms *jus cogens*, obligations *erga omnes* and international crimes, and the rise of the objective treaty regime all point to a move from strict positivism, absolute equality of consent and unanimity towards decision-making that is either majoritarian (General Assembly) or universalist (*jus cogens*).[111] In particular there has been a tendency to accord General Assembly resolutions normative force. In academic writings and in decisions of the ICJ, these resolutions are regarded

---

[105] Another form of inequality establishes a threshold for any sort of participation within the international system or within a particular international organisation or within the international order (recognition, admission). I discuss this in a later section on existential equality.

[106] *Asylum Case* (1950) ICJ Rep. 266 at 278.

[107] Or as signatories they are bound to observe the objects and purposes of the treaty (VCLT Article 18).

[108] See, e.g. VCLT Articles 60–2.

[109] See, e.g. Jonathan Charney, 'Universal International Law' (1983) 87 AJIL 529.

[110] Starke's *Introduction*, 104.

[111] See discussion of hierarchy in Chapter 2 and anti-pluralism in Chapter 8.

as (at least indirect) sources of obligation.[112] As one academic put it, 'the licensing, authorising, recognising and constitutive powers of the recommendations of the General Assembly . . . largely account[s] for its political potency'.[113] The *Nicaragua Case* and Judge Tanaka's famous and influential dissent in the *South West Africa Case Second Phase*, for example, point towards the use of General Assembly Resolutions as components of custom (even where voting is not unanimous).[114] In *Nicaragua*, the Court held that '*opinio juris* may, with all due caution, be deduced from, *inter alia*, the attitude of the parties and the attitude of States towards certain General Assembly resolutions . . .'.[115]

As well as allowing the development of forms of universal law (binding on objector states), legislative equality is affected by distinctions existing between different classes of state on the basis of their influence or power. The Great Powers possess constitutional privileges within international organisations or dominate the law-making process at international conferences (see Chapters 4 to 7). A strong form of legislative equality would regard as impermissible the special law-making powers of the states of the first rank. The powers and privileges afforded the Great Powers in the Security Council, in voting procedures in important financial organisations and in the creation of new legal regimes are examples of these special law-making powers and tend to suggest that strong legislative equality does not exist in international law despite a general commitment to sovereign equality.[116] This legalised hegemony is one of the primary subjects of the book. In the following chapters I ask how it arises or when it is converted from political domination and I discuss the ways in which it is reconciled with a form of sovereign equality.

The law-making privileges of the Great Powers are reflected most explicitly in the doctrine of specially affected states; a form of legislative inequality that, does offer special law-making power to Judge Shi's

---

[112] See, e.g. M. Reisman, 'A Hard Look at Soft Law' (1988) 82 *Proceedings of the American Society of International Law* 371; R. Higgins, 'The United Nations and Law-Making: The Political Organs' (1970) *Proceedings of the American Society of International Law*; I. Brownlie, 'The United Nations as a Form of Government' (1972) 13 *Harvard Journal of International Law* 421.

[113] G. Gottlieb, 'Global Bargaining' in N. Onuf (ed.), *Law-Making in the Global Community*, 109 at 122–3.

[114] *South-West Africa*, Second Phase (1966) ICJ Rep., at 248.

[115] *Nicaragua Case*, para. 188.

[116] I discuss later the argument that these hierarchies are derived from the egalitarian practice of equal consent, i.e. that the UN membership has consented in advance to the superior powers of the UN Security Council.

'appreciable sections' of the international community. In the *North Sea Continental Shelf Cases*, the judgement of the Court distinguishes between the practice of, say, land-locked states and that of specially affected states. According to the Court, the practice of these latter states contributes to a greater degree to the creation of custom.[117] As Judge Tanaka states in another dissenting opinion: 'We cannot evaluate the ratification of the Convention by a large maritime country . . . as having the same importance as similar acts by a land-locked country which possesses no particular interest in the delimitation of the continental shelf.'[118] In an analysis of the cases, Hersch Lauterpacht noted the particular importance of the great maritime powers in establishing state practice for the purposes of delimiting the continental shelf.[119] As he put it, 'with regard to the continental shelf and submarine areas generally, the conduct of the two principal maritime powers [at that point, the United States and Great Britain] inaugurated the development and their initiative was treated as authoritative almost as a matter of course from the outset'.[120]

Existential equality

I want to conclude this section by turning to those legal hierarchies that operate as modes of exclusion or that classify states according to culture or civilisation or democracy rather than power. These hierarchies offend a principle of existential equality that arises out of a recognition by the international community that an entity is entitled to sovereign statehood and that equality is the immediate product of fully recognised sovereignty. Existential equality, then, is the foundation of a pluralist conception of international legal order.

In discussing sovereign equality, Hans Kelsen endorsed a version of equality that emphasised the independence and immunity of states; so that while not all states have the same positive rights each possesses a threshold of negative rights or immunities and certain minimal rights of participation.[121] Existential equality, then, includes a

---

[117] *North Sea Continental Shelf Cases* (1969) ICJ Rep., at para. 73.

[118] D. J. Harris, *Cases and Materials on International Law* (4th edn), 36.

[119] See, too, C. de Visscher, *Theory and Reality*, 155 (arguing that the Great Powers were 'always decisive in the formation of customary international law'). Only these powers can give the rules effectiveness. He gives as an example the role of the United States in the formation of custom at the turn of the century.

[120] (1969) ICJ Rep., para. 3.; (1950) 27 BYIL 376 at 994.

[121] The mere enjoyment of statehood does not assure an entity of full participation in international organisations. Not all states are members of the United Nations. States

state's sphere of domestic jurisdiction (Article 2(7) of the UN Charter), its right to territorial integrity, its right to political independence and its right to participate in international institutions. Existential equality encompasses also states' dignity. As Philip Jessup put it, 'States have "feelings"'.[122]

When publicists refer to states as having the same rights, this existential equality is often what is meant. States have a set of sovereign rights in common while other rights are distributed unequally. These rights in common are, in Heffter's words, 'based upon its existence as a state in the international society'.[123] This form of equality is basically coterminous with conventional understandings of sovereignty and independence. Each state possesses a sphere of jurisdictional supremacy and immunity as well as a right to territorial integrity and a qualified immunity from intervention. Associated with this is the right to exist in a form of a state's own choosing. This pluralist element within existential equality derives from states' rights to self-determination and is usually expressed as 'the right freely to choose and develop its political, social, economic and cultural systems'.[124] The internal characteristics of states are not relevant to the concept of sovereign statehood (once possessed).[125] (I discuss the various incursions into this existential right later.) Existential equality, then, is defined as a right to exist (territorial integrity), the right to choose the manner of existence (political independence) and the right to participate in the international system as a consequence of the first two rights: so, that the corollary of existential equality is the norm of non-intervention and the right to choose one's own form of government free from external interference.[126] The Cuban delegate at San Francisco captured this idea in the following terms: 'Every state has a right to exist . . . to organise itself as it sees fit . . .'.[127] This was reaffirmed in *Nicaragua* when, in the process of deploring what it termed ideological intervention, the Court noted that 'adherence by any

do not have an automatic right to participate in the regulation of international organisations The UN like other international organisations has a right to regulate its own membership *pace* M. Sibert, *Traité*, 267 in Broms, *Doctrine of Equality*, 57. See *Conditions of Admission of a State to Membership in the United Nations* (1948) ICJ Rep. at 57.

[122] P. Jessup, *A Modern Law of Nations*, 28.

[123] *Volksrecht*, secs. 26–7 (quoted in Dickinson, *Equality of States*, 137).

[124] General Assembly Special Committee on Friendly Relations (1963) GA Res. 1966 (XVIII), (16 December 1963).

[125] Simma, *Commentary*, 87.

[126] But see, e.g. Phillimore, *Commentaries*, Section 162, 149 (arguing that these rights belong to the category of independence and not equality).

[127] Cuban Proposals on Dumbarton Oaks, UNCIO III at 496, Doc. 2 g/14(g) 2 May 1945.

state to any particular doctrine does not constitute a violation of international law' before going on to say that such a principle makes a nonsense of 'a fundamental principle of international law, state sovereignty, and violates the freedom of choice of the political, economic, social and cultural system of states'.[128]

Existential equality is central to the broad commitment to pluralism that has proved relatively durable in international affairs since Westphalia. The notion that states have certain immunities and rights to choose their own political system is well established. Of course, states have disappeared sometimes to re-appear (Poland), sometimes not (the Kingdom of Bohemia), but the overall logic of the system has insisted on the preservation of a territorial integrity and political independence for those entities privileged enough to be recognised as states.[129] As Hedley Bull has argued, 'the attempt to remould a states system on principles of ideological fixity is likely to be a source of disorder'.[130]

Existential equality is compatible with quite pronounced inequalities in voting power (legislative inequality).[131] However, I will argue in this book that a strong commitment to existential equality is not compatible with the forms of anti-pluralism found in the nineteenth and twentieth centuries (Chapters 7–8) and is being challenged by theories of democratic governance and liberal exceptionalism in the twenty-first (Chapter 9). States consigned to the margins of the international system do not enjoy the rights associated with this principle. The legal structures that designate and treat states as outlaws or criminals or failed states deprive this small proportion of states of their sovereign rights. These states become unequal sovereigns in relation to the generality of states within the system. This anti-pluralist movement radically changes the basis of war and peace in international society. Most critically,

---

[128] *Nicaragua* (Merits) at para. 263. See, too, Letter of 20 November 1991 (issued as United Nations document A/46/844 and S/23416) where Libya emphasised that the Charter 'guarantees the equality of peoples and their right to make their own political and social choices, a right that is enshrined in religious laws and is guaranteed by international law' (quoted in *Case Concerning Questions of Interpretation and Application of the Montreal Convention Arising from the Aerial Incident at Lockerbie, United Arab Jamahiriya v. The United Kingdom* (Preliminary Phase), Dissenting Opinion, Judge Oda at para. 30).

[129] Of course, there are occasionally challenges to the existence of individual states (e.g. the Iraqi invasion of Kuwait) but even these are exceedingly rare in the international order. See M. Koskenniemi, 'The Future of Statehood' (1991) 32:2 *Harvard International Law Journal* 397–410.

[130] Bull, *Anarchical Society* (2nd edn), 240.

[131] See, e.g. M. Korowicz, *La Souveraineté des Etats et l'avenir du droit international*, 78–9, quoted in Broms, *Doctrine of Equality*, 55.

enemies are converted from adversaries in the context of sovereign equality into 'outlaws of humanity' on the plane of anti-pluralism.[132] This tension between the pluralist commitment to existential equality and anti-pluralism is the subject of the third part of this book.

Tolerated inequalities

The purpose of this chapter has been to demonstrate that sovereign equality contains three separable elements (formal equality, legislative equality and existential equality). I will go on to show that the latter two are heavily qualified in practice by exercises of legalised hegemony that have recurred in international law since 1815 and an anti-pluralist conception of international community that can also be traced back to the early nineteenth century.

I now want to end this chapter by noting some inequalities among states that are relatively uncontroversial under a classic conception of sovereignty. In particular, I discuss the material inequalities sanctioned by the principle of sovereign equality (or about which sovereign equality has nothing to say).

The doctrine of sovereign equality, no matter how interpreted, is compatible with an array of tolerated social inequalities. Most obviously, there is no strong principle mandating substantive or economic equality between states in international law. Material inequalities flourish in the inter-state system and international law at the level of structure or concept has little to say about these. This is not to suggest that there are not specific regimes designed to ameliorate inequality nor that individual states do not attempt to remedy the most visible inequalities nor is it to suggest that certain principles embodied in soft law could not ultimately generate a stronger version of sovereign equality.[133] However, it is clear that there is no general duty or obligation to produce material parity or even relief in the international system.[134] There is no general principle requiring affirmative action on behalf of disadvantaged states.[135]

---

[132] See Schmitt, *Concept of the Political*, 54.

[133] See R. Tucker, *Inequality of Nations*, *passim*.

[134] But see, e.g. *The Stockholm Declaration on the Human Environment* at http://www.unesco.org/iau/tfsd_stockholm.html adopted on 16 June 1972.

[135] See *Libya-Malta Continental Shelf* (1985) ICJ Rep. at 13; Warbrick, 'The Principle of Sovereign Equality', 208. See, too, K. B. Lall, 'Economic Inequality and International Law' (1974) 14 *Indian Journal of International Law* 7; Thomas Franck, 'Is Justice Relevant to the International Legal System?' (1989) 64:5 *Notre Dame Law Review* 945–63. For a later, different view, see T. Franck, *Fairness in International Law and Institutions*.

At the political level, inequalities in the capacity to effect legal solutions or to exact compliance with legal norms are part and parcel of an international system based to a large extent on self-help. The right to self-defence or the capacity to take counter-measures are largely dependent on military or economic capabilities.[136] The unequal distribution of power also affects the capacity of states to influence legal outcomes through informal pressures. When the United States threatened sanctions against Yemen for its failure to support Security Council Resolutions against Iraq, it was using precisely this form of power. Distasteful as this may seem in some quarters, there is nothing illegal about it. This, too, is regarded as a tolerable inequality.

Indeed, inequalities exist and are justified in international society for the same reason they exist in domestic societies. Liberty, in this instance the liberty or sovereignty of states, is a powerful barrier to the imposition of egalitarian initiatives. State self-interest is the default position and any obligations to weaker members of the community have to be established through the creation of certain legal rules. Accordingly, states are entitled to prefer particular states as their trading partners and are not required to abide by non-discrimination norms in any of their practices outside the formal rules set out in the GATT/WTO.[137] In this way, sovereign equality and economic or political inequality are not simply co-existent but co-dependent. Without rights to sovereign equality, states would be unable to pursue the very economic projects that differentiate them from one another.[138]

---

[136] Warbrick, 'The Principle of Sovereign Equality', 209.

[137] An exception to this may lie in the area of expropriation of foreign property but this exception is not designed to achieve redistributive outcomes. See, e.g. *Amoco International Finance Corp.* v. *Iran* paras. 140–2.

[138] The position within the GATT is more ambiguous. Article I of the GATT demands that all contracting parties be treated equally in regard to tariff concessions conceded by a state party. In other words, all imports are to be treated in the same manner. (See W. F. Schwartz and A. O. Sykes, 'Toward a Positive Theory of the Most Favoured Nation Obligation and its Exceptions in the WTO/GATT System' (1996) 16 *International Review of Law and Economics*, 27.) On the other hand, the GATT permits a number of economic inequalities to exist with the purpose of protecting developing nations, e.g. preferential tariff rates are permitted between former colonies and their 'parent' states (see Trebilcock and Howse, *The Regulation of International Trade*, 369). In addition, the Generalised System of Preferences and the Lomé Convention permit a measure of derogation from the GATT's MFN rules in favour of developing states in general (see Trebilcock and Howse, *Regulation of International Trade*, 373). For a discussion of differential treatment in international law in the environmental area arguing that such treatment is a beneficial deviation from the principle of sovereign equality, see Phillipe Cullet, 'Differential Treatment', 549.

This tension between formal equality and economic liberty is caught nicely by Georg Schwarzenberger when he states: 'International law does not ordain economic equality between states nor their subjects. Economic sovereignty reigns supreme.'[139] It is not impossible that states could agree to institute some overarching policies of redistribution while retaining their economic sovereignty. However, this remains unlikely partly because, while agreement can be reached on the injustice of certain types of absolute deprivation, there is wide-ranging disagreement on the preferred methods for ameliorating these deprivations and substantial disharmony on the desirability of measures designed to achieve more substantive equalities.[140]

Indeed, all sorts of complications are raised when we consider the question of what sort of equality is due to states in the international system. David Miller explores some analogous questions in his essay 'Justice and Global Equality'. He begins by noticing the moral discomfort we experience on reflecting that Tanzanians enjoy an average per capita GNP of $140 as compared to the equivalent German figure of $25,000 (188–9). Our concern here, however, seems to be about absolute deprivation.[141] In a world of great wealth it seems unconscionable that some have so little or, worse, too little to survive. But this sense of injustice may well spring not from concerns about equality but rather from concerns about absolute deprivation. As Thomas Schelling puts it, in another context, we may agree on closing the gap but disagree profoundly about by how much the gap should be closed.[142]

The issue is further complicated if we think of the differences in per capita GNP enjoyed by Spaniards and Germans ($13,000 as against $25,000). Again, it may be that many of us would regard this as an acceptable and tolerable accident of history and geography. We may conclude that Spaniards enjoy a reasonable standard of living. The relative disadvantage suffered by the average Spaniard does not engage our moral concern because of our sense that the citizens of Spain enjoy a standard of wealth that in absolute terms is acceptable. However, such differences

---

[139] Georg Schwarzenberger, 'Equality and Discrimination in International Economic Law' 25 Yearbook of World Affairs 163. Article 1 of the WTO is an attempt to change this.

[140] See David Miller, 'Justice and Global Equality' in Hurrell and Woods, Inequality, 188–9.

[141] It is the fact that Tanzanians live in poverty that tends to offend us here, not the degree to which this poverty stands in contrast to Germany's wealth. German wealth is relevant because it proves that there are sufficient resources to go around. For a discussion of relative deprivation see the comparison between Spain and Germany.

[142] Schelling, Causes and Consequences: Perspectives of an Errant Economist.

will not always be tolerable simply because the disadvantaged group exists above the poverty level. For example, if Spain was a province of Germany the position of the Spanish might then adopt a more sinister form. To take one final example (drawn from Miller), if Tanzania was a province of Germany we might regard the difference in GNP as 'a flagrant violation of social justice'.[143] In other words, if this were the case, it might seem even worse to us or more objectionable a difference than that found in the first instance (where Tanzania and Germany are two separate states).[144]

These examples suggest a number of ways to proceed in our thoughts about sovereign equality and hierarchy in the international system. First, according to the classical liberal view of international law, certain levels of inequality would be tolerable providing they do not result in a loss of sovereignty.[145] What David Held calls 'the classic regime of sovereignty' accepts that entities are able to function as states with a certain degree of legal and political independence even in the face of quite severe material deprivation.[146] The concern over Somalia, reflected in its configuration as a 'failed' state, arose out of a sense that Somalia lacked independence or sovereignty and not because it was a shockingly poor country. Similarly, Kampuchea's sovereign equality was thought unimpaired by the policies of the Khmer Rouge (despite the devastating impact of those policies on the Cambodian people and the level of economic deprivation suffered by the country as a whole). Conversely, the Vietnamese invasion

[143] Miller, 'Justice and Inequality', 187.
[144] There are some who would find all inequalities intolerable. These observers would take a more cosmopolitan view of the Tanzanian-German instance and conclude that the change in circumstances makes no difference. The duty of equality exists towards individuals not states (see, for a parallel example, though one lacking the sharply redistributive dimension, e.g. Tesón, 'Kantian Theory', 53–102). Others might point to the presence of de facto Tanzanias within wealthy Western societies, e.g. South Eastern LA and the Aboriginal communities in Australia's Northern Territory. The classical liberal international law position on inequality has accepted that inequality is a matter for internal remedy or a natural concomitant of sovereign equality. Neither the severe economic disadvantage felt by states within the international political order nor that experienced by groups within states was a matter of international concern. This position was modified during the 1960s when the United Nations began imposing sanctions against governments practising apartheid. However, it was the particular form of racism (neo-colonial) that was deemed offensive rather than racism itself (compare the reaction to the (ongoing) treatment of the Kurds by Turkey at this time or the disadvantage experienced by the Irish Catholics in Northern Ireland) or economic inequality generally.
[145] I discuss what it means to adopt such a perspective in Chapter 3.
[146] See Held, *Cosmopolitanism*, Paper on file with author.

of Cambodia was widely condemned not because Cambodia was worse off (it was not) but because formal sovereign equality had been adversely affected by a breach of territorial integrity.

It is this attitude towards sovereign equality that provides the rationale for the inaction of the international community in situations such as those outlined in the Tanzanian example above because it permits international lawyers to view Tanzanians and Germans as belonging to fundamentally different communities. This would not be the case if Tanzania was a province of Germany (a change of circumstance bringing a different set of moral assumptions to bear). Miller makes the point that inequalities may become a matter of injustice when these inequalities arise within societies or communities. He claims that membership in a community creates some presumption of equal treatment. 'Thus suppose a nation-state were to give unequal voting rights to different classes of citizens . . . this would inevitably be experienced as humiliating by those placed in the category of second-class citizens'.[147] Because Tanzanians are not citizens of Germany the resultant inequalities do not appear to be as intuitively unjust. This argument resembles one made by Thomas Franck where he suggests that the inter-state system is incompatible with the pursuit of strong forms of equality precisely because it is founded on a sovereignty that regards arbitrary distinctions based on place of birth as justifications for radically different treatment.[148] There are other structural hierarchies that are perfectly compatible with most plausible understandings of sovereign equality. The distinction between states and non-states is the most obvious way in which inequality structures the operation of the system itself.[149]

---

[147] Miller, 'Justice and Inequality', 189.

[148] See e.g. T. Franck, 'Is Justice Relevant to the International Legal System?', 19. This argument accepts some basic assumptions about the validity of the sovereign-state system. However, it looks less convincing viewed from the perspective of some brands of cosmopolitanism (emphasising world citizenship and denying the legitimacy of the state/non-state distinction) and those elements of radical internationalism that deny the acceptability of massive economic inequalities in the global order. See R. Falk, 'The Pursuit of International Justice: Present Dilemmas and An Imagined Future' (1992) 52:2 *Journal of International Affairs* 409–44; R. Falk, *A Study of Future Worlds*; Armstrong 'Law, Justice and the Idea of World Society'. For a radical internationalism see I. Wallerstein, *After Liberalism*. Meanwhile, realists have tolerated sovereign equality as well as attempts to effect economic redistribution only providing these do not interfere with balancing structures and security interests, i.e. necessary inequalities.

[149] See Chapter 3. This was a difficulty Westlake understood when he distinguished between protectorates over states and protectorates in uncivilised regions (see Westlake, *Chapters*, xiv).

So, the classic principle of sovereign equality can accommodate, and indeed, justify a number of material hierarchies. These latter material and structural inequalities are not directly the subject of the book.[150] However, it is important to understand how these inequalities relate to the idea of sovereign equality so that the legalised hierarchies I am most concerned with can be brought into relief.

It is to these hierarchies and their relationship to anarchy and equality that I now turn in the following chapter.

---

[150] For an example of structural inequality see the background political ideas that structure our understandings of world order, e.g. the talk of first, second and third worlds in the cold war and the split between developed states and underdeveloped or developing states.

3   Legalised hierarchies

Introduction

States possess differing prerogatives in the international legal order. Some are Great Powers, capable of, and legally authorised to, project force in ways that would be unlawful for other states in the system. Other states are outlaws, denied the basic protections of sovereignty. In this chapter I define what I mean by legalised hierarchies before going on to discuss more explicitly the concepts of legalised hegemony and anti-pluralism. All of this prepares the ground for an historical account of the interaction between hierarchy and equality in the workings of the international system and in theories about that system (Chapters 4 to 10).

It should be clear already that I adopt an inter-disciplinary perspective on this relationship but I do not want to overstate the degree to which the book integrates the two disciplines of international law and international relations. This is primarily a work about international law. When I speak of hierarchy or equality, I am concerned mainly with their operation in legal settings or when they adopt legal forms. Nevertheless, I do not believe it is possible to approach these matters from an exclusively legal perspective. The book is partly about the impact of different theories of international order on the way institutions and doctrines are structured. These theories of international order cannot be described as either public international law or international relations theories (Chapter 1). This chapter, in fact, relies heavily on readings drawn from international relations since it is work in this field that has had the most to say about inter-state hierarchies.

The chapter is divided into four sections. In Section 1, I consider how hierarchy operates in conditions of anarchy. I set out, then, my conception of hierarchy and contrast it with two broader categories of hierarchy drawn from the public international law literature and the international relations literature. Sections 2 and 3 focus on the two forms of hierarchy with which the remaining chapters of this book are most concerned. The first is *legalised hegemony*, i.e. the juridical dominance of the Great Powers acting in concert. The second form of hierarchy, *anti-pluralism*, encompasses a number of different legal hierarchies and exclusions operating within the state system based on culture and ideology rather than power. The idea of anti-pluralism is taken up in much greater detail in Chapters 8, 9 and 10. In Section 4, I discuss some hierarchies that do not fall within these two conceptions.

Hierarchy and anarchy

Hedley Bull's major contribution to international thought, *The Anarchical Society*, characterises the international order as anarchical not because it is chaotic or disordered but because it lacks a centralised law-making and law-enforcing authority.[1] States find themselves in a state of anarchy in the sense that they acknowledge no legal superior. To a certain extent, then, sovereignty and anarchy are mutually supportive institutions within the international order: sovereignty being a zone of exclusive legal authority; anarchy the co-existence of these sovereigns.[2]

Debate about the compatibility of law and anarchy is a permanent feature of the intellectual landscape in international law and relations. The question: 'Is international law, law?' derives from an assumed mismatch between conditions of anarchy and the existence of law. John Austin famously questioned the existence of public international law on precisely these grounds. In the absence of a single over-arching world sovereign how could there be law among sovereigns? Latter-day legal positivists, such as H. L. A. Hart, were more sympathetic to international law but nevertheless remained unsure of its precise status because of problems related to validity, coercion and identification.[3]

---

[1] See, e.g. H. Bull, 'Society and Anarchy in International Relations', in H. Butterfield and M. Wight (eds.), *Diplomatic Investigations* ('anarchy it is possible to regard as the central fact of international life and the starting-point of theorising about it' (33)).

[2] But see A. Wendt, *The Social Theory of International Politics* (for a discussion of the contingent nature of anarchy).

[3] Hart believed international law was a 'primitive' system of law: his word for what the likes of Bull call 'anarchy'. According to Hart, primitive societies lacked secondary rules or a valid and transparent law-making machinery. However, he might have accepted that these societies were hierarchical in the sense that law was enforced by, say, chieftains or Great Powers in a semi-formal style. See H. L. A. Hart, *The Concept of Law* (1st edn), 3, for parallels between international law and primitive law.

International legal positivists shared the concerns of their domestic counterparts. They, too, believed that valid law required compulsion, identifiability and certainty. However, international legal positivists responded to the conditions of anarchy by dropping the requirement that law depended on the central authority of a Hobbesian Leviathan. For them, coercion was possible in a decentralised (anarchic) order through the mechanism of self-help while certainty could be achieved through strict requirements relating to the identification of genuine state consent.[4] Later, the concern for coercion and compulsion gave way to an examination of compliance as the key attribute of a successful international legal order.[5] The point of all these projects was to demonstrate the compatibility of law and anarchy and to show how international law was more than international morality.[6]

Confusion arises when hierarchy is introduced into this picture of anarchy. Hierarchy, for the purpose of this book, remains compatible with anarchy but signifies the presence of *formal* status differentiation among the actors within a decentralised system of authority and law, i.e. *constitutional or legal* hierarchies (compare the international relations usage) situated *within* an anarchical order (compare domestic legal orders or world government). States acknowledge no central legal superior and there is no stable locus of supreme sovereignty within the system. However, there are gradations in the sort of legal power and status held by the various actors within the system. Directorates of the Great Powers arise from time to time and states are often subject to procedures of differentiation on the basis of their moral or political qualities. These are the hierarchies I characterise as legalised hegemony and anti-pluralism.

This idea of hierarchy ought to be contrasted with other possible meanings of the term. Often, the term hierarchy is used to describe legal orders in which there exists centralised or vertical decision-making and enforcement. The municipal legal order is often characterised in this way. The sovereign (executive, legislature and judiciary) regulates the behaviour of private individuals within the society. These private

---

[4] Watson, 'A Realistic Jurisprudence'; P. Weil, 'Towards Relative Normativity in International Law?' (1983) 77:3 *American Journal of International Law* (1983) 413–42.

[5] H. Koh, 'Transnational Legal Process' (1996) 75:1 *Nebraska Law Review* 181–207; T. Franck, 'Legitimacy in the International System' (1988) 82:4 AJIL 705–59.

[6] For a discussion of the movement between psychological and material theories of consent, see M. Koskenniemi 'The Normative Force of Habit: International Custom and Social Theory' (1990) 1 *Finnish Yearbook of International Law* 77–153.

individuals are assumed to be subordinate to the sovereign.[7] The Hobbesian movement between the state of nature (anarchy) and the social state (hierarchy, the Leviathan) perhaps best exemplifies this sort of hierarchy. By definition this form of hierarchy describes a situation that is non-anarchical.

In public international law, this centralised order does not exist. 'Private' actors (i.e. sovereign states) within international legal relations are self-regulating. This is the very essence of sovereignty. The international system has tended to operate in this way since at least Westphalia (Chapter 2). However, there have been periods prior to that where certain international legal orders were 'centrally guided'.[8] The Holy Roman Empire or, indeed, any imperial structure with universalist aspirations, could be described as a centralised model operating within an international system.[9]

Another use of the term hierarchy is that adopted by international relations scholars to describe a system in which political, economic and social status among the actors is highly differentiated even though these actors enjoy some measure of formal sovereign equality.[10] Hierarchy, here, does not refer to the existence of a Leviathan or supreme sovereign. In fact, it has no legal or constitutional connotations at all. It simply refers to the grading of states on the basis of relative capacity. These distinctions explain why many international relations scholars (sometimes to the bafflement of international lawyers) can speak of hierarchy and anarchy as core attributes of the international order.

For international relations theory this is unproblematic. States of widely differing capabilities (hierarchy) co-exist in a decentralised social order (anarchy). Indeed, for realists, hierarchy and hegemony are desirable qualities in an international system.[11] It is a given for realists that a small elite of large powers will be vested with managerial responsibilities

---

[7] The picture is complicated by the idea of a social contract where the sovereign is regulated by the constitution or embodies the will of the people, or 'is' the people.

[8] R. Falk, *Revitalizing International Law*, chap. 1.

[9] This might include, for example, the Empires of the eighteenth and nineteenth centuries with their vertical ordering structures, the projects of cosmopolitanism (for a discussion see D. Zolo, *Cosmopolis: Prospects for World Government*, and, potentially, the European Union with its increasingly centralised bureaucracy and authority structures.

[10] See, generally, I. Clark, *Hierarchy*.

[11] See R. Evans, 'All States are Equal, but . . .' (1981) 7:1 *Review of International Studies* 59–66 at 59.

Table 3.1 *Centralised Legal Order   Anarchical Legal Order*

Centralised Legal Order	Anarchical Legal Order
United Kingdom, USA	Public International Law
Holy Roman Empire	
World Government	Post-Westphalia Inter-State System
Cosmopolis	

in any particular world order and that these states will enjoy special legal privileges within that order. Hierarchy is the structuring principle that permits Great Powers to order the international system either by pursuing the logic of the balance of power among themselves or by imposing on small and middle powers principles and norms of international order.[12] Hegemony stabilises the international order through the security guarantees of the hegemon or because the hegemon is able to anchor the international political economy.[13] To put it even more bluntly, inequality is what the international system is about since there does not exist the sort of normative and institutional framework found in the domestic system that might leaven these inequalities.[14]

These two usages of the term hierarchy (centralised governmental authority and material hierarchy) are not adopted here. In describing any movement from an anarchical order to one with 'hierarchical' decision-making (i.e. forms of world federation or government), I shall use terms such as 'centralised' instead.[15] One might usefully compare two different *legal* systems here. The first is a system of non-anarchic hierarchy found in a centralised legal order (e.g. the United Kingdom's legal system) and the second is legalised hierarchy (e.g. the international legal order). These legal orders, in turn, can be contrasted with a political order in which hierarchy and anarchy cohabit the system but in which hierarchy has no legal significance (e.g. the state of nature, a realist view of international affairs, see Table 3.1).

[12] See Hurrell, 'Security and Inequality', in Hurrell and Woods, *Inequality*, 254.
[13] This is the import of Robert Gilpin's book, *The Political Economy of International Relations*.
[14] See, generally, Bull, *Anarchical Society*.
[15] I appreciate that the special position of the Great Powers has been described as 'governmental' in some IR literature. However, I prefer to differentiate government (a high degree of centralised control and authority exercised through permanent bureaucratic structures) from legalised hegemony (a directorate of the Great Powers that nevertheless lacks a permanent secretariat and direct legislative authority). But see Coral Bell, *The Debatable Alliance: An Essay in Anglo-American Relations*, 111–13, for a description of the handling of the Cuban Missile Crisis as 'government' (quoted in Carsten Holbraad, *Superpowers and International Conflict*, 3).

My argument is that the international legal order is an anarchical system with constitutional pretensions to egalitarianism but one in which legal hierarchies are present, if muted.

Legalised hegemony: the Great Powers in concert

Two forms of hierarchy provide the basis for the inquiry undertaken in this book. In one case, either membership or the quality of that membership in the international community is subject to certain gradations in status based on culture or ideology (anti-pluralism). In the other case, the subject of this present section, certain states are accorded a position of pre-eminence or dominance by virtue of their superior 'power' (legalised hegemony).[16] The Great Powers have stood slightly apart from the rest of the Family of Nations since the early nineteenth century. In 1815, the Congress of Vienna was organised, administered and choreographed by the 'P5' of the time. It seemed natural to them that they should occupy a formally distinct position in international regimes constructed at that time (Chapter 4). This de jure separation of the elite from hoi polloi has continued to be carved into the various regimes constructed since then at Versailles, at San Francisco, at Bretton Woods and during the Kosovo intervention.

The material fact of greater power or political capacity combined with cultural advantage was converted into legalised hegemony at the beginning of the nineteenth century.[17] This legalised hegemony is composed of four elements. First, there is a constitutional or legal basis to the dominance of certain powers. Their superiority is reflected in legal norms and in the institutions of particular eras. The phenomenon of legalised hegemony arises only in the context of an international society. Second, there is a form of sovereign equality existing among the powers themselves

---

[16] I use this term in a highly qualified, preliminary fashion. As I go on to indicate 'power' is not necessarily the decisive consideration. Culture and ideology do play a part in the construction of the category 'Great Power'. Still, at this stage, the contrast is a useful one.

[17] It is not my concern here to assess the moral or instrumental implications of an international order in which the Great Powers have a special role. There is little doubt that the Great Powers can play a useful role in promoting 'order' in its neutral sense. See Bull, *Anarchical Society*, 202–30. They also make the task of the political scientist simpler: 'The inequality of states in terms of power has the effect of simplifying the pattern of international relations' (206). For a more jaundiced view of the role of the Great Powers in European affairs see Misha Glenny's *The Balkans, 1804–1999: Nationalism, War and the Great Powers*.

(in spite of actual material differences existing between these powers). Third, the directorate of Great Powers acts in concert to achieve certain ends within the international order. These powers have an interest in and prerogatives over, not only their own narrowly defined interests, but over the whole international system. Fourth, legalised hegemony is both imposed from above by the Great Powers and also accepted by consent from below by the other powers within the system.

Legalised hegemony, then, is the term I use to describe the following phenomenon: *the existence within an international society of a powerful elite of states whose superior status is recognised by minor powers as a political fact giving rise to the existence of certain constitutional privileges, rights and duties and whose relations with each other are defined by adherence to a rough principle of sovereign equality.*

Much of the discussion in Chapter 4 is about how these political facts are converted into legal realities. For present purposes, I want to sketch out the meaning of the category 'Great Powers' and discuss some complications associated with use of the term before providing a brief summary of some attributes of a typical hegemonic coalition.

The origins of the term are untraceable but a stable elite of states with managerial aspirations and an inclination to realise these aspirations in legal or institutional form arises as a political fact only at the beginning of the nineteenth century. Obviously, great powers have been with us since the organisation of human relations into large centralised territorial units.[18] Alexander's Greece, Imperial China, Caesar's Rome and the mediaeval Vikings were great powers in this sense. Each controlled substantial swathes of territory and each constituted the dominant military force of its period. However, these powers tended to be exceptional or sole powers. The structuring principles that we have come to associate with the *Great Powers*, i.e. balance, alliance, concert and legal form, were not yet present.

Although the growing maturity of the inter-state system increased the prospect of the establishment of the category Great Powers, two elements of the mediaeval or pre-modern period had prevented the crystallisation of this category. The first was the continuing existence of the Holy Roman Empire. The reality of centralised, spiritual and, to a lesser

---

[18] I use the capitalised term 'Great Powers' when discussing either the management of international legal order by an elite group of states (the idea of the Great Powers) or historical examples of this institution (the Great Powers at Vienna in 1815). Lower case usage refers simply to empires or states whose military and political might have defined a certain era but who did not act in concert.

extent, material power in Europe meant that the idea of a directorate of great territorial states could not develop. Sweden and France (and, to a lesser extent, England) were large powers but their concern was to establish their own status vis-à-vis the Empire. This was not conducive to self-consciousness about Great Power status. Though they occasionally formed temporary alliances their concern was to achieve parity with the Empire rather than manage international relations themselves.

The second obstacle lay in the nature of the Westphalian period (1648–1815). This was an era in which squabbles over status and diplomatic precedence meant that the formation of stable elite groups was rendered unlikely. In addition, this phase was marked by multiple bilateralism rather than the sort of multilateralism that is the catalyst for Great Power coalitions.[19] It was not until Vienna (or at least the period leading up to the Congress) that 'this concern with standing was secularised, gradually transmuting into the ideas that there were "Great Powers" endowed with special rights and obligations in international society'.[20]

The idea of 'special rights and duties' suggests that the category Great Powers is itself a legal category. I want to argue that this idea of the Great Powers is, in many important respects, a juridical idea but that it has been presented as a material fact. More primitive definitions tend to focus on 'power'. Sometimes, the Great Powers are said to possess greater 'actual power'.[21] This superior material power, in itself, is insufficient to establish primacy. Obviously, a state must do something with its material advantage. Ninic calls this the 'capacity for political action'.[22] Hedley Bull, too, in his chapter on the subject of the Great Powers in *The Anarchical Society*, begins by focusing on the projection of political power.[23] According to Bull, membership of this group does not require that a state be able to ensure its own survival but it does require a clear supremacy in military capacity and the ability to project military power without the help of allies.[24] Great Powers maintain spheres of influence, establish primacy over allies and put pressure on client states

---

[19] Christian Reus-Smit, *The Moral Purpose of the State: Culture, Social Identity, and Institutional Rationality in International Relations*, stating 'the general tendency was to disaggregate a systemic conflict into dyadic sub-conflicts' (108).

[20] *Ibid.*, 109.   [21] Ninic, *The Problem of Sovereignty*, 126.   [22] *Ibid.*

[23] He rejects, for example, the claim that Japan had become the world's first militarily weak 'Great Power' by virtue of its economic successes. Bull regards military power as indispensable. Bull, *Anarchical Society*, 200–29.

[24] The advantages offered to the aggressor in a nuclear age make it impossible to guarantee survival in any meaningful sense. Self-sufficiency is an idea derived from Leopold Ranke, *The Great Powers*, in T. H. Von Laue (ed.), *The Formative Years*, 203.

to behave in certain ways. But as well as maintaining specific spheres of influence, at Vienna and in the subsequent Concert, the Great Powers were defined as those states with an interest in all European affairs. These powers were thought to be entitled in some way to regulate the affairs of Europe and, on questions of territorial distribution, were regarded as having exclusive rights and responsibilities.[25] This interest in the generality of international relations is crucial to the establishment of legalised hegemony.

However, an additional element is required to propel a state into the Great Power league. In Bull's words, 'great powers are powers recognised by others to have and conceived by their own leaders and peoples to have, certain special rights and duties'.[26] In other words, hegemony is a juridical category dependent on the 'recognition' of 'rights and duties' and the consent of other states in the system. This, of course, makes legalised hegemony much more effective, on the whole, than other forms of dominance.[27]

This presents a challenge to most orthodox accounts of international law. These accounts of the relationship of states in the international legal order tend to recognise the superior material capacity of the Great Powers, the occasional institutional privilege and perhaps, in more challenging accounts, the special influence states have over law-making. However, the Great Powers do not only have greater influence on the way rules are developed but also have special rights and duties consolidated within these legal regimes. Latterly, these special rights and duties have become more transparent and, thereby, more controversial. Two examples from later chapters of the book will illustrate this point. In the Kosovo intervention, a coalition led by a group of Great Powers intervened in a sovereign state without gaining express approval from the Security Council and in the absence of any reliance on an Article 51 right to self-defence. These states, though, argued that they had a right to intervene in cases of humanitarian catastrophe. In many instances, states and scholars endorsed this argument and supported this right. What they were supporting though was not a general, universalisable right to humanitarian intervention but a special right on the part of

---

[25] See the discussion of legalised hegemony at Vienna in Chapter 4.
[26] Bull, *Anarchical Society*, 202.
[27] For a wider discussion of the Gramscian implications of all this, focusing on the presence of ideological legitimation in the international system, see Robert W. Cox, 'Social Forces, States and World Orders: Beyond International Relations Theory' (Summer 1981) 10:2 *Millennium* 126–55 at 153, n. 27.

the Great Powers to intervene in such cases. Similarly, the Afghanistan intervention can be understood best as a further expansion and development of a special norm of self-defence exercisable by the Great Powers and their coalition partners. This enhanced doctrine of self-defence is not intended for use by the majority of states nor would its use by those states be endorsed by other states in the system or by scholars assessing the legality of such actions. Instead, there is an implicit recognition of legalised hegemony in scholarly pronouncements and in state responses to such actions (Chapter 12).

Two other dimensions of Bull's definition are salient. First, and this becomes clearer in light of the Vienna manoeuvrings, the existence of a Great Power concert requires the operation of a robust norm of equality between the Great Powers themselves. As I will go on to demonstrate, the importance of sovereign equality in certain circumscribed spheres is not limited by the existence of legalised hegemony in others. This element of equality need not have complete correspondence to material realities. Prussia, for example, was a relatively small Great Power during the period of the Concert and the current status of the United Kingdom and France as Great Powers at the Security Council is only partially diminished by their obvious political inferiority. It is here that I depart from Bull who argues that material equality is necessary.[28] It strikes me that formal equality between the hegemons operates in a similar way to sovereign equality among states generally; it overlays a regime of equality upon a highly differentiated material reality.[29] I also argue, though Bull is more equivocal here, that the presence of some sort of directorate is necessary. The Great Powers must act (in some ways at least) as a group. There can be fracturings and even inter-power wars as there were in the mid-nineteenth century but the possibility of joint action must always be present. The term 'concert', I believe, conveys the idea of a coalition of Great Powers acting in unison to achieve certain ends over a substantial period of time using legal and institutional processes (e.g. regular formalised meetings or hierarchically structured international organisations).[30]

---

[28] Though he argues that China was a Great Power at the height of the Cold War despite obvious material failings. The important factor for Bull seemed to be a combination of actual power, official rhetoric of the power concerned and the degree of acceptance by other states in the system (Bull, *Anarchical Society*, 204).

[29] For a discussion of the different, political category, 'superpowers' see *ibid.*, 203, 208–28.

[30] Holbraad distinguishes between 'concert': 'an informal association of major powers which attempted to manage the international affairs of the world by habitually

Second, and crucially, the directorate of Great Powers can only arise within a society.[31] There must be sufficient integration of states within a network of norms and expectations for the category to acquire any meaning. Raw power must be given some normative meaning. This is important because, if Bull is right, it means that the brute reality of power is a lesser consideration in assessing the status and existence of Great Powers than the element of legality or constitutionality. A basic conceptual tool of a sort of instinctive realism ('the Great Powers dominate international relations and disregard the law') is heavily dependent on the existence of a state of affairs (legality, society) that this realism otherwise undervalues and deprecates.[32]

Let me expand on this relationship between legality and status. Bull makes the point that the special privileges accorded the Great Powers in bodies like the Security Council are derived from the rights and duties they already possess and not the other way round.[33] So, presumably, the Vienna and Versailles arrangements were merely institutional confirmations of already existing normative structures. However, Bull mistakenly assumes that these normative relations (the recognition of rights and duties) can be divorced from considerations of legality. At one point in his discussion of the instrumental value of the Great Powers he says: 'If states were equal in power *as they are in law* . . .'.[34] Yet, his whole discussion up to this point has been premised on an inequality of rights and

---

consulting each other and occasionally co-ordinating their efforts' (*Superpowers and International Conflicts*, 151) and pentarchy or hexarchy which he characterises as a directorate with quasi-governmental functions (151). In discussing the Concert of Europe, he distinguishes between the early period of 'pentarchy' (governmental) and the looser (post-1822) period of 'concert'. I agree with Holbraad that the period 1815–22 is to be distinguished from the later operation of the Concert. However, I adopt the term 'concert' to describe both phases. In each case, legalised hegemony was a feature of the international order. This hegemony was more overt and legalistic in the congressional phase (1815–22) but remains part of the international system throughout the nineteenth century. In this book, I make no distinction between the terms pentarchy, directorate or concert since each conveys the central idea of a small elite of powers managing international affairs. The different usages reflect different intensities of coordination.

[31] Bull, *Anarchical Society*, 202.

[32] This idea is clarified in Bull's statement that Nazi Germany was not a Great Power. It was a military power, of course, but it did not view itself as possessing rights and duties within an international society. In fact, it rejected the whole idea of society and legality (*ibid.*, 202). States like Nazi Germany and Napoleonic France practised what Martin Wight would have called 'a catastrophic revolutionism' that was incompatible with any sense of obligation towards the existing order. See M. Wight, 'Anatomy', 221–5.

[33] Bull, *Anarchical Society*, 202.   [34] *Ibid.*, 205.

duties, i.e. legalised hegemony.[35] Bull, in other words, fails to distinguish several aspects of 'sovereign equality' discussed in Chapter 2. In fact, the hegemony of the Great Powers results in a form of legislative inequality that is undoubtedly legal in nature. Bull equates legal equality with a narrow view of sovereign equality that I have called formal equality but the contrast between this form of sovereign equality ('legal equality') with a series of inequalities ('political inequalities') does not capture the nuanced nature of inequality within the legal order nor does it sufficiently recognise the legal nature and effects of other inequalities (such as the legislative and existential equalities that are the subject of this book).[36]

This legalised hegemony operates alongside a capacity or will to act in a 'concerted' fashion. Legalised hegemony implies a capacity to 'exploit their [the Great Powers] preponderance in relation to the rest of international society by . . . joint action, as is implied by the idea of a great power concert or condominium'.[37] What this requires and what was lacking in the case of the superpowers is some degree of formalisation (regular meetings) and 'a theory . . . of world order'.[38] I appreciate that grey areas can arise here. Was the Great Power Concert of the 1815–50 period a legal regime? I have treated it as such because the relationship between the Great Powers and the medium and smaller countries was institutionalised, regularised and formalised for the first time. The European powers met regularly, developed a set of legal rules

[35] Bull may have been referring to political rights and duties. However, it is difficult to see how these rights are to be understood in the absence of law.

[36] Much of the rest of the discussion concerns the nature of the norms establishing the role of the Great Powers, e.g. their spheres of influence. Here, Bull notes that: 'If such operational rules do exist, there are difficulties in assessing precisely what the content is . . .' (ibid., 212). He speaks of spheres of influence as possessing legal content. Bull also argues that 'the Great Powers cannot formalise or make explicit . . . their dominance for fear of losing legitimacy'. There are two points to be made here. First, such non-formalised rules can still have legal content in custom. Second, the Great Powers do formalise many of their privileges in international institutions, as I will go on to show (228).

[37] This is the sixth of six features described by Bull. I am less interested in the others because (a) I suspect these features could exist in the absence of 'Great Powers' and (b) legalised hegemony, if taken as a sub-set of the concept of the Great Powers, is about concerted action on the part of a small elite.

[38] The Holy Alliance possessed one; it is probable that the Quadruple Alliance did also (albeit one that is less obviously ideological). According to Bull, the Security Council has one but it remained, in 1977, 'unactivated' (Anarchical Society, 227). The Atlantic powers (post-1999) have one (a belief that sovereignty can be suspended in cases where there are mass human rights violations or a threat of terrorist attack).

to manage areas of international social life and they took as their constituting moment a semi-formal meeting to order international relations
(the Congress of Vienna). One can compare this *legalised* hegemony with
the distinction made in the Cold War between the superpowers and the
rest. This latter formulation was politically crucial in this period but it
is doubtful whether it had any explicit legal status.[39] This is because the
superpowers did not seek to manage the system through formal mechanisms of control in the way the nineteenth-century powers did.[40] It
has been argued that the Cold War had certain legal effects such as the
implicit acknowledgement of spheres of influence and the concomitant
effect of these spheres on the non-intervention norm.[41] However, I do
not find this argument persuasive. The superpowers may have entered
into a tacit arrangement in delimiting each other's sphere of influence
(this is the thrust of Paul Keal's *Unspoken Rules and Superpower Dominance*)
but whether this was converted into a legal rule is debatable.[42] The
Soviets claimed a right to intervene in Eastern Europe but argued that
this complied with international law because these interventions were
designed to secure the territorial integrity and independence of their
satellites from the threat of counter-revolution or Western intervention
(the Brezhnev Doctrine). The Americans made similar arguments in relation to the modified Monroe Doctrine. In other words, neither party
suggested that the norm of non-intervention had been abandoned.[43]

Legalised hegemony is distinguishable from superpower dominance
in that the former requires a commitment to long-term *collective* action

[39] This would not have been the case had the Security Council been composed of only
two members: the Soviet Union and the United States.

[40] For an exception, see Treaty on the Non-Proliferation of Nuclear Weapons (1968) 729
UNTS 161.

[41] See Bull, *Anarchical Society*, 211 (noting the debate over whether these spheres
generated legal norms of mutual recognition).

[42] See, generally, Keal, *Unspoken Rules and Superpower Dominance*.

[43] For a discussion of nineteenth-century spheres of influence and their status in
international law see Keal, *ibid.*, 179–81. International lawyers agonised over how
international law should respond to the existence of such spheres. See the
equivocation in Keal, *ibid.*, 190–2 and in Falk. Falk cautions against too much
formalism or realism in approaching this question but ends by recommending weakly
'an intermediate position, one that maintains the distinctiveness of the legal order
while managing to be responsive to the extra-legal setting of politics, history and
morality', in R. Falk and C. Black, *The Future of the International Legal Order: Trends and
Patterns*, vol. I, 34 (discussing 'the interplay of Westphalia and Charter conceptions of
international legal order'). But see Martti Koskenniemi on the impossibility of
developing a coherent intermediate position in such matters, in 'The Politics of
International Law' (1990) 1:1/2 *European Journal of International Law* 1–31.

together with a formal constitutional validation of these collective goals and processes. The superpowers were not 'Great Powers' according to this definition. They did not exercise legalised hegemony through concert. They were the greatest powers in the system but they did not act responsibly in order to maintain the system through some sort of concert.[44] Even in the heady days of détente it is hard to discern the outlines of concert or condominium.[45] It is true that usually chilly US–Soviet relations were punctuated by the odd collaboration (over Suez or non-proliferation) but this did not amount to the sort of cooperation and management necessary for legalised hegemony.[46]

I want to conclude this section by noting two peculiarities of legalised hegemony. The first concerns the relationship between power and culture. The hegemony of the Great Powers at Vienna had a cultural basis as well as a military or material one. The European elite, for all its history of strife, was able to come together and form a constitutional system because of certain shared understandings and an assumption of cultural superiority over non-Europeans. The Ottomans, for example, were still a power in the early nineteenth century. They certainly eclipsed Prussia territorially and were a match for the Austrians militarily. Yet, they were excluded from the Concert and the Family of Nations until 1856. The treatment of Japan at the turn of the nineteenth century and Communist China in the post-Second World War era are other examples of cases where the superior power of an entity was not enough to offset its perceived cultural liabilities and afford it entry into the hegemonic elite.

A second aspect of legalised hegemony worth commenting on is that it may not reflect, entirely, the material inequality present in the system. Bull goes further by suggesting that it cannot do so for, 'to make explicit the full extent of the special rights and duties of the great powers

---

44 Holbraad, *Superpowers and International Conflicts*, vii.

45 The term 'condominium' is likely to generate some confusion among international lawyers. A condominium implies joint ownership of land. In international law, it was used to signal a joint sovereignty over a piece of territory. Holbraad mentions the German Confederation (1816–48) and Austro-Hungarian/Ottoman joint sovereignty over the Balkans between 1879 and 1908 in this regard. Among political scientists, it has been used to describe either a 'concert' of two Great Powers or a high degree of joint control by two powers over international relations. According to Holbraad, such a situation has never arisen. Duopolies are unstable and do not give rise to high degrees of trust and joint endeavour (Holbraad, *Superpowers*, 1–10).

46 After studying four events in which the superpower relationship was implicated (Taiwan, Suez, the Six-Day War and Cuba), Holbraad calls the cold war a period of minimal dual crisis management, *ibid.*, 15–114.

would be to engender more antagonism than the international order could support'.[47] This implies that there are certain prerogatives that must occupy a borderland between legality and illegality (Bull gives the example of a right to enforce global peace). It is this borderland that is explored in the forthcoming chapters and in particular Chapter 7 on Kosovo and Chapter 12 on Afghanistan.

Legalised hegemony, then, is based on the constitutional recognition of a Great Power concert within the system combined with a recognition of a form of sovereign equality within the coalition itself. This form of hegemony arose in the early nineteenth century. Not only did, 'the institutionalisation of the special status of the Great Powers probably originate[d] with the Concert of Europe' but the whole concept of 'Great Powers' originated here in a moment of constitutional revolution. Since that time there has been, in the words of Marcus, '. . . in international law, in addition to the *de iure* recognition of a government or state, the *de iure* recognition of a state as a Great Power'.[48]

Liberal anti-pluralism

The second type of hierarchy I want to discuss is anti-pluralism and, in particular, liberal anti-pluralism. Liberalism has supplied international law with two conceptions of political community among states. I characterise these as *liberal pluralism* and *liberal anti-pluralism*. I associate liberal pluralism, in its contemporary manifestation, with the reluctance of the United Nations to question seriously the democratic or humanitarian credentials of its members. Liberal anti-pluralism finds its most prominent manifestation in the recent work of Fernando Tesón, Michael Reisman, Thomas Franck, John Rawls and Anne-Marie Slaughter where, in each case, the internal characteristics of a state has the potential to determine that state's standing in the Family of Nations.[49] I argue

---

[47] Bull, *Anarchical Society*, 228–9.

[48] Marcus, *Grand puissances, petites nations et le problème de l'organisation internationale*, 144 (quoted in Ninic, *The Problem of Sovereignty*, 126).

[49] For a constructivist take on liberal theory from the international relations side, see, e.g. Chris Reus-Smit's 'The Strange Death of Liberal International Theory' (2001) 12 (3) EJIL, 573–94. See, also, José Alvarez's doubts about the explanatory and predictive power of liberal anti-pluralism, 'Do Liberal States Behave Better?', *passim*. Other commentaries from international lawyers include Susan Marks, 'The End of History? Reflections on Some International Legal Theses' (1997) 8:3 EJIL 449; B. Kingsbury, 'Sovereignty and Inequality'; David Kennedy, 'The Disciplines of International Law and Policy' (1999) 12 *Leiden Journal of International Law* 9.

that one criticism of these writers, i.e. that they seek to introduce divisions and distinctions between states, abolished in contemporary international law, misses the prevalence of anti-pluralism in both theory and practice throughout the life of international law. In fact, the legal order since, at least, the beginning of the nineteenth century has been structured around a tension between pluralistic conceptions of community and theories based on the sorts of distinctions re-introduced by Tesón *et al.*[50]

Robert Frost defined a liberal as someone unable to take his own side in an argument.[51] In a similar vein, Flanders and Swann wrote in one of their songs that 'eating people is wrong' in a parody of one particular, liberal gentleman who was able to see virtue in almost all other forms of human behaviour.[52] In a different key altogether, Francis Fukuyama announced in 1989 that history had ended and went on to say that, 'liberalism remains the only coherent political aspiration'.[53]

When we think about liberalism today we seem to be confronted with at least these two competing images.[54] First, there is a 'classical' liberalism emphasising the virtues of tolerance, diversity, openness together with an agnosticism about moral truth. This classical version is epitomised by Frost's indecisive liberal and Flanders's ironic injunction against cannibalism. John Stuart Mill's work is imbued with some of this ethos of tolerance and, more recently, John Gray, the English political philosopher, has referred to it as the 'modus vivendi', i.e. the idea of

[50] The book here is deliberately parsimonious. I want to show that there are similarities between these various anti-pluralisms, not that they are the same. Each is hostile to a common egalitarian conception of international law that relies on sovereign equality as a foundational norm but beyond this there are clear dissimilarities. Note, however, the tendency of each successive generation of anti-pluralists to disassociate itself from the preceding one. In the case of the Victorians, the Chinese were rebuked for mistaking unequal treaties for 'the offspring of the piratical bloody-mindedness of our earliest forerunners in the China trade' (R. Gilbert, *The Unequal Treaties*, 5). Meanwhile, Anne-Marie Slaughter cautions us to appreciate the distinctions between the democratic governance standard and the standard of civilisation that underpinned these unequal treaties (Slaughter, 'Liberal Theory of International Law', paper delivered at ASIL, 8 April 2000, on file with author).

[51] Robert Frost, quoted in Thomas Nagel, 'Moral Conflict and Political Legitimacy' (1987) 16 *Philosophy and Public Affairs* 215.

[52] Michael Flanders and Donald Swann 'The Reluctant Cannibal', *At the Drop of a Hat*, Parlophone Records, PCS 3001 (1959).

[53] Francis Fukuyama, *The End of History and the Last Man*.

[54] I say 'at least' because there are many ways to distinguish liberalisms ranging from Isaiah Berlin's *Two Views of Liberty* to the disputes between egalitarian liberals (represented by the John Rawls of *A Theory of Justice*) and libertarians represented by the likes of Robert Nozick or Frederich Hayek.

liberalism as a procedure for organising relations among diverse communities.[55] It is also reflected in a disinclination within at least one *liberal* strand of international law to make judgements about the internal politics of the state (one that favours the strong conception of sovereign equality in this regard). The UN's approach to membership after about 1950 (as anticipated in the *Admissions Case*) is an example of this strain of liberalism.[56] However, there is a second image of what it means to be a liberal. This is liberalism (sometimes characterised as neo-liberalism) endowed with a sort of moralistic fervour, a conviction and, at times, an intolerance of the illiberal. Louis Hartz, in his study of American liberalism, described it as 'this fixed, dogmatic liberalism of a liberal way of life' and traced its roots in American liberalism's lack of internal enemies and resultant lack of plausible alternatives.[57] This liberalism produces a profoundly illiberal 'conformitarianism' according to Hartz. In various writings about international affairs, Francis Fukayama's liberal triumphalism is the starkest example of this liberalism but it is there, also, in Fernando Tesón's strident Kantian theory of international law, Michael Reisman's peremptory dismissal of the illiberal in his pro-democratic intervention work and, to a lesser extent, in Anne-Marie Slaughter's distinctions between liberal and non-liberal states.[58] This is the liberalism of certainty, or what I want to call 'liberal anti-pluralism'; a liberalism that can be exclusive, and illiberal in its effects. In international law, it differs from the liberal pluralism identified above most obviously in its lack of tolerance for non-liberal regimes.

---

[55] John Gray, *The Two Faces of Liberalism*. Louis Hartz located this liberalism in a European tradition in which there was a 'sense of relativity . . . acquired through an internal experience of social diversity and social conflict' (*The Liberal Tradition in America*, 14). This view of liberalism emphasises the idea of open political process and pragmatic compromise over the competing idea of absolute rights and legal standards. It is liberalism as a mechanism for making political choices in a world of disagreement as opposed to liberalism as a system designed to erase those disagreements altogether.

[56] *Admissions Case* (1948), ICJ Rep. See discussion in Chapter 9.

[57] Hartz, *Liberal Tradition*, 8–9. Hartz associates this with the constitutional fetishism which sees the Supreme Court 'resolve' moral dilemmas for the nation. It may be that this escape from politics and ethics is peculiarly American. Certainly, the ascendancy of liberal-democracy has been proclaimed by American scholars and these American scholars have embraced a sort of legalism to pursue liberal ends at the international level.

[58] See, e.g. Tesón, 'Kantian Theory', 54. Also see T. Franck, 'The Emerging Right to Democratic Governance' (1992) 86 *American Journal of International Law* (1992) 46; Slaughter, 'Liberal States', 3.

To illustrate the difference between these two liberalisms consider John Rawls. Rawls, in his recent book on international law, which I take up later, might be characterised as an old liberal in style and a new liberal in substance.[59] His tone is full of the sort of equivocation often found in liberal scholarship. He says at one point, 'we . . . conjecture . . . that the resulting principles will hang together . . . Yet there can be no guarantee'.[60] This sounds like Frost's caricature of liberal coyness, and such phrases are scattered throughout *The Law of Peoples*. On the other hand, Rawls's distinction between 'decent' and 'outlaw' peoples places him in the camp of the new liberals. In substance, Rawls's 'Law of Peoples' is a philosophical justification for one form of liberal antipluralism or the liberal intolerance of intolerant governments.[61] This, in turn, can be distinguished from Rawls's liberal pluralism found in the sketch of international law in *A Theory of Justice* where an international original position produces the norms of classical, Charter liberal pluralism and the strong conception of sovereign equality, most notably an equality of nations, 'analogous to the equal rights of citizens in a constitutional regime'.[62]

The way liberalism splits into these two traditions – an evangelical version that views liberalism as a comprehensive doctrine or a social good worth promoting and the other more secular tradition emphasising proceduralism and diversity – is reflected in some of the major debates in international studies.[63] To begin with, the whole discipline often has been

---

[59] See John Rawls, *The Law of Peoples*.   [60] *Ibid.*, 99.

[61] It is this combination of liberal doubt combined with theoretical certainty that Lea Brilmayer and others have found so exasperating. See 'What Use is John Rawls' Theory of Justice to International Relations?' (2001) 6:2 *International Legal Theory* 36.

[62] Rawls, *Theory of Justice*, 378. For a similar conclusion from the international law side see Thomas Franck, 'Is Justice Relevant?' For a critique of this application of Rawls to the international system see Fernando Tesón, *Humanitarian Intervention: An Inquiry into Law and Morality*, 58–71.

[63] From the international relations side, liberalism has been conventionally understood as a response to the realist tradition in IR scholarship. The realist–liberal divide was the key debate in IR theory for a substantial part of the post-war era. However, this liberalism is, itself, highly unstable. For example, it is both derivative of and distances itself from the Wilsonian liberalism of the inter-war period (itself disparaged by realists as 'legalist-utopianism'). This liberalism fragments into quite distinct intellectual projects. Michael Doyle has pointed to three quite different liberal traditions in IR drawn from Kant, Machiavelli and Schumpeter. See Michael Doyle, 'Kant, Liberal Legacies and Foreign Affairs: Part 1' (1983) 12 *Philosophy and Public Affairs* 205–35 at 216–17. Jim Richardson has referred to 'contending liberalisms' in 'Contending Liberalisms: Past and Present' (1997) 3:1 EJIR 5–34. Others contrast the strong neo-Kantian version with a weaker liberal institutionalism (the former

characterised as 'liberal', emphasising qualities of rule of law, autonomy, rights and equality. This liberalism is reflected in various doctrines and principles within the international legal order, e.g. the territorial integrity of states and their entitlement to sovereign equality. According to this liberal view of international law, states in the international system are in an analogous position to individuals in a domestic political order. Orthodox international law, then, is based on a classical liberalism transplanted onto the international relations between nation-states.[64] This is what I have called *liberal pluralism*. The principles underlying this approach find their highest expression in the text of the UN Charter. The point of this approach is to treat all states equally, to allow them each the same rights afforded to individuals in a liberal society (i.e. domestic jurisdiction, equality, non-intervention) and to, if not celebrate, at least tolerate the diversity produced by these norms.[65] This liberal pluralism is associated with the idea of existential equality developed in Chapter 2 and is based on a norm of inclusion entwined with a policy of strategic engagement. Undemocratic or illiberal states are admitted into international society so that society may be universalised and those states domesticated.

As Wolfgang Friedmann put it, 'the most basic principle of international law is the equal claim to integrity of all states regardless of their political or social ideology'.[66] It almost goes without saying that this liberalism gives ontological priority to the state; it is states that are given rights and immunities, not individual human beings. This is the liberalism that José Alvarez refers to when he contrasts Anne-Marie Slaughter's work with 'the pluralistic project that has characterized contemporary international law'.[67]

Compare, then, this 'pluralistic project' of the Charter with liberal anti-pluralism, where the idea is to *distinguish* between states on the basis of their internal characteristics. As Slaughter notes, 'Liberal theory permits more general distinctions among different categories of states based

---

emphasising the prospects of pacification and the latter having the more modest goal of deeper cooperation).

[64] For a fuller analysis see G. Simpson, 'Imagined Consent: Democratic Liberalism in International Legal Theory' in M. Koskenniemi (ed.), *Sources of International Law*.

[65] See Chapter 2 for more detail. Articles 1(2), 2(7) and 2(4) are the most obvious textual props of this liberalism but the way that Article 4 has been interpreted has also been a key element of this liberal approach.

[66] W. Friedmann, 'Intervention, Civil War and the Role of International Law' in Richard Falk (ed.), *The Vietnam War and International Law*, 151.

[67] J. Alvarez, 'Liberal States', 239.

on domestic regime type.'[68] This new liberal anti-pluralism lays empha-sis on the rights of individuals themselves and the norm of democracy as defining qualities of a workable international order. To this extent, international human rights law with its intellectual roots in the en-lightenment and its emphasis on popular sovereignty and civil rights is the engine of this new liberal anti-pluralism. This liberalism (which includes neo-Kantianism, liberal internationalism and democratic gov-ernance theory) seeks to undermine the present (over?)inclusive orienta-tion of the international legal order and replace it with one in which the status of states is determined by their adherence or non-adherence to certain individual rights (say, free expression) and international norms (say, the embryonic standard of democracy). According to the strong ver-sion of this anti-pluralism, the strong sovereign equality that underpins the Charter conception of liberalism has become an absurdity. Aaron Fellmeth, for example, describes it as a 'superannuated mystery', the moral theory by which 'the integrity of a fascist dictatorship is entitled to as much respect as the government of a social democracy'.[69]

In this, liberal anti-pluralism individuals are given ontological priority. Indeed, Tesón calls this 'normative individualism'.[70] I term this theory of liberal international law 'liberal anti-pluralism' in order to emphasise both its roots in a liberal-humanitarian tradition and some of its 'illib-eral' implications.[71] Georg Schwarzenberger, in an important book about

---

[68] Slaughter, 'Liberal States', 509.

[69] A. X. Fellmeth, 'Feminism and International Law: Theory, Methodology and Substantive Reform' (2000) 22 *Human Rights Quarterly* 658 at 703, fn 171.

[70] Tesón, 'Kantian Theory', 54.

[71] José Alvarez has characterised this as Illiberal Theory and it is illiberal from the perspective of the state system since it accomplishes that very illiberal result, the exclusion of certain entities from a political order on the basis of their ideological position (see 'Liberal States' at 238). From a different perspective, as Alvarez recognises in his paper, it is, of course, highly liberal. It promotes liberalism within states. In many ways, this debate over terminology strikes at a deeper dilemma for liberalism. To what extent should it tolerate illiberal elements in its midst? The original idea of the liberal state was to produce a tolerant polity rather than one that merely replicated its absolutist predecessors by replacing one absolute truth with another.
My choice of language in relation to 'pluralism' also will strike some people as peculiar. Surely, it is the new liberals that deserve the label 'pluralists'. It is they who have developed models which take seriously the preferences of non-state actors in the system. In addition, their support for democracy within states signals a preference of the sort for pluralism that functions best in such polities. These claims are plausible and perhaps the new liberals are right to be proprietorial concerning the label 'pluralist'. This book, though, is about states and inter-state relations. It compares two

the League of Nations, neatly summed up this difference. When one of the representatives at the Conference to establish the League of Nations spoke of admission to the League being open to 'free' states, Schwarzenberger remarked that the word 'free' was 'somewhat ambiguous, as it does not necessarily refer to the internal conditions of an applicant state, but may be read as synonymous with "independent" or "sovereign".[72] The ambiguity identified by Schwarzenberger is in some respects an encapsulation of the two liberal approaches to equality in international law discussed in this study.

It is impossible to do justice to the many nuances of these two liberalisms and to the part they play in various aspects of international law. In the latter part of this study, then, I want to concentrate on the question of status and membership of the international community. Chapters 8, 9 and 10 are about liberalism as a theory about how political society should be constituted, who should be part of that community and who should be excluded. The debate over regulation of membership in the international community since the early to mid-nineteenth century can be seen partly as a conversation between these two liberalisms or two views of society. It is also a conflict between a strong conception of sovereign equality (encompassing existential equality) and the weaker version in which this equality is severely compromised. These chapters are given over to a discussion of three periods in which this debate was brought sharply into focus. Chapter 8 reveals how Victorian international lawyers justified the exclusion of certain states from the inner circle of international law by virtue of their lack of civilisation or inability to protect the liberal rights of non-citizens. The failure of entities such as China and Korea to embrace liberal norms marked them out

approaches to state heterogeneity, one of which (Charter liberalism) seeks to preserve diversity among states, the other, liberal anti-pluralism, which favours systems of like-minded democratic states.

All of this makes John Rawls's work a little difficult to situate. I have labelled him an anti-pluralist yet his whole life's work has been dedicated to a defence of pluralism and the construction of a decent society in the face of the fact of pluralism. His work on the international order is pluralist in one sense. He wants to accommodate illiberal but decent states in his *Law of Peoples*. Reasonable states (illiberal and liberal) can and do disagree it is up to a reasonable law of peoples to 'find a shared basis of agreement' (*Collected Works*, 530) between these peoples. This marks Rawls out from, say, Fernando Tesón, for whom decency and republican democracy are identical. On the other hand, Rawls is a liberal anti-pluralist because his project violates the basic principle of Charter liberalism, i.e. the sovereign equality of states. Outlaw states and burdened states do not enjoy sovereign equality.

[72] G. Schwarzenberger, *League of Nations*, 88.

for exclusion from the core. This view, though, came under increasing challenge from liberalism's universalist face, one that sought to extend membership of the international community as widely as possible. This was the liberalism of tolerance and diversity (or liberalism in its anti-colonial mode).

A second moment of controversy occurred at San Francisco in 1945, when, again, there was disagreement about the extent to which the international community should be inclusive and heterogeneous in nature. Here, the liberalism of state diversity and sovereignty came into conflict with liberal anti-pluralism and its pursuit of democratic standards within states. What eventually prevailed was a Charter liberalism that advocated flexibility in the standards required for the admission of states to the United Nations community. I discuss the San Francisco meetings in Chapter 9.

Finally, I look at the new liberal anti-pluralists: Rawls, Franck, Reisman, Tesón and Slaughter and their challenge to what Anne-Marie Slaughter calls the 'prevailing account of liberalism in international law' (liberal pluralism) which, she says, denies 'the possibility of distinguishing between states or looking within them'.[73] I supplement a reading of these writers with an analysis of two regimes of anti-pluralism: the criminal regime and the democratic governance regime (see Chapter 10).

Other hierarchies

This book is about the operation of legalised hegemony and liberal anti-pluralism among states. I want to conclude this section by comparing inter-state constitutional hierarchies with two other formal hierarchies operating in the system: the class distinction between states and non-states and the hierarchies produced by the tendency to internationalise certain territories.

First, status hierarchies operate to distinguish full members of the international system (states) from non-states. The story of self-determination is about the struggle of non-state groups arranged on ethnic, territorial or national lines to reach the other side of this divide.[74] In contemporary international law there has been a move from a system in which status was stratified to one in which there are basically

---

[73] A.-M. Slaughter, 'Liberal Theory'.
[74] G. Simpson, 'The Diffusion of Sovereignty' (1996) 32:2 *Stanford Journal of International Law* 255–86.

only two positions for groups – the state and the non-state actor; participant and non-participant.[75] This explains the difficulty posed for international law by self-determination movements (who possess some form of popular sovereignty but no territorial jurisdiction) and indigenous peoples (whose notions of sovereignty are often incompatible with the sovereignty of the state in which they are located and the theory of exclusive sovereignty on which the international legal order is based).

In relation to such groups, international law's exclusionary strategies operate at a number of different levels. The whole idea of statehood and sovereignty operates as a discourse of exclusion and hierarchy. Equality is possessed by sovereigns and states are universally subject to international law. Yet, for all its geographical univeralism, international law defines relevant political space very narrowly. The state has monopolised international legal life to the exclusion of other forms of political organisation. So that, though equality is a principle of the system, this equality (even in its most generous versions) extends only to those social groups willing to adopt orthodox political designs. This is the paradox at the heart of self-determination. Admission to the Family of Nations is only open to those who would play the part of the state. Richard Olney, writing in 1909, enunciated this principle in a brutal form: 'savage tribes and scattered nomadic and casual collections of men may be disregarded'.[76] This partly explains international law's ambiguous relationship with indigenous peoples over the years. These groups did not organise themselves as states and therefore could be accorded no recognition in the system. Worse still, unlike ethnic self-determination movements, many indigenous groups have no interest in establishing the sort of centralised territorial authority with rational, hierarchical legal systems that is the mark of the Weberian nation-state.[77]

A second form of hierarchy, alongside the one distinguishing between states and non-states, operates to suspend sovereignty in a particular area. The protectorates established over Kosovo and East Timor may prefigure a return to nineteenth-century forms of deferred sovereignty.[78]

---

[75] During the high point of statism (1945–99), state sovereignty was qualified by human rights but the state was not challenged by other legal forms to the extent that it was, say, in the nineteenth or sixteenth centuries.

[76] R. Olney, 'The Development of International Law' (1909) 1:2 AJIL 421.

[77] Some cases, e.g. *Coe* v. *Commonwealth of Australia* (1979) 24 ALR 118, 137 are strategic exceptions to this rule where Aboriginal people use Western concepts to challenge existing legal orders.

[78] Very recently, it has sometimes seemed as if international law was moving back to a nineteenth-century system in which sovereignty could be dispersed within a single

These hierarchies (protectorates, condominia, dependencies, dominions, trust territories and mandates) were thought to have been abolished by the middle of the twentieth century. In a way, hierarchy had become blunter and less refined by 1960. Until very recently, the system was composed of either states or non-states. Entities either possessed full sovereignty or no sovereignty at all. This is the classical orthodox model of sovereignty. However, it may be that the nineteenth-century model will revive as part of a general movement in the direction of more stratified forms of sovereignty.

This book is not about these hierarchies but about the juridical distinctions that operate between states.[79] It is the gradations in sovereignty that interest me not the denial of sovereignty. So, the first category of distinctions, between states and non-state actors, is not a primary focus of this book. I touch on the second category (the stratification of sovereignty) only to the extent that it supports the thesis about sovereign inequality. The main brunt of my argument is found in a different set of distinctions within statehood, among states, i.e. the status differentiations existing among the community of sovereign states. My primary interest is in how these dualities and hierarchies influence and mark the development of legal norms and legal institutions and what they tell us about the hierarchy/equality relationship in relation to states and the state system. This story of exclusion and hierarchy in the nineteenth century is the subject of the first section of Chapter 8 and its renewal by a group of scholars and policy-makers associated with the anti-pluralist tendency is reviewed in Chapters 9 and 10.

These status hierarchies, in the nineteenth century and early twentieth century, distinguished between civilised states and non-civilised or partially civilised states. The distinction here is not so much between states and non-states but between states belonging to the Family of Nations (initially Western European) and those civilisations or empires on the periphery. Japan, China, the Ottomans and other states were denied full membership either because they were uncivilised or because they were not fully sovereign. These two categories were mutually reinforcing

---

territory (see, for example, in East Timor and Kosovo, SC Res. 1244 (10 June 1999), on Kosovo; SC Res. 1272 (25 October 1999), in East Timor establishing UNTAET).

[79] Given what I have said about the stratification of sovereignty in the nineteenth century this may cause complications. However, I think it was still fairly clear which entities in the system were sovereign states at that time. The fact that they were deprived of certain sovereign prerogatives did not deprive them of sovereignty. They possessed sovereignty but not sovereign equality.

in that the lack of civilisation was deemed a reason for derogating from sovereignty. Thus the West 'participated in a status degradation ceremony, where Asian and African polities were publicly denounced as outside and in opposition to a self-referentially valid progress'.[80] The nineteenth century was an imperial project founded on the division of humanity. Strang tells of the efforts of peripheral entities to gain some sort of recognition or a protected level of sovereignty and how these efforts were either a total failure (Burma), a partial success (Siam) or a complete success, at least latterly (Japan). There are signs of a return to these status hierarchies in the legal conditions imposed on the likes of Iraq, Libya and Yugoslavia in the post-cold war era and in the language used to characterise the international order.[81] This is the subject of Chapter 10.

Conclusion

Before concluding with two brief illustrations of the relevance of hierarchy to some current international legal doctrines, I want to make a couple of supplementary points about the relationship of hierarchy and equality in the international system.

First, the tension between the two is not capable of final resolution within an anarchic system regulated by international law. It is not envisaged that hierarchy will give way to equality within the inter-state system nor, indeed, that it necessarily should. There is a permanent tension within the present system; one that is unlikely to be resolved by anything less than a revolutionary change in international human relations.[82] Second, I do not view either hierarchy or equality as related in any particular way to stability. Just as surely as the high point of sovereign equality doctrine after Westphalia heralded a period of relative stability so too did the hegemonic system, introduced at Vienna, inaugurate fifty years of peaceful relations between the Great Powers.

Let me conclude this chapter's discussions of hierarchy, while at the same time prefacing the largely historical analysis to come, by signalling the relevance of some of these patterns of hierarchy and equality to two

---

[80] See David Strang, 'Contested Sovereignty' in Weber and Biersteker (eds.), *State Sovereignty as Social Construct*, 44.

[81] See reference to a 'family of states' threatened by terrorism and rogue states in US National Security Strategy (2002) at http://www.whitehouse.gov/nsc/nss5.html

[82] World government and international socialist revolutions are two (highly unlikely) methods by which resolution might be effected.

problems of contemporary international law: sovereign immunity and the use of force.

The traditional view of sovereign immunity was that states and their representatives had immunity from prosecution in the courts of another state. This rule was derived from the broader principle of sovereign equality and the commitment to existential equality in international law. Sovereign immunity applied to all sovereigns no matter how nefarious, undemocratic or uncivilised they might be. The doctrine of sovereign immunity ensured that all sovereigns would be treated equally in deference to their position and regardless of the substantive politics they pursued in their own countries. In recent years, this liberal pluralist rule has come under attack from a number of different perspectives, each grounded in a particular world-view or theory of international law. Human rights advocates have argued for a category of exceptions based on crimes against humanity, war crimes and various other human rights offences. The idea is that sovereign equality should give way to prevailing notions of justice and morality and that individual leaders, by virtue of their behaviour, should be denied immunity from criminal proceedings.[83]

Another fundamental norm of international law, derived from sovereign equality, is the right of each sovereign state to have its territorial integrity respected by other states and by international organisations. This right (or immunity) is expressed in Article 2(4) of the UN Charter prohibiting uses of force 'against the territorial integrity and political independence of any member state' and is derived from classic liberal rights to property and to bodily autonomy and security.[84] Here, the legalist orthodoxy reflects a literal reading of the Charter. The use of force is deemed unlawful unless it falls within one of two exceptions (collective security or self-defence). The idea is that the legal rule prevails over other, sometimes compelling, moral and political considerations.[85]

---

[83] *Regina v. Bow Street Metropolitan Stipendiary Magistrate, ex parte Pinochet Ugarte* (No.1) [2000] AC 61, (No.2) [2000] AC 119, (No.3) [2000] AC 147. For an example of an illiberal anti-pluralism as applied to sovereign immunity see the radical internationalist tendency to disregard immunities based on sovereign prerogatives. The taking of the Teheran hostages is a good example of this sort of radical resistance to classic international legal norms, *US Diplomatic and Consular Staff in Teheran Case* (1980) ICJ Rep. at 3 (1981) 61 ILR 504.

[84] For an intelligent discussion of this issue see Karen Knop, 'Feminist Re/Statements' (1993) 3:2 *Transnational Law and Contemporary Problems* 293–345.

[85] For a more detailed discussion see Chapter 7.

As I will demonstrate later, this Charter reading of use of force law has come under challenge from liberal anti-pluralists who have called for an expanded doctrine of intervention in order to promote human dignity, world order and democracy or to punish outlaw states for various 'crimes'. In some cases, this right would be exercisable only in illiberal 'zones of war'. The Charter norms have also been challenged by the tendency of small coalitions of like-minded states to use force in order to impose a set of values on recalcitrant states (see Chapter 7).[86]

The point is that in each case the orthodox reading based on state equality has been challenged by contending ideas emphasising hierarchies (of power) or (moral) inequalities between states and quite often these readings have become part of the legal landscape and the argumentative structure of international law. In each case hierarchy and equality remain in tension. This tension helps us understand what is going on in these doctrinal disputes.

The rest of this book is about the tension between sovereign equality (in particular, legislative and existential equality) and legalised hierarchy (in particular, legalised hegemony and liberal anti-pluralism). In the remaining chapters, I describe and analyse the way in which these various legal forms interacted in the design and creation of organisations and regimes and in the construction of juridical sovereignty from 1815 onwards.

---

[86] Of course, the two forms of hierarchy that form the focus for this book do not represent the only challenges to Charter norms of non-intervention and non-violence. Realists have always believed that force is acceptable if its use is required to promote state interests, for *raison d'état*. The only relevant consideration when deciding whether to employ force is the likelihood of success and the fit between the military action and the foreign policy goals to be pursued (see, e.g. D. Acheson, 'The Arrogance of International Lawyers' (1963) 57 ASIL *Proceedings* 14). Radical internationalism has taken many different forms. Marxist versions have tended to regard territorial integrity as a bourgeois norm designed to protect dominant class interests or counter-revolutionary forces and to give these interests territorial security (e.g. the Brezhnev Doctrine). Islamic or radical Third World versions have tended to view it as an impediment to just territorial revision (see Iraqi justification for the invasion and annexation of Kuwait). Other forms of radical internationalism have seen territory as a carry-over from illegitimate statist systems of governance. See, e.g. generally, I. Wallerstein, *After Liberalism*.

Part III Histories: Great Powers

4   Legalised hegemony: from Congress to Conference 1815–1906

> The constant intrusion, or potential intrusion, of power renders meaningless any conception of equality between members of the international community.[1]

Introduction

In the next four chapters, I consider the relationship between sovereign equality and a particular form of hierarchy I have called *legalised hegemony*.[2] I explore four moments of regime design or redesign in which the potentially contradictory principles of sovereign equality (or more specifically, legislative equality) and legalised hegemony were managed and brought into some sort of balance. These moments occurred at Vienna, The Hague, San Francisco and during the Kosovo intervention. These are significant because each of these constitutional 'moments' defines a particular era in the history of international law. In particular, these are moments where the tension between equality and hierarchy adopts a specific form, one that proves to be the defining characteristic of the period following it. In this chapter, I focus on the Vienna settlement.

In 1815, a post-Napoleonic directorate of Great Powers sought to manage and order European affairs and re-formulate international law.[3] This process represented a repudiation of the existing Westphalian consensus based on sovereign equality and challenged the underlying assumption that reform of the state system would take place on the basis of that

---

[1] E. H. Carr, *The 20 Years' Crisis 1919–1939* (2nd edn), 166.   [2] See definition in Chapter 3.
[3] The Great Powers were traumatised by the Napoleonic Wars and, consequently, built a series of structures designed to prevent a repeat of Bonapartist aggression. In this sense, they were like their successors at Versailles and San Francisco. However, they were, perhaps, less self-conscious about legal innovation than their counterparts.

equality.[4] At Vienna, the Great Powers were successful in forging a Concert system in which they played a dominant role. Though this hierarchical system was controversial and remained in place for less than half a century, it was a forerunner to the international organisations of the twentieth century. Section 1 of this chapter is a description and analysis of the revolutionary moment at Vienna, perhaps the apogee of legalised hegemony. In this section, I make two supplementary arguments. First, I describe the way in which legalised hegemony in the international order often requires a highly formalistic commitment to sovereign equality in relations between the hegemons. Second, I note the prevalence of other forms of legalised hierarchy even among those smaller states most tied (at least rhetorically) to the ideals of sovereign equality.

This book is largely about the practice of states but it is also about the role of international lawyers in defending, adjusting and modifying the principle, and explaining departures from it in this practice of states. Throughout the thesis, the work of intellectuals in the field is central. In his recently published book, *The Gentle Civiliser of Nations*, Martti Koskenniemi remarks that 'it may be too much to say that international law is only what international lawyers do or think. But at least it is that . . .'.[5] Parts of this book are inspired by this sentiment and while this book is not just about the professional sensibilities of international lawyers, it nevertheless takes seriously their role both in making the language of the world order and, in justifying, challenging and explaining the exploits of those who remake the world at large. To take one simple example, the 'outlaw state' is partly the product of Security Council resolutions or judicial decisions but it is also formed in the minds of men and women by the intellectual efforts of experts such as international lawyers and political scientists.

Section 2, then, examines how nineteenth-century international lawyers tried to explain the apparent contradiction between the principle of sovereign equality and the imposition of a form of legalised hegemony in 1815. At one level, this can be seen as a debate between formalists operating in the classical mode ('fidelity') and pragmatists working in the modern style ('repudiation'). The formalists (e.g. Oppenheim, Hall) wished to defend the integrity of the sovereign equality norm against

---

[4] See, e.g. Kooijmans, *Doctrine of the Legal Equality*, 99.
[5] M. Koskenniemi, *The Gentle Civiliser of Nations: The Rise and Fall of International Law 1870–1960*, 7.

the depredations of the Vienna system. Meanwhile, pragmatists such as Lorimer and Lawrence argued for the abandonment of the principle altogether in the face of political 'realities' and institutional 'facts'. A third group, represented here by the English scholar John Westlake, was ambivalent about the precise legal effects and implications of the Vienna arrangements ('equivocation').

This debate among scholars continued into the late nineteenth century but by this time diplomatic practice was changing. The legitimacy of legalised hegemony was being challenged by the newer states. The Second Hague Peace Conference represents the culmination of a series of defections from the congressional system of legalised hegemony. In 1907, the newly enfranchised smaller states organised around a uniquely strong form of sovereign equality in order to defeat the proposals for a Permanent Court of Arbitral Justice structured along hegemonic lines.

However, this resulted in another re-evaluation of the sovereign equality principle by international lawyers. This time the majority view among scholars was that the principle, at least in its strong legislative form, had to be abandoned in order to clear the way for the establishment of centralised international organisations. The Court fiasco demonstrated to them the futility of creating international organisations on strongly egalitarian lines. Legalised hegemony, albeit in a modified form, was endorsed as a necessary part of the architecture of international legal order. These developments are the subject of Chapter 5.

The Congress of Vienna and the inception of legalised hegemony

At the Congress of Vienna, Great Power dominance and sovereign equality both competed with each other and mingled with a nascent institutionalism, expressed initially through a Concert system developed there for the first time. This clash of two ideals – the supremacy of the Great Powers and the equality of states – translated into a dialogue between the advocates of management through legalised hegemony and those who preferred a more egalitarian, representative system of European governance. Vienna is a critical moment, though the conflict is a feature of the Concert period generally. The point to understand in approaching Vienna is that the Congress introduced a new regime into European politics. As Lande says:

During the 18th century the principle of equality of states was not disputed, and no legal superiority of the Great Powers was asserted.[6]

Lande's claim may surprise those who assume that relative power has always been the key to understanding international relations. In Thucydides' famous dialogue between the Melians and the Athenians, Athens rejects the claim by Melos that it (Melos) is entitled to equal respect, proclaiming, famously, that 'the strong do what they will and the weak do what they must'.[7] It is undeniable that this conflict between might and right has been a feature of the international political landscape for centuries. However, in this book I explore two relatively new phenomena, albeit ones related to this ancient problem. One is the principle of sovereign equality introduced at Westphalia, the other is the principle of legalised hegemony developed at Vienna.[8] It is the clash between these two principles that is new and not the eternal tension between the great and the good.

The Vienna Congress occurred at the end of a period of turmoil in European history precipitated by the French Revolution and culminating in Napoleon's attempt, and subsequent failure, to dominate Europe. By the time the Congress had dissolved, Napoleon was nine days from Waterloo. Following Waterloo, the restoration of Louis XVIII took place, a European balance of power was reinstated and the reconstruction of Europe commenced. The presence of a defeated would-be hegemon and a weary but victorious coalition with a shared commitment to collective security and a mildly reformist sensibility gives Vienna the feel of other post-war settlements at San Francisco and Versailles.

There were, however, key differences. The Congress of Vienna did not lead to the creation of any significant *standing* international legal

---

[6] A. Lande, 'Revindication of the Principle of Legal Equality of States 1871–1914' (1947) 62 *Political Science Quarterly* 406. See, too, Dickinson, 'Equality of States', 354 (stating 'prior to the French Revolution only the vaguest notions of the supernational authority had made their appearance in European politics'). For a plausible explanation of these changes see Lande, 'Revindication', 407.

[7] *The Landmark Thucydides*, 380.

[8] The Peace of Westphalia, concluded in two treaties, the Treaty of Münster and the Treaty of Osnabrück, was by no means a perfect expression of sovereign equality. Most obviously, the legal capacity of the Holy Roman Empire and that of each of its constituent units was weak in relation to the powerful nation-states of the period (notably France and Sweden). See Chapter 2 for details. See Peace of Westphalia 1648 at http:/www.yale.edu/lawweb/avalon/westphal.htm; Treaty of Münster, 24 October 1648, in *Major Peace Treaties of Modern History, 1648–1967*, vol. I (ed. F. Israel) (1967) 7–49; Treaty of Osnabrück 1648, in *The Consolidated Treaty Series, 1648–1649*, vol. I (ed. C. Parry) (1969), 198–269.

organisations nor did it overhaul the rules of international law.[9] The Concert of Europe was a much less formal institution than either the League of Nations or the United Nations.[10] It lacked the universalist pretensions of its twentieth-century successors (though the Great Powers at Vienna saw themselves as 'Europe' and Europe as the centre of world affairs, they had little interest, at this point, in regulating the rest of humanity). The Concert operated with a view to keeping the peace in Europe and trading over colonial possessions occurred only as part of that process. Its scope was limited in other ways. There was no attempt to deny the applicability of the balance of power as the favoured instrument of social control. Indeed, the Concert was designed to manage the balance rather than abolish it and there was little question that the Great Powers would do the managing.[11]

Yet, in international law, the doctrine of sovereign equality among states had become received wisdom; its pedigree stretching back at least to Westphalia. In this section, I undertake an examination of the encounter between the legalised hegemony of a powerful elite and the idea of sovereign equality. This was to develop into a relationship between a hierarchical structure in which a small number of states regulate, through law, the affairs of the rest and a system in which sovereign states interact with each other as free, equal and independent entities. For the first time, the international system institutionalised the congress method (though no formal organisations were created). This institutionalisation also meant a certain degree of formality and, more arguably, legal regulation. But it also meant legal recognition of sovereign hierarchies.[12] How did international lawyers respond to this, given their concern for sovereign equality? How did statesmen reconcile sovereign equality with great power management? And finally, how did the Great

---

[9] See I. Clark, *Hierarchy*, 112. At least one *regional* or *federal* organisation arose from the Congress of Vienna. As Nussbaum says: 'The new German Confederation which it established . . . was constructed as a permanent league among sovereigns, hence as an institution of international law' (*Concise History*, 179).

[10] The Congress of Vienna in 1815 was not an Assembly, far less an international organisation. Indeed, the Congress did not actually meet as such. The minor powers merely constituted an 'expensive background' (see Genevieve Peterson, 'The Equality of States as Dogma and Reality II. Political Inequality at the Congress of Vienna' (1945) 60 *Political Science Quarterly* 532 at 550).

[11] See Clark, *Hierarchy*.

[12] For the argument that a system of juridically sovereign states was introduced for the first time at Vienna (rather than Westphalia), see Murphy in Weber and Biersteker, *State Sovereignty*, 96. However, this sovereignty was surely highly differentiated and hierarchical.

Powers persuade the smaller states of Europe to accept the various inequalities imposed on them?

The Congress of Vienna: a brief account[13]

At the beginning of 1814, the Four Powers (Great Britain, Prussia, Russia and Austria) signed a Secret Protocol at Langres in which they agreed to make all the major decisions concerning post-war reconstruction themselves.[14] The Langres Protocol affirmed that the balance of power and not sovereign equality was the idea of the time. Article 1 stated that: 'relations from whence a system of real and permanent Balance of Power in Europe is to be derived, shall be regulated at the Congress upon the principles determined upon by the *Allied Powers themselves . . .*' (my italics).[15]

At Chatillon, an early attempt to reach agreement with the French failed but the Great Powers vowed to make peace with France 'in the name of Europe forming a single whole'.[16] In the light of Napoleon's continuing ability to threaten European security, the Four Powers established their defensive alliance, the Treaty of Chaumont (10 March 1814), where the objectives of big powers were defined again and an early version of the Quadruple Alliance came into effect.[17] This Treaty is important for three reasons. First, there was the first legal expression of the idea of Great Powers.[18] Phillips underscores this unique combination of hegemony and constitutional authority:

The significance of the European Coalition during the eight years that followed the signature of the Treaty of Chaumont is, that it represented . . . an experiment in international government, an attempt to solve the problem of reconciling central and general control by a European Confederation with the maintenance of the liberties of its constituent states, and thus to establish a juridical system.[19]

---

[13] This form of legalised hegemony practised, in a steadily diluted form, by the Great Powers can be seen at various points between 1815 and 1871. Vienna is significant because it establishes the normative and procedural framework for the Concert of Europe.

[14] *The Langres Protocol* of 29 January 1814.

[15] This was confirmed in the *Additional, Separate and Secret Articles to the First Paris Peace Treaty*, 30 May 1814, Article 1. See E. Hertslet, *Map of Europe by Treaty*, vol. I (1875–91), 18.

[16] Comte d'Angeberg, *Le Congrès de Vienne*, vol. I (Paris, 1864), 105, quoted by H. Nicolson, *The Congress of Vienna: A Study in Allied Unity.*

[17] The Alliance was renewed by the Definitive Treaty of Alliance and Friendship, Paris, 20 November 1815 (Hertslet, *Map of Europe*, 342).

[18] According to Harold Nicolson, 'this expression now entered diplomatic vocabulary' (*Congress of Vienna*, 81).

[19] W. A. Phillips, *Confederation of Europe: A Study of the European Alliance, 1813–1823* (2nd edn), 9.

Second, these Great Powers began to see themselves as the sole guarantors of peace in Europe for a substantial period. Indeed, for some purposes, they became 'Europe'.[20] Third, they agreed to form a perfect concert and hold a general congress at the conclusion of the war. It was this coalition that prevailed over Napoleon who capitulated to the Allies in April 1814 and was exiled in Elba.[21]

A defeated France then entered into seven treaties with its major former adversaries (UK, Prussia, Russia, Austria, Spain, Sweden and Portugal). These are collectively known as The First Treaty of Paris (30 May 1814). Article 32 of The Treaty of Paris called on the sovereign powers of Europe 'engaged on either side of the present war . . . to settle in a general congress the arrangements which are to complete the disposition of the present treaty'. However, the content of this public treaty concluded by the Eight Powers was predetermined by a series of secret articles, drawn up by the Four Great Powers, that 'pledged the congress in advance'.[22] These secret articles, in turn, merely restated the position of the Allies as expressed in a series of agreements concluded during the war with France.[23]

The First Treaty of Paris contained some useful ambiguities. On the one hand, all the powers were to be invited to the Congress (sovereign equality, universality), on the other hand, the Great Powers fully intended to dominate the post-war system (legalised hegemony). This represents a curious paradox because it meant that the two major features of the Congress system were in opposition to one another. The Congress embodied the idea of a World (or at least, European) Congress open to all coincidental with the introduction and high point of legalised hegemony. This is reflected, too, in the Final Treaty concluded at Vienna in 1815. In its Preamble, the Great Powers are said to have assembled at Vienna 'with the Princes and States their allies to complete the provisions of the said Treaty (First Treaty of Paris)' (my italics).[24] The

---

[20] See Peterson, 'Political Inequality', *passim*; Klein, *Sovereign Equality Among States: The History of an Idea* (1974), 12; Nicolson, *Congress of Vienna*, 81. As Gordon Craig argued, 'For all practical purposes, Europe meant the four states which were considered . . . to be Great Powers', G. A. Craig, *Europe Since 1815* (3rd edn), 11.

[21] See *Treaty of Fontainebleau* (Napoleon's Abdication). But see, too, Lande, 'Revindication', 258. Lande dates this claim to legal superiority from this initial conference at Chatillon on 5 February 1814.

[22] J. Westlake, *Chapters*, 95. The eight powers were Austria, France, Great Britain, Portugal, Prussia, Russia, Spain and Sweden. Portugal, Spain and Sweden were excluded from the negotiations of the Secret Articles.

[23] See BFSP, vol. 2, 49–773.

[24] General Treaty between Great Britain, Austria, France, Portugal, Prussia, Russia, Spain and Sweden (Vienna 9 June 1815 (Final Act)) in Hertslet, *Map of Europe*, 208.

Assembly was universal in its pretensions but the Great Powers issued the invitations.

Two contradictory sets of expectations, then, began to converge as the moment for the Congress approached. The Great Powers favoured legalised hegemony. The central powers did not much care how obvious this claim was to the smaller powers though the British, anticipating the rationales for later Great Power coalitions, preferred an approach that assuaged the concerns of the smaller powers and allowed a larger role for France. Meanwhile, the small and middle powers expected a Congress in which they participated equally. France played a spoiler's role, at first supporting the principle of sovereign equality as a way of preventing the Big Four from dominating the Congress before switching sides when admitted to the big power coalition.[25]

In the summer and autumn months of 1814, the four victorious powers (UK, Russia, Prussia and Austria) met with a view to engineering certain outcomes at Vienna. In September, in a series of pre-Congress meetings in Vienna itself, the Foreign Ministers of the Four Powers agreed to increase their number with a view to accommodating the interests of two other big powers, Spain and France. The only point of agreement at this stage was that the Great Powers would make the decisions and that 'the conduct of the business must practically rest with the leading powers'.[26] An effective cabinet composed of six large powers was to be created with France and Spain added to the big four.[27] There seemed to be some disagreement among the Four Powers as to the precise role of France and Spain in this executive body. The British, keen to mollify French sentiments, wished these two states to be treated as equals. These six, the putative directing Committee for the Congress, were, for Castlereagh, 'Powers of the first order'.[28] The Prussians had no such qualms however. They supported a 22 September Protocol asserting that 'only the four powers can decide on the distribution of states . . . the two other powers can be admitted in order that they give their opinions'.[29] Eventually, the Four Powers agreed on a compromise whereby there was Four

---

[25] The Great Powers have often supported legal equality for some political or strategic purpose, e.g. France in 1815, Britain's support of Greece in 1878 and the Soviet support of Belarus and the Ukraine in 1945.

[26] *Dispatch of Viscount Castlereagh* to the Earl of Liverpool, Vienna, 24 September 1814, FO Continent 7.

[27] Peterson calls this the 'first expression of the idea of Great Powers, with rights as such, distinct from any derived from treaties' ('Political Inequality', 534).

[28] *Dispatch of Castlereagh.*

[29] See Protocol of 22 September 1814, BFSP, vol. 2, 554, 556.

Power decision-making, Six Power consultation and 'respect' for the little powers.[30]

The next problem concerned the nature of the Congress itself. Was it to be an Assembly or a collection of negotiators? How would the Congress be managed? An initial proposal suggested that the Congress itself appoint an executive committee of some sort. This would have meant constituting the Congress in the plenary form and allowing it to take the lead in establishing the structure of negotiations for the post-war order. The Prussians were hostile to the idea of a democratic assembly, preferring to leave such matters in the hands of the Six Powers. Lord Castlereagh believed the first method was too risky and the second too blatant.[31] His preference was that the Congress be induced to support the creation of an executive body composed of the Great Powers.[32] In setting out the advantages of such a method, he delivered a speech that reveals much about the way in which Great Power primacy is secured alongside sovereign equality:

The advantage of this mode of proceeding is that you treat the plenipotentiaries as a body with early and becoming respect. You keep the power by concert and management in your own hands, but without openly assuming authority to their exclusion. You obtain a sort of sanction from them for what you are determined at all events to do, which they cannot well withhold . . . and you entitle yourselves, without disrespect to them, to meet together for dispatch of business for an indefinite time to their exclusion . . .[33]

Under the terms of the 22 September Protocol, the Four Powers met formally on 30 September. This and subsequent meetings, as well as the response to these meetings, demonstrated the various tensions between

---

[30] Alan Palmer, *Metternich, Councillor of Europe*, 132.

[31] The first was too uncertain because it would have prejudged all sorts of decisive preliminary questions which the Allied powers wished to resolve prior to the Congress, e.g. the mode and functions of the Congress, the membership of the plenary and the structure of the Committee work and decision-making procedures. See also R. Klein, *Sovereign Equality*, 13, and *Dispatch of Viscount Castlereagh*.

[32] As Peterson puts it: 'Considerable ingenuity was expended by the ministers of the allied Powers to find a scheme whereby the delegates to the Congress would seem to take part in the discussions without actually having any part in the decision' ('Political Inequality', 535). Castlereagh was under no illusions as to the nature of the whole arrangement. He makes this quite clear in a private letter to the Duke of Wellington in which he describes the role of the Congress in approving the Treaty as 'more a formality, when approved by the eight powers than a substantial proceeding' (*Correspondence of Viscount Castlereagh*, Ser. 3, 10 at 218, Letter of 17 December 1814).

[33] Peterson, 'Political Inequality', 536–7; *Peace Handbooks No 153*, Appendix III, 'Two Projects of Castlereagh on the Method of Opening Congress', Vienna, September 1814.

particular views of equality and hierarchy. France and Spain demanded full 'political equality' with the Great Powers, Portugal argued for its inclusion at these meetings, and other states within Europe protested their exclusion from the Group of Eight (e.g. Bavaria, Denmark).[34] These protests were ignored and throughout October the Great Powers met in informal sessions from which France and Spain were now excluded.[35]

France began agitating for a more prominent role in the Great Power coalition. Protests by small powers, with France in the leadership role, called for equal treatment. This proved to be an unstable alliance. France supported legislative equality in theory but, as Klein makes clear, Talleyrand saw it as unworkable in practice. He was worried about there being too many minute states with too little power.[36] The strong doctrine of sovereign equality was useful as an irritant against the Four Powers but was to be abandoned once France claimed its place among the Great Powers.[37] In the interim, Talleyrand's compromise solution was to allow smaller powers to be represented where their interests were affected and to have a Committee of Eight run the Congress.

The Congress was postponed again while the Great Powers decided first, how hierarchies should be arranged and legitimised and second, how the Congress should be managed. The Four Powers continued to meet throughout October in informal settings and the Committee of Eight met, to inconclusive effect, in late October to deal with the questions of credentials.[38] Another postponement in effect marked the end of any aspirations for a full plenary meeting of the Congress.

At the end of 1814, the Congress finally moved into a more formal phase with the convening of various committees.[39] With the idea of a full congress of European powers shelved, the Committee of Eight

---

[34] Peterson, 'Political Inequality', 538; G. Ferraro, *The Reconstruction of Europe: Talleyrand and the Congress of Vienna, 1814–1815*, 153.

[35] The original idea was that France would be admitted once the Four Powers had come to an agreement among themselves and that Spain would be part of any negotiation affecting her directly. After the initial meetings, France and Spain were invited to an audience with the Great Powers at which Castlereagh said: 'The object of today's conference is to acquaint you with what has been done by the Four Courts since we have been here' (quoted in Ferraro, *Reconstruction of Europe*, 145, 153–4).

[36] Klein, *Sovereign Equality*, 19.   [37] *Ibid.*

[38] With Portugal, Spain, Sweden and France now included (Palmer, *Metternich*, 133).

[39] Though the use of the word 'formal' is perhaps misleading given the degree to which decisions were made without any 'constitutional' authority. As Palmer puts it, 'nobody had the faintest idea of the rules governing this particular diplomatic game . . .' (*ibid.*, 139).

initially took over the administration of the Congress of Vienna.[40] Even this state of affairs was to be short-lived when the disposition of Poland became part of the agenda.[41] For this question, the Big Four again excluded all others apart from France, which, by then, had been admitted to the inner circle.[42] A Committee of Five thus took over the running of the more significant aspects of the Congress's affairs. By this time, it was clear that Vienna had become 'the Congress that was not a Congress'.[43]

It might be said that France joined the Great Powers and abandoned legal equality on 9 January 1815 when the Committee of Five was officially convened. This Committee became the de facto directing Committee of the Congress. From this point on, the Congress took the form of two directing committees (the Committee of Eight and the powerful Committee of Five) and a number of sub-committees, which reported to these two.[44]

---

[40] This committee, in turn, established several sub-committees to deal with major issues facing Europe, e.g. the question of navigable rivers, the rank of diplomatic representatives and the quantification of territory and population conquered by Napoleon. These committees were rather informally constituted by today's standards. A committee to discuss the future of Germany was created without any express authorisation from the Congress or any Great Power group.

[41] In a way, Poland had never been off the agenda but the Great Powers had put aside their differences in the spirit of cooperation that, occasionally, informed their alliance against Napoleon. However, with Napoleon defeated, Prussian aspirations in Germany (their claim to Saxony), Russian requirements in Poland, Austrian anxieties in Central Europe (fear of an enlarged Prussia and an extended Russia), claims in Italy and the Balkans and, finally, British security interests (Antwerp, demands over the high seas and concerns about the balance of power in Central Europe) meant that the Congress would have to reconcile a variety of sometimes contradictory interests among the Great Powers. This proved to be fertile ground for the French, and Talleyrand cleverly exploited his opportunities. In the end, Prussia mobilised in 1814 and Great Britain, France and Austria entered a defensive alliance on 3 January 1815 after the French developed a compromise plan for the partial dismemberment of Saxony and partial partition of Poland. The consequence of all this is that harmony among the Great Powers took precedence over justice for the small. Great Britain and Austria needed France so France was admitted as a Great Power. France desired the label 'Great Power' and so gave up any pretence to champion the rights of the small powers. Meanwhile, Saxony was divided and parcelled and Poland was allowed to die. On Saxony, see Article 15, *Final Act of Congress of Vienna*. On Poland, see Articles 1–13, *Final Act of Congress of Vienna*.

[42] This was formalised at Aix-la-Chapelle in 1818.

[43] Talleyrand, quoted in Palmer, *Metternich*, 139.

[44] There were in fact ten sub-committees created: a Drafting Committee, a Statistical Committee, a Committee on International Rivers, a Committee on Diplomatic Precedence, a Slave Trade Committee and various committees on regional affairs including the important German Committee.

At the Congress itself, the large powers made most of the important decisions in private, extra-plenary meetings.[45] This was not uncontentious. Spain objected to the lack of transparency and the smaller states claimed admission to the conferences, neither with any success. In the end, the Final Act of the Congress was adopted by the five Great Powers (Austria, Britain, Prussia, Russia and France) on 9 June 1815 as well as by two of the declining European powers: Portugal and Sweden. Spain refused to sign.[46] Adoption occurred three months after Napoleon's escape from Elba and nine days before he met his defeat at Waterloo.

The Congress of Vienna, understood here as the Committee meetings in Vienna, the treaties signed subsequently and the various informal sessions before and after, represents a curious combination of responses to the problem of institutionalisation, hierarchy and equality. As befits a system with no precedents in international law, there is a quality of *ad hoc* experimentalism about the whole affair. The major figures, Castlereagh, Talleyrand, Metternich, von Humboldt and Alexander I, were making policy, law and institutions on the run. What resulted was a system in which one can already see the outlines of future institutional structures, debates and controversies.

Hegemony and hierarchy at Vienna

In considering hierarchy and equality, there are four separate sets of relationships to consider. First, there was the distinction between the Great Powers and the rest (a relationship based on *legalised hegemony*).[47] Second, there were relations among the Great Powers themselves (marked by a reliance on *sovereign equality*). Third, there were the various hierarchies operating among the small powers. Fourth, there were the future relations between the French and the Allies (this is what we would characterise now as the question of enemy or outlaw states and is discussed later in the book).[48]

Legalised hegemony

The most obvious tension existed in relation to aspects of sovereign equality (notably legislative equality) and legalised hegemony. Of course,

---

[45] 'The basic mechanism of the Congress consisted of regular morning meetings in Metternich's apartment' (Brison Gooch, *Europe in the Nineteenth Century*, 57).

[46] Spain refused to sign the General Act of Congress, claiming that 'the act included many articles which had not been reported at the meeting of the plenipotentiaries of the great powers' (Westlake, *Chapters*, 97). She acceded to the Treaty in 1817.

[47] This included relations between the Great Powers and the larger middle powers such as Sweden, Portugal and Spain.

[48] See Chapter 8.

the category 'Great Powers' had existed prior to Vienna but only as a *political* idea. With the Congress there was, for the first time, recognition of a phenomenon I characterise as legalised hegemony.[49] This was a significant innovation in a European system that had previously known systems of hierarchy only within vertical or supranational structures of governance.[50] The situation prior to Westphalia was hierarchical but the Holy Roman Empire represented a form of imperial hierarchy that was the opposite of anarchy.[51] Westphalia introduced a system of anarchy in which state sovereignty and equality supplanted the vertical authority of the Church.[52] At Vienna, the 'democratic' system introduced after Westphalia gives way to a hegemonic or oligarchic system that was to be the mark of the Concert order.[53]

In this section, I want to discuss three associated questions. First, what was the nature of this legalised hegemony and what made this form of domination legal rather than merely or purely political? Second, when did this hegemony arise? Third, who possessed this form of constitutional power and how did they come to do so?

The first question forces us to confront the process by which political realities are transformed into legal rules in revolutionary situations. This is a particularly acute problem for international lawyers whose rules of recognition possess modest descriptive and legitimising power. There is significant latitude for disagreement (e.g. some international lawyers denied the existence of legalised hegemony altogether, asserting that Vienna imposed no change on the basic Westphalian model).

The separation or intermingling of law and politics is a problem for any legal or political order. Whole schools of legal theory have arisen

---

[49] See, e.g. Arnold Heeren, *Handbuch der Geschichte*, 443–4, Holbraad, *Concert of Europe*, 82; recognising the novelty of the aristocratic system.

[50] See Chapter 2.   [51] See Goebel, *Equality of States*, 30–58.

[52] See, e.g. Ferraro, *Reconstruction*, 147 (arguing that the 22 September Protocol had contravened eighteenth-century international law by permitting the Allied powers to dispose of territory as if they constituted a judicial or legislative body for the whole of Europe).

[53] See the interesting ideas of Karl Salomo Zacharias (1841) expressed in his *Vierzig Bucher vom Staate*, v220 (quoted in Holbraad, *Concert of Europe*, 65). Zacharias characterises the development of European society from monarchy (Pope) to the revolutionary (Reformation), to Westphalian ('democratic') to Napoleon's attempted re-imposition of monarchy and finally the triumph of oligarchy at Vienna. The Great Powers did not simply impose hierarchy but used all sorts of techniques to achieve consensus in relation to this hierarchy, e.g. in the Regulation of the Eight Powers concerning Rank and Precedence of Diplomatic Agents, the Eight simply 'invite those of the other Crowned Heads to adopt the same regulations' (Annex 17, Vienna Congress Treaty).

out of the different assumptions concerning this relationship.[54] In international law, it results in at least three over-simplifying tendencies. According to one group, law can be detached from politics and studied as an entirely separate phenomenon (see Oppenheim, Hall below). Another group collapses law into politics or believes law 'reflects' politics (e.g. Lorimer and Lawrence in a tendency decried by Goebel).[55] A third group seeks to implicate something called 'politics' in the ruination or compromise of something called 'law'.[56] None of these ideas possesses an entirely satisfactory conception of law. Ultimately, the idea that 'law is politics' is true on one, trivial, level. Of course, treaty-making is political – it seeks to secure political ends and it involves a pooling of political aspirations. As Hans Kelsen describes it, law is 'a specific social technique for the achievement of ends prescribed by politics'.[57] Indeed, law could have no meaning in the absence of politics. Law is politics transformed.[58] It can neither be reduced to politics nor can it be incubated from politics. The Congress of Vienna was neither simply politics nor was it legal regulation tainted by political manoeuvrings. Complicating the matter is the fact that at Vienna a new international regime was being created. There was no law to regulate the creation of the Concert. Three possibilities therefore arise. The Concert could continue to be described as a political body divorced from law or as an unlawful regime or as a moment of legal innovation.

I characterise what happened at Vienna as a novel legal form because it involved law at both a procedural and substantive level. The Congress was established according to a series of treaties signed by either the Eight Powers or the Four. The Protocols by which the Four proposed to dominate the Congress were legal instruments. The results of the Congress were set out in treaty form and ratified by the major European states with the acquiescence of the small powers.[59] At the substantive level, the Congress was concerned with territorial redistribution[60] and

---

[54] For recent studies see T. Franck, *The Power of Legitimacy Among Nations*; Michael Byers, *Custom, Power and The Power of Rules*.

[55] I discuss this separation in greater detail in Simpson, 'Magic Mountain', 70–92.

[56] See, generally, M. Cherif Bassiouni, 'From Versailles to Rwanda in Seventy-Five Years' (1997) 10 *Harvard Human Rights Journal* 11 (calling for an international criminal justice system safeguarded from political compromise).

[57] Hans Kelsen, *The Law of the United Nations*, xiii.

[58] See W. Levi, *Revue De Droit Int'l*, April–June 1995, 126 (arguing that: 'Without political decisions a legal norm could have no rational content . . . legal norms are the translation of political decisions into legally binding rules of behaviour').

[59] See discussion in Kooijmans, *Doctrine of Legal Equality*, 100.

[60] A neutralised Switzerland, a reconstituted union of Belgium and Holland and a German Confederation.

the technical legal rules relating to watercourses, rivers, questions of precedence and other matters central to international law.[61] It also resulted in an agreement to abolish the slave trade.[62] In fact, the treaties concluded around the Congress were remarkably legalistic.[63] So, while Westphalian sovereign equality may have been in retreat here, the idea of legalism was not. It is remarkable to reflect on the role of international law in, for example, resolving questions related to private debts incurred during belligerency.[64]

The Great Powers not only enforced their will on Europe but regarded themselves as possessing a right to do so. They not only instituted a new political order in European affairs but did so using legal techniques that sought to entrench this dominant position.[65] The Great Powers not only had greater influence in the political sphere, they also excluded small powers from representation at the Congress, drafted secret protocols prior to the Conference and possessed superior legal power as a consequence of their greater diplomatic clout. For Ian Clark, 1815 marks the moment when there was 'a final de jure recognition of the inequalities that had always existed de facto in the balance of power system'.[66] The Concert of Europe legalised hierarchy. Or, as Adolf Lande puts it, the Concert was a system of inequality: 'What in 1814 had been a legal

---

[61] For territorial matters see Protocol on the Neutrality of Switzerland and Protocol Cessions made by the King of Sardinia to the Canton of Geneva (Hertslet, *Map of Europe*, 67–71). For the watercourses see *Regulation for the Free Navigation of Rivers*, Annex 16, Vienna Congress Treaty, March 1815 (Hertslet, *Map of Europe*, 75).

[62] This was seen as the primary aim of the Congress by many domestic constituencies in the United Kingdom. Yet, in truth, Castlereagh spent very little time on this matter. Much of the correspondence he received from the UK during the Vienna meetings concerned this emotive issue but his attitude to it can be seen from his response to William Wilberforce in a letter sent from Vienna on 11 November 1814 where he concedes that he 'has not yet been able to enter upon this object . . . but I will seize the first favourable opportunity for doing so . . .', *Correspondence of Viscount Castlereagh*, Ser. 3, 10 at 199. See, too, Annex 15, Vienna Congress Treaty of 9 June 1815 containing a Declaration of the Eight Powers Relative to the Universal Abolition of the Slave Trade (Vienna, 8 February 1815) (Hertslet, *Map of Europe*, 60). This described the trade as repugnant and degrading to Europe but allowed a margin of appreciation as far as outright abolition was concerned. See also First Treaty of Paris, Additional Articles, Great Britain and France, 30 May 1814, Article 1, Abolition of Slave Trade (Hertslet, *Map of Europe*, 20).

[63] It was here that the legalisation of human rights began in earnest. See, e.g. Article 15, First Treaty of Paris, Hertslet, *Map of Europe*, 60 (protecting the right to express a political opinion in the restored and ceded territories).

[64] *Correspondence of Viscount Castlereagh*, Ser. 3, 10 at 170.

[65] The proliferation of treaties, the language of rights, the procedure of regular meetings and the references to sovereign equality all indicate a move to legality.

[66] Clark, *Hierarchy*, 2.

usurpation became later a widely held, though not generally accepted, legal opinion.'[67]

Vienna was the classic case of a revolutionary social practice transforming itself into a new constitutional order through a combination of political will, legal usurpation and subsequent democratic ratification. As with all revolutionary situations, tracking the moment when a practice casts off its illegality and creates the conditions for its own validity is not simple. However, and here I turn to the second question, it is surely possible to see the period in September 1814 as one in which just such a transformation was wrought by the acts of the Great Powers and the tacit acquiescence of the other states in Europe.[68]

The precise moment when this legal usurpation takes place is disputed by historians but many agree that it occurred during the preparatory sessions for the Congress and is given the blessing of Europe's major powers in the Vienna Treaty. In meetings preceding the Congress – at Chatillon, at Chaumont and at Langres – the Great Powers referred to their predominant power in, and their rights over, European affairs.[69] It seemed natural, inevitable and legitimate that they should form the directing committee of the Congress and manage European affairs through the Concert system.[70] At Aix-la-Chapelle, France was invited to join the Great

---

[67] Lande, 'Revindication', 259.

[68] This apparent conundrum is not unique to international law. It is a major question of constitutional origin and transformation in domestic settings, also. See, e.g. V. Jackson and M. Tushnet, *Comparative Constitutional Law*, stating: 'What is the relationship between crisis, extra-legal behaviour, and constitution-making? What is the relationship between coercive power and consent in establishing a constitution? . . . Some would argue that several of our [United States'] most transformative constitutional moments have been characterised by questionable legality', 251.

[69] As early as the First Treaty of Paris, the Allies were claiming a right to regulate European affairs. See First Treaty of Paris, 30 May 1814. In fact, the Treaty of Paris was six separate treaties concluded between France and the Great Powers (see Hertslet, *Map of Europe*). Article 2 stated that the Great Powers 'shall devote their best attention to maintain, *not only between themselves*, but, inasmuch as depends upon them, between all the States of Europe that harmony and good understanding . . .' (my italics).

[70] For scholarship supporting this idea that political hierarchies adopted legal forms at Vienna see Lande, 'Revindication' (dating the imposition of legalised hegemony to the September meetings in Vienna); Klein, *Sovereign Equality*, 11–14 (stating that at Chatillon 'the Four laid the groundwork for their claim to pre-eminence over the secondary states of Europe'); C. K. Webster, *The Cambridge History of British Foreign Policy, 1783–1919*, vol. II (1923), 49–50, quoted in Klein, *Sovereign Equality*, 14 (asserting that the September 1814 negotiations were the moment when the concept of Great Powers as bearers of legal rights first was formulated); Peterson, 'Political Inequality' (describing 15 September 1814 as the moment when agreement is reached that a cabinet of great powers should direct congress (534)). See, too, R. Albrecht-Carrié, *Diplomatic History*, 12.

Powers and assume 'the place that belongs to her in the European system'.[71] The Union of Powers could now operate to ensure the general peace of Europe through a system within which they formed the constitutional pinnacle.

It is important to realise that these rights were not simply asserted by the Great Powers but also were conceded by most of the small powers.[72] Like the smaller powers at San Francisco, the minor powers at Vienna were disappointed with certain outcomes and disliked the superior attitudes of the big powers but nonetheless did not question the pre-eminent role of the major states. This is not to suggest that questions of sovereign equality did not arise. In fact they did, but mostly in relation to the failure of the Great Powers to convene a full congress with universal representation.[73] The small and middle powers did not expect a leadership role but they did want their voices heard.[74]

Finally, who were the Great Powers? In most revolutionary moments, the Great Powers present themselves 'naturally' (as opposed to being nominated through some formal legal process). They tend to be the major victors after a conflict; the indispensable members of the coalition formed to defeat a large revisionist power. Indeed, in the post-war moment, military power will tend to play a larger role in defining 'greatness' than at other times in history.[75] However, the fact of power is insufficient to establish superior status. Great Powers possess a range of non-material resources such as diplomatic experience and cultural acceptability, which can compensate for a lack of raw power (Austria 1815,

---

[71] Protocol of Conference, between the plenipotentiaries of Austria, France, Great Britain, Prussia and Russia. Signed at Aix-la-Chapelle, Hertslet, *Map of Europe*, 571–2.

[72] This for Treipel is the very essence of hegemony, where 'the feeling of oppression has been changed into a feeling of joyful subordination' (Section. 44), *Die Hegemonie, Ein Buch von fuhrenden Staaten* (1938) (quoted in Kooijmans, *Doctrine of Equality*, 96).

[73] In fact, 216 *chefs de mission* attended Vienna. These were the representatives of all European powers apart from Turkey. See Dickinson, 'Equality of States', 357.

[74] Representations were made concerning the dominance of the Great Powers prior to Aix-la-Chapelle. Metternich responded by arguing that the oligarchy was endorsed by the Treaty of 20 November 1815 and that discussions at Aix-la-Chapelle would be restricted to matters anticipated by the treaty. After the Congress of Verona, there was a further attack by the King of Wurttemberg. Metternich responded by asking why the Great Powers needed the consent of small powers in law for such meetings (aside from the functional considerations). The system is variously described as pentarchy, political preponderance and, more negatively, 'quadruple despotism' (Holbraad, *Concert of Europe*, 45).

[75] Unless, of course, the enemies remain military powers, e.g. France in 1815 and Germany in 1918, in which case power will tend to be offset by the fact of a recent defeat.

Britain 1945).[76] Conversely, the absence of such qualities can handicap Great Power aspirants (China 1945). This leaves some scope for disagreement as to membership of this privileged group.

At Vienna, the Great Powers were distinguished from smaller nations, most obviously by their relative power. However, the definitions most often used at Vienna to distinguish the Great Powers from the rest did not mention power. Instead, Great Powers were said to have wider interests in European security and territorial redistribution than the small and middle powers.[77] René Albrecht-Carrié characterises a Great Power as one 'with general interests, meaning by this, one which has automatically a voice in all affairs, by contrast with a Power of lower rank, or power with limited interests'.[78] All states had parochial interests, only the Great Powers had interests transcending geography.[79] Baron von Humboldt, the Prussian Foreign Minister, modified these distinctions further, claiming that matters of general interest could be settled by the Six Powers (including France and Spain), regional questions by the powers involved and territorial matters by the members of the Quadruple Alliance alone.[80] Other definitions emphasise the responsibilities of the Great Powers (to be correlated with their rights).[81] These definitions and practices conform to the definition of legalised hegemony adopted in Chapter 3 where emphasis was laid on these non-material attributes of Great Power identity.

Sovereign equality in the service of legalised hegemony

These definitions, however, did not render the issue of membership of the Great Power grouping any less contentious.[82] Questions of hierarchy and equality had the potential to arise among the Great Powers themselves (and did in fact arise in a much more acute form between the Great and would-be Great Powers, as I discuss later). I want to argue here that sovereign equality operated most successfully among the Great Powers in order to facilitate cooperation between them and prevent disputes arising about status within this group. So, paradoxically, legalised hegemony as between the Great Powers and the rest, in order to

---

[76] See Chapters 3 and 6.   [77] Ninic, *The Problem of Equality*, 126.
[78] Albrecht-Carrié, *Diplomatic History*, 22.   [79] Alfred Lande, 'Revindication'.
[80] Bernard Gilson, *The Conceptual System of Sovereign Equality*, 476.
[81] For similar arguments made during the drafting of the Charter, see Chapter 6.
[82] A number of states agitated for membership, e.g. Sweden, which was thought to have the support of Alexander I. See Castlereagh, *Dispatch*.

work effectively, requires a formalistic commitment to sovereign equality *among* the Great Powers themselves.

At Vienna, there was little doubt that Russia, Austria, Prussia and
Great Britain were states of the first rank. They claimed this position
by virtue of their size, military capacity and economic power. However,
even among the four Great Powers hierarchies existed. Britain was regarded as the most powerful by the other states and saw itself as the
neutral arbiter and guarantor of Europe's security.[83] States such as Spain
and Portugal, as we have seen, viewed themselves as Great Powers and
resented their exclusion from the inner councils.

Among the Great Powers themselves, the question of legalised hierarchy did not appear to arise at all. All this tends to suggest that in
thinking about sovereign equality it is a mistake to assume that it applies either to relations between all states in the system or does not
apply at all. In fact, the doctrine of sovereign equality was applied most
unerringly to relations among and between Great Powers. At Vienna, a
Committee was established to set out in explicit detail the ranking of
the various powers including the resolution of questions of precedence
among the Great Powers themselves. The result of this was a series of
rules that attempted to preserve the ritualistic elements of sovereign
equality. For example, it was determined in the resulting regulations
that ties of consanguinity or existing alliances between Courts should
confer no special status on diplomatic representatives (Article VI). Similarly, the question of precedence in relation to the signature of treaties
was to be determined by ballot (Article VII). It was inconceivable that
any of the Great Powers at Vienna would have accepted a lesser status
regardless of any actual disparities in power. The same might be said for
the San Francisco arrangements. In the political world, the Soviet Union
and the United States were superpowers but in the legal world of the
UN Charter, they were accorded equal status (voting rights, veto powers)
with the other much weaker Great Powers (France, UK and China).

Ultimately, then, sovereign equality became an indispensable requirement of harmony between the Great Powers even where material inequalities were salient.[84] The very arguments used to sustain the practice

---

[83] See Peterson, 'Political Inequality', 551. The position had changed considerably from
that of 1813 when the United Kingdom was excluded from the inner circles of the
anti-Napoleonic alliance and was obliged to 'demand an equal voice in Coalition
policy' (Nicolson, *Congress of Vienna*, 58).

[84] The idea of 'legalised hegemony' then depends on an artificial assumption of equality.
So, while sovereign equality is declared unworkable because it fails to take into

of legalised hegemony and temper the application of sovereign equality doctrine to the body of states in general (i.e. the reality of material differences) are silenced when relations between the Great Powers are arranged. Here, sovereign equality becomes the dominant norm and hierarchies are regarded as illegitimate and dangerous.[85] A standard international relations account of equality and hierarchy suggests that equality is a fiction and hegemony the expression of some underlying reality in the international order.[86] In fact, hegemony appears to require the fiction of equality (albeit extended only to the hegemons themselves) in order to sustain it.

Other hierarchies

I have tended to refer to legalised hegemony as a product of the division of powers into great and small. However, hierarchies developed in other relationships. A fascinating aspect of the Vienna process was the incessant jockeying for position among the various participants. Hierarchy tended to work itself out in many different forms. So that, though the small powers argued for sovereign equality as an abstract principle, they nevertheless embraced any opportunity to differentiate themselves from the pack.

This occurred in a number of different ways. First, there were those erstwhile or aspirant major powers who sought inclusion in the 'G5'. Sweden, Spain and Portugal each had some claim to this distinction but none entered the elite. In order to satisfy the demands of these powers, the Group of Six was formed (to accommodate Spain and France) along with a Committee of Eight (the signatories of the Treaty of Paris, which added Sweden and Portugal to the group). Meanwhile, Denmark and the Netherlands hovered around the edges of this expanded Eight Power group but were not admitted.[87] In the end, the Committee of Eight

---

account the physical inequalities between nations, legalised hegemony is no more realistic. It, too, fails to take into account significant differences, in the interests of equal representation and equality. At the time of the Congress of Vienna, Austria was only barely hanging on to its Great Power credentials (as well as its existence) while Prussia had only recently been elevated from the rank of a third-class power. See, e.g. Nicolson, *Congress of Vienna*, 15, 17–31.

[85] The Council of the League of Nations is a stark example of this. Italy's position on the Council is an anomaly considering its weakness compared to, say, the UK. See Fenwick, *International Law*, 2nd edn, 156.

[86] See R. Evans, 'All States are Equal but some . . .', 59, arguing that equality is only possible between evenly matched powers.

[87] Klein, *Sovereign Equality*, 25.

took formal leadership but it was the Committee of Five that met most frequently and made the crucial decisions. The *Commission de Redaction* (with a representative from each of the Eight Powers) drafted the Final Act and all but Spain signed this Final Act. Of the sixty-seven protocols drafted at the Congress only seventeen were signed by the delegates of Portugal, Sweden and Spain. The rest were the business of the Great Powers alone.

The way the various Committees and sub-committees were organised was also hierarchical. The small powers had not given up their claims to some sort of representation at the Congress. The German principalities, in particular, wished to be represented on those committees that were to deal with German affairs. In this, they were successful.[88] But claims for equality were tempered somewhat by the preference that hierarchy operate even at this lower level, e.g. Baron de Haske of Baden argued for 'equal representation' on the German Committee but not for every principality. Baden was to have a special role by virtue of its pre-eminence.[89] On 14 October, there was a meeting on German affairs attended by the five most powerful German states. As D'Angeberg put it:

This committee must only be composed of plenipotentiaries from the five courts of Austria, Prussia, Bavaria, Hanover and Wurttemberg, either because a larger number might hold up proceedings, and in any case the five courts named must be considered the most powerful, or because other states had submitted beforehand to the arrangements which might be required by the order to be established for the preservation of German independence.[90]

Others took an even more radical position, arguing that a German Confederation should take its place among the Great Powers leaving the small powers behind. In the end, the body established by the German

---

[88] See J. L Chodzo, *Le Congrès de Vienne et les traités de 1815*, 295–6 (quoted in Bengt Broms, *Doctrine of Equality*, 89). This was in part due to the fact that the quadruple alliance needed a strong confederated Germany in order to repel future French intrusions. Of course, the Germans could not be too strong for fear of German expansion. Europe has always been threatened by a Germany that is either too weak (it becomes a playground for French and Russian interests) or too strong (it embarks on foreign adventures). See Henry Kissinger, *Diplomacy* (1995), Chapter 2.

[89] Klein, *Sovereign Equality*, 26. The number of sovereign and semi-sovereign entities in Europe at this time seems large when viewed from a twentieth-century perspective. Klein mentions seventy little states, nineteen autonomous Swiss Canons and thirty seven German principalities (at 10). A population size of between 10,000 and 70,000 was the norm.

[90] D'Angeberg, *Le Congrès de Vienne et les traités de 1815* (1863), 289, quoted in Ferraro, *Reconstruction*, 179.

Committee, the German Confederacy, perfectly illustrated the way the principle of sovereign equality is asserted in international law only to be modified by substantive principles based on legalised hierarchy. Article III of the Treaty, creating the Confederacy, declared that 'all members are equal' but Article VI went on to introduce weighted or unequal voting based on state hierarchies.[91]

Conclusion

At Vienna, sovereign equality remained, at best, a background claim. The small powers did advocate forms of legislative equality (though not in as vehement a manner as their successors in 1907) and the whole idea of a Congress was premised on a tentative notion of sovereign equality. Also, the small states had anticipated a plenary form in which they would participate as equals in public fora (even if there was general acceptance that some major issues would be dealt with by committees). This did not occur. Vienna had its Security Council, but the international system was not yet ready for a General Assembly. Hegemony and hierarchy were the preponderant practices at Vienna. Only the most minimal lip service was paid to the principle of sovereign equality (except among the Great Powers themselves). Castlereagh understood its appeal from a rhetorical perspective but he had no intention of letting it interfere with the agenda of the Great Powers.

All three facets of legislative equality were heavily compromised at Vienna. The Great Powers made the law and the middle powers signed the resulting Treaty. The smaller powers, meanwhile, were erased from consideration. As far as representation was concerned, the European

---

[91] These justifications reappear in debates preceding each of the diplomatic conferences and moments of institution-building studied in this book. This Treaty was signed on June 8 and appended to the Congress of Vienna. See Gilson, *Conceptual System*, 398. See Vienna Congress Treaty, Final Act, Articles 54 to 64. Article 55 states that: 'The members of the Confederation, as such, are equal with regard to their rights . . .'. The Germanic Confederation was to be composed of a Federative Diet (in which all states of the German Confederation were entitled to one vote each) and a more powerful General Assembly wherein the Germanic states were allocated votes on the basis of size or prestige, e.g. Austria had four votes, Baden three, Holstein two and Saxe-Weimar one (Article 58). In the German Confederation Treaty of 1820 much of this was confirmed by the Final Act of the Ministerial Conference, Vienna 15 May 1820 (Hertslet, *Map of Europe*, 636). In this Act, the states of the Confederation are said to have 'reciprocal and equal rights' within the entity and are said to constitute a collective power for external purposes. There is no right to secede from the Confederation, however (Article 5). Here, again, were the various justifications for hierarchy: greater power, the need for efficiency and the presumed tacit consent of the smaller powers.

powers were arranged according to an elaborately hierarchical pattern. Voting did not take place at Vienna so the question of weighted votes for the Great Powers did not arise. Still, the Great Powers did not require weighted votes because they were in the majority in the two major committees and utterly dominated proceedings in other respects. Equality of consent was respected in the most formal and, sometimes, meaningless, manner possible. The small powers consented to the resulting arrangements because they were given little choice. The Saxon King, for example, gave his consent (as 'an equal') to the amputation of half his sovereign territory but only after being threatened with continued incarceration. The consent of the smaller states was required as a matter of form and etiquette but it was far from indispensable. Legislative equality was regarded as an impediment to the success of the Conference.

Formal equality, the principle that states will be protected in their enjoyment of the rights they already possess in courts of law, was not particularly relevant at Vienna. A whole new order was being drawn up by the delegates and that order did not anticipate the establishment of judicial bodies to determine the claims of states.

Albrecht-Carrié suggested that the Congress's approach to legislative and existential equality could be distinguished, with the latter right surviving the move to hegemony: '[the] legitimate right of all to exist is a very different concept from the democratic notion of equality . . . The democratic idea was anathema in Vienna, where instead the concept that power implies rights no less than responsibilities was frankly acknowledged . . .'.[92]

In fact, the territorial integrity and political independence of the various principalities and kingdoms that had been absorbed by Napoleon and who, optimistically, had regarded the Congress as the opportunity to claim back their independence by gaining representation at Vienna, were little respected.[93] States were divided, territories amputated and principalities confederated.[94] In particular, a large part of Poland was incorporated into Russian territory and the 300 pre-war German principalities and kingdoms were merged into the 30-member German Confederation.[95]

---

[92] Albrecht-Carrié, *Diplomatic History*, 12.   [93] Klein, *Sovereign Equality*, 11.

[94] Castlereagh, for example, argued that Flanders was better off amalgamating with the Netherlands in order to stave off threats to its security. Sovereignty was best preserved by giving it away.

[95] The Holy Alliance provided a new and different threat to the idea of existential equality (see Chapters 7 and 8).

Ultimately, sovereign equality in many of its manifestations was poorly served at Vienna. The existence of states was insecure, their votes were often worthless, there was no formal representation for many states and new laws and organisations were foisted on the smaller European powers with only minimal levels of consent. Following Vienna, the Five Powers managed European international relations in the first half of the nineteenth century through the Concert system. However, their domination was not converted into the sort of permanent bureaucratic hierarchy that existed in Geneva or now exists in New York. This is what prevents us from describing the Vienna system as an organisation.[96] Article VI of the Second Treaty of Paris, signed on 20 November 1815, resulted in an agreement to consult on matters involving the future of Europe. This was in essence the Concert system. The Great Powers were to regularly, 'consider measures . . . the most salutary for the repose and prosperity of nations and for the maintenance of the peace of Europe'. The Concert was reaffirmed by a Protocol of the Treaty in 1818 mandating the Great Powers to continue their meetings (though by this time in the absence of the British who left the Congress system and elected to play a detached broker's role in future European affairs). In the end, the Concert was neither a full-blooded international organisation nor a continuation of eighteenth-century forms of anarchy. To adopt late-twentieth-century nomenclature, it was a regime or an institution and one that surprised its detractors and disappointed its ardent advocates. As Castlereagh's witty summary put it following the first meeting of the Concert at Aix-la-Chapelle:

It is satisfactory to observe how little embarrassment and how much solid good grow out of these reunions, which sound so terrible at a distance. It really appears to me to be a new discovery in the European Government, at once extinguishing the cobwebs into which diplomacy obscures the horizon, bringing the whole bearing of the system into its true light, and giving to the Great Powers the efficiency and almost simplicity of a single state.[97]

Was the refusal to countenance strong forms of sovereign equality a problem? There are those who argue that a stable international order requires a hegemon.[98] Many of the realists of the twentieth century

---

[96] Though it is described variously as an idea, a practice, a confederacy, a system, an institution. See Holbraad, *Concert of Europe*, 4.

[97] Letter from Castlereagh to Liverpool, 20 October 1818 (cited in Albrecht-Carrié, *The Concert of Europe* (1968), 43).

[98] See, generally, Gilpin, *Political Economy*.

(e.g. Henry Kissinger) remember the Concert as a period of stability. The departures from the doctrine of sovereign equality were the price to be paid for a successful international order.[99] There were others who thought the Concert lacked legitimacy because it had been imposed on Europe from above. For them, this accounted for its fragility.

Whatever one's views on this question there seems little doubt that Vienna proved to be the high point of legalised hegemony in international affairs. In Edwin Dickinson's words, Vienna was 'absolutely irreconcilable' with legal rights to political equality.[100] The informal meetings of the Great Powers in Metternich's Vienna apartment instituted a practice that 'accustomed the participants to the idea of the Great Powers making basic decisions for not only themselves but also the second-ranked states. This viewpoint extended through the nineteenth century.'[101] Of course, such distinctions continued to exist (as at Versailles and San Francisco). Nonetheless, never again would differentiation on this scale occur. Nor would there again be a failure to convene a General Assembly in tandem with the establishment of an executive body. The Congress introduced an extreme version of legalised hegemony but was also its high-water mark. In a similar manner, the Hague Peace Conference of 1907 introduced, and yet at the same time heralded the demise of extreme sovereign equality. From 1815, hegemony slowly gave ground to aspects of sovereign equality. After 1907, legalised hegemony reasserted itself but in a form mediated by elements of sovereign equality.

International legal scholarship: fidelity, repudiation and equivocation

Following Vienna, and for the rest of the nineteenth century, international law publicists grappled with the consequences of this novel system in much the same way that contemporary international lawyers look back to the system created at San Francisco in order to understand the contemporary scene. International lawyers were obliged to explain two apparent anomalies in a system supposedly based on sovereign equality. These anomalies arose from Great Power dominance, on the one hand, and the belief in European cultural superiority, on the other (see Chapter 8).

---

[99] Kissinger, *Diplomacy*, 81.   [100] Dickinson, 'Equality of States', 357.
[101] Gooch, *Europe in the Nineteenth Century*, 57.

The nineteenth-century and early twentieth-century international lawyers were confronted with a system of European administration in which legalised hegemony had become a founding principle and sovereign equality appeared to have been relegated to the level of cosmetics. In this section, I consider, first, the various ways in which one group of scholars ('fidelity') reconciled their continued allegiance to legalism and sovereign equality with their realisation that Vienna had transformed the diplomatic scene. These writers appreciated that Vienna had introduced a set of new procedures into international relations. However, there was an effort made to ensure that legal equality stood apart, uncontaminated by these diplomatic or political occurrences. Lawyers like Oppenheim, Hall and Wheaton embraced a radical separation of law and politics and thereby anticipated an ongoing theme in the literature and doctrine on sovereign equality.[102]

Meanwhile, another group of international lawyers regarded Vienna as a moment of transformation in legal relations between states ('repudiation'). The likes of Lawrence and Lorimer rejected strict adherence to sovereign equality in international legal doctrine and jettisoned certain elements of sovereign equality (notably the idea of legislative equality) when it ceased to describe what they perceived as objective legal relations between sovereign states. The position of the Great Powers in the Concert system had fashioned a set of new relationships and doctrines. The scholarship of these writers accommodated these changes and saw in them the possibility of better facilitating political relations between states and the establishment of international organisations with permanent administrative and executive bodies. For some of them, the hegemony of the Great Powers was a step towards the cosmopolitan dream of world government, for others it was simply a juridical recognition of harsh political realities. Finally, there was John Westlake's equivocation, which mirrored that of the discipline as a whole.

Fidelity

Nineteenth-century legal scholars were unanimous in their recognition that the Great Powers existed as a social category. Studies of the Vienna Congress and the early workings of the Concert system confirmed

---

[102] Some writers do not feel the need to say anything at all about equality. Such writers would regard themselves as having dealt with all issues relating to equality in the various sections on territory, sovereignty and independence. See, e.g. Wm. Oke. Manning, *Commentaries on the Law of Nations*.

the dominance of this group and their determination both to manage European affairs and to have that management sanctioned in law. However, many international lawyers were reluctant to play the role of handmaiden or apologist for the Great Powers and expended considerable scholarly energy to deny legal effect to Great Power hegemony.

Three strategies were employed (sometimes interchangeably) by these lawyers. In the first case, a clear demarcation was made between the political domination of the Great Powers and the legal equality of states (e.g. Oppenheim). However, this separation of the legal and political domains was hard to sustain in the face of Great Power activism in the legal sphere. A second strategy involved demonstrating that the Great Powers had acted with the consent of other states in the system. Either that consent had been given prior to the construction of the Vienna system (implicitly or explicitly) or was a device used to ratify decisions made by the Great Powers at Vienna (e.g. Holland). In both cases, sovereign equality was reconciled with various forms of hegemony. A third group of lawyers adopted a different course and declared that the hegemony of the Great Powers was an unlawful exercise of power contrary to principles of legal equality (e.g. Nys). In some respects, this is the opposite of the first argument because it accepts that the legal and the political overlap to a large extent and that the activities of the hegemons were susceptible to legal regulation or, at least, condemnation.

Lassa Oppenheim's scholarship epitomised the first of these strategies.[103] Legalised hegemony, he said, was a nonsense: 'however important the position and influence of the Great Powers may be, they are by no means derived from a legal basis or rule'. Any doctrine that made the mistake of abolishing sovereign equality or recognised legalised hegemony 'confounds political with legal inequality'.[104] Arthur Nussbaum agreed, describing the phrase 'Great Powers' as 'a political rule rather than a legal term'.[105] On the other side of the Atlantic, Henry Wheaton, in his *Elements of International Law*, declared that the 'primitive equality of nations'[106] was unaffected by differences in power and unimpaired by either 'occasional obedience' to another state or even the 'habitual influence of other states' (i.e. the pre-eminence of the Great Powers).[107]

---

[103] For a later argument along similar lines see Kooijmans, *Doctrine of Legal Equality*, 107–16.

[104] Oppenheim, *International Law* (3rd edn), vol. I, 162–4.   [105] *Ibid.*, 181.

[106] Wheaton, *Elements of International Law* (8th edn), 158.

[107] *Ibid.*, 33. This strict separation was sustained rather uneasily. For example, he went on to concede that equality was affected by 'express compacts'.

None of these practices or habits was thought to have any bearing on the equality of states as it operated in the juridical sphere.[108]

Oppenheim's and Wheaton's bald distinction between political and legal inequality leaves a number of interesting questions unanswered.[109] Did the Great Powers acquire their position in an extra-legal context or did they acquire it illegally? Was the position of the Great Powers in European public life a matter of politics alone? At what point would the special position and influence of the Great Powers become a matter of law? Writers in this camp were not blind to the increasing authority of the Great Powers. They conceded that hegemony existed but not in the juridical sphere. How, then, was this juridical sphere demarcated? Holtzendorff referred to 'social superiority'.[110] In a similar vein, Rivier spoke of a political hegemony that does not affect questions of right; a form of domination compatible with sovereign equality providing, for example, that 'when resolutions are adopted in a congress a great power has no more voice than a small one'.[111]

Typifying a rhetorical commitment to the principle of sovereign equality, common among international lawyers in this age, Richard Wildman, writing in 1849, declared that: 'No principle of public law is more generally acknowledged than the perfect equality of nations. Russia and Geneva have equal rights.'[112] In Wildman's view, this equality encompasses equality, 'in contemplation of the law' and equal rights with regard to three matters: territory, choice of government and 'extent of resources'.[113] However, Wildman accepted that this perfect equality did not encompass legislative equalities nor was it affected by relationships that twentieth-century lawyers would view as illegitimately hierarchical,

---

[108] This anticipated the decision in *Austro-German Customs Union* where Judge Anzilotti distinguishes Austria's political or de facto dependence on Germany from her legal independence or continued exercise of sovereignty (Separate Opinion of Judge Anzilotti, *Austro-German Customs Union Case*, PCIJ Rep., ser. A/B, no. 41 (1931)).

[109] Others, of course, believed that the creation of hegemonic elites offended natural law or was bad policy. See, e.g. Frederick Eden, *An Historical Sketch of the International Policy of Modern Europe*, deploring the Congress for extinguishing so many states and forming an elite of super states.

[110] F. V. Holtzendorff (1900) 2d ser. 2 RDILC 22 (quoted in Dickinson, *Equality of States*, 128).

[111] Rivier, *Droit des gens*, vol. I, 125 (quoted in Dickinson, 'Equality of States', 162).

[112] Richard Wildman, *Institutes of International Law*, vol. I, 13. See Marshall CJ in *The Antelope Case* (discussed in Chapter 2). This has been updated. The comparisons are more likely to be between Malta and the United States (Shaw, *International Law*, 148). For other examples see, e.g. A. Walker, *The Science of International Law*, 112; J. T. Abdy ed., *Kent's Commentaries on International Law*, 40.

[113] Wildman, *Institutes*, 39.

e.g. he regarded equality as compatible with unequal treaties, 'so long as the state retains the right to self-government'.[114] This was the case even where 'some pre-eminence is conceded to its ally'.[115] The pre-eminence accorded collectively to the Great Powers at Vienna was therefore reconciled with sovereign equality.[116]

At the same time, the continued vigour of the ranking system of states appeared also to undermine sovereign equality. Wheaton described this ranking system as a 'vain pretension' but he conceded that an elaborate system of ranking continued to exist in the custom and usage of European states during the nineteenth century.[117] The Royal Honours system had developed into a complex hierarchical structure that accorded precedence on the basis of form of government. Its compatibility with sovereign equality could be maintained only by characterising this form of hierarchy as purely ritualistic. Procedural inequalities that would be regarded as intolerable today were thought to be quite consistent with a larger commitment to sovereign equality in the nineteenth century. For Woolsey, writing in 1860, 'legal equality' was compatible with inequalities of honour, rank and respect and did not include commercial or political equality.[118] Instead, it was taken to mean 'simply equality of state rights . . . the possession of all the same rights which other states possess'.

The writers discussed above distinguished the sovereign equality of states from both the substantive hegemony of the great states and the formal ranking of states in the European system on a hierarchical basis. Sovereign equality existed, then, in a sphere bounded on one side by an

---

[114] *Ibid.*, 67.   [115] *Ibid.*

[116] See, too, W. E. Hall, *International Law*, noting that there had been a transformation from hierarchy pre-Westphalia (the apex of this hierarchy occupied by papal legislation or imperial dictates) to equality (Westphalia and beyond). An associated debate occurring around this time questioned the precise status of the balance of power in international law. Did this idea and, by inference, the hegemony of the Great Powers, operate as a legal principle? In his *Four Lectures on Subjects Connected with Diplomacy* at 95–6, Montague Bernard argued that it was a mistake to confuse a rule of international law (sovereign equality) with a method by which it is secured. See, for the opposite view to Bernard, Travers Twiss, *The Law of Nations Considered as Independent Political Communities* (1st edn), i, 153; see, too, Phillimore, *Commentaries*, vol. I, 456. Various treaties of the period do explicitly refer to the balance of power, including the First Treaty of Paris itself. See also Preamble to Treaty between Prussia and Russia, relating to Poland, Vienna Congress Treaty (3 May 1815), Annex 2, purporting to found the disposition of Poland on 'the principles of a just balance of power', (Hertslet, *Map of Europe*, 106).

[117] Wheaton, *Elements*, 8th edn, 154.

[118] T. Woolsey, *Introduction to the Study of International Law* (1860), 83.

expanding domain of hegemonic politics and on the other by a slowly receding complex of hierarchical ritual and form.[119]

Another strategy adopted by the legalists involved accepting that the Great Powers at Vienna had pretensions to legalised hegemony but declaring that their actions were breaches of the law.[120] Ernst Nys, in his study of the Congress of Vienna, adopted this position. This hegemony, he said, was in 'positive contradiction' to sovereign equality and the nature of the international legal order. He maintained that it ought therefore to be rejected by international lawyers.[121] Nys warned against international legal science's tendency to legitimise retrospectively unlawful acts. Legalised hegemony, he argued, had no 'rational basis or historical foundation'.[122] Chrétien was just as vehement. The Great Powers had violated a central principle of international law by arrogating to themselves quasi-judicial power.[123] These nineteenth-century scholars, then, attempted to deny the existence of legalised hegemony by describing these Great Power privileges as violations of sovereign equality or exceptions (with no legal effect) to a general rule.[124] A third group refused to recognise even a latent tension between equality and hegemony at Vienna. What the Great Powers had claimed for themselves had been given willingly by the smaller states. T. E. Holland, for example, argued that the formation of oligarchies was consented to by the vast majority of European states and so did not interfere in the slightest with equality.[125]

---

[119] In a similar vein, Halleck, after ascribing to states an equality before the law (derived from nature) regardless of any political inequalities, then devoted a great deal of attention to the problem of precedence and ranking (G. Sherston Baker (ed.), *Halleck's International Law*, 3rd edn, 120–1). Though in a later edition he stated: 'Nevertheless, the Great Powers of Europe have obtained such a position of authority that they are able to exercise predominance over other states. This position is now well recognised.' Halleck, *International Law*, vol. I, chapter 5, sec. 2, 126.

[120] See, e.g. Holtzendorff (quoted in Dickinson, 'Equality of States', 128).

[121] Nys, *Etudes de droit international et de droit politique*, vol. II, 3.   [122] *Ibid.*, 3.

[123] Dickinson, 'Equality of States', 166. Interestingly Chrétien appears to accept that ceremonial and diplomatic rankings are compatible with sovereign equality in a way that legalised hegemony is not. Precisely the opposite would be the case in the modern period (Chrétien, *Principes de droit international public* (Paris, 1893), sec. 174 in Dickinson, 'Equality of States', 166).

[124] See, e.g. F. de Martens, *Traité de droit international* (trans. A. Leo) (Paris, 1883–7), vol. I, 380 (distinguishing practice of inequality from law of equality); George Streit, 'Les Grandes Puissances dans le droit international' (1900), 2nd ser., 2 RDILC 17, describing departures from sovereign equality as infractions no more capable of destroying the principle than infractions of municipal law destroy its rules (quoted in Dickinson, 'Equality of States', 151).

[125] Holbraad, *Congress of Vienna*, 188 (quoting T. E. Holland).

To conclude, among the group of international lawyers who denied any effect to the Vienna settlement, one group viewed hegemony as political and therefore not relevant to a consideration of international law (Oppenheim) while another group saw it as operating in the area of law but as an unlawful usurpation of power. Sometimes these were combined to produce somewhat illogical results, e.g. Nys claimed that the Concert system was contrary to sovereign equality and yet also described the hegemony produced as a 'political fact . . . not a juridical principle'.[126] Kebedgy also shifted between these two positions in an essay written at the turn of the century. For him, the hegemony of the Great Powers was a violation of international law and could not 'abolish right by denying it. Still less is it well founded to consider its violation as capable of establishing a rule of law.' However, a little later in the same passage he declared that these inequalities produced by hegemony were 'juridically insignificant' and, 'not opposed to the existence of the rule of equality for all before the law'.[127]

What each of these writers in this camp was keen to accentuate was their fidelity to an uncompromised norm of sovereign equality.

Repudiation

For another group of lawyers, these various attempts to cast about for justifications and rationales for the Vienna system were fruitless and wrong-headed. Instead of reconciling hegemony with existing doctrines of legal equality, international legal scholars, they believed, were obliged to adopt a more pragmatic posture. These arguments fell also into three broad categories. At the descriptive level, writers in this group simply could not accept the distinctions between the legal and the political drawn by the likes of Oppenheim. For them, the hegemony of the Great Powers was a fact with legal consequences. The Powers represented a legislative elite and the law was obliged to recognise this fact. Political inequality rendered a strong form of sovereign equality null or fictitious or purely theoretical.[128] The reality of international law was that states

---

[126] Nys, *Etudes*, 3.

[127] Neue Folge (1900) 19 ZSR 88–90 (quoted in Dickinson, 'Equality of States', 152).

[128] These arguments reappear more forcefully in the post-Hague period. See, e.g., Brown, 'Theory of Independence' (1915) 9 AJIL 305 at 326–9; R. Olney, 'Development of International Law' (1907) 1 AJIL 419; J. B. Scott, *Hague Peace Conferences*, vol. I, 169, 503. For the opposite view arguing that it is legalised hegemony that is 'theoretical', see Johann Droysen, describing the centralisation of power and the establishment of pentarchy in Europe as 'a theory, usurpation and pretext' (*Die politische Stellung Preussens* (1845), quoted in Holbraad, *Concert of Europe*, 55).

were unequal and had unequal rights. Sovereign equality was an ideal but one that could never be realised. These writers were less concerned with democratic deficit or institutional progress and more with the need to bring international law into line with political 'reality'.[129]

Other arguments carried a normative dimension. Here, legalised hegemony was seen as necessary to the establishment of international organisations and advanced forms of international law. Sovereign equality, at least in its stronger forms, was thought to be an anachronism and a barrier to the future development of international administration. A complex version of this position, articulated in the late nineteenth century, saw sovereign equality as a principle applying to general relations between states but not to the practices of international organisations.

Finally, there was the familiar argument from justice or democracy. This was the idea, expressed by Pillet, that sovereign equality was a denial of fair or equal representation.[130] The very quality that supporters of the principle emphasised (the equality of Geneva and Russia) became its chief defect. When Russia and Geneva were treated equally, the inhabitants of these territories were being accorded highly unequal treatment.

Thomas Lawrence and James Lorimer were perhaps the most able and prominent exponents of the first view that sovereign equality had the potential to retard the development of international organisations in the nineteenth century but they were not alone. For Bonfils, the pentarchy possessed 'a superior right, a quasi-legislative authority . . . as the directorate of the international society'.[131] Legalised hegemony was not just consistent with legal organisation; it *was* international organisation. There seemed to be acceptance that the Great Powers had some form of legal authority or preponderance within incipient international organisations. This was produced, according to some, by 'voluntary submission'.[132] Here, 'superiority of fact' was converted into 'superiority of right' by the formal consent of smaller states.[133] Others viewed coercion as a necessary evil in order to promote what we would now recognise as collective security.[134] For Cobbett, this was primarily political control,

---

[129] See, e.g. T. Funck-Brentano and Albert Sorel, *Precis du Droit des gens* (1877) (quoted in Kooijmans, *Doctrine of the Legal Equality*, 103–4).

[130] See examples in Dickinson, 'Equality of States', *passim*.

[131] H. Bonfils, *Droit International Public*, sec. 278 at 165 (quoted in Dickinson, 'Equality of States' 174).

[132] Holtzendorff (1900) 2 RDILC sec. 4 at 16 (quoted in *ibid.*, 175).

[133] Pillet (1898) 5 RGDIP 71 (quoted in *ibid.*, 176).

[134] Brusa (1888) 9 *Annuaire Institute De Droit* 296 (quoted in *ibid.*, 175).

but when it became a propensity to order territorial distribution it was transformed into something 'scarcely in keeping with the theory even of legal equality'.[135] These views tended to confirm that legalised hegemony existed but provided divergent rationales for tolerating it (right, ratification and the special status of territorial distribution).

At the very end of this period, and immediately prior to The Hague, Beale equated the move from sovereign equality to legalised hegemony with a larger process in which the private law of nations was giving way to a form of international constitutional law.[136] He believed that Vienna and the various conventions signed at The Hague and Geneva all pointed to the official, constitutional domination of the Great Powers. Beale saw great merit in this process whereby the Great Powers could act for the common good by, for example, suppressing the slave trade and outlawing various classes of weaponry.

Others justified legalised hegemony less on functional grounds and more on grounds of legitimacy and representation. Anticipating the arguments of Thomas Franck a century later, Pillet, for example, regards equality as not just unrealistic but potentially unjust. Pillet goes further than Franck, though, in wishing to distinguish between, for example, 'civilized and partially civilized states [and] between sovereign and partially sovereign states'.[137] Lawrence was the most forthright in his condemnation of the sovereign equality principle. As he put it, 'the doctrine of equality is becoming obsolete and must be superseded by a doctrine that a Primacy with regard to some important matters is vested in the foremost powers of the civilized world'.[138] In *Essays*, he was unapologetic about the need to give legal recognition to the primacy of the Great Powers. According to Lawrence, international law was returning to its pre-Westphalian form of common superior or universal authority. The Congress of Vienna marked a complete transformation in the nature of international society in which there was a shift from sovereign equality and consent to hegemony and authority by coercion and degree.[139] In a later edition of his treatise, he stated that 'there is no moral or jural necessity about the doctrine of equality'.[140]

---

[135] Cobbett, *Cases and Opinions* (3rd edn), vol. I, 50, 76.
[136] Note (1905) 18 *Harvard Law Review* 274–5.
[137] Dickinson, 'Equality of States', 169; Franck, *Fairness*, 477–84.
[138] Lawrence, *Principles of International Law* (3rd edn), 242.   [139] Lawrence, *Essays*, 209, 232.
[140] Lawrence, *Principles of International Law* (4th edn), 277. See also *Essays*, 230: 'the six Great Powers have by modern international law an authority superior to that of other states . . . a primacy among fellows'.

James Lorimer, in a typically caustic polemic, made the claim that:

No principles have been repeated more frequently or more authoritatively than the equality of states ... except perhaps their counterparts, the balance of power and the status quo; and all of them may now, I think, be safely said to have been repudiated by history, as they always were by reason.[141]

He then went on to describe the theory of state equality as 'baseless'.[142] In Lorimer's writings, there was an almost mathematical concern for differentiation: 'Even within the sphere of plenary political recognition, States are no more equal to each other in the absolute sense, than their citizens are equal. They differ in powers, and consequently in rights . . .'.[143] For Lorimer, the prevalent view of state equality was 'a more transparent fiction than the equality of all individuals'.[144] This was because states were unequal in ways that citizens were not. There were no limits to the possible differences in power and importance existing between states.[145] Ultimately, Lorimer rejected the equality of states and the balance of power in preference for a finally graded hierarchy based on doctrines of interdependence.

To summarise, the rejectionists tended to divide into three camps. There were those who wanted to bring international law into line with reality. Sovereign equality was clearly an obstacle to this given the manifest inequalities existing between states. A second group was concerned that a commitment to sovereign equality would inhibit the development of hierarchically ordered international organisations. The third group worried about the unrepresentative nature of sovereign equality. According to them, treating states as equals meant treating individuals unequally.

Equivocation

John Westlake's equivocation on the subject of sovereign equality mirrored that of the discipline at large. In Westlake's earlier work from this

---

[141] J. Lorimer, *Institutes of International Law*, 44.
[142] *Ibid.*, 170–1. Though he is no happier with two competing conceptions of international order – universal monarchy and oligarchy (legalised hegemony).
[143] *Ibid.*, 103–4.   [144] *Ibid.*, 171.
[145] Lorimer argued that individual inequality was limited by the constraints imposed by the human mind and body. There was only a certain level of physical difference between humans. This was not true of states which differed widely in their material capacities. Having said this, Lorimer was of the view that small states do have rights that must be preserved. These are the rights associated with, what I have called, existential equality (*ibid.*, 170–1).

period, *Chapters on the Principles of International Law* (1894), he insisted on describing the Vienna outcomes as 'political inequality'.[146] In assessing the Berlin arrangements, where the practice was repeated (1878–81) and where again the Great Powers dictated boundary changes, Westlake argued that those states directly affected by the boundary changes who were not parties to the convention (Romania, Serbia and Montenegro) had subsequently tacitly 'accepted' the arrangements. Westlake's conclusion was that 'when no such acceptances were thought to be even formally necessary to a declaration of the will of Europe on several matters, we can appreciate that political inequality is compatible in the European system with legal equality'.[147]

Yet, at the same time, Westlake saw the moral pentarchy at Vienna as a 'controlling authority'.[148] This authority possessed 'moral weight'[149] but adopted 'legal forms'.[150] Indeed, it resembled the British House of Commons because the legal basis of its authority was capable of being understood only by studying the operation of convention across time.[151] Finally, all this, according to Westlake, 'may prove to be a step towards the establishment of a European government'.[152]

How though can a political hegemony, which adopts legal forms and is founded on some legal basis, be reconciled with legal equality? In his *Collected Papers*, Westlake elaborated by taking the view that the subsequent consent and ratification of small states converted political acts into legal ones. The smaller states of Europe were in 'a situation of political inferiority . . . yet their legal equality is not necessarily infringed thereby'.[153] The political authority of the Great Powers remained merely political until it was converted into legalised hegemony by consent, i.e. by the exercise of sovereign equality. The will of sovereign equals produces legalised hegemony. This is a position somewhere between that of Oppenheim and that of Lawrence. According to Lawrence the 'consent' of the small states was consent to the idea of legalised hegemony.[154] For Westlake, the idea of consent of the small states reconciled the doctrine of sovereign equality with forms of hegemony.

Later, however, Westlake moved closer to the rejectionist view of Lorimer and Lawrence when he anticipated a situation in which international order would become centralised. As he said in 1904: 'The world in which the largest intercourse of civilised men has been from time to

---

[146] Westlake, *Collected Papers*, 101.   [147] *Ibid.*, 100.   [148] *Ibid.*, 99.   [149] *Ibid.*
[150] *Ibid.*, 98.   [151] *Ibid.*   [152] *Ibid.*, 101.   [153] *Ibid.*, 92.
[154] *Principles of International Law*, at sec. 114, 275 (quoted in Dickinson, 'Equality of States', 178).

time carried on has not always been distributed into equal and independent states, and we are reminded by what we see that it may not always continue to be so distributed.'[155] When oligarchy became habitual the principle of legal equality was eroded. By 1904, Westlake's intellectual development from a strong formalism to a knowing pragmatism seemed to have mirrored a more general movement in international law.

These various disagreements among international lawyers were reflected in the dispute over permanent judicial dispute resolution at The Hague. The question remained: how was the creation of hegemonically based international organisations to be reconciled with the Westphalian commitment to sovereign equality? It seemed at this stage as if the arguments of the rejectionists were prevailing. Yet, in 1907, arguments based on strong legislative forms of sovereign equality were revived. How did this occur? In the final section of this chapter, I supply a brief sketch of three late-nineteenth-century developments each of which pointed towards an increasing re-acceptance of strong sovereign equality.

Towards the Hague Peace Conferences

While some international lawyers were willing to accommodate 'the reality' of legalised hegemony in the late nineteenth century, three countervailing tendencies were pushing the system back in the direction of a sovereign equality, in which legislative equality played an important role, and preparing the ground for the South American assertion of extensive sovereign equality rights at the Hague Peace Conferences.

First, the late nineteenth century saw the mutation of the Concert system into a much looser framework in which a weakened legalised hegemony continued to have a role in organising both European and non-European relations. For all their 'realism', it is not clear that Lorimer and Lawrence prevailed immediately in the battle of the books recounted above. Certainly, they seemed better able to explain the Concert system from a legal perspective and there is little doubt that after 1907 international lawyers came to accept the need for legalised hegemony. However, Alfred Lande's argument is that the post-Congress era represented a gradual move away from the practice of legalised hegemony.[156] True, the Great Powers imposed legal obligations on the small powers during the period of the Concert but the level of

---

[155] Westlake, *International Law* (1st edn).   [156] See Lande, 'Revindication', *passim*.

representation for these small powers rose steadily throughout the nineteenth and early twentieth centuries.

Three years after Vienna, at the Congress of Aix-la-Chapelle in 1818, the Concert system came into operation but already, as Broms argues, the doctrine of sovereign equality was having a restraining effect on the Great Powers.[157] For example, on 15 November 1818, the Big Five issued a Protocol claiming to observe the rights of nations and arguing that their sole concern was to keep the peace in Europe.[158] Principle 4 of this Protocol introduced a system of regular meetings in which the affairs of Europe were to be discussed and ordered but,

in the case of these meetings having for their object affairs specially connected with the interests of other states of Europe, they shall only take place in pursuance of a formal invitation on the part of such of those States as the said affairs may concern.[159]

Despite this, initially at least, legalised hegemony continued to operate as the predominant institutional form in a series of further congresses that took place.[160] At the 1878 Congress of Berlin (concerning problems of the Near East) participation was restricted to those states which had signed the 1856 and 1871 treaties. Here, again the Great Powers claimed to be speaking on behalf of Europe and disposed of territories on that basis. The Commissions formed at Berlin were all based (putatively) on the legal equality of participating states. However, hierarchies continued to assert themselves. At the first level were the signatories of the 1856 Paris Peace Treaty, at the second level were those permitted to present their views (Greece (an independent state), Romania (about to be independent) and Persia (a non-Christian state not part of the European system of public law)). At the third level were entities not even permitted this dignity (e.g. Bulgaria, Serbia).[161]

---

[157] Broms, *Doctrine of Equality*, 92.   [158] See Klein, *Sovereign Equality*, 30.

[159] The Declaration of the Five Cabinets, signed at Aix-la-Chapelle, 15 November 1818, makes broadly the same promise. See Union of Five Powers, 15 November 1818, in Hertslet, *Map of Europe*, 572. Aix-la-Chapelle was to 'complete the political system' introduced at Vienna but it was to do so while respecting the rights of nations and the principle of non-interference (573). Similarly, in the Treaty of London, regarding the pacification of Greece, the British, French and Russians promised that they would seek no advantage that is not conferred equally on all other nations: Article 5 (771).

[160] The Conference of London in 1830 revised the Final Act of Vienna and permitted a Belgian secession from the Netherlands.

[161] Broms, *Doctrine of Equality*, 99–100. See, too, P. Thornberry, *International Law and the Rights of Minorities*, 38–57; Lande, 'Revindication', 268–9.

At the later Conference of Berlin (1884–5), a significant change could be discerned. With the Concert now in abeyance, legalised hegemony had given way to more participatory techniques of administration in relation to the future of the Congo Basin. Here, the equality of nations was vouchsafed by the major powers in speeches made at the conference.[162] In fact, what happened was a form of differentiation based on interest rather than power (resulting in a Committee composed of only some Great Powers, and the exclusion of Russia altogether until the later stages of the Conference).

In planning for the 1906 Conference of Algeciras (for the settlement of Great Power claims to Morocco), a Committee was formed to explore the matters to come before the Conference. This Drafting Committee was initially composed of only five states but eventually pressure was placed on the Committee to open deliberations to all states. Invitations were extended on the basis of signature to the Convention of Madrid, 1880; a form of limited equality.[163] The equality of states again proved to be a matter of some importance both in terms of representation and voting. Some of the Great Powers found themselves in a privileged contractual position but mainly because of their special interest rather than overwhelming power (e.g. Spain).

Bengt Broms summarises this period by remarking on the difference between Vienna and the late-nineteenth-century congresses. By the end of the century, he argues, representation was granted on a near universal basis, interest replaced status as the criterion for participation and there was no binding law produced by these congresses without the agreement of other states.[164] Lande agrees but sees the process as less unidirectional. He divides sovereign equality into three components: participation, procedure and outcome/substance. Having made these distinctions he then argues, like Broms, that sovereign equality acquired more and more purchase as the century progressed. From 1814 to 1871, status was very much the defining quality of participation in international congresses. However, in 1871, status gives way to interest as the key principle (the Conference of Berlin is a landmark in this regard). Legalised hegemony could not be sustained. The Franco-Prussian War of 1871 had put an end to the idea that the Great Powers were capable of acting as a quasi-supranational authority in legal and political matters. The equality of states had re-attained its functional primacy within the system.

---

[162] Lande, 'Revindication', 274.   [163] BFSP, 71 at 814.
[164] Broms, *Doctrine of Equality*, 102.

A second development towards stronger forms of legislative equality occurred within the codification or functional conferences of the nineteenth century. The hegemony of the Great Powers was much less pronounced at these conferences partly because they were thought, by the larger powers, to be less important or contentious.[165] The result was an egalitarian functional regime coexisting alongside an initially hierarchical political system. This functional regime can be seen in the drafting process of the 1864 Geneva Convention on Soldiers Wounded in Battle, which was open to all states, and in the voting procedures under the Sugar Convention.[166]

At this point, then, legalised hegemony was becoming increasingly diluted in political organisations and institutions and had ceased to exist in relation to many of the technical conferences of the time.

The third and final important development, which had the effect of buttressing the efforts of the egalitarians at The Hague, was the elaboration of the sovereign equality idea by South American states. The rising power of the United States was the single most important phenomenon in the Western hemisphere in the nineteenth century and the development of legal equality within the Americas can only be understood in the light of this fact. The political preponderance of the United States had the paradoxical effect of producing a distinctively American approach to the question of equality. The United States was most concerned in

---

[165] For example, Great Britain took no part in various conferences on the codification of Private International Law.

[166] Article 9. See Dickinson, 'Equality of States', 282. The 1868 Revision Conference was similarly open (ibid., 282). The Austrians and Russians were absent from both the Revision Conference and the initial meeting. Economic matters proved an exception to this general flow in the direction of equality. Weighted voting in economic organisations becomes more pronounced during this period. This institutional innovation occurs at the same time as general sovereign equality surges. At the International Office of Public Health (1907) votes were proportional to contribution. In the Convention for the Creation of an International Agricultural Institute (1905) (Articles 3 and 7) a similar system existed. The Universal Postal Union (1878) provided for additional votes in the case of those (large imperial states) with dependent territories. As early as the Treaty of Vienna itself (Article 13, Annex 16) the votes of the Rhine Navigation Commission were allocated according to the extent of riparian river territories. See, e.g. Lande, 'Revindication', 403. This would tend to indicate that international law was more and more inclined to adopt a pragmatic approach to equality in the economic sphere and a principled approach in the political sphere. Legalised hegemony was slowly being supplanted by a form of legal equality that was nonetheless prepared to countenance functional inequalities in economic spheres of activity. This reversed the earlier distinction (discussed in the text) between hierarchical political organs and egalitarian codification conferences. For an interesting analysis see Lande at 401–2.

the nineteenth century to prevent any outside interference in American affairs. So, initially, the Monroe Doctrine was a response to the interventionist rhetoric of the Holy Alliance. The idea was to liberate the Americas from the corrupting influence of European diplomacy. In this sense, the Monroe Doctrine is anti-interventionist though it is commonly understood in retrospect as a rationale for US intervention in the American sub-continent. The American states were to be 'free and independent' in law even if the United States regulated the politics of the region through its overwhelming material superiority.

Having created a cordon around the Americas, the United States was willing to tolerate the egalitarian preferences of the South and Central American states. The Inter-American system was inaugurated on precisely this note by James G. Blaine, the US Secretary of State in 1899:

> The delegates can show to the world an honorable, peaceful conference of seventeen independent American Powers, in which all shall meet together on terms of absolute equality.[167]

The principle of sovereign equality was to have its uses for both the United States and its hemispheric neighbours. For the Americans, it was used mainly as a device to legitimise the Monroe Doctrine. Slowly, this unilateral expression of state interests was converted into a system of collective security in which, according to Theodore Roosevelt, speaking in 1913, states were to participate 'on a footing of equality'.[168] The system also came to resemble a more consensual version of the Holy Alliance, where states agreed to combat external and 'internal' aggression.

At the same time, the small and middle powers saw the principle of sovereign equality as a way of claiming in the juridical sphere that which they clearly lacked in the political. Accordingly, throughout the development of the Inter-American system, these states accentuated and revitalised the equality idea. They drew on the US Declaration of Independence as their inspiration and articulated particularly strong versions of the equality principle.[169] This did not prevent the unequal allocation of

---

[167] First International Conference of American States, Minutes, 11 (quoted by Robert Herrera, in 'Evolution of Equality of States in the Inter-American System' (March 1946) 61 *Political Science Quarterly* 90–119). The Americans had in mind here the legislative and formal equality I referred to in Chapter 2.

[168] Herrera, 'Evolution', 93.

[169] See, e.g. Dr Juan A. Buero, Uruguay, arguing that sovereign equality rights cannot be limited 'even with the consent of the concerned state'. See Conference on Central American Affairs (Washington, 1925), 80 (quoted by Herrera, 'Evolution', 97).

representation in committees at the various International Conferences on Inter-American Affairs but voting rights remained equally distributed. Overall, sovereign equality was a dominant feature of the legal rhetoric of the Pan-American system and this distinctively egalitarian philosophy was to be a major influence on the approach of the South Americans to the Second Hague Conference.[170]

---

[170] Herrera 'Evolution', 95. See also, e.g. Article 4, Montevideo Convention on the Rights and Duties of States (1933); Inter–American Juridical Committee, 'Reaffirmation of Principles of International Law', Project of Resolution submitted to the governments, Members of the Pan American Union in (1943) 27 AJIL 21–3.

5 'Extreme equality': Rupture at the Second Hague Peace Conference 1907

Even among the angels, inequality is indispensable to order.[1]

Introduction

Many of international law's great romantic projects originated at The Hague Peace Conferences. Students of the laws of war remember them as the moments when the idea of humanising armed conflict was secured in convention form. International organisations scholars look back fondly at the blueprints for international order sketched at The Hague. Procedurally, the conferences in 1899 and 1907 ushered in the expectation that congresses of states would be inclusive and universal. International arbitration, too, was formalised here following the success of various ad hoc schemes in the eighteenth and nineteenth centuries.[2] This chapter, though, is about, predominantly, The Hague Conferences' greatest failure: the project to create an international court of justice. In particular, I explore the role of two diplomats (a North American and a South American) whose views of international order clashed resulting in the decision to abandon, temporarily, the pursuit of international court-based justice. James Brown Scott was the United States delegate at The Hague Conference in 1907. He was also one of the most eminent American international lawyers of his generation: a president of the American International Law Institute, the solicitor-general of the United States Department of State and an editor of the *American Journal of International Law*. Scott wanted to build an international legal order

[1] Goebel, *Equality of States* (quoting Gregory the Great), 16.
[2] E.g. the Jay Treaty (US–UK) and the Alabama Claims Tribunal (US–UK).

that was effective and enforceable. To this end he argued for a judicial institution in which Great Powers were given special representation. However, like Castlereagh before him, and the Big Five at San Francisco, he attempted a balance between legalised hegemony and an attenuated principle of sovereign equality. Rui Barbosa, his Latin American adversary, was Brazil's delegate at The Hague, a diplomat representing one of the newly admitted sovereign states and determined to secure sovereign equality for these states. Barbosa was a staunch republican (author of Brazil's first Republican constitution) and a former Brazilian finance minister. His opposition to the United States at The Hague earned him the sobriquet 'The Eagle of The Hague' but ensured that he would not represent Brazil at Versailles (because of US opposition to his presence). He became a judge at the Permanent Court of International Justice in 1922.

This chapter develops the ideas discussed in Chapter 4 but takes up the question of sovereign equality/legalised hegemony at the moment when the process of institution building in international law begins to deepen. The chapter also provides a bridge from the legalised hegemony seen at Vienna to the modified collective security system found at San Francisco.

In the chapter, I focus on the Second Hague Peace Conference and its aftermath. There are three subjects considered here. The first is a proposal made at The Hague by the Great Powers to establish a Permanent Court of Arbitral Justice (PCAJ). The intended composition of the bench was based on a form of legalised hegemony, i.e. special representation for the larger states. This proposal, and the powerful response to it on the part of the smaller states, is the primary focus of Section 1, though I also touch on some other relevant aspects of The Hague negotiations (e.g. the creation of an International Prize Court and the form of voting at the Conference in general).

The second subject consists of the response of international lawyers and political scientists to the failure of the PCAJ. In Section 2, I outline these responses and demonstrate how they paved the way for a re-acceptance of hegemony in the construction of international organisations. The subject of the third section is the Peace Conference in 1919 and the establishment of the League of Nations and, in particular, the way in which the relationship between sovereign equality (and in particular legislative equality) and legalised hegemony was structured in discussions at Versailles and in the ensuing arrangements. In Section 4, I trace some of the themes present in the history of this relationship between 1815 and 1920 as a prelude to analysing the San Francisco Conference and the Charter era (Chapter 6).

. . . .

Why is the Second Hague Peace Conference important to the thesis pursued in this book? First, because the statements made in Committee B of the First Sub-Commission were the earliest self-conscious articulations of support for a return to strong sovereign equality (by the smaller states) and legalised hegemony (by the Great Powers) in the context of international treaty making. At these meetings, state plenipotentiaries and legal advisers were obliged to give their reasons for supporting various forms of equality or hegemony. These meetings represent, then, a rich source of 'jurisprudence' for our understanding of the two principles.

Second, The Hague represents a sort of apotheosis for the principle of sovereign equality. The arguments made in favour of sovereign equality were both unique and, in retrospect, extreme. For the first time the principle was thought, by a significant group of states, to mean the absolute equality of state representation in the organs of an international body. This understanding resulted in a need to articulate fully the counterarguments in support of a form of legalised hegemony.

The third reason The Hague is so important to our understanding of sovereign equality is that it was followed by a consensus among international lawyers that the principle was operational only in a diluted form. The outcome of the debates discussed below was a recognition that the future of international organisations, as the likes of Lawrence and Beale had predicted (see Chapter 4), depended on a willingness to embrace modified models of legalised hegemony.[3]

More specifically, I argue in this chapter that the conflict at The Hague between the doctrinaire legalism of Barbosa and pragmatic institution building of Scott resolved itself in a post-Conference reassessment of the sovereign equality doctrine. The protagonists were unable to convince one another at the Conference itself and the Great Powers were unwilling or incapable of enforcing their will on the majority at that time. The result was the failure to create a permanent judicial body.

---

[3] While most international lawyers were reacting to the failure of the proposals for the Permanent Court of Arbitral Justice, others embraced The Hague Peace Conferences as a new way of organising international affairs around the idea of vertical integration. The failure of the PCAJ was a mere blip on the way to international union. This form of vertical hierarchy is not the subject of this book (except where the Great Powers form the apex of such a union). See, for arguments that The Hague created quasi-legislative bodies or a union of states, T. J. Lawrence, *International Problems and the Hague Conferences*, 42; Walter Schucking, *The International Union of the Hague Conferences* (trans. Charles Fenwick).

Following this, international lawyers rejected Barbosa's strong form of sovereign equality, which was viewed as responsible for this failure and, during the first half of the century, scholars such as Pitman Potter and Edwin Dickinson began to characterise strict sovereign equality as an obstacle to institution-building and acknowledged the inevitability of institutional hierarchy. After 1907, the strong theory of sovereign equality fell out of favour among traditional international lawyers, partly out of a sense of disillusionment with the radical egalitarianism expressed at The Hague.

There are two complicating factors. First, while there was a retreat from extreme theories of equality, there was also a greater commitment to a more inclusive world order. The Second Hague Peace Conference was a turning point in the international system. The European state system was expanded to include the South American states, China, Siam and Japan, as fully fledged members of the community.[4] One form of inequality, the inequality of exclusion (*anti-pluralism*), was in (temporary) recession but the inequalities of status that have been the mark of relations between even full members of the Family of Nations continued to flourish (*legalised hegemony*).

A further irony lies in the fact that the Conference resulted in a retreat from unmodified forms of equality (or extreme legalism) despite the appeal of Barbosa's rhetoric. The arguments made at The Hague on behalf of the small powers would not resurface again. On the other hand, Vienna had represented a form of extreme hegemony that proved ultimately unacceptable in a system committed to certain liberal principles of participation. It was simply impossible to regulate inter-state relations at the level of stratification seen at Vienna. For some time after The Hague, international lawyers became reconciled simply to managing these tensions (see Chapter 6).

From an inter-disciplinary perspective this has some bearing on the way we view the development of the two disciplines of international

---

[4] In 1899, Mexico was the sole representative of South and Central America. By 1907, this position had dramatically changed with all the states of that region now present. In addition, there were a number of other states in existence on the peripheries who were admitted to the conference, notably Ethiopia, Siam, Afghanistan, Persia and, of course, Japan and China. Twenty European, two American and four Asian states congregated at the 1899 Conference. These represented twenty-six out of approximately fifty-nine states existing in the world. Notable omissions included South Africa and the Orange Free State. By 1907, the number had increased to forty-four out of fifty-seven, with that increase accounted for almost entirely by the addition of the South and Central Americans. For an interesting examination of the reasons why these states were able to survive as independent entities at the height of colonisation, see David Strang, 'Contested Sovereignty' in Biersteker and Weber, *State Sovereignty*, 37–43.

law and international relations. The typical tale told of the inter-war period and the Second World War is of idealist lawyers, discredited by the failure of their institutions and norms, transforming themselves into political scientists.[5] Hence, the birth of a science of international relations at the moment of legalist apostasy.[6]

However, the League of Nations, instead of representing a high point of zealous legalism, in fact rejected at least one form of legalism, i.e. the commitment to a radical version of sovereign equality. In fact, the consensus among international law publicists prior to 1945 seemed to have assumed a disjunction or fundamental contradiction between equality on one hand and the whole idea of institutionalism on the other. Philip Marshall Brown's view in 1915 is emblematic of the period: 'It would, however, seem not only impossible, but grotesque to conceive of a world organisation in which England (*sic*) and Liberia would be treated as having an equal status.'[7] Lawyers had already accepted at least one of the hierarchical premises of the realists. This reading of the inter-war period would pose a direct challenge to the idea that, in some sense, international law was 'responsible' for the Second World War and the failure to respond to Hitler, and would cast doubt on the systematic portrayal of international law as a utopian (and therefore marginal) discipline.

Rui Barbosa and James Brown Scott

At The Hague, the twentieth century began in a spirit of legalism and, to a certain extent, idealism. International law became bureaucratised and judicialised in a manner with no precedent in the nineteenth

---

[5] In most retrospectives of the period, the two disciplines of international law and International Relations are assigned particular roles, e.g. International Relations responds to international law's legalism of the 1920s by embracing a hard-nosed realism in the 1940s and 1950s. But these histories seem less compelling when particular writers are under discussion. If anything, international relations may have been reacting to its own idealism (and often in a highly unpredictable manner: Martin Wight's response to the failure of the League (of which he was a great supporter) was a Christian Pacifism (see H. Bull, 'Martin Wight and the Study of International Relations' in Wight, *Systems of States*, 3). International law, meanwhile, reached its legalist high point in 1907 and became much more pragmatic in the inter-war period. One distinction worth keeping in mind here is that between the views associated with Wilsonian idealism and the attitudes of the international law mainstream. International Relations literature has a tendency to merge the two.

[6] G. Simpson, 'The Situation on the International Legal Theory Front' (2000) 11:2 *European Journal of International Law*, 439 at 448–50.

[7] Brown, 'Theory of the Independence', 332. Ironically, one of these entities, Liberia, is now regarded as a failed state while the other, England, is not a state at all.

century.[8] Where the nineteenth century was largely the era of big power rapprochements, the balance of power and colonial allocation, at The Hague there was a self-conscious effort to create a new order based on the equality of states and the civilising effects of law.[9] In retrospect, a clash was inevitable. International law was being created in the image of universality and equality yet the large European and North American powers continued to expect a special role in the system.

This tension became most acute in the debates over the composition of the proposed Permanent Court of Arbitral Justice (a forerunner to the PCIJ and ICJ). Prior to the 1907 Conference, there already existed the Permanent Court of Arbitration created in 1899. This body posed few difficulties in relation to sovereign equality since arbitrators were to be chosen by the parties to the dispute, exercising their sovereign prerogatives. The composition of the Permanent Court of Arbitration (PCA) was, therefore, not an issue in 1899. The Convention for the Pacific Settlement of Disputes (1899) was open-ended; allowing states to choose a menu of options, most of them highly consensual.[10] These included

---

[8] There was a heated debate among German scholars in particular as to the extent and permanence of this process. Had The Hague Conferences changed the international order? Was this change really juridical? The debate is outlined in Schucking. There were those who saw The Hague in the same light as the Concert meetings. Others accepted that there was something peculiarly legalistic about the two Peace Conferences. If it was not a disorganised anarchy was it a federation, union or community of states? (Schucking, *International Union*, 79). Schucking himself argued that The Hague created an International Public Union of states with an existence independent of these states. The Hague Peace Conferences certainly departed from nineteenth-century precedents by establishing permanent, multilateral arbitration systems and an incipient international bureaucracy to maintain that system. See, e.g. the International Bureau and the International Administrative Council (see Schucking, *passim*). Though this debate is not central to our concerns here, the idea of equality was important in establishing the precise form of the Conference. For example, James Brown Scott claimed that the combination of regular meetings and sovereign equality 'offers the advantage of federation without the disadvantage' (J. B. Scott, *The Hague Peace Conferences 1899 and 1907*, vol. I, 750).

[9] The Hague is really an institutional anomaly in a period of international anarchy. The Congress of Vienna had broken down, nationalism and expansionism were everywhere in Europe, colonisation was reaching its heights in the 'scramble for Africa' and a sort of Darwinian experiment in social evolution was occurring with states seeking to survive, expand and conquer. This was the environment in which the powers met at The Hague. With the benefit of hindsight one can see that the logical consequence of these forces was the Great War and not The Hague Peace Conferences.

[10] See Convention for the Pacific Settlement of Disputes, 18 October 1907 in Igor Ivar Kavass, US Treaties and Other International Agreements (as published in *Statutes at Large*, Malloy, Miller, Bevens, Buffalo, NY: Hein (1975)). See, e.g. Article 87. The 1907 Convention was a modified version of the 1899 original.

good offices, mediation and the use of 'seconds' as well as arbitration itself.[11] The crucial point of difference between the 1899 system and the 1907 proposals was the issue of permanence. Despite its name, the PCA was simply a list of arbitrators from which the disputants could choose individuals to decide a particular dispute.[12] By 1907, the idea of a Permanent Court of Arbitral Justice was on the table and it proved much more contentious.[13] Along with the question of compulsory arbitration, the composition of this Court was *the* problem of the Conference.[14]

However, prior to debate on matters of substance, the participants at The Hague faced the problem of voting and levels of representation. Sovereign equality was also heavily implicated here. It was generally assumed during the nineteenth century that the equality of states required a form of unanimity, in the adoption of a convention or treaty.[15] This is the equality of consent I discussed in Chapter 2 under the general heading 'legislative equality'. At The Hague, many delegates began to accept that unanimity, as an aspect of strict sovereign equality, retarded the development of international organisations and international law. Schucking described as a 'prejudice' the idea that 'the equality of states required that legislative conferences shall adopt no resolution [except by unanimous decision]'. This was, he believed, 'the fetish of unanimity'.[16]

---

[11] See David Bederman, 'The Hague Peace Conference 1899–1907' in Mark Janis (ed.), *International Courts for the 21st Century*, 9–11. On the use of 'seconds', see 1899 Convention, Article 8.

[12] See Articles 23 and 24 of *The Convention on the Settlement of International Disputes*. For a short discussion of the PCA see William E. Butler, 'The Hague PCA' in Janis (ed.), *International Courts*, chap. 4.

[13] The terms are confusing. The First Hague Court functioned as an Arbitral Tribunal with the arbitrators attempting to reach a compromise rather than state or develop law. The term Court is a little misleading as is the convention establishing the Court which enjoins it to apply law. The proposed Court of Arbitral Justice or Judicial Arbitration Court was a prototype for the Permanent Court of Justice and the International Court of Justice. The word 'arbitral' in the title is a source of confusion. Wehberg calls the Court of Arbitration designed in 1899 a 'mongrel institution' (Wehberg, *The Problem of an International Court of Justice* (trans. C. G. Fenwick), 79). Many states objected to the early drafts of the PCAJ Statute on the basis that states would be unable to choose all the judges on an ad hoc basis. They claimed a loss of sovereignty. Note that the International Prize Court called for compulsory jurisdiction and permanent judges.

[14] These discussions took place in four fora, the Sub-Commission, the Committee of Examination (Committee B), the Commission and in the Plenary. The Conference programme, like that at Vienna, was largely directed by an unofficial steering committee of the Big Seven.

[15] See, e.g. Schucking, *International Union*, 210, 216.

[16] *Ibid.*, 206 (quoting La Fontaine, the Belgian delegate at the Inter-Parliamentary Union of 1908).

The voting procedures at The Hague attempted to move beyond unanimity. In the end, there was majority rule in the plenary and commissions and quasi-unanimity in the adoption of the Second Conference resolutions and Acts.[17] This quasi-unanimity allowed for the adoption of Acts either where recalcitrant states agreed that their rejection was to have no effect on the outcome of the Conference (Brazil in the case of the Prize Court) or where the number of dissenting states was small and their status low. The Second Hague Peace Conference, then, represented the beginning of a move from unanimity (based on strict equality) to majority (based on modified notions of hegemony).[18]

However, for all this innovation, it remained the case that the Great Powers were unwilling to have the idea of majority rule imposed on *them*. Ironically, this departure from the principle of equality (majority rule) would have been tolerable to these states only in circumstances where there was a gradation in voting (i.e. the denial of equality to small states).[19] Only a scheme such as this could have avoided what the Great Powers most feared, i.e. 'an ochlocracy of the smaller states'.[20] The difficulty of apportioning seats on the basis of power, culture or population meant that this general principle of gradation was never discussed at The Hague in relation to these matters.

This was not true in the exceptional case of the PCAJ proposal where a number of imaginative schemes along these lines were suggested, each presenting itself as conformable to sovereign equality.[21] The US delegation was under instructions to work for a Permanent Court and, to that end, presented a draft to the Conference envisaging a fifteen-judge bench.[22] Later proposals included one which contemplated strict

---

[17] A similar situation obtained at the First Conference in 1899. Conventions required unanimity while resolutions (or declarations as they were known) were adopted in the face of rejection by various states. Schucking, *International Union*, 217–21.

[18] Of course, sovereignty was preserved by the fact that these Conventions required ratification on the part of the states that adopted them.

[19] In fact, this occurred in one egregious instance. At both Hague Peace Conferences, the State of Montenegro was represented by Russia, meaning that Russia had, in effect, two votes on each issue where every other state had one. See J. Choate, *The Two Hague Conferences*, 54.

[20] Schucking, *International Union*, 222.

[21] After the failure of the PCAJ, these ideas continued to circulate. See, e.g. F. C. Hicks, *New World Order*, 530; Lawrence, *International Problems*, 23, 74; Schucking, *International Union*, 222.

[22] See J. B. Scott, *American Addresses at the Second Hague Peace Conference*, 206. This was one of two proposals put before the Conference on the first day of discussion. The other, a more minimalist model proposed by the Russians, was taken no further. See A. Pearce Higgins, *The Hague Peace Conferences*.

equality (forty-five judges representing the forty-five nations), a variation on the fifteen-judge proposal, which divided the forty-five judges into three groups (on an alphabetical basis) of fifteen each with each group of judges serving for a period, various schemes of regional representation, a distribution based on population and a final proposal involving a free vote.[23]

The proposal that gained the greatest number of adherents was the seventeen-judge rotation system whereby each state appointed a judge but judges would sit for unequal periods. The Great Powers were given permanent representation while other states were represented for periods of either ten, four, two or one years depending on a classification scheme that took into account diversity of legal systems, population, political position and territory.[24] It was this 'ingenious'[25] proposal that gained enough support at the First Sub-Commission stage to be sent to Committee B for examination.[26] In Committee B, this joint US-German-British proposal superseded the original US proposal.

In the debates at Committee B, there appeared to be general agreement on the need to preserve the doctrine of sovereign equality but substantial disagreement on the parameters of that equality. Scott, in a statement to Committee B, reaffirmed the Americans' commitment to some form of sovereign equality:

> The exclusion of a single state from the proposed court, or the denial of the right of a single state to appoint, would proclaim the principle of juridical inequality and vitiate in advance the project.[27]

The trick then was to negotiate a delicate balance between three ends. First, the major powers wished to be seen to advance a plausible version

---

[23] See Mr Choate's Proposal, Scott, *Proceedings of The Hague Peace Conferences*, Conference of 1907, vol. II, 683. See Wehberg, *The Problem of an International Court of Justice*, 70. There were other proposals including one that envisaged the Conference itself choosing judges, another involving a general vote by the Conference and yet another suggesting the establishment of a committee to choose the judges. See *ibid.*, 73.

[24] This was a complex arrangement. The Great Powers, Germany, United States, Austro-Hungary, France, Great Britain, Italy, Japan and Russia were given permanent representation. Spain, Turkey and the Netherlands (the great empires of previous ages) were accorded ten years. A large group containing a number of South American and European powers was given four years. This group included Brazil and China. Bulgaria, Persia, Serbia and Siam had two years. A final group of small states (all South and Central American apart from Luxembourg and Montenegro) was to have judges sit for one of the twelve years.

[25] W. Hull, *The Two Hague Conferences and their Contribution to International Law*, 423.

[26] The US proposal was adopted by twenty-eight for, with twelve abstentions.

[27] Scott, *Proceedings*, 609.

of legal equality.[28] Second, they wanted to implant in the scheme a hierarchical principle. Third, they had to ensure that this principle emerged in an acceptable manner. The hierarchical system chosen was one that had to exclude the 'uncivilised' big powers, Turkey and China. (The Chinese were enthusiastic about various hierarchical schemes but, awkwardly, they preferred 'democratic equality'.[29] Inequality was to be avoided by distributing judicial seats on the basis of population. Any other system based on either an excessively formal reading of legal equality or a legalised hegemony based on special representation for a self-selecting group of 'Great Powers' was unacceptable to them and, it was made clear, would result in a Chinese abstention.)[30]

Scott's rhetorical efforts in support of this impossible synthesis were strenuous but ultimately unsuccessful. In his original proposal, he emphasised sovereign equality then showed how it had to be modified.[31] His equality was a right to representation. States were each to have the same right to representation on the Court but the exercise of that right was to be regulated according to the rotational scheme designed by the Great Powers.

Although, eventually, Rui Barbosa led a South American revolt against the proposals, initial responses to the rotation idea were less coolly received. The Argentinian delegate, Luis Drago, for example, spoke in favour of rotation providing foreign commerce was used as the marker of progress and civilisation.[32] Scott's response to this was to concoct a system of legal inequality that took into account factors other than simply population. These included the claims of industry and commerce and the right of representation belonging to the 'systems of law at present existing in the civilised world', traditions of the past and political geography.[33] At another point, Scott argued that the conflicting interests of great states were the source of the majority of disputes in the world.[34]

---

[28] The United States proposal was intended to ensure representation for the various systems of law and procedure and the principal languages within the personnel of the Court. See Pearce Higgins, *Hague Peace Conferences*, 512.

[29] One proposal included China and Turkey. See Calvin De Armind Davis, *The United States and the Second Hague Peace Conference*, 240. This was met with dismay by the Western powers. They liked hierarchy but only in certain forms. Instead, these powers developed a ranking scheme for membership with the 'two Oriental empires' (267) being moved from the first rank – in China's case to the third! (268).

[30] Scott, *Proceedings*, 606.   [31] Hull, *Two Hague Conferences*, 415.

[32] Scott, *Proceedings*, 325; Wehberg, *The Problem of an International Court of Justice*, 175; Hull, *Two Hague Conferences*, 418.

[33] Scott, *Proceedings*, 610.   [34] *Ibid.*

It was only appropriate, therefore, that they be over-represented numerically on the Court designed to resolve these disputes.[35] All this was to result in a table of distribution based on 'juridical equality'.

What did Scott mean by this term? There are a number of possibilities. Perhaps, sovereign equality was a thin principle offering a minimal right to some representation but not necessarily equal representation. A more generous assessment of Scott's tactics might view him as expanding sovereign equality to accommodate a thicker notion of equality that encompassed physical qualities (e.g. industrial capacity). However, this substantive equality also had the potential to legitimise distinctions based on cultural attributes (civilisation) and degree of development. A third interpretation, and I think the more plausible one, is that the Great Powers had a view of sovereign equality which they held to in theory but were willing to depart from in practice. So, in Scott's comments at the Conference, and in subsequent work, he often emphasised his support for the formal doctrine but warned against an over-zealous application of it to the practice of states. Thus, the rotational scheme reconciled juridical equality with 'the facts of daily life'.[36] At other times, however, it was a particular version of the theory that was criticised, i.e. one that insisted on 'absolute and rigid equality' or one that was 'literal and, therefore absurd'.[37]

In the end, Rui Barbosa effectively killed the big power proposal by insisting on a particular form of strict numerical equality.[38] In Examination Committee B, he brought forward a proposal to expand the existing Hague Arbitration Court with each of the states appointing members. These judges (of whom there might be forty-five if all states made an appointment) would then be divided on an alphabetical basis. The judges would sit on a three-yearly circuit.[39] This was a way of ensuring that the right to legislative equality remained inviolable.

[35] This was a recognition that national identity does matter when it comes to choosing judges. At other times, the delegates of the Great Powers denied this.

[36] Scott, *The Hague Peace Conferences*, vol. I, 457.

[37] *Ibid.*, 500–1 (quoting M. Renault, 'The Work of The Hague' Paris Lecture, 5 June 1908, School of Political Science).

[38] There are suggestions in the literature that Barbosa was simply hostile to the whole notion of a permanent court and felt that advocating sovereign equality was the best way to defeat the proposal. See, e.g. Wehberg, *The Problem of an International Court of Justice*, 28. This seems unlikely given his 'republican' history.

[39] The hope was that some states would choose not to take up their places on the Court and that others would combine. In the end, Barbosa withdrew this proposal but remained implacable in his opposition to the idea of a Court. See Hull, *Two Hague Conferences*, 424.

What Barbosa objected to in the Scott proposal was what he called 'a proclamation of the inequality of national sovereignties'.[40] He characterised all deviations from the strong version of sovereign equality as 'arbitrary'[41] and argued that the Scott scheme was inconsistent with the vows made at the 1899 Conference to the effect that all states were to have an equal representation on the Court.[42] Scott's distinction between the right and its exercise did not convince him, especially here where the 'rights are more or less subordinated to the conditions of necessary exercise'.[43] For Barbosa, there were two equality rights at issue: the right to appoint and the right to sit. One was realised, the other was violated. In addition, he remarked that the scale of importance was 'noticeably partial in favour of certain European countries'.[44]

These categories of sovereignty, claimed Barbosa, 'humiliated' the smaller nations and countries. Sovereign equality was the only card they possessed and now it, too, was to be forfeited. The calculations used to determine the precise workings of hierarchy were criticised for their provocative and demoralising effects and for the 'mute and sorry' fashion in which cultural attributes were to prevail over material factors.[45] Ultimately, all of this culminated in a critique of Euro-centrism. Barbosa insisted that the nations of South America were not tributary nor were they coming to the end of their development as nations. Unlike the old nations of Europe, they were maturing as civilisations and as nations.

In order to further discredit the idea of rotation or inequality, Barbosa characterised it as completely novel. The Anglo-German-American proposal, he claimed, was based on a principle of rotation or sovereign inequality arising '*for the first time in international law*'.[46] It was, he continued, a 'revolutionary audacity'.[47] So, he argued, 1907 marked the occasion on which the international community was obliged to pronounce itself as between the 1899 principle of equality and the novel principle of inequality.[48]

Rui Barbosa's comments at The Hague are a brilliant distillation of the arguments in favour of the strong position on sovereign equality. The whole point of his counter-proposal was, in his own words, 'to illustrate

---

[40] Scott, *Proceedings*, 619.   [41] *Ibid*.

[42] These points were made in three different venues: Committee B (on 17, 20, 27 August; 5, 11 September), Examination Committee (17, 22 September) and in the Plenary (10 September).

[43] Barbosa's position is that conditions of exercise are acceptable providing these, too, are equally applied (Scott, *Proceedings*, 628).

[44] *Ibid*., 620.   [45] *Ibid*., 646.   [46] *Ibid*., 623   [47] *Ibid*., 643.   [48] *Ibid*., 623.

by a concrete example the kind of Court consistent with both the unimpaired equality of nations and the exercise of sovereignty'.[49] He even went as far as to appeal to America's 'liberal' genius to bolster his rejection of the idea of hierarchy.[50] For him, juridical equality was the one point of 'moral commensuration' in an international system in which inequality was pervasive.[51] Without juridical equality, the big powers received in law what they already possessed in power. This is why he denounced the illiberal project of assigning a 'tariff of the practical value of the sovereignties'.[52] Most of the delegates from South America and other parts of the developing world supported either Barbosa or forms of hierarchy based on material factors that did not necessarily favour the big powers. Of those who supported him, none approached either Barbosa's skills as an advocate or his vehemence. The Chilean delegate, Matte, did, however, provide an interesting supplementary argument in favour of sovereign equality when he linked it to the unanimity rule. As he pointed out,

If each state at the Conference votes as a unit for the adoption of each . . . resolution of the Conference, why should there be a different representation in the judicial organisation entrusted with putting these resolutions into effect?[53]

The Western powers found themselves in an impossible position. Strict legal equality was undesirable since it constituted a reduction in Western power. Legalised hegemony was acceptable but could not yield the desired results if based on a 'material' doctrine of inequality (one that took into account, say, territory or population).[54] At The Hague, Scott, perhaps inadvertently, disclosed the Western agenda when he stated, in some exasperation, that no matter how the various doctrines of inequality and equality were reconciled, 'we must insist that no distinction be made between the States of Europe and of America possessing approximately the same qualifications'.[55] This combined the rhetorical commitment to universal juridical equality with the revelation that legalised hegemony or 'substantive' equality was to be founded, not on economic or population factors, but on cultural and civilisational ones.

---

[49] Scott, *The Hague Peace Conferences*, vol. I, 459.
[50] Scott, *Proceedings*, 646.   [51] *Ibid.*, 647.   [52] *Ibid.*, 647.
[53] Scott, *Proceedings*, 180; Wehberg, *The Problem of an International Court of Justice*, 75. See also Judge Huber quoted in Wehberg, *ibid.*, 76, supporting this proposition.
[54] Huber noted that finding a rational basis for the rotation scheme was 'impossible' (see Wehberg, *ibid.*, 77).
[55] Scott, *Proceedings*, 610.

In the end, the Committee adopted a resolution designed to defer the question of composition to a later stage. The full Commission voted in favour of this compromise after a number of statements were made supporting the idea of sovereign equality or legal equality.[56] A Draft Convention for the Establishment of a Judicial Arbitration Court was thus adopted by the Conference. The devil remained in the detail.

Ultimately, Scott's rotation scheme, a subtle form of hierarchical management, was regarded by many as hostile to both equality and the whole idea of legality.[57] It secured for the Great Powers permanent representation on the Court. To that extent, it operated in an unequal fashion. However, this structure also reflected a view that judges somehow represented the state. This was thought to be directly contrary to the ideals of judicial impartiality and, more broadly, the internationalisation of justice.[58]

. . . .

For those who decry the proliferation of international tribunals today, the 1907 Conference delegates must appear profligate. There were proposals for a revamped Court of Arbitration, a Permanent Court of Arbitral Justice and an International Prize Court. The PCAJ, as we have seen, raised questions concerning sovereign equality. The International Prize Court debates aired a similar set of concerns. Here, again, the question was whether any proposal for such a court could reconcile the claims of hegemony and equality.[59] A German proposal advocated an arbitral method of determining composition whereby the disputants chose two judges, two neutrals chosen by the two states who, in turn, chose another two judges and a third neutral picked a final judge to sit on a five-person bench. The British Plan was more patently elitist in nature. It called for 'each of the signatory powers whose merchant marine, at the date of signature of this Convention, is more than 800,000 tons [to]

---

[56] This resolution or 'voeu' was adopted by thirty-eight votes for and six abstentions.

[57] Schucking claimed that 'all of the states except the Great Powers declared this system of rotation unacceptable, because they saw in it an attack upon the principle of legal equality' (*International Union*, 223).

[58] Thirty-five Articles were eventually adopted by the Conference providing for qualifications, terms of office, procedure and other matters. The vote was in the Commission and thirty-eight for, with six abstentions in the Plenary. The selection of judges remained the only point of serious contention.

[59] There were three issues in contention, apart from composition – the question of permanence, whether the Court should be a Court of Appeal from national courts of the first instance or the last resort and whether the owner of the seized 'prize' could bring an action directly.

designate one judge'.[60] The Germans then denounced this plan as lacking in equity. The problem of the state with 780,000 tons was raised as well as that of states with five million.[61]

The British Plan was rejected in this form but it represents an interesting attempt to create a form of hierarchy that reflects not the status of the Great Powers but the special interests or functions of certain powers. Russia and Austria were to be excluded from the Court's permanent seats while maritime powers such as Norway and The Netherlands were to have permanent representation. This original plan was favoured by the likes of Schucking who saw in it the beginning of legal hierarchies based on interest not status. His concern was that a status-based category like 'The Great Powers' was unstable and variable (see Chapter 4).[62] In the end, a revised British Plan calling for fifteen judges (eight representing the Great Sea Powers based on merchant marine tonnage, value of maritime commerce and strength of naval forces) was adopted 38-5-1. Interestingly, the landlocked Great Powers were unperturbed by this state of affairs. One source of contention, though, was Rui Barbosa who this time worried not so much about the lack of equality but rather about how inequality was to be managed.[63] The pure doctrine of sovereign equality was defended by the Venezuelans who abstained because the composition of the Prize Court, 'flatly contradicted the principle of equality of sovereign states'.[64] Most of the states who had rejected the PCAJ arrangements, however, seemed to accept the proposition that the Prize Court was exceptional and that there was a difference between arbitral jurisdiction requiring absolute equality of representation, and prize, 'which would be called upon to adjudicate only one special kind of international difference'.[65] Max Huber, too, believed that such tests worked for functional arrangements but not for general institutions.[66]

. . . .

The Hague, then, represented a number of different tendencies in the development of the principle of sovereign equality. In one respect, George Grafton Wilson, writing in 1910, was correct to argue that the endorsement of equal voting rights at The Hague vindicated legal equality

---

[60] Hull, *Two Hague Conferences*, 438.   [61] *Ibid.*, 459.

[62] Schucking, *International Union*, 232.

[63] Brazil had been ranked in the fourth class.   [64] Hull, *Two Hague Conferences*, 447.

[65] *Ibid.*, 447. States in this category included Romania, Norway, Greece, Belgium and Serbia. Six nations abstained and one voted against, Brazil. It was also true, of course, that the small powers had more to gain from an IPC since such an institution would limit the then unfettered power of the large seafaring nations.

[66] Schucking, *International Union*, 232.

in international law.[67] Certainly, the use or threatened use of these votes to defend other aspects of sovereign equality would seem to be a confirmation of this belief. The rejection of compulsory jurisdiction can also be viewed as an assertion of a certain form of sovereign equality, i.e. the idea that states will not be bound to a certain form of dispute resolution against their will.

However, the negotiations in The Hague also point in a quite contrary direction. First, there was the beginning of a deviation from the practice of unanimity in voting at international conferences. Majority rule was introduced here for a limited range of matters. This broke the link between sovereign equality and unanimity of consent in international law. Second, there was the acceptance that states could be classified in international administrative bodies, according to contributions. This idea was to be carried forward to institutions such as the World Bank and the IMF and harked back to the original composition of The Universal Postal Union.[68]

Most significantly, the strong conception of sovereign equality was to be besieged subsequent to The Hague. The Great Powers proved adept (if not with any immediate success) at manipulating the principle to accommodate the idea of executive power and elite representation on international institutions. The minor powers advocated a version of sovereign equality that, in retrospect, was quite easy to discredit on the grounds of its apparent incompatibility with institution building in international law. Barbosa had stymied the Court initiative but he simultaneously paved the way for a reformulation of the idea and limits of sovereign equality.

The unintended consequences of Barbosa's efforts can be measured in the fact that international lawyers, after The Hague, abandoned the principle, realising that support for international legal institutions was more important to the discipline than a continued adherence to the strict formal equality doctrine. I now turn to a consideration of these early twentieth-century jurists and the culmination of their efforts at Versailles and then San Francisco.

Hegemony revived

Prior to Versailles, the ground was clear for the re-evaluation of sovereign equality. There was a realisation that the creation of international organisations required recognition in law of the real inequalities existing

---

[67] See G. G. Wilson, *Handbook*.   [68] See Chapter 6.

between states. It seemed to lawyers that the Second Hague Conference had demonstrated what happens when an excessively fervent legalism clouds the minds of negotiators. In particular, Rui Barbosa's position was now regarded as marginal, a little foolish and full of immature exuberance.[69] He had taken sovereign equality too seriously. According to Pearce Higgins, Barbosa had single-handedly 'wrecked the scheme' with 'heated speeches'.[70] Equally, the practice of quasi-unanimity and the structure of the proposed IPC both suggested that the strict construction of sovereign equality, based on legislative equality, was anachronistic and inappropriate.

The Great War, of course, had a profound impact on the way sovereign equality doctrines were approached. First, the war seemed to confirm to lawyers that international organisations modelled along realistic, feasible, hierarchical lines were necessary to prevent future human catastrophe. Second, the blood expended by the Allied countries in repelling the Central Powers seemed to confirm for those countries that legalised hegemony was both instrumentally and morally desirable.

As a result of this, in the League of Nations era, the doctrine of legislative equality, encompassed within the idea of strong sovereign equality, was rejected altogether by a number of leading scholars. There was widespread agreement that the doctrine was descriptively wrong and, in the light of the aborted Hague Court, dangerous and retrograde. It failed to represent with any fidelity the (legalised) reality of Great Power concerts of the nineteenth century and the continuing need for collective security in the twentieth. It also threatened to undo the great institutional projects of the twentieth century. It was descriptively inaccurate because it failed to account for the various principles and legal schemes embodying legal inequality. These included capitulations, the presence of semi-sovereign states, intervention doctrines and unequal treaties. Baker, writing in the *British Yearbook of International Law*, argued that the minorities regime ought to be added to this list on the grounds that:

They, too, came to be accepted as part of the public law of Europe, to such an extent that in 1919 they were imposed as of right on practically all states with

---

[69] There had been some doubts expressed before the Conference that the expansion in numbers would allow 'rough customers' as delegates to the Conference given the 'various grades of civilisation'. In fact, Choate, for one, believed that even the smaller states had managed to send able and cultivated men. Choate, *Two Hague Conferences*, 57.

[70] Pearce Higgins, *Hague Peace Conferences*, 513. This is the same word used by Schucking to describe Barbosa's efforts (*International Union*, 97).

mixed populations which took part in the Peace Conference. There can be no doubt that . . . these states were *pro tanto* unequal in rights under international law with other states.[71]

Baker also noted that legal equality was ultimately undemocratic since it treated unequals equally and skewed representation in international organisations.[72]

International lawyers and political scientists were not slow, then, to assert the claims in favour of hegemony.[73] The theory of equality associated with the small powers at The Hague came to be viewed as an example of an idealism that needed to be expunged from international studies:

the theory of equality is a striking instance of the effect of idealism on the world's history. Nothing can be more certain than that the theory, in municipal law truistic, is, when applied to the position of states, inept and misleading.[74]

Such a theory was simply redundant in a system where there was no central authority and bilateral action was regarded as the appropriate mode of redress. Albrecht-Carrié saw the dangers in this legalist idealism when he spoke of

the legalised fiction of the equality of states. Fictions are not necessarily devoid of utility in the operation of politics, as witness the success of the underlying egalitarian assumption in at least some democratic states. But a fiction too far divorced from reality may in itself constitute a danger by diverting men's thoughts and attention away from the hard facts of power and life.[75]

This anticipated the realism of Carr and Morgenthau. Soon legal scholars joined in. Brown called sovereign equality 'a theory in patent antagonism with the facts'.[76] Olney described it as 'theoretically true . . . but an anachronism and a mistake' and Scott argued that the doctrine would bring the push for international institutions to a standstill.[77]

---

[71] P. J. Baker, 'The Doctrine of Legal Equality of States' (1923–4) 4 *British Yearbook of International Law* 1–21 at 10. See, too, e.g. Badinter Arbitration Commission, *Opinion No 2* (1992), 92 ILR 167 (imposing additional obligations on aspiring states).

[72] Baker, 'Doctrine of Legal Equality', 19.

[73] This move to realism may have also been facilitated by the fact that many international lawyers were political scientists at this time or, at least, were located within political science departments rather than law schools.

[74] F. E. Smith, *International Law* (1911), 37.   [75] Albrecht-Carrié, *Diplomatic History*, 308.

[76] Brown, 'Theory of Independence', 327.

[77] R. Olney, 'The Development of International Law' (1907) 1:2 AJIL 419–20 (quoted in J. D. Hughes, 'International Law' in Grant *et al.*, *An Introduction to the Study of International Relations*, 13).

One of the most forthright thinkers of this era was the Professor of International Law at Princeton, Philip Marshall Brown. In two books, *International Realities* and *International Society*, he developed an idiosyncratic approach to international law. For him, both the balance of power and the legalisation of international politics had been causes of the Great War. The former failed to reckon with the primal forces of nationalism while the latter was based on a combination of excessive bureaucratisation and a belief that foreign policy could be managed democratically. He had no time for the cosmopolitan view that popular control over international relations would have a pacific influence. Following De Toqueville and anticipating Kennan, he argued that democracy was best quarantined in the domestic sphere. In foreign relations, it was 'dangerous'.[78] What were the implications of all this for his view on equality? Brown was an ultra-realist on this question. His view that 'the claim to equality stands squarely in the way of world organisation itself' was typical of the time if somewhat at odds with his dislike of legalisation in international affairs.[79]

Brown was a supporter of the theory of legalised hegemony, describing the Council of the League of Nations as an organ in which 'the equality of nations [finds] its full repudiation in the organisation and control of the Council'; a development anticipated at the London Naval Conference of 1909 where only the Great Powers were represented.[80] These, then, were the facts of international social life. Sovereign equality was merely a pretty theory. Brown was particularly scathing about the idea of a right to equality, noting that rights were based on recognised interests and not on the aspirations of, say, the American Institute.[81]

In a similar, if more temperate vein, Nicolas Politis, a former Greek Foreign Minister, delivered a series of lectures at Columbia University in 1927 in which he explained how compromised sovereign equality had become and why change was necessary. There were three elements to his argument. First, the requirement of unanimity derived from sovereign equality was having a paralytic effect on the creation of new, indispensable laws. Only by moving in the direction of a majoritarian system

---

[78] Brown, *International Realities*, 174.   [79] *Ibid.*, 15.   [80] Brown, *International Society*, 127.
[81] See J. Watson, 'A Realistic Jurisprudence', 265–85. In a later book, post-dating the creation of the League of Nations, Brown's *International Society*, a different image of international order was conveyed. This time, alongside 'the necessary primacy' (48) of the Great Powers was found the need for international courtesy. In a similar vein to Castlereagh 100 years previously, Brown warned against 'affronting the susceptibilities of other nations, great or small' (49).

of law-making could international law develop quickly enough to keep pace with developments in the political and economic spheres.[82] Second, strict constructionist readings of legal equality were resulting in obstructive tendencies towards the creation and functioning of international organisations. Third, the doctrine was already seriously undermined by the practice of international law and diplomacy. At Vienna and Aix-la-Chapelle, the representatives of the Great Powers had taken precedence in diplomatic ranking over those of the smaller powers and, a century later, the Prize Court established at The Hague had provided the eight large powers with permanent representation among the judges. Polites, in common with other writers, did not reject sovereign equality altogether. Juridical and legal equality (or what I have termed 'formal equality') remained important but these did not encompass other derivative or analogous forms of equality.[83] Lassa Oppenheim, for example, dismissed the notion of equal apportionment on the basis that the composition of the Court was irrelevant to sovereign equality. Sovereign equality, he argued, was protected by the consensual jurisdiction of such courts.[84]

In this manner, scholars were beginning to distinguish certain aspects of sovereign equality (e.g. formal equality) from other aspects (e.g. legislative equality). Pearce Higgins, for example, argued that the small states at The Hague had supported a crude dogma that failed to distinguish equality before the law and equality of influence. He continued: 'The "Primacy of the Great Powers" is a fact, if it is not a legal principle.'[85] (Though it was still not clear, even in forthright statements such as this, what were the legal effects of this primacy.) Walter Schucking made a similar point in relation to the unanimity/majority vote disagreement arguing that it would be absurd to allow 'the opposition of a . . . state which has just been adopted into the Family of Nations from the group of half-civilised states to obstruct a work of the civilised states as a body'.[86]

Huber, meanwhile, cast a backward glance at the Vienna arrangements in arguing that 'the so-called community of states . . . cannot be

---

[82] E.g. N. Politis, *Les Nouvelles Tendances du Droit International*, 28 (quoted in Starke, *Introduction*, 104): 'The unanimity rule, conceived as the safeguard of the minority, has, through exaggerating the doctrine of equality, become an instrument of tyranny against the majority.'

[83] N. Politis, *The New Aspects of International Law* (1928), stating: 'Neither did equality imply an equal participation in the constitution and functions of the organisations which administer the interests of the international community' (9).

[84] See Oppenheim, *Die Zukunft des Volkerrechts*, 43.

[85] Pearce Higgins, *Two Hague Peace Conferences*, 517.   [86] Shucking, *International Union*, 216.

considered a commonwealth, unless it is desired to assign to the community of the great powers a control over the other states'.[87] Schucking supported this view, arguing that the further one moved towards international union the more sovereign equality must recede into the background. However, he was only prepared to concede so much to the Great Powers. 'Special influence in the creation of substantive rules' was to be discounted (see Chapter 2).[88] Voting in universal organisations was to remain equal though gradation was tolerable in specialised administrative agencies. Schucking called this 'relative equality' and explained it in the following manner:

> the great states will not merely claim a position of preference in the new international institutions by reason of their political leadership, but an endeavour will be made to discover a standard according to which a classification can be made of all the members of the international union, which will then be to the corresponding advantage of the great powers.[89]

The idea was to distribute seats and voting in functional organisations on the basis of interests and representation in general and in universal organisations on the basis of population.[90] This was the 'objective' test. 'Is not the interest of a world power of 65 million citizens in a new and permanent international court much greater than that of a small state of four million inhabitants?' asked Schucking.[91] This was contemplated in discussions outside The Hague but was rejected on the basis that countries such as Turkey and China would then be over-represented in the same way as the Great Powers. Schucking supported this objective test but made it clear that, 'naturally, this principle could not be followed to its logical consequences. Otherwise the Chinese nation, with its 400 million, which has but recently been taken into the Family of Nations, would overwhelm all the Great Powers of Europe.'[92] For Schucking, merely stating this argument revealed its innate absurdity.

Pitman Potter, writing in 1924, took a similar view, supporting equality before the law as litigants (formal equality) but not political or legislative equality.[93] Potter believed that to regard sovereign equality as encompassing parity of this sort 'is to become the victim of some subtle form of legalistic superstition', or to embrace 'an outworn metaphysic'

---

[87] *Ibid.*, 116.   [88] *Ibid.*, 230.   [89] *Ibid.*, 231.   [90] *Ibid.*, 233.

[91] Schucking's preference was for electoral districts based on population (*ibid.*, 233–4).

[92] *Ibid.*, 233.

[93] See too A. Hershey, *The Essentials of International Public Law*: 'But legal equality, or equality under the protection of the law, does not necessarily imply equality of voting power' (247).

or 'a dogma'.[94] Again, even from one sympathetic to international law, there was the scathing reference to extreme legalism, i.e. the lawyer's failure to take a cool, scientific view of the true basis of international relations as opposed to 'the fictions of diplomacy and legal theory'.[95] At the same time, Potter found a democratic justification for this realism. Legislative inequality was deemed necessary simply because it was unjust that a citizen of Panama be given 200 times the legislative power of a citizen from the United States. No mention was made of Chinese representation.[96] In addition, big states contributed more and cared more about international organisations.[97] It was appropriate that they be afforded weighted representation.

Finally, imperialism itself remained at this stage a *justification* for greater representation because '. . . within the confines of colonial empires are many states in everything but name'.[98] There was no suggestion that these 'states' be represented directly. Still, their existence legitimated the formalised hierarchies operating in favour of the big powers.[99] Not that the big powers presented things in this light. Leon Blum addressed the Assembly of the League of Nations in the following terms:

There is not, and we trust never will be, an order of precedence among Powers forming the International Community. Were a hierarchy of states to be established . . . the League would be ruined.[100]

And yet hierarchy was a vital aspect of the League's drafting, its structure and the substantive rules it applied. The Allied Powers dominated the discussions on Versailles and, importantly, the Covenant was

---

[94] P. Potter, *Introduction to the Study of International Organisations*, 254, 332, 334.

[95] *Ibid.*, 287.   [96] *Ibid.*, 286.

[97] But see Léon Bourgeois, *Pour La Société des nations*, arguing that the states at The Hague were, 'all equal in point of consent and responsibility' (quoted in Choate, *Two Hague Conferences*, xi).

[98] Potter, *International Organisations*, 286.

[99] Not all scholars supported this view. Hans Wehberg, writing in 1918, argued that the rotation scheme was contrary to both the idea of sovereign equality and the requirement of impartial, international judges (Wehberg, *The Problem of an International Court of Justice*, 75). Hull also refused to see The Hague in this overwhelmingly negative light, arguing that the Conference had achieved a 'golden mean' between world empire and 'the particularist ideal of absolute and isolated autonomy on the part of each nation' (*Two Hague Conferences*, 496). Julius Goebel argued strongly against the idea that law should simply fall into line with the facts of international politics. To undermine the doctrine of sovereign equality was a mistake. According to Goebel, 'this trifling with the law will bring it into contempt' (*Equality of States*, 1).

[100] Quoted in Levi, *Law and Politics*, 123.

included as part of the Paris Peace Treaties. This was a signal that the Allied powers had no intention of relinquishing their grip on the post-war reconstruction. Equally, outside the League the big powers continued to dominate in other institutional settings and through less formalised regimes.[101] Prior to the Great War, and just after the Hague Peace Conferences, the British, for example, determined that the 'mistakes' of The Hague were not to be repeated. In the British Foreign Office Blue Book of 1908, there was a warning that the Great Powers might be driven to act by themselves if 'the second and third-rate states' continued to claim absolute equality. This threat took on a material reality when the Naval Conference in London was convened with only the Great Powers present.[102]

Versailles

The tension between sovereign equality and legalised hegemony was evident in the debates leading up to Versailles and found expression in the Covenant itself. However, it would be wrong to characterise the debate as one between international lawyers, on one hand, and realist politicians, on the other. In fact, by 1919, most lawyers had come to accept many of the realist premises. By the time of Versailles, many international lawyers regarded the strong version of sovereign equality as bankrupt. There was little professional attachment to a central idea of legality, i.e. equality.

The creation of the League of Nations, as with each of the moments of institutional design I have considered, required a compromise between two world order projects and these two projects, in turn, generated a conflict over membership and status within the institution. The conflict this time existed between the Great Power management project (realism) and the Wilsonian liberal project (democratic liberalism) as well as in, to a lesser extent, Lenin's 'democratic' internationalism.[103]

The realists acknowledged the failure of the European balance in 1914 and preferred a system of legalised hegemony where the major European and North American powers managed international affairs (as they had

---

[101] See John Dunbabin 'The League of Nations' Place in the International System' (1993) 78 *History*, 425 in Hurrell and Woods, *Inequality*, 254.

[102] At least, the powerful naval countries – Germany, US, UK, France, Austria-Hungary, Spain, Italy, Japan, the Netherlands and Russia.

[103] Though the idea of a League of Nations was originally developed by Lord Robert Cecil and the English international lawyer Robert Phillimore.

always done) but this time within the setting of a formal international organisation. The major powers had won the war, achieving victory through an alliance among themselves. It seemed natural to assume the burden of designing and managing the post-war settlement. This, in turn, required a legalised or, at least, institutionalised form of hierarchy.

Against this was a strongly negative view of the performance of both the system (balance of power, concert, secret diplomacy) and the Great Powers themselves. The Wilsonian perspective called for the abolition of these elements of the international order that had directly contributed to the Great War. For these liberal cosmopolitans, the balance of power was unstable, recurrent war was unthinkable, the old diplomacy was anachronistic, the concert system irregular and slow and, finally, the special position of the major powers untenable. Cosmopolitan liberals called for adherence to the ideals of equality (the impetus in this case being a combination of liberal democracy and self-determination) but for revolutionary ends. Indeed, for these policy-makers, mere legal equality was insufficient. Drawing on the third of Wilson's Fourteen Points, calling for 'the establishment of an equality of trade conditions among all nations . . .', they supported substantive equality and economic equality.[104]

These larger conceptual conflicts played out in three aspects of the League of Nations system: the process of its creation, the structure of its constituent organs and the substantive rules developed within the framework of the League.

The negotiations in Paris involved both peace treaties and institution making. The purpose was to conclude the Great War and create the League of Nations. The combination of a punitive peace treaty and hortatory Covenant was to prove an unhappy one. Twenty-seven nations were present but again the plenary form was eschewed in preference to a series of summits and informal private meetings among the Big Three (with occasional Italian and Japanese representation). This form mirrored arrangements at Vienna and was a departure from the more transparent style adopted at The Hague.[105] In the drafting of the Covenant,

---

[104] See R. S. Baker, *Woodrow Wilson and World Settlement*, vol. III.

[105] Though even at The Hague, the Great Powers enjoyed certain advantages, almost by accident and partly because of the vagaries of the alphabet and a little linguistic manipulation. The five Great Powers were each seated close to the front – Russia as the host, France, Great Britain, 'Allemagne' and 'America'. The Conferences at Vienna, Versailles and San Francisco resembled each other in that each was part of a post-war reconstruction. In addition, each was hosted by a Great Power; Austria in 1815, France

the spectre of Vienna again hovered over proceedings. A Commission, entrusted with the drafting of the instrument, was appointed by the Plenary. This was composed exclusively of Allied powers and their associates. The Five Great Powers each had two representatives while five representatives were elected by the smaller powers. These smaller powers were dissatisfied with this arrangement and managed to leaven the effects of legalised hegemony by appointing a further four representatives and by setting in place a form of communication between the Great Powers on the Drafting Committee and excluded neutrals.[106] However, there is little question that the major players continued to be the Great Powers.

An important preliminary question, preceding the larger issue of institutional structure, concerned the membership of the League. International lawyers found congenial the idea of an organisation based on some form of legalised hegemony with a special role for the Great Powers. A number of important politicians were of the same mind. Colonel House, for example, went as far as to suggest to Woodrow Wilson that since the issue of voting power was 'an almost insurmountable obstacle', the small powers should not become members of the League at all.[107] Wilson could not accept this proposition given his liberal inclinations and commitment to a universal international organisation.[108] This was especially true in light of the last of Wilson's Fourteen Points in which he declared that the new international organisation be,

a general association of nations . . . formed under specific covenants for the purpose of affording mutual guarantees of political independence and territorial integrity to great and small states alike.

In the end, membership was relatively open but the Great Powers nevertheless demanded a special role in the newly created body.

Hegemony and equality were partially reconciled at Versailles. The major powers were successful in building a big power council into the

in 1919 and the United States in 1945. The Hague is an exception to both these rules. Even the Tsar remarked on the significance of The Hague, favouring it as a neutral place for '. . . a work in which all countries of the universe are equally interested'. See Hull, *Two Hague Conferences*, 6.

[106] Georg Schwarzenberger, *League of Nations and World Order*, 20–1.

[107] House's suggestion was that these small powers should be neutralised in the same way as Switzerland. See Schwarzenberger, *League of Nations and World Order*, 24, quoting Seymour, *The Intimate Papers of Colonel House* vol. IV, 49.

[108] Schwarzenberger, *League of Nations and World Order*, 24.

Covenant while the liberal internationalists ensured that small powers were represented on the Council and that the egalitarian Assembly was given greater weight. This, of course, in turn, prefigured the United Nations Charter arrangements. To sum up, three techniques were employed to offset legalised hegemony within the structure of the League. First, there was a nominally equal second chamber with concurrent responsibilities for peace and security.[109] Second, states were equally represented on this second chamber; each member had one vote.[110] Third, there was some representation for small and medium powers within the first, and more powerful, chamber. Indeed, this non-permanent membership was increased to eleven, further diluting the hegemony of the Great Powers.[111] As Schwarzenberger puts it, this all represented a compromise between, 'the schematic application of the principle of absolute equality' (The Hague) and, 'the limitation of membership in the Council . . . to Great Powers' (Vienna).[112]

The design of a judicial institution proved less irksome than had been the case at The Hague. Indeed, the PCIJ structure mimicked the overall constitution of the League itself. The Permanent Court of Justice proposals to secure places for the five Great Powers on its fifteen-judge bench were uncontroversial. As Politis put it, 'in 1920 a solution could be adopted which in 1907 had seemed impossible'.[113] The PCIJ drafters avoided the problems of The Hague Court by using the concept of national groupings and by requiring a majority vote of both the Assembly and Council in the election of judges. This could then be claimed as a victory for a softened form of sovereign equality while lurking in the background was the de facto veto power of the Great Power-dominated

---

[109] Article 3(3). But see, for exceptions, Article 6(3), Article 16(4), Article 22(7–9). Compare Article 3 of the Covenant with Article 24 of the UN Charter. Article 3 states: 'The Assembly may deal at its meeting with any matter within the sphere of action of the League affecting the peace of the world.' See, too, J. Brierly, *The Charter and the Covenant* (for general comparison of the two constituent instruments).

[110] Article 3(4).

[111] Article 4 had envisaged that the Principal Allied and Associated Powers (France, the United Kingdom, the United States, Japan, Italy and Russia) would be represented on the Council along with four other states. The increase in number of the other states meant that the Powers (or those that took up their seats) lost their majority on procedural matters. However, a principle of unanimity applied on substantive issues meaning that all states on the Council possessed a de facto veto.

[112] *Power Politics*, 304. What Schwarzenberger called 'absolute equality' is what I have referred to as 'legislative equality' (Chapter 3).

[113] Politis, *New Aspects*, 9.

Council as well as the fact of special representation for the Allied powers. This was a perfect expression of the melding of a soft legalism with a basically hierarchical structure. Of course, at Versailles, it was the jurisdiction of the Court that proved a major obstacle. It was the large powers (Great Britain, France, Italy and Japan) who rejected compulsory jurisdiction of the PCIJ on the basis that such jurisdiction threatened a hegemony that had been established at some cost.[114]

In addition to the procedural aspects of the equality/hierarchy relationship, sovereign equality and legalised hegemony both found some measure of implementation in the two dominant substantive principles of the Wilsonian system. These were collective security and self-determination.[115]

Wilson was not so much of an idealist that he did not appreciate the need for some sort of collective enforcement structure in his new world order. So, amidst all the talk of democracy, representation and the accommodation of small and middle powers, hierarchy continued to exist as an operating principle in the area of security. As Ninic argues, drafters 'built . . . a broader and substantially novel system of collective security'. If this is so, it was a mild form of collective security by the standards of the UN Charter. The League's Council possessed nothing like the power of the Security Council. Peaceful resolution was less obligatory under the Covenant. True, Article 10 called for action against malefactors but this action was to be taken by members of the League with 'the advice' of the Council. Article 16 contained stronger provisions but again the Council's role is to 'recommend' action to be taken by all the members of the League against those states who violate the Covenant. So, the role of the Allied-dominated Council in collective security remained relatively small. The Great Powers had to wait until San Francisco before they could (almost) entirely colonise the field.[116]

On the face of it, self-determination reflected Wilson's more egalitarian leanings. Here was an idea that called for the equality of peoples. Yet, the principle of self-determination had an ambiguous relationship with that of sovereign equality. Certainly, a primary motivating factor behind the push for self-determination was the desire to secure equal status on the part and on behalf of those peoples outside the state

---

[114] Potter, *International Organisations*, 237.
[115] These principles continued to dominate the scene at Yalta in 1945 and in the post-1989 reconstructions of world order. They intersect in the former Yugoslavia.
[116] See, e.g. Article 24 United Nations Charter.

system. Colonised and ethnic peoples wanted sovereign equality. However, it would be a mistake to view them as having been deprived of equal status in the same way as, say, Turkey or Japan were in the nineteenth century. These latter entities were sovereigns denied equal status. They were 'unequal sovereigns'. The ethnic groups of Central Europe and the colonised peoples of Africa and Asia did not possess sovereignty at all. Their claims were for statehood (and concomitantly equality) rather than equality by virtue of their already existing status as states. In any case, the promotion of self-determination proved to be a highly irregular business. Some ethnic groups acquired statehood (the Hungarians, the Romanians) while others (the Bohemians) had to make do with minority status. As for Africa and Asia, the colonised peoples of these regions were designated mandate territories or denied altogether any status independent of that of the imperial powers.[117] The most interesting effect of self-determination on the principle of sovereign equality is that it was used to burden certain new states in Europe with duties towards their minorities. These duties were not universally applicable but affected only a small minority of states. The principle of self-determination, manifested in the minorities treaties, resulted in a new form of hierarchy in the relations of states.

Ultimately, in the drafting of the Covenant, in its institutional structure and its substantive provisions, the tension between sovereign equality and legal hierarchies is present. In some cases (e.g. drafting processes) hegemony prevails, in other areas a delicate balance is sustained. Ultimately, the League of Nations was the partial realisation of many of the predictions made by that group of scholars I described under the heading 'Repudiation' in Chapter 4. These writers and their twentieth-century successors saw hegemony as an indispensable element of institutionalism. There is no question that it appeared in many forms throughout the drafting of the Covenant and in its structural design and substantive doctrine but it continued to be modified by the principle of equality of states.[118]

---

[117] See Simpson, 'Diffusion of Sovereignty'.

[118] These inequalities were related to the position of the Great Powers rather than any diminution of 'sovereignty'. So, e.g. when Garner suggested that the League of Nations rested on 'abandoning the doctrine of sovereignty and equality of states' (Garner, *Recent Developments in International Law*, 401 (quoted in Ninic, *The Problem of Sovereignty*, 25)), he is speaking not of legalised hegemony (inequality between members of the organisation) but what he perceives, over-optimistically in my view, as the withering away of sovereignty in the face of a powerful centralised international organisation acting in the interests of humanity.

From Vienna to Versailles: some preliminary conclusions

In this final section, I briefly summarise some of the major trends present in the 1815–1920 period with a view to setting the scene for a discussion of the operation of legalised hegemony/sovereign equality in the United Nations system and beyond. In one sense, this was a period 'both marked by inequality and structured around it'.[119] This hierarchy operated as a more diffuse legalised hegemony replacing the centralised hierarchies of the Holy Roman Empire. Legal authority no longer reposed in one powerful central body but was possessed, sometimes tenuously, by the Great Powers. This new form of hierarchy inevitably came into conflict with the principle of sovereign equality but this tension adopted a number of different forms.

In the first place, there was a tension between a growing political commitment to equality and the consolidation of material hierarchies in the international order. The industrial revolution increased the power and capability of the state and widened existing power differences between states. All this consolidation of economic and political power resulted in a system in which some states enjoyed complete dominance. The Great Powers became less reliant on smaller states for the purpose of military action and they were able to act as a unit, relatively unencumbered by commitments to smaller states. At the same time, enlightenment philosophies of equality had begun to migrate from the domestic to the international order. At first, this apparent contradiction manifested itself in a series of institutional developments in which the appearance of equality was somewhat undercut by the machinations of the Great Powers.

Two contradictory processes emerged from this tension. In one case, equal rights in the international system emerged as an idea in the eighteenth century but suffered a setback at Vienna in 1815 where the system was transparently hierarchical.[120] In the other case, diplomatic precedence (kings, princes, republics), dominant in the eighteenth century, was in recession by the time 1815 came round and was replaced by modern conceptions of pluralism, equality and liberalism.[121] Ritualistic hierarchies gave way to sovereign equality at the same moment in history that sovereign equality was compromised by legalised hegemony.[122]

---

[119] Hurrell and Woods, *Inequality*, 248.
[120] See Bull and Watson, *Expansion*, 6. See, too, Lande, 'Revindication', 406.
[121] 'Not a principle of equal rights' according to Bull and Watson, *Expansion*, 7.
[122] See Hurrell and Woods, *Inequality*, 251.

A second theme revolves around the realisation among many international lawyers that international institutions were dependent on a regulated hierarchy among states combined with equality and balance between the Great Powers themselves.[123] The relationship between the growth or, indeed, possibility, of international organisations and principles of hierarchy and equality begins to exercise the minds of international lawyers. In the nineteenth century, many international legal positivists simply ignored the Congress of Vienna and refused to concede its relevance to developments in the law of sovereign equality. They characterised Great Power hegemony as 'politics' and, more plausibly, they were able to argue that the Congress was not, or did not establish, an international organisation but was simply a collection of agreements combined with a vow to meet again. With the rise of the international organisation, there came a growing realisation that such bodies could only be successful if they embraced hierarchical forms. So, by 1945, there was relatively little angst among international lawyers about the veto power and the special role of the P5.

The more interesting period occurs between the late nineteenth century and Versailles where international lawyers were agonising over the nature of international society and the place of hegemony in it. Streit, for example, fretted over the meaning of hegemony and its implications for international organisations in a manner that seems scarcely plausible to us now. For him, international organisations were impossible because they *did* require hierarchy and international law was incompatible with such hierarchies. Providing hierarchy was removed to the social sphere, the basis of international law remained untouched. With the creation of an international organisation, hierarchy was transposed from the political to the juridical, thus destroying the basis of international society.[124]

---

[123] See Albrecht-Carrié, *Diplomatic History*, 12.

[124] George Streit, 'Les Grandes Puissances dans le droit international' (1900) 2e series, 2 RDILC 5–25 (quoted in Dickinson, *Equality of States*, 128) RDILC (1900) 2e ser., Vol II, 5–25. The author is referring to universal political organisations along the lines of the yet-to-be-created League of Nations and United Nations rather than international organisations per se. The Universal Postal Union, for example, had already been established at this stage. Interestingly, Holtzendorff states that '. . . juridical hegemony . . . appears neither *to indicate* nor to be possible as the beginning of an organization of international society'. This appears to concede the potential existence of the phenomenon of legalised hegemony but argues that such hegemony would exist apart from questions of international organisation.

Admittedly, even at the turn of the century, this was an unusual position for an international lawyer to hold. Most of Streit's contemporaries agreed that organisational development required hierarchy or hegemony but they believed that a new approach to international law could accommodate this hegemony either through a more liberal reading of sovereign equality or abandonment of the strong version of that principle altogether.

Third, there was, following The Hague, rejection not of legalism per se but rather of extreme sovereign egalitarianism or the strong conception of sovereign equality. Most of the lawyers in this period believed that strict equality represented a threat to the project of building a new functional world order in which law, nonetheless, remained central (e.g. Scott). So that these lawyers were both realistic about equality and legalistic about world order. This is why when realists look back on the inter-war years and see failed legalist utopianism (where there ought to have been prudence and suspicion), they describe only half the story. Though these international lawyers were highly reform-minded and advocated a form of peace through law, they based that law, and the organisations given the job of applying it, on hierarchical principles congenial to the realist attitude to world order.[125]

Fourth, it was equally true that the overt hegemony exercised at Vienna was not to be repeated.[126] It could not be reconciled with the ideas of democracy and representativeness that were beginning to flow from domestic political orders into the international order. In addition, the Congress of Vienna, for all the stability it brought to Europe in the early nineteenth century, was regarded as a failure. The Great Powers had begun to feud amongst themselves and the idea of a beneficent European Public Order taking root through the interactions of these powers had come to seem implausible.[127] The smaller powers were beginning to demand representation and equal voice and with their numbers increasing, their influence also increased. In this respect, the post-1900 atmosphere resembled that of the late-1950s with a swelling in state

---

[125] Fried, in fact, calls them 'revolutionary pacifists' though this seems too strong. See Wehberg, *The Problem of an International Court of Justice*, 7.

[126] But see Ferrero, arguing that the impossibility of legalised hegemony was already manifest at Vienna: 'The Congress was neither a secret conclave of the Great Powers, as the victors had desired, nor a general European Assembly of both great and small powers as Talleyrand had proposed.' (Ferrero, *Reconstruction*, 266).

[127] Indeed, Ferrero counter-poses the sovereign law of Europe with the sovereignty of the Great Powers (208). The Franco-Russian War had split the Great Powers (see, too, Lande, 'Revindication', 409).

numbers also signalling a change in the structuring principles of the system.

Fifth, the Great Powers themselves came to appreciate the need to base legalised hegemony on a form of sovereign equality in relations among themselves. This point was well made by Pitman Potter when he remarked that: 'At all events, the rule of equality and unanimity was not effective, in fact, except, in a mild way, *among the Great Powers themselves.*'[128] This even extended to the treatment of enemies and their eventual rehabilitation at Vienna (though Versailles marks a departure from this). So, a curious phenomenon arose. It was precisely those institutions structured around forms of legalised hegemony that were most dependent on a form of sovereign equality existing among the elite states or Great Powers. The 1815 declaration was partly that the imposition of hegemony on any of the Great Powers by one of their own was somehow against the rules. The political hegemony of any single power was declared unlawful at precisely the moment when the legalised hegemony of the Great Powers was set in place.[129]

Finally, it becomes apparent in this period that equality is inevitably a difficult notion to apply in a transparent way. Even the strict constructionists or legalists could not really satisfy all claims to equality.[130] For example, there was a suspicion among European powers at The Hague that strict equality would lead to unequal representation because of the de facto influence of the United States on Central and South American states.[131] Another problem, and one that has haunted the United Nations since its inception, was that of the fluid nature of power. The application of hierarchical models of social organisation was an attempt to reflect power differentials institutionally. However, the degrees or preponderances of power or status used to supply the rationale for these distinctions are never fixed. Particular hegemonic models are often rendered anachronistic, almost at their inception. The presence of France and the UK, and the absence of Japan and

---

[128] My emphasis, Potter, *International Organisations*, 347.

[129] Legalised hegemony, in effect, gave the balance of power a normative dimension.

[130] The Brazilian Plan could also accommodate actual inequalities. The idea was to ensure that all states could be represented equally, not that all states *would be* represented equally. Note that Barbosa was not suggesting a variant on the contemporary notion of substantive equality or welfare equality. States may, in actual fact, not send a judge to The Hague, may choose to be represented by another state or may amalgamate around one judge. There was no provision to guarantee the substantive exercise of the right (Scott, *Proceedings*, 650).

[131] See *Lake Mohonk Conference Report* (Mohonk Lake, NY: 1910), 86.

Germany on the Security Council are the most familiar examples of this phenomenon.[132]

This was simply one of the problems facing the delegates at San Francisco. After the Second World War, the makers of world order again were faced with the problem of reconciling, more broadly, the imperatives of hegemony with the demands of equality. This effort is the subject of the next chapter.

[132] It is true, also, that even the staunchest advocates of strict sovereign equality can regret the inequalities produced by this doctrine. Rui Barbosa recognised that the treatment of Brazil as an equal with other Latin American states was a form of inequality (but one swallowed by a bigger principle (see Scott, *Proceedings*, 651)).

6   The Great Powers, sovereign equality and the making of the United Nations Charter: San Francisco 1945

Introduction

Much of this book concerns the intersection of law and power. I have used a familiar but neglected principle of international law, that of sovereign equality, to investigate some dilemmas of international legal and political order. As I demonstrated in Chapter 2, the principle of sovereign equality is associated with the notion that states are formally equal or are entitled to some sort of equality under or before or in the creation of the law.[1] I juxtapose against this principle of international order two images of the state that are just as familiar to international lawyers but, perhaps, are under-theorised by them. These are, respectively, the image of the 'Great Power' and the portrayal of some states as outlaw states or criminal states. This chapter continues an analysis begun in Chapters 4 and 5 of the legalised hegemony of the Great Powers. In this chapter, I consider the efforts made at San Francisco to construct an international organisation that reconciled the requirements of the Great Powers for legalised hegemony and the demands of the middle and smaller powers for some form of sovereign equality.

This is not a political history of the United Nations nor an investigation into its working practices. Instead, this chapter has the more modest goal of showing how the practice of legalised hegemony was given legitimacy at San Francisco despite the reluctance and anxieties of the weaker powers. The institution of a council of Great Powers deciding the fate of humanity goes back further than 1945, of course. Nonetheless, it was in San Francisco that the idea was most fully realised. The four-policeman model of international order is the most potent symbol of the

---

[1] This hardly does justice to the nuances of sovereign equality. For a classic account see Dickinson, *The Equality of States* and Chapter 2.

institution-building that took place during the post-war era. Yet, at the same time, the UN organisation was thought capable of ensuring that states had equal standing in the inter-state system. The principal concern of this chapter, then, is the drafting of the Charter itself. As with Vienna, The Hague and, in the next chapter on Kosovo, I am interested primarily in the foundational moments of a new regime rather than its subsequent operation. So, I contrast implicitly statements made by Castlereagh *et al.*, at Vienna with the positions adopted by Barbosa and Scott in 1907 and by the participants at the drafting of the Charter in 1945.

．．．．．．．．．．

The standard textbooks on international law have not been concerned, to any significant degree, with the problem of the Great Powers. One exception is Don Greig's *International Law*, published in 1974. In a forthright passage, Greig considers the problem of the UN Charter. In particular he asks, what are the basic principles underlying it? For Greig, there is little doubt that it is 'the principle of great power hegemony upon which the Council and Charter is based'.[2] This view, though, is at odds with that found in some of the specialist texts on the Charter. Goodrich and Hambro, for example, argue that it was sovereign equality that, 'determined the fundamental character of the proposed organisation'.[3] Bleckmann justifies his agreement with this position by arguing that any exceptions to the principle of equality were 'based on pragmatic reasons and cannot be interpreted as a general feature of the Charter . . .'.[4]

I want to take Greig's comments as my point of departure in thinking about sovereign equality and legalised hegemony. In the end, I disagree with both him and the likes of Goodrich and Hambro.[5] In this chapter,

---

[2] D. Greig, *International Law*, 2nd edn, 709. Greig is not alone. See, e.g., P. E. Corbett, *Law and Society in the Relations of States*, 264–5 (writing that the Charter contained merely a 'salute' to the principle of sovereign equality) and Bengt Broms, *Doctrine of Equality*, 166 (dismissing Article 2(1) as 'an act of homage' with little legal significance).

[3] L. M. Goodrich and E. Hambro, *Charter of the United Nations*, 2nd edn 7.

[4] A. Bleckmann, 'Article 2(1)' in Simma, *Commentary*, 77, 89.

[5] Of course, this hardly exhausts the range of possible attitudes towards the UN. For some, the organisation represents either a move towards world government or the indefinite postponement of that fantasy. For others, it is viewed as a workable compromise between balancing power and creating just order (though this belief was tested in the post-war period of Great Power domination and intransigence). Yet another group saw the UN as a return to the disastrous institutional utopianism of the inter-war period. For a general discussion, see A. Roberts and B. Kingsbury, *Presiding Over a Divided World: Changing UN Roles, 1945–1993*, ch. 1; A.-M. Slaughter, 'The Liberal Agenda for Peace: International Relations Theory and the Future of the United Nations' (1994) 4 *Transnational Law and Contemporary Problems* 377.

I argue that the Charter effects a (perhaps unremarkable) compromise between the political requirements of hegemony (or what was termed the 'special responsibility' of the Great Powers) and the juridical commitment to equality (or the dignity and sovereignty of the smaller states). Of course, throughout the past fifty-eight years, the particular ways in which equality and hegemony have been configured have themselves changed. What has remained stable, though, is the original constituting text of the world organisation.[6] Accordingly, this chapter focuses on the debates at San Francisco and how these debates shaped this text and determined the contours of the tension between sovereign equality (and, in particular the practice of legislative equality) and legalised hegemony. I consider the operation of legalised hegemony and sovereign equality in the drafting history of the United Nations Charter in order to demonstrate how, not for the first time, institution-building in the legal order required an attempt at reconciliation between these two core values.[7] All of this, in turn, has contemporary significance in the light of recent debates concerning reform of the UN. Though I do not make any explicit links in this chapter, it will be obvious to the reader that many of the patterns of debate found in 1945 are being replayed in present discussions.[8]

Going to San Francisco

At the Fairmont Hotel

In 1945 a number of states met at the Fairmont Hotel in San Francisco to establish a new international organisation and to design its constituent instrument, the UN Charter.[9] At this time, the world community was split along (at least) three axes: the Great Powers, the small and middle powers, and the enemy states. Each represented a different bloc of

---

[6] With some exceptions, e.g. Articles 23 and 27 of the UN Charter were amended in 1965 (providing for an enlarged Security Council).

[7] In this book I have focused exclusively on international organisations so there is no discussion of sovereign equality and legalised hegemony in, e.g. the Council of Europe or other regional organisations. For an interesting discussion see Greig, *International Law*, 717–23.

[8] For reform proposals see B. B. Ghali, *Supplement to An Agenda for Peace*, UN Doc A/50/60-S/1995/1, 1–24; S. Touval, 'Why the UN Fails' (1994) 73 *Foreign Affairs* 44. On the cyclical nature of 'reform' see D. Kennedy, 'A New World Order: Yesterday, Today and Tomorrow' (1994) 4 *Transnational Law and Contemporary Problems* 329.

[9] This group made up the majority of already existing sovereign states. Excluded were the Axis powers, states that had supported the fascists (e.g. Argentina) and states whose government remained contested (e.g. Poland).

interests and presented a distinct set of difficulties for the re-negotiation of international political community.

The Great Powers arrived at San Francisco convinced of the merits of their proposals for a world order devised at Dumbarton Oaks and based on legalised hegemony.[10] The 'Four Policemen' model was a central element of these proposals and the idea of an executive-led, collective security regime dominated the thinking of the US, the UK and the USSR delegates in particular. The small and middle powers brought to California a set of anxieties about the shape of order expressed in the Dumbarton Oaks proposals.[11] They worried about the entrenchment of Great Power privilege in the UN Charter. There was widespread acceptance that the Great Powers occupied a special position in the international system but many of the delegates believed that the Dumbarton Oaks proposals had exaggerated the role of the Great Powers in the areas of dispute resolution and enforcement. There was a belief that the new organisation threatened to convert potentially ephemeral material inequalities into immutable constitutional certainties. The Netherlands government, for example, in responding to the Dumbarton Oaks proposals, regretted the fact that these proposals perpetuated 'and *legalised* an existing de facto position of inferiority'.[12]

Finally, there were the enemy powers. They were the outsiders against whom the other nations were to be 'united'. They were to have no role in drafting the new Charter and were to be excluded, initially, from the resulting organisation. Their existence meant that the early outlines of the organisation could not be fully universal. The concept of the 'enemy state' was thereby ingrained in the formative moments of the new international organisation.[13]

The push for hegemony

How were all these positions to be reconciled? In particular, would or could sovereign equality be reconciled with the idea of Great Power

---

[10] The Dumbarton Oaks meetings were a series of preliminary negotiations among the Great Powers. The discussions at Dumbarton Oaks focused almost entirely on security issues and, in particular, the role of the Great Powers in policing the international order.

[11] These are discussed below.

[12] Suggestions presented by The Netherlands Government Concerning the Proposals for the Maintenance of Peace and Security Agreed on at the Four Powers Conference of Dumbarton Oaks, 9 October 1944, January 1945, Doc 2 G/7(j), III, United Nations Conference on International Organisations (UNCIO) 306, 315 (emphasis added).

[13] This story is taken up in Simpson, 'Two Liberalisms' and in Chapter 9.

privilege? For those committed to the ideal of equality among nations, the opening scenes of the conference (albeit that they took place off-stage) must have seemed inauspicious, to say the least. Clemens von Metternich, who hosted the important 'informals' prior to the Vienna Congress in 1814, would have recognised the scene (and endorsed the procedure) as the Big Five met in a penthouse suite on Nob Hill at the Fairmont Hotel in San Francisco to discuss the outcomes of the conference to establish the UN system.[14] The idea of pre-arranging a post-war order in anticipation of a plenary conference of all nations had an established history by this time. The outlines of the UN system itself are found in the wartime councils of the great allied powers at Moscow (1941) and Yalta (1944) and in the technical agreements at Dumbarton Oaks.[15] The smaller states were excluded from all these preliminary but defining conferences. It was accepted among the Great Powers, therefore, that the system would be hegemonic in style and structure (though the euphemism 'collective security' was preferred).

At first, following Yalta, President Roosevelt, whose administration was the intellectual engine-room for this new world order, envisaged a policing mechanism as the central element of international organisation.[16] The Big Three (the US, the UK and the USSR) were to possess exclusive enforcement capacity over a disarmed majority (with the possibility of some review by a watchdog body of neutrals). In cases of recalcitrance, 'the policing powers could then threaten to quarantine the offending state and, if that did not work, to bomb some part of it'.[17] Later, at Dumbarton Oaks, the Americans developed the idea of an Executive Committee in which three of the Big Four (China was now added to the list) could initiate action with the support of some smaller states.[18]

[14] See C. Eagleton, 'The Charter Adopted at San Francisco' (1945) 39 *American Political Science Review* 934, 936. See, too, H. V. Evatt, *The United Nations*. For a discussion of the meetings in Metternich's apartment see B. Gooch, *Europe in the Nineteenth Century*, 57.

[15] See Dumbarton Oaks, Washington Conversations on International Peace and Security Organization, 7 October 1944, http://www.ibiblio.org/pha/policy/1944/441007a.html.

[16] United States Department of State, 'Report on the Crimea Conference: Message of the President to Congress' (1945) 12 *Bulletin* 321; R. Wedgwood, 'Unilateral Action in the UN System' (2000) 11 EJIL 349, 350.

[17] R. Russell, *A History of the United Nations Charter: The Role of the United States 1940–1945*, 98. In fact, Roosevelt's plan was to have two forms of collective security, one aimed at minor transgressors to be dealt with through the quarantine method (sanctions), the other by the full-scale collective enforcement method (against larger states). The problem of Security Council members breaching the peace was not raised at Teheran because the United States was keen to get the Union of Soviet Socialist Republics involved at this stage, *ibid.*, 156.

[18] See H. Notter, *Postwar Foreign Policy Preparation, 1939–1945*, 611–19.

The British favoured this concept of an executive body though they were keen for it to have a European focus. In October 1942, the British issued their Four Power Plan, which anticipated an international organisation under the 'supreme direction' of the four Great Powers with 'an international police'.[19] This policing metaphor is found repeatedly in other statements of President Roosevelt, Mr Sumner Welles, Premier Joseph Stalin and Prime Minister Winston Churchill around this time.[20]

That the UN was to be based on a form of legalised hegemony struck most observers as inevitable. However, it was justified in a number of different ways. One rationale was based on the special responsibilities of the Great Powers.[21] Anthony Eden made this explicit in his address to Parliament following the Moscow Conference where he began by allaying fears that the Three Powers had any intention of creating a 'dictatorship'. On the other hand, he continued, 'special responsibilities do rest on our three powers and we did at Moscow try to devise machinery and agree on a policy that would enable us to give full expression to that sense of our responsibility'.[22] A number of Roosevelt's wartime statements reflect the same assumptions. In his Postwar Security Organisation Program of 15 June 1944, he refers to those states 'bearing responsibilities commensurate with their individual capacities'.[23] Andrei Gromyko, the Soviet Ambassador to the United States, justified the special position of the Great Powers on the correspondence of this position with the 'responsibilities and duties that would be imposed on them'.[24]

Interestingly, though, the Great Powers did not wish to have this justification articulated in the UN Charter itself. Mexico sought to spell out the reasons for the special position of the Big Five in the Charter. Permanent seats would go to those states with 'greatest responsibility for the maintenance of peace' because of the 'juridical principle that more extended rights were granted to those states which have the heaviest obligations'.[25] The proposal that these justifications be expressed in the

---

[19] Ibid., 103.   [20] See Slaughter, *Liberal Agenda*; G. Kennan, *Memoirs 1925–1950*.

[21] See Russell, *History of the United Nations*, 17, 241; and Goodrich and Hambro, *Charter of the United Nations*, 199.

[22] Russell, *History of the United Nations*, 146. As a United States State Department Memo said, prior to the Dumbarton Oaks meetings: 'This principle of equality should not extend, however, to the field of enforcement, in which the states having greater responsibilities should have correspondingly greater powers' (quoted in Russell, *History of the United Nations*, 405). See, too, discussion of Bull, Chapter 3.

[23] Fourth Meeting of Commission III, 22 June 1945, Doc 1149 III/11 XI UNCIO, 103, 108.

[24] Ibid., 109. Note here the genuine belief on the part of the Great Powers that they had not sought this position but acquired it as a burden or duty 'imposed' on them by the international community.

[25] Russell, *History of the United Nations*, 650.

Charter, though, was rejected by the five Great Powers.[26] Another view advanced at this time regarded a place on the Security Council as a 'reward' for the great burden borne by the major allied powers during the war.[27] These powers, it was said, had a unique role in preserving peace in light of their wartime sacrifices and, in a stronger version of this view, they had, as a result, come to embody the general interest.[28]

Ironically, one of the primary justifications for hegemony was, and continues to be, linked to the idea that 'substantial' sovereign equality could best be preserved by resort to legalised hegemony. According to this view, the sovereignty and existence of small states could only be secured through some form of hierarchically based centralised international organisation. To give a contemporary example, the preservation of Kuwait's sovereignty could be attributed to the special privileges and powers of the Security Council without which the Great Powers would be disinclined to intervene in order to preserve the sovereign equality of a member state.[29]

Finally, there were the ghosts of Vienna and, most notably, Versailles to exorcise. The Great Powers were determined to avoid the lack of consensus apparent shortly after Vienna, and the fatal dispersal of power and the overall lack of centralised, mandatory authority found at Geneva.[30] The principal failing of the post-Great War settlement was thought to lie in its lack of enforcement potential combined with the absence of certain key powers from the elite arm of the organisation. It was regarded as vital that these defects be remedied at San Francisco.[31] Equally, Vienna, while it created a loose and inclusive enforcement arm of the Great

---

[26] There is, of course, very clear inequality of responsibility in the apportionment of the expenses of the organisation among member states. This is relatively uncontroversial now (legally at least) but when the first scale was released the United States baulked at its 50 per cent allocation on the basis that the UN was an organisation of 'sovereign equals': Goodrich and Hambro, *Charter of the United Nations*, 184.

[27] The Position of the Government of Uruguay, 28 September 1944, Doc 2 G/7(a), III UNCIO, 26.

[28] Ninic, *The Problem of Sovereignty*, 130.

[29] I leave aside here arguments relating to the legal justification for the action as collective self-defence under Article 51 of the Charter or as an exercise of an inherent right to self-defence.

[30] The Council of the League of Nations was able to recommend enforcement measures but it could not compel members to take action in the way envisaged by the UN Charter.

[31] N. Bentwich and A. Martin, *A Commentary on the Charter of the United Nations*, xi. The League was dissolved in April 1946 at its final meeting. This meant that the existence of the League of Nations and the UN overlapped for a short period. For an evocative (fictionalised) account of this temporary co-existence see Frank Moorhouse, *Dark Palace*, 635–57.

Powers in the Concert of Europe, lacked a permanent institutional structure. The Second World War Allies preferred a concert built on firmer organisational foundations.

These various inclinations resulted in a process that was, initially, openly elitist, and a series of proposed norms that reflected or confirmed the dominance of this elite. The big powers met in various combinations prior to San Francisco with the smaller powers waiting in the wings for portents of the new international order. The Washington Declaration[32] was signed by all of the, then, twenty-six allied states, but even this gesture to equality was undermined by the unusual practice of having the major Four Powers sign the document first. According to Ruth Russell, this was a procedure 'not accepted without resentment by many of the smaller states'.[33]

So, throughout the pre-San Francisco period, the big three continued to meet and discuss drafts. There was little inclination to ask the small powers to participate lest they ask awkward questions of their larger allies. International organisation was to be worked out in advance by the elite states. The 'Vienna' procedures were preferred over transparency or democratic decision-making. This was the case in both the political discussions at Moscow and Potsdam and in the important technical meetings at Dumbarton Oaks. Often, the decisions reached at these meetings formed the substance of the final texts in the UN Charter.[34]

But there remained the tricky question of who was entitled to Great Power status or designation. This issue had arisen at Vienna where the Great Powers had been similarly mismatched and where France's role had proved so ambiguous.[35] It is typical of any period of hegemony that

---

[32] Declaration by the United Nations, 1 January 1942 (Washington Conference) (1941), *A Decade of American Foreign Policy: Basic Documents, 1941–9* (1950), at http://www.yale.edu/lawweb/avalon/decade/decade.03.htm.

[33] Russell, *History of the United Nations*, 54.

[34] The text of Article 27 is virtually unchanged from that agreed upon at Yalta (Bentwich and Martin, *Commentary*, xviii).

[35] The question of what to do about enemy states who are also Great Powers arose more acutely at Vienna where, arguably, France, though an enemy state, remained a Great Power in defeat. At San Francisco, both Germany and Japan were severely weakened states and demoralised societies. There could be no question of inviting them into the Big Five of the Security Council. Of course, the inevitable renaissance of these powers meant that these questions had simply been left to a later date. At Vienna, France was admitted to the Great Power councils towards the end of the Congress only as a result of a number of successful power-plays by Talleyrand and because France was viewed (by the British and Austrians) as useful in maintaining the balance of power against Russia and Prussia. The rehabilitation of Germany and Japan can be explained on similar grounds.

the identity of the hegemons themselves will often be controversial. The category is inevitably contentious and in order to supply some stability to membership a rough notion of sovereign equality has often been employed in relations *among* the Great Powers despite obvious differences in power, capacity and influence.

At the conclusion of the Second World War, the US, the USSR and the UK formed a natural alliance (though even within this group there was a United States-United Kingdom predominance that gave rise to a great deal of suspicion on the part of Stalin).[36] However, the question of China's and, later, France's membership quickly became an issue of contention. The British were against Chinese membership, believing the Chinese to be unworthy of this status, while the Soviets refused to even talk to the Chinese as equals.[37] These disputes resulted in two separate conversations at Dumbarton Oaks, one between the United States, United Kingdom and the Soviet Union, and the other involving the United States, United Kingdom and China.[38] In the end, the American interest in having the Chinese as (junior) policing partners in the Pacific prevailed over more material criteria and China was admitted to the Great Power grouping.[39] In contrast, the United States attitude towards France was quite negative. Roosevelt believed it to be a small power, which would be disarmed as part of the general post-war settlement. By mid 1944, however, pressure was rising to allow France a place at the table and France was eventually admitted in 1945. As at Vienna, it was partly because of the fear that France would become a leader in the Assembly of the smaller European powers that it was co-opted onto the Security Council.[40]

The result of all this was the present composition of the permanent members of the Security Council (the 'P5'). It is worth remembering that the make-up of the P5 was far from settled even as late as 1945. It is not the case that reform of the Security Council membership today is necessary because the current membership has become an anachronism. It always was an anachronism. When Goodrich and Hambro argued that

[36] Russell, *History of the United Nations*, 128.   [37] *Ibid.*, 103.

[38] The Soviet phase lasted from 1 August to 28 September 1944 and the Chinese phase from 29 September to 7 October 1944.

[39] Interestingly, the Americans also believed that the presence of China would deflect criticism that the UN was to be a Western-controlled body: Russell, *History of the Unied Nations*, 128.

[40] *Ibid.*, 272. The Anglo-French alliance and the force of de Gaulle's personality enabled France to be admitted to the inner sanctum in 1945 after its liberation or when it 'recovered its greatness' (*ibid.*, 114).

Article 23 imposes a 'static arrangement' because 'the great powers to-day . . . [may not] always continue to be so', they were only half right.[41] At least two of the P5 powers of 'today' were in fact, already in 1945, the Great Powers of yesterday.[42]

This need not have been the case. There were a number of proposals in circulation after Dumbarton Oaks that sought to mitigate the element of permanence and lack of flexibility in arrangements concerning the identity of the Great Powers. The Mexican Plan reflected the overall thrust of some of these plans (others included The American-Canadian Technical Plan and The United States Technical Plan) in calling for an 'Executive Council' based on a distinction between non-permanent and *semi*-permanent members. Article 12 of the Mexican Proposal read:

> The semi-permanent Delegates shall represent the States whose responsibility for the maintenance of peace is more considerable in the international community. It shall be the duty of the Assembly to decide, every eight years, which shall be these states.[43]

This was justified on the grounds that history is partly a history of the rise and fall of individual Great Powers. As the Explanatory Memorandum put it, 'there is no State whose relative international importance fails to suffer with the passage of time'.[44] This proposal, too, was rejected. The Great Powers wanted privilege to follow power but only to a certain extent. They did not wish to have the enjoyment of these privileges subject to the continued possession of commensurate power. A norm of sovereign equality, then, created a level of artificial parity between the Great Powers themselves in the Security Council just as legalised hegemony ordered relations between the core and the peripheral states.[45]

---

[41] *Ibid.*, 199.

[42] Attempts were made by the smaller powers to have the permanent members unnamed in the Charter to take into account changing circumstances. Unsurprisingly, this was rejected by the Great Powers.

[43] Opinion of the Department of Foreign Relations of Mexico, 23 April 1945, Doc 2 G/7(c), III UNCIO, 54, 111.

[44] *Ibid.*, 117.

[45] There was still a need to determine how other states in the Security Council were to be chosen. Britain suggested military contributions and the Soviet Union, general contributions. The United States feared that this would lead to three levels of states: the P5, those with military power, and others (with these others being effectively excluded from the council should such a proposal be successful). In the end, Article 27 embodied a principle by which non-permanent members would be chosen on the basis of regional representation and contributions. (In practice, this operates

This combination of parity and hegemony became a mark of the new international legal order.

To conclude, the four (and subsequently five) 'great' powers, for all their disagreements, did reach a consensus on the idea that they were to be the principal players in the new organisation. This agreement was born out of two concerns that were prevalent at Dumbarton Oaks. The first, as I have said, was the strong belief that this new world organisation should not repeat the mistakes of its predecessor, the League of Nations. In order to accomplish this end, the Dumbarton Oaks delegates settled on a system in which there was very little diffusion of responsibility and power in the organisation and in which there was the potential for rapid military action against potential aggressors. The second concern flowed directly from the solution to the first concern and resolved itself as an anxiety on the part of the four powers that majority voting in the security branch of the new organisation combined with strong enforcement powers might lead to a situation in which one (or more) of the four might be obliged to provide military support for an action of which it was not in favour.[46]

The pull of equality

At the same time, the sovereign equality of *all* states, as opposed to a specific equality ordering relations among the elite powers, was recognised as a founding principle of the UN system from its period of gestation during the Second World War through to the final drafting process in 1945. As early as 1943 in Moscow, where the four major Allied powers initiated the planning of a future world organisation, they acknowledged, in Article 4, the need to establish 'at the earliest practicable date a general international organisation based on the principle of sovereign equality of all peace-loving States and open to membership by all such states, large and small'.[47] This was partly a matter of form and partly a response to the anxieties of smaller powers alarmed by Roosevelt's policing metaphor.[48]

---

through a system of rotation and political preference rather than 'merit'.) But see the inequalities of representation in the General Assembly caused by Byelorussia's and the Ukraine's admission to the UN as member states, as well as, more debatably, the premature admission of some of Britain's former colonies.

[46] Broms, *Doctrine of Equality*, 156–7.
[47] The Moscow Declaration 1943 (Joint Four-Nation Declaration, October 1943).
[48] Russell, *History of the United Nations*, 110.

Roosevelt, himself, saw parallels between sovereign equality and the rights enjoyed by individuals within the American republic. The idea that the large would dominate the weak was rejected as having been the principle adopted by the enemy states.[49] Cordell Hull, in an address to Congress after the Moscow Conference, called equality 'the cornerstone of the future international organisation upon which the future international organisation will be constructed' and he laid particular emphasis on the special significance of the norm for the 'American family of nations'.[50] The mantra was repeated at Dumbarton Oaks.[51]

Meanwhile, in international legal practice, the principle of sovereign equality was influencing the Great Powers in some of their direct dealings with minor states. At the Teheran Conference,[52] for example, there was an exchange of notes between the UK/Soviet Union and Iran in which the Soviets and British agreed to 'do their best to secure that Iran will be represented on a footing of equality in any peace negotiations affecting her interests'.[53]

But while the Great Powers were paying lip-service to the idea of equality, the smaller states were naturally alarmed at the prospects of four policemen in a world in which they were to be disarmed. Many states worried that the Dumbarton Oaks proposals had concretised a system of permanent alliance among the Great Powers to the detriment of the 'rights and aspirations of the so-called small and medium nations'.[54] The problem for the drafters of the UN Charter was exactly that which faced Castlereagh in Vienna and the likes of James Brown Scott during The Hague Conference of 1907. How could the principle of sovereign equality and, in particular, the *amour propre* of the smaller states, be reconciled with the realist imperatives of Great Power hegemony?[55] In each case, the Great Powers attempted to assuage the feelings of the 'jealous' small powers. At the Congress of Vienna, the Big Four co-opted

---

[49] Opinion of the Department of Foreign Relations of Mexico, 106.

[50] *Ibid.*   [51] Goodrich and Hambro, *Charter of the United Nations*, 7.

[52] The Teheran Conference, 28 November to 1 December 1943, Declaration of the Three Powers, 1 December 1943, *A Decade of American Foreign Policy: Basic Documents, 1941–9* (1950).

[53] Treaty of Alliance between the UK and the Soviet Union and Iran, 29 January 1942, Cmd 6335, Persia No 1, 2, 5.

[54] Observations of the Government of Venezuela, 31 October 1944, Doc 2 G/7(d)(1), III UNCIO, 189.

[55] H. V. Evatt, the Australian delegate, remarked, towards the end of deliberations at San Francisco, that 'the smallest nations had a sense of dignity and self-respect which was really the basis of their international life' (Fourth Meeting of Commission, Evatt, *The United Nations*, 129).

France, involved selected small powers in committee deliberations and adopted Castlereagh's scheme of ensuring that legalised hegemony was introduced gently or surreptitiously. At The Hague Peace Conference in 1907, the small powers rejected Scott's rotation scheme for the constitution of an international court of justice and instead advocated a strong form of absolute sovereign equality (with every state represented on the Court) that rendered centralised decision-making rather problematic.[56]

By the time of San Francisco, developments at Versailles (and the backlash against legalism engendered by the Second World War and the 'failure' of the League of Nations) meant that the time was more propitious for the imposition of some form of legalised hegemony. Nevertheless, the Allies remained wary of forcing such a system on the other states. Weighted voting on the basis of material power was rejected on precisely these grounds. The United States State Department, for example, discussed the possibility of plural voting 'but it was agreed that the smaller states would strenuously resist any unequal voting methods in the Conference'.[57] Such a system was thought to be too transparent a departure from sovereign equality and had provoked a powerful reaction at The Hague. Instead, the large Allied powers preferred an 'indirect' form of legalised hegemony. The United States Staff Charter, developed in anticipation of the San Francisco meeting, was explicit on this point:

Such a system [weighted voting] would provoke the traditional resistance of a majority of states to overt denials of the equality of states, and it would be difficult to secure general support for any index of power with its corresponding system of voting. While weighted voting may well be utilised in the organisation of certain technical agencies, it constitutes too direct a violation of the traditional system to be proposed for the plenary body of the United Nations. It was considered more satisfactory to provide for the special position of the larger states in the United Nations by more indirect means, particularly through the composition of the Council and the voting privileges accorded states with indeterminate tenure on the Council.[58]

This document argued for a Council in which the small powers were to be represented so as to downplay the appearance of hegemony. Other changes were more cosmetic but nonetheless reflected Great Power sensitivities, for example, the term 'members with indeterminate tenure' replaced 'permanent member' in relation to Security Council

[56] A. Ross, *A Textbook on International Law.*   [57] Russell, *History of the United Nations*, 353.
[58] *Ibid.*, 357. By 1944, the Moscow Declaration had led to the proposal to establish the Interim Consultative Security Commission (ICSC).

membership.[59] Britain also wanted more small states represented on the Council, 'in order to prevent criticism that the major powers wanted to rule arbitrarily'.[60]

A Draft Four Power Agreement circulated by the United States State Department in 1943 tried to formulate a proposal that would satisfy Roosevelt's desire for a measure of legalised hegemony as well as the concerns of the small powers. The four-policeman model was inserted into a scheme in which the principles of equality of nations and universality were central. However, this draft was modified after discussions at the State Department because of a belief that 'equality' implied a 'factual equality' incompatible with collective security. As a compromise, 'sovereign equality' replaced 'equality of nations' on the basis that sovereign equality was a principle more consonant with the dominance of the Great Powers.[61] All of this reflected Roosevelt's preference for a system in which hegemony dominated in one sphere (the security arena) while a form of egalitarianism was permitted to operate in the economic and social zone.[62]

Understandably in the circumstances the small nations approached the San Francisco conference in a state of suspicion and anxiety. The Mexican response to the Dumbarton Oaks conversations exemplified this mood. The Mexicans were concerned that the Dumbarton Oaks proposals deprived the organisation of its democratic basis by limiting the powers and functions of the General Assembly. Such a limitation violated the principle of sovereign equality 'theoretically consecrated' in the Dumbarton Oaks proposals.[63]

Nevertheless, even among the small powers, there was an appreciation of the need to find some reconciliation between the two principles of sovereign equality and legalised hegemony. The Uruguayan government issued a statement in 1944 that attempted to find just such a middle ground. At the same time as calling for an international league, 'in which there are no differences of prerogatives and treatment among its members . . . with identical rights', the Uruguayans also accepted that the Great Powers, because of the weight they had carried in the war, should assure themselves of places on an executive council during a transition period.[64]

[59] *Ibid.*, 241.   [60] *Ibid.*, 272.   [61] *Ibid.*, 111.   [62] *Ibid.*, 206.
[63] Dumbarton Oaks Proposals, Article 1, ch 2; Opinion of the Department of Foreign Relations of Mexico, 107.
[64] Position of the Government of Uruguay, 26.

Ultimately, there was agreement on three points. First, sovereign equality was to be a cornerstone of the new international system. Second, departures from the principle or, at least, deviations from the strict implementation of the principle, would be necessary to give the new international security regime some teeth. Third, these departures would have to be justified on the basis either of competing legal principles or by reference to overwhelming political necessity.

At San Francisco

Procedurally, the conference at San Francisco was a Great Power affair in one respect: it was sponsored by the Great Powers themselves rather than in the name of an international organisation.[65] However, in other respects there was an egalitarianism or democracy that had been missing at, say, Versailles or Vienna. Though the Big Five held consultations throughout the conference, the adoption process was much more egalitarian than at Versailles, where the Great Powers controlled the steering committee and acted as gatekeepers for any proposals. At San Francisco, proposals circulated more freely and a two-thirds majority was required before proposals could be adopted. This meant that the Great Powers were obliged to convince, or at least cajole, other states into accepting their schemes (embodied in the Dumbarton Oaks proposals) for post-war international organisation.[66] It also meant that the small powers were sometimes able to prevail on relatively important matters.[67] Offsetting this was the fact that only the Great Powers were represented in each of the San Francisco committees and sub-committees.[68]

In substance, most of the debate concerning sovereign equality/legalised hegemony revolved around the Security Council and its powers.

---

[65] France, yet to be accorded status among the Great Powers, declined the invitation to become one of the sponsoring powers.

[66] The P5 hinted that they would cease to participate if there was not general agreement on the security provisions and veto power. Senator Connolly gave this threat a graphic reality when he tore up the proposed Charter in order to demonstrate what a vote against the veto meant. See II UNCIO 493.

[67] Goodrich and Hambro, *Charter of the United Nations*, 17; Broms, *Doctrine of Equality*, 160; L. M. Goodrich, 'Pacific Settlement of Disputes' (1945) 39 *American Political Science Review* 956, 958.

[68] Broms, *Doctrine of Equality*, 159. The San Francisco Conference resembled the Vienna Congress in the sense that all the important work was completed in committees and sub-committees. A number of important committees handled the procedural aspects of the Conference while the substantive issues were under consideration by four commissions and twelve sub-committees.

It was assumed that the principle of sovereign equality would appear in a prominent place in the Charter. The sole issue remaining was to what extent it would be compromised by or mediated through the entrenchment of Great Power authority. The small and middle powers expended virtually all their energies in Commission III (on the Security Council) in an attempt to dilute the effects of legalised hegemony. The form of constitutional organisation envisaged at Dumbarton Oaks was heavily weighted in favour of the idea of executive action on the part of an international elite composed of the Great Powers and it was this aspect of the Dumbarton Oaks proposals that came under heaviest scrutiny in the various committees at San Francisco.

Unease about the Dumbarton Oaks proposals was reflected in a number of counter-proposals. In general, the most visible advocates of this egalitarian revisionism were the 'Western' middle powers (notably the Netherlands and Australia) and the smaller Latin American countries such as Peru or Ecuador, whose contributions were very much in the spirit of Rui Barbosa at The Hague and the special Latin approach to equality.

These counter-proposals were organised around four different strategies: the attenuation of the veto power itself, the dilution of Great Power hegemony within the structure of the Security Council (including the review of permanent membership, the status of that membership and the number of non-permanent members), the subjection of Security Council action to either procedural or normative constraint and the enhancement of the General Assembly's role and powers.[69]

Attenuating the veto

Now, I think if we start from the basis of the inevitability of the veto even the most orthodox person must agree that it is a realist approach, and we are told we must be realists.[70]

Voting, of course, was a matter of intense debate among delegates and a rich array of amendments to the Dumbarton Oaks proposals was suggested. Inevitably, there were those states that wished to do away

[69] It is remarkable how similar these 'reform' proposals are to some of the current schemes for redesigning the Security Council to bring it into line with international 'realities'.

[70] Statement of Questions by the Delegate of New Zealand and of Replies by the Delegate of the United Kingdom at Ninth Meeting, 17 May 1945, Doc. WD3, XI UNCIO 317, 319. See Statement of the Delegate of the United Kingdom, *ibid.*, 323.

with the veto altogether.[71] However, the majority of the smaller powers accepted the need for the special voting rights of the Great Powers in the Charter and focused their energies on softening the effects of the veto. Some states, for example, sought to re-define the veto power by broadening the category of procedural matters that could be carried by a simple majority. The Australian delegation reluctantly accepted the need for a veto but argued that by removing its application from settlement of disputes (Chapter VI), its use could be limited to cases where the Security Council was taking enforcement action.[72] This was a position shared by many other states.[73] The Australians also proposed that the veto power should be suspended in cases involving the amendment of the Charter.[74] The Egyptian delegate argued that action under Chapter VII ought to be permissible when four of the five permanent members wished it.[75]

The response of the Great Powers was negative. The greatest fear seemed to be that any loss of veto power would have the potential to compromise the special position of the Great Powers altogether. There was a particular concern that a move to majority decision-making in Chapter VI would carry over too readily into Chapter VII and that a member of the P5 could become embroiled in a dispute resolution process against its will which would then become an enforcement action. Ultimately, allowing changes in voting in Chapters VI and VII might lead to an unstoppable chain of events in which the loss of veto power at the beginning of the chain would lead to its elimination at the end. Justifying the veto, per se, the British delegate argued that the veto was just an extension of the unanimity requirement under the League of Nations

---

[71] Fifth Meeting of Commission III, 22 June 1945, Doc 1150 III/12, XI UNCIO 163.

[72] Debates occurred over whether the veto applied to both Chapters VI and VII; to both recommendations and decisions; to procedural matters or substantive matters; and to all actions or only those not involving superpowers. Whatever the discussion, as Senator Vandenberg wrote, 'this veto bizness (sic) is making it very difficult to maintain any semblance of the fiction of sovereign equality among nations' (quoted in Russell, *History of the United Nations*, 725–6, also 717–18; A. H. Vandenberg Jr (ed.), *The Private Papers of Senator Vandenberg*, 200).

[73] Fifth Meeting of Commission III, 165.

[74] Verbatim Minutes of Fourth Meeting of Commission III, 123. H. V. Evatt justified this approach by arguing that Chapter VII powers ought to be distinguished from Chapter VI duties. Only the former were susceptible to the use of the veto (Verbatim, 108). The Great Powers themselves seemed to be leaning at this point in the direction of allowing discussion regardless of the objection of a P5 member but were not willing to go further and permit the full menu of conciliation measures to be recommended (Verbatim, 124).

[75] Amendments to the Dumbarton Oaks Proposals Presented by the Egyptian Delegation, 5 May 1945, Doc 2 G/7(q)(1), III UNCIO 453, 458.

Covenant but with the veto withdrawn from the minor or 'secondary' powers.[76] The British delegate agreed that while the veto rule 'may be considered to be unequal treatment . . . I would like to submit that it is not entirely unreasonable'.[77] The British also argued that the special position of the Great Powers, while not democratic or egalitarian, was necessitated by the nature of international life:

Well, we in my country are inclined sometimes to boast of our democracy . . . but we can only justify that boast by periodically introducing and passing redistribution bills adjusting the constituencies to a shift in population . . . You can't do that in the international field. You have to accept the inequalities you find, and you can't alter them in any rough and ready way.[78]

This was a classic statement of the realist belief in the disjunction between a domestic zone of constitutionality and democracy and an international zone of hierarchy and anarchy. It was this view that prevailed with only minor modifications.

Modifying the membership

Alongside the attempt to limit the matters over which the veto could be exercised, there was also a debate about the membership of the Security Council not unlike the one that took place over the composition of the Permanent Court of Arbitral Justice at The Hague. Once again a number of schemes were suggested. Liberia proposed membership based on the alphabet, a special position for middle powers was suggested by Holland, India preferred a criterion based on population (taking up China's arguments from 1907) and Australia wanted re-election for non-permanent members.[79] The Egyptians proposed an imaginative scheme, which involved an executive based on regional zones corresponding to 'electoral constituencies'.[80] The UK wanted contributions to security to be the main qualification. The Latin Americans insisted on a special seat to be reserved for a state from that region.[81] Some of these proposals

---

[76] Russell, *History of the United Nations*, 716.   [77] Ibid., 717.

[78] Statement of Questions by the Delegate of New Zealand and of Replies by the Delegate of the United Kingdom at Ninth Meeting, 320.

[79] Russell, *History of the United Nations*, 648.

[80] Suggestions of the Egyptian Government on the Tentative Proposals of Dumbarton Oaks under Examination at the United Nations Conference at San Francisco, 16 April 1945, Doc 2 G/7(q), III UNCIO 446, 449; and Amendments to the Dumbarton Oaks Proposals Presented by the Egyptian Delegation, 457.

[81] Brazilian Comment on Dumbarton Oaks Proposals, 2 May 1945, Doc 2 G/7(e), III UNCIO 232.

were special pleading. All the proposals were summarised in the Report of the Rapporteur of Committee III/1. In that report the Committee listed the various criteria suggested in discussions as,

full equality of all member nations, geographical distribution, population, contributions . . . guarantees concerning the active defense of the international order . . . combination of elements including population, industrial and economic capacity, future contributions in armed forces and assistance pledged by member states.[82]

The small powers were pushing for a combination of ends. They wanted an increase in the number of non-permanent members in order to loosen the hold of the Great Powers on decision-making in the chamber and some form of special representation for discrete categories of regional powers.

Alongside attempts to modify the membership of the Council, there were proposals seeking to render the membership of the P5 less permanent. A number of delegations proposed that permanent membership be subject to review after ten years (see above). Legalised hegemony was to operate on a flexible basis. It was pointed out that the identity of Great Powers was subject to serious fluctuation and that any entrenchment of specific Great Powers in the Charter would render it an anachronism. The Mexican position, discussed above, questioned the very validity of permanence and suggested replacing it with a structure in which some states occupied a seat on a semi-permanent basis.[83]

The Brazilians supported the idea that the Security Council should begin in hegemonic mode but should become more 'democratic' once the transition period was over.[84] This came to be associated with another unsuccessful proposal that the Security Council's mandate should be reviewed after eight or ten years.[85] There was also a genuine concern about the extent of the Security Council's transitional powers in the Charter. It was believed that Great Power hegemony might operate for a significant period outside the parameters of the already expansive

---

[82] Report of the Rapporteur of Committee III/1 on Activities of Committee III/1 (Structure and Procedures for the Security Council), Concerning Chapter VI of the Dumbarton Oaks Proposals, 17 June 1945, Doc 1050 III/1/58, XI UNCIO 675, 678.

[83] Summary Report of Seventh Meeting of Committee III/1, 16 May 1945, Doc 338 III/1/14, XI UNCIO 289; Opinion of the Department of Foreign Relations of Mexico, 111.

[84] Brazilian Comment, 236.

[85] Fourth Meeting of Commission III, 116; Fifth Meeting of Commission III, 163.

Charter system, though this fear proved unfounded.[86] Again, the Great Powers prevailed and the current membership of the P5 remains unchanged since 1945.

Constraining the Council

Committee I of Commission III was given the task of determining the structure of the UN Security Council and it was during these meetings that a number of further attempts were made to limit the effect of hegemony in the Charter. Most of these efforts revolved around the important question of whether Council decisions could be constrained by any principles of law and whether there could be any review of Council decisions under Chapter VII by other bodies (notably the General Assembly or the International Court of Justice (ICJ)). These two matters were, of course, linked, since the idea of normative constraint presupposed some form of review.[87] The most radical of these proposals focused on the potential of the General Assembly as a body capable of supervising the Security Council and endorsing or censuring actions.[88] The Venezuelans argued for a 'better balance' between the General Assembly and the Security Council through mechanisms that would allow the General Assembly to act 'as a control on some decisions of the Council'.[89] Other delegations went further, suggesting that the essence of the relationship between the General Assembly and the Security Council was one of delegation from the plenary body to the executive.[90] For the Costa Ricans, the General Assembly's role was to safeguard the principles and purposes of the UN in relation to the Security Council.[91]

---

[86] Statement on Behalf of the Australian Delegation Regarding the Report of Committee 3 of Commission III on Chapter XII (Transitional Arrangements) Annex to Fifth Meeting of Commission III at 198.

[87] Though not necessarily judicial review, see J. Alvarez, 'Judging the Security Council' (1996) 90 AJIL 1.

[88] Verbatim Minutes of the First Meeting of Commission III, 13 June 1945, Doc 943 III/5, XI UNCIO 12, 13. Another possibility was that states not members of the Security Council play a larger role in the Council's deliberations either when the interests of these states were at issue or when it was envisaged that these states might have to contribute military forces in Council action (*ibid.*, 14).

[89] Observations of the Government of Venezuela, 189, 196. The Venezuelans also called for a larger role for the ICJ with the possibility that it might 'intervene' in political conflicts, *ibid.*, 209.

[90] Observations of the Guatemalan Government Regarding the Proposal for the Establishment of a General International Organisation for the Maintenance of Peace and Security in the World, 23 April 1945, Doc 2 G/7(f), III UNCIO 254.

[91] Comments of the Government of Costa Rica, 5 December 1944, Doc 2 G/7(h), III UNCIO 274.

Other states were content to outline the normative limitations on Security Council action either by suggesting that Council action be limited by the purposes and principles of the Charter or by the operation of a rule stating that the Security Council should not 'establish or modify principles or rules of law'.[92] As a corollary, the possibility that the Security Council be *required* to act in cases of aggression was mooted. This would have left the Council free to determine the existence of lower levels of violation (threats and breaches of the peace) but would have made action automatic in cases of aggression. Committee III/1 rejected this proposal on the time-honoured grounds that a definition of aggression could not be agreed upon.[93] On the other hand, as we have seen, there were those who wished to diminish the effect of the veto when the Council was acting in its quasi-judicial mode. The idea here was to distinguish action under Articles 41 and 42 from determinations under Article 39 and Chapter VI. This was the thrust of the Netherlands proposal and the Australian position discussed above.[94]

Another dispute revolved around the status of 'principles and purposes'. Could not these be written in such a way as to bind or circumscribe action under Chapter VI or VII? This too was rejected by the Conference with the Big Five arguing that this specification would open a loophole for challenging any particular action of the organisation as being unjust. The Security Council, they emphasised, should be able to prevent fighting as a policeman does, deferring inquiry into the rights and wrongs of a situation until later.[95]

In the end, the small states were successful in modifying the Dumbarton Oaks proposals in respect of the General Assembly's right to be kept abreast of all questions being dealt with by the Security Council (Article 12(2)),[96] but virtually every other modification was rejected by the P5. Article 24 contained a reference to the principles and purposes of the UN but at the UN Conference on International Organisations,

---

[92] Fourth Meeting of Commission III, above n. 23, 113; Verbatim Minutes of the First Meeting of Commission III, 16.

[93] Verbatim Minutes of the First Meeting of Commission III, 17; Russell, *History of the United Nations*, 671–2.

[94] Summary Report of Ninth Meeting of Committee III/1, 18 May 1945, Doc 417, III/1/19, XI UNCIO 305. *Ibid.*, 309.

[95] Russell, *History of the United Nations*, 656. See also *Case Concerning Questions of Interpretation and Application of the 1971 Montreal Convention Arising from the Aerial Incident at Lockerbie (Libyan Arab Jamahiriya v. UK) (Libyan Arab Jamahiriya v. US)*, (1998) (Preliminary Objections) ICJ Rep. 115.

[96] Goodrich and Hambro, *Charter of the United Nations*, 173.

a decision was made 'to leave to the Council, the entire discretion as to what constitutes a threat to the peace . . .'.[97] The middle and small powers were left with the forlorn hope that the P5 would treat the veto as a 'sacred trust'[98] to be wielded sparingly and only in the interests of the international community. There was a recognition that special privileges were at variance with the principle of sovereign equality, 'from a democratic, legal and theoretical point of view', but that these privileges were politically necessary.[99]

As a result, hegemony is entrenched in the resultant institution. The Security Council's powers are 'generous', especially in the field of peace and security where it has primary responsibilities.[100] Chapter VII outlines a procedure that offers the Council a high degree of latitude in defining its own powers to act either forcibly or non-forcibly.[101] Each member of the P5 wields a significant amount of power within the system.[102] Most of this power is what might be called 'negative power', permitting P5 states to prevent certain action being taken by the UN on a range of issues. So, for example, a permanent member of the Security Council is able to veto any amendment of the Charter, prevent the appointment of a candidate for the Secretary-General's position and restrict efforts to have states admitted or expelled from the organisation.[103] These are not merely theoretical powers. P5 states have been active in

---

[97] VII UNCIO, 505, quoted in G. Nolte, 'The Limits of the Security Council's Powers and its Functions in the International Legal System: Some Reflections' in M. Byers (ed.), The Role of Law in International Politics: Essays in International Relations and International Law, 315, 317.

[98] Fifth Meeting of Commission III, 163.

[99] Suggestions Presented by the Netherlands Government, 314.

[100] Goodrich and Hambro, Charter of the United Nations, 29. The Council has in recent years established ad hoc criminal courts, e.g. SC Res. 827 (1993); imposed new obligations on states, e.g. SC Res. 687 (1991) and acted as a quasi-judicial body, e.g. SC Res. 705 (1991). It has also considerably expanded the category 'threats to the peace and security' to include failed states, internal wars and failure to comply with disarmament treaties.

[101] The extent of these powers is itself the subject of controversy among scholars. One group argues for a 'constitutional' reading of the Council's powers based on the Charter's principles and powers or the constraining effects of the Charter's text: see T. Franck, 'Fairness in the International Legal and Institutional System: General Course on Public International Law' (1993) 240 Collected Courses of the Hague Academy 189. Another group adopts a 'realist' position denying to the Charter (or even international law) any restraining potential (see, for a discussion, Alvarez, 'Judging the Security Council', 87).

[102] Article 23. Note that Russia has 'succeeded' to the Soviet Union's seat at the Security Council in 1990 and the People's Republic of China replaced Taiwan as the Chinese representative in 1971.

[103] Article 110 also required the ratification of each of the P5 before the Charter could come into force. Only a majority of the other states was required.

ending the ambitions of sitting Secretary-Generals, for example, the United States's failure to support Boutros Ghali's quest for a second term, and have regularly vetoed admission of states to the UN system.[104] The requirement that P5 states all agree on any fundamental reforms of the UN system makes the various efforts to change the composition of the P5 highly problematic.[105] The veto, then, is a 'central norm of decision-making in the UN'.[106]

It is in the area of collective security that the operation of legalised hegemony is most remarkable.[107] A P5 state can veto any enforcement action by the Security Council or by regional organisations, though by a customary law modification of the Charter neither an abstention nor absence is any longer regarded as a de facto veto.[108] The effect of the collective security provisions is to entrench a form of sovereign inequality. It is not just that the Great Powers enjoy special powers in the realm of enforcement and institutional management but that their position in relation to the former has an effect on their sovereign power vis-à-vis other states.[109] Chapter VII of the Charter, in effect, grades sovereignty

---

[104] See, too, the 'implacable hostility' shown towards Trygve Lie by the Soviet Bloc after the Korean enforcement action. See H. G. Nicholas, *The United Nations*, 156. The Security Council also shares certain powers with the General Assembly (e.g. powers of election relating to membership of the organisation and the choice of judges at the ICJ).

[105] K. Annan, Secretary-General, Presents Annual Report on Work of Organisation, as 55th General Assembly Begins General Debate, GA/9760, 200. For the distinction between reform of the UN requiring amendment and reforms that can be carried out more informally, see L. Sohn, 'Important Improvements in the Functioning of the Principal Organs of the United Nations That Can Be Made Without Charter Revision' (1997) 91 AJIL 652.

[106] B. Fassbender, *UN Security Council Reform and the Right of Veto: A Constitutional Perspective.*

[107] Article 106 also permitted the P5 some latitude to use force outside the Charter scheme pending the coming into force of Article 43 (and thus Article 42). Some scholars, of course, argue that Article 43 has never come into force (see, e.g. Higgins, *Problems and Processes*). Do the P5 thereby retain their powers under Article 106?

[108] See *Legal Consequences for States of the Continued Presence of South Africa in Namibia (South West Africa) notwithstanding SC Res. 276 (1970)* (Advisory Opinion) (1971) ICJ Rep. At 16. The veto operates only in respect of non-procedural matters. For a discussion of the difference between procedural issues and non-procedural matters see Greig, *International Law*, 707–9. One could argue that the Rules of Procedure provide for a dilution of hegemony by permitting the President of the Council to declare procedural or non-procedural a draft resolution (Rule 30). Such a ruling can only be reversed by a nine-member majority. The permanent members of the UN are also permanent members of the now largely moribund Trusteeship Council. In fact, the P5 are now the sole members of that Council. See Ninic, *Problem of Sovereignty*, 132.

[109] Bentwich and Martin, *Commentary*, xvi, even suggest that the relationship of UN members to the Security Council was a principal/agent relationship in which members delegated authority to the Council.

on the basis of degrees of immunity or territorial integrity. The P5 enjoy complete de facto immunity from the enforcement jurisdiction of the Security Council while other states are subject to increasingly intrusive doctrines of intervention.[110] While the Great Powers could argue that this was simply an application of the unanimity principle found in a number of international bodies prior to the Charter, it resulted in an inequality in the Charter because in other respects, and for other states, majority rule was now the accepted procedure in international organisations.[111] The unmodified unanimity procedure was a rule of equality. As Brierly remarked in 1944, the unanimity rule (dominant at The Hague) means that a state could 'refuse to have its own rights or duties changed' whereas the veto permits a member of the P5 to 'debar other states from introducing changes which are only to affect itself'.[112] This is the case for all actions under Article 25 and most obviously in regard to the amendment procedures under Articles 108 and 109. In addition, as Fassbender has argued, the veto has enormous influence in cases where it is never used, by virtue of its utility as a bargaining tool.[113]

Enhancing the Assembly

If the small and middle powers were unsuccessful in their attempts to constrain the Security Council, they were more successful in expanding the domain of the General Assembly. The egalitarian chamber is putatively the General Assembly though even this equality has highly unequal effects if approached from the perspective of say, fairness to individuals or representation of non-governmental entities.[114] On the inter-state plane, though, there is little doubt that the General Assembly is the 'most representative organ of the United Nations'.[115] All members of the UN are represented on the General Assembly and there are no special privileges for Great Powers.[116] Article 9(2), specifying the number

---

[110] Ninic, *Problem of Sovereignty*, 132. See, e.g. SC Resolution 794 (1992) and 837 (1992) on Somalia.

[111] On the transition from unanimity to majority voting see, e.g. T. J. Lawrence, *International Problems*; Schucking, *International Union*.

[112] J. Brierly, *The Outlook for International Law*, 99, quoted in Fassbender, *Security Council Reform*, 280.

[113] *Ibid.*, 281.   [114] Franck, *Fairness*, 484.

[115] Goodrich and Hambro, *Charter of the United Nations*, 25.

[116] The Soviet Union ended up with two extra seats (those of Byelorussia and the Ukraine). Stalin had placed enormous pressure on the United States in this regard, arguing that the Soviet republics were at least as important as Liberia or Guatemala and at least as independent as the Philippines and India. Secretary Stettinius

of delegates permitted to sit in the General Assembly, also has its roots in an egalitarian sensibility. There was a concern, at San Francisco, that the large states would swamp the small states with their larger number of delegates at the General Assembly and 'wound their [the small states]' delicacy'.[117]

Of course, the representative nature of the General Assembly does not in itself demonstrate that the UN is in any way an egalitarian organisation. Indeed, in a typical image of the UN it combined a powerful core (the Security Council) and an irrelevant talking shop (the General Assembly).[118] On this reading, the mere presence of a weak General Assembly would barely detract from the hegemonic essence of the organisation.

This interpretation of the General Assembly's role, though, misrepresents both its constitutional power and its symbolic impact. In fact, the General Assembly possesses quite extensive powers even if it cannot legislate as such.[119] It is from the General Assembly that a number of other UN organs derive their powers.[120] The Trusteeship Council and the Economic and Social Council report to the General Assembly and take instructions from that body and both the Security Council and Secretary-General are obliged to provide annual reports of their activities to the

described this frankly as 'the multiple membership of the Soviet Union': quoted in Russell, *History of the United Nations*, 535. Roosevelt confirmed this interpretation in Malta when he distinguished the admission of the British dominions and that of the Soviet Republics: 'it was not a question of a new country but of giving one of the Great Powers three votes instead of one in the Assembly' (Malta and Yalta Documents, 775, quoted in Russell, *ibid.*, 538). The Soviets suggested that the United States also get two extra votes in order to secure equality (*Foreign Relations of the United States: Diplomatic Papers, The Conferences at Malta and Yalta (1945)*, United States Government Printing Office (Washington, 1955), Department of State Publication 6199, 967, cited in Russell, *ibid.*, 539). However, this raised the question of why the United Kingdom had six votes (these votes being the Dominion votes controlled by the United Kingdom delegate) and the United States and the Soviet Union only one and three respectively (Russell, *ibid.*, 596).

[117] Observations of the Government of Venezuela, 195.

[118] For a discussion of some of these images of the UN, see Roberts and Kingsbury, *Divided World*, ch. 1.

[119] The legal effects of General Assembly resolutions were a matter of some discussion among international lawyers in the 1960s and 1970s. Prima facie, the General Assembly's recommendations have no law-making effect. The General Assembly is the 'open conscience' of the world: Goodrich and Hambro, *Charter of the United Nations*, 150, and, as with all consciences, it has no direct legislative capacity. However, General Assembly resolutions can contribute to the formation of the *opinio juris* limb of customary international law: see R. Higgins, *The Development of International Law Through the Political Organs of the United Nations*. See discussion in Chapter 2.

[120] Goodrich and Hambro, *Charter of the United Nations*, 25.

General Assembly for consideration.[121] The International Law Commission is mandated to complete certain tasks at the behest of the General Assembly.[122]

Then there are the various functions of the Assembly. These include the peaceful settlement clauses of the Charter permitting the Assembly to initiate studies, promote cooperation and 'recommend measures for the peaceful adjustment of any situation, regardless of origin'.[123] Finally, there are the elective and financial functions.[124] The General Assembly has control over the organisation's budget and it elects its own members on a recommendation from the Security Council as well as the non-permanent members of the Security Council and the members of the Economic and Social Council.[125]

Given all this, it would be peculiar to adopt the position that the UN is overwhelmingly hegemonic in structure. Indeed, one might claim that the significant reforms to the system have been in the direction of sovereign equality or, at least, democratisation. There are more states than previously represented at the Security Council, more states on the Economic and Social Council and a general diluting of the power of the P5.[126] Even in the Security Council, the P5 cannot act without the support of at least three non-permanent members (this is sometimes referred to as the sixth veto). The early history of the UN is marked by regular attempts, some successful, on the part of the General Assembly to accrue more power over areas of international regulation (security, political matters) and specific issues which prima facie fall within the jurisdiction of the Security Council.[127] Even in cases where the San Francisco delegates refused to adopt a specific mechanism, the General

---

[121] See Articles 15, 98, 16, 60 and 85.   [122] Article 13(1)(a).

[123] Articles 17, 18 and 61. In addition, the General Assembly can discuss and make recommendations relating to any matter 'within the scope of the present Charter' (Article 10) providing it does not trench on Security Council action under Article 12.

[124] These categories are found in Goodrich and Hambro, *Charter of the United Nations*, 26.

[125] The General Assembly is also involved in the election of judges to the ICJ (Article 4 of the Statute of the ICJ) and in the appointment of the Secretary-General (Article 97).

[126] The General Assembly has tried to chip away at the power of the Security Council in the admissions process by making recommendations to the Council and by initiating an Advisory Opinion on the powers of Security Council members; in the peace-enforcing realm with its *Uniting for Peace Resolution* (GA Resolution 377 (1950)) and in the peacekeeping area where it possessed primary responsibility during the first phase of peacekeeping operations. On enforcement, see GA Resolution 376 (1950); on peacekeeping see *Certain Expenses of the United Nations* (Advisory Opinion) (1962) ICJ Rep. 151; on admissions see *Membership Case* (1948) ICJ Rep. 57.

[127] Perhaps the most famous being the *Uniting for Peace Resolution*, *ibid*. See also the discussions of the Palestine and Spanish cases in Goodrich and Hambro, *Charter of the United Nations*, 153–63.

Assembly has used its extensive powers under Article 13 to broaden its role. The now routine practice of having the General Assembly submit multilateral treaty proposals to the community of states is an example of this.

Sovereign equality is also preserved in relation to the formal weighting of votes at the UN. (It is 'formal' because, obviously, the institution of the veto adds significant weight to the negative vote of a member of the P5.) The principle of one state, one vote has never been departed from in the procedure of a universal political organ. Article 18(2) of the Charter was adopted with little dispute.[128] In the decades immediately following the adoption of the Charter, a number of suggestions were made concerning the calibration of votes. The most politically weighty of these proposals came from John Foster Dulles, who argued for voting strength to be allocated on the basis of power.[129] Others asserted that voting privileges should correspond to financial contributions (along the lines of the International Monetary Fund and the World Bank) while another group worried about the democratic deficit in giving one vote to each state.[130] None of these proposals resulted in any modification of the sovereign equality principle as it applied to voting.

Finally, of course, there are the references to equality in the Charter itself. The equality of states was regarded as a basic principle of the new international organisation. Articles 2(1) and 78 make this explicit while Articles 1(2) and 55 indicate that promoting the equal rights of peoples is a purpose of the UN.[131] These articles clearly do not preclude organisational hierarchies but they do confirm that the UN continues to be based on both some idea of state sovereignty and an insistence that 'UN organs must also treat states equally'.[132]

---

[128] See a proposal from the Canadian Delegation that a category of 'middle powers' be recognised in the Charter: Ninic, *The Problem of Sovereignty*, 119.

[129] J. F. Dulles, *War and Peace*, 197, quoted in Ninic, *The Problem of Sovereignty*, 119.

[130] This time the representation of the citizens of Iceland and the United States was compared: see Romulo, first session of the GA, UNGAOR 1252, cited in Ninic, *The Problem of Sovereignty*, 120.

[131] There has been some debate about the precise meaning of 'peoples' in this regard. It seems unlikely that it was to apply to peoples in the decolonisation sense because self-determination was not regarded as a right in the Charter. However, the terms 'peoples' and 'states' are employed loosely in the Charter and it does not seem absurd to suggest that what Articles 1(2) and 55 represent are attempts to link sovereign equality to economic development and the promotion of human rights within states. For confirmation of this view, see Bentwich and Martin, *Commentary*, 7.

[132] Bleckmann, 'Article 2(1)', 78. Bleckmann goes on to suggest that sovereign equality also means that the UN 'must not infringe [state] sovereignty'. This hardly seems a plausible reading of the Charter now (see Article 2(7)) but in 1945 many states regarded the principle in this light.

Equality and hegemony revisited

In the end what was produced in San Francisco was a dialectical structure in which an attempt was made to satisfy the imperatives of hegemony and the requirements of equality. None of the views expressed at the beginning of this chapter is entirely accurate: Greig's because it overstates the weight of legalised hegemony; Goodrich's and Hambro's because they do the opposite; and Bleckmann's because he is wrong to suggest that hegemony can be consigned to some non-legal zone leaving a pristine area of equality-based legal regulation (and because the distinction between the political and legal features of the Charter is unsustainable).[133]

At San Francisco, the drafters of the Charter succeeded in accommodating equality and hegemony where the delegates at The Hague failed and in a manner not even attempted at Vienna. It is true that on the central question of Security Council privileges, the Great Powers could not be budged. Famously, the small powers were faced with the choice of a Charter with Great Power privilege or no Charter at all.[134] However, in other respects, the sovereign equality of states was bolstered by the Charter. The main plenary body, the General Assembly, became a principal egalitarian organ. Voting and representation was to be equal in the decision-making practices of this body. While the existence and constitution of the Security Council was a reflection of the hegemonic imperative in international affairs, even here it must be remembered that the Great Powers had only one vote each (albeit one capable of being exercised as a veto). The principle of weighted voting had been rejected as a breach of the norm of sovereign equality.[135]

Is the Charter, then, a reconciliation of the two principles? The Charter creates an international order in which the sovereign equality of

---

[133] Greig, *International Law*; Goodrich and Hambro, *Charter of the United Nations*; Bleckmann, 'Article 2(1)'.

[134] Fifth Meeting of Commission III, 163.

[135] Weighted voting did, of course, feature in the Bretton Woods Agreements. For a consideration of voting procedures at the International Monetary Fund and World Bank, see L. Sohn, 'Weighting of Votes in an International Assembly' (1944) 38 *American Political Science Review* 1192; J. Gold, *Voting and Decision in the International Monetary Fund: An Essay on the Law and Practice of the Fund*; W. Gainaris, 'Weighted Voting in the International Monetary Fund and the World Bank' (1990–1) 14 *Fordham International Law Journal* 910. See also the existence of plural voting at the International Labour Organisation, the International Atomic Energy Agency and the International Maritime Organisation.

all states was adapted to the prerogatives of the Great Powers.[136] It represents neither the vindication of sovereign equality (in spite of the references to the principle in Articles 2(1) and 55) nor its passing (despite Chapter VII and Article 25). Instead, sovereign equality needs to be understood as a raft of principles, some of which survive the creation of semi-centralised constitutional orders, others of which are severely compromised as a consequence. In the case of the Charter, a thin formal equality persists in, for example, the rules concerning the ICJ and the acceptance of the idea that the organisation 'in deciding on disputes between its members must act impartially, unmoved by considerations of power'.[137] What might be termed the existential equality of states is protected by a series of non-intervention provisions and by a general commitment to independent statehood and organisational pluralism.[138] Legislative equality, the equal power to make or influence international law, meanwhile, finds some measure of protection in the General Assembly's powers but is severely compromised in the governing principles of the Security Council.[139] Ultimately, the Charter enacts a weakened form of legal equality alongside a mildly constrained constitutional hegemony.[140]

---

[136] It is sophistic to argue that legalised hegemony is an expression of sovereign equality because sovereign states have contracted together to form an international organisation with legalised hegemony at its heart (this argument is described in Fassbender, *Security Council Reform*, 289). Perhaps hierarchy can be defended on voluntaristic grounds but only at the cost of saying anything meaningful about the way the Charter was created, the ways in which it actually operates and, in particular, the manner in which the whole collective security regime is premised on radical inequality.

[137] Bentwich and Martin, *Commentary*, 12.   [138] E.g. Articles 2(4), 2(7) and 2(1).

[139] I have given the word 'legislative' a liberal definition here. What I mean is that the General Assembly has played a critical role in the development of international law through custom and through its Sixth Committee and the International Law Commission. I realise that there is another sense in which it is clearly not a legislative body. Indeed, arguments have been made that the Security Council lacks direct law-making authority in the classic sense even though it can establish 'norms'. I find these arguments unpersuasive. See e.g. M. P. de Brichambaut, 'The Role of the United Nations Security Council in the International Legal System' in Byers, *Role of Law*, 269.

[140] Equality of consent, too, is diminished by the Charter's embrace of the majority idea. All UN organs decide either by simple majority or some form of special majority. Compare this to the League of Nations's preference for unanimity: Bentwich and Martin, *Commentary*, 11.

7   Holy Alliances: Verona 1822 and Kosovo 1999

Introduction

In each of the three moments of regime building discussed in the previous chapters, a tension between sovereign equality and legalised hegemony has been the mark of a foundational moment in the development of the international legal order. In the early nineteenth century, the Great Powers established the institution of legalised hegemony through the procedures and substantive law of the Congress of Vienna (Chapter 4). The Concert of Europe began as a 'usurpation' but ended by legitimising hegemony and endowing it with an institutional respectability it had hitherto lacked. The idea of legalised hegemony seemed to have, at least for the time being, and despite the exertions of some of the smaller powers, trumped the Westphalian principle of sovereign equality. Throughout the nineteenth century, public international lawyers wrestled with this new phenomenon. Some rejected hegemony as 'illegal' or 'political', others viewed it as a new constitutional norm. At the same time, in international legal practice, legalised hegemony, in the uncompromised form found at Vienna, was, by the late nineteenth century, giving way to a more participatory and egalitarian international legal order (Chapter 4). In particular, the newly admitted smaller states began agitating for greater representation in international institutions (Chapter 9). The Great Powers, however, were not disposed to give up too much of their authority.

This tension culminated in a moment of crisis at the Second Hague Peace Conference in 1907. At The Hague, the Great Powers continued to expect a special role in the system (not dissimilar to the one they enjoyed at Vienna) while some of the smaller powers lobbied for a form of 'extreme' sovereign equality (Chapter 5). This tension, reflecting in part the debate among the scholars of the late Victorian period, could not be resolved and led to the failure to create a new Permanent International Court of Justice. Extreme equality appeared to have prevailed at the cost of creating new judicial organs and this signalled to the next generation of scholars and statesmen that 'extreme sovereign equality' or the strong conception of sovereign equality could not coexist with a modern international law of institutions. The major institution building of the first half of the twentieth century, then, was premised on the need to build legalised hegemony into the international order while at the same time attempting to temper it with various constitutional constraints favouring the minor powers. This was the story of the San Francisco Conference and, to a lesser extent, the Versailles Peace Conference.

In Chapter 6, I dissected some of the tensions played out at the San Francisco Conference. In particular, I showed how the apparent contradiction between sovereign equality and legalised hegemony was managed at the Conference and in the text of the Charter itself. The overall picture presented was of a constitutional order configured around a founding text in which both hegemony and equality were brought into precarious systemic balance. I presented an image of the UN system as a hegemonic collective security order embedded in a, sometimes, egalitarian structure of principles and procedures. After 1945, there were no major modifications to this system. The United Nations scheme worked rather fitfully and the hegemons themselves built coalitions outside the UN order. However, these coalitions were directed at primarily political ends.[1] There was no attempt to usurp the collective security functions of the Security Council.[2] The Council, of course, did not function in the manner hoped for by its founders. It is notorious that the United Nations collective security regime foundered on rising East–West antagonisms. This was not something entirely unanticipated. Throughout the San Francisco Conference and before, there were those who suppressed their pessimistic instincts about the prospects for superpower relations and agreed to build an international order on the slim hopes

---

[1] Though these alliances were placed on a legal footing by treaty. See P. Malanczuk, *Akehurst's Modern Introduction to International Law*, 8th edn, 5. For a discussion of the difference between legal and political regimes, see Keal, *Unspoken Rules*.

[2] For example, Nato did not regard itself as having a right to intervene in areas outside its jurisdiction and the Warsaw Pact was similarly cautious in the scope of its interventionist counter-revolutionary policy. See Article 5, North Atlantic Treaty (1949) 34 UNTS 243; The Warsaw Security Pact Treaty (14 May 1955) at http://www.yale.edu/lawweb/avalon/intdip/soviet/warsaw.htm

of congenial Great Power relations.[3] It was not to be and throughout the long second phase (1947–87) in the existence of the UN security order (the first phase being the formalisation of the contours of that system at San Francisco), collective security was virtually moribund. The Military Staff Committee remained in abeyance and the international system was organised around spheres of influence (in the Western Hemisphere and in Europe) and spheres of competition (in Africa and Asia). This led to many collective interventions (by the OAS or by the Warsaw Pact) but only very few by the UN or in the name of the UN. The UN interventions that did occur (in the Congo and Korea) were anomalous both procedurally and substantively.[4]

I characterise these spheres of influence as political sub-systems rather than legal orders (see Chapter 2). Accordingly, I argue that the international legal structure designed and established at San Francisco (1945) gave way shortly thereafter to a series of regional, political sub-systems in the period 1948–87.[5] During what may prove to have been a brief interregnum between 1987 and 1998, the Security Council began to function as had been intended. The enforcement action against Iraq was in response to exactly the sort of transparent inter-state aggression by a middle power that the Charter drafters viewed as paradigmatic. This classic enforcement action was followed by a series of interventions that, while

---

[3] See, e.g. Churchill's view in the period prior to the San Francisco Conference (discussed in Chapter 9).

[4] See R. Higgins, *Problems and Process*, 254–66; T. Franck, *Fairness*, 224–42. The intervention in Korea was procedurally unusual because of the initial absence of the Soviet Union from the Security Council during some of its critical votes on the Korean question (e.g. Security Council Resolution of 25 June 1950), and because the General Assembly's activism, expressed in the *Uniting for Peace Resolution* (GA Res. 377 (V), 3 November 1950; GAOR, 5th Sess., Supp. 220 para. 10), enjoyed an insecure constitutional authority. The case of the Congo is just as peculiar. In this instance the UN arguably encouraged a secession in Katanga and was ultimately complicit in the removal of Patrice Lumumba, the Congolese Prime Minister who had requested the aid of the UN in the first place (see Linda Melvern, 'Dispatching Lumumba' (September 2001) 11 *New Left Review* 147–54).

[5] I do not mean to suggest that the United Nations was inactive during this period. In fact, of course, it carved out for itself a prominent peacekeeping role not envisaged by the UN Charter but legitimated by reference to Article 39, the principles and purposes of the UN Charter and an ICJ decision (*Certain Expenses of the United Nations* (1962) ICJ Rep., UN Doc. S/5653; (1964) 3 ILM 545). The possible dates for the commencement of the third period are 1987 (the year of the Security Council mandated ceasefire in the Iraq–Iran war), 1989 (the end of the cold war) or 1991 (the first full enforcement action authorised by the UN Security Council with the support of the P5). See, e.g. SC Res. 661, 6 August 1990, (1990) 29 ILM 1325; SC Res. 678, 29 November 1990, (1990) 29 ILM 1565; and SC Res. 598, 20 July 1987, (1987) 26 ILM 1479.

novel in substance (implicating as they did 'humanitarian intervention'), nonetheless remained, with one possible exception, within the bounds of the UN Charter.[6] So, the international security order, until the Kosovo intervention, had undergone three distinct phases: Legalised Hegemony Formalised (1945), Political Hegemony (1946–87) and Legalised Hegemony Realised (1987–98).

This chapter assesses the argument that the Kosovo intervention is an example of a new form of legalised hegemony; a moment of regime innovation in which the hegemons break out of the existing legal constraints and establish a new legal order along the lines of the Vienna Congress of 1815. It compares that argument with the view expressed by some of the main protagonists that the intervention in Kosovo was a unique one and not to be repeated, a deviation from the collective security system established in the UN Charter or, more typically, an enforcement action implicitly authorised under existing UN instruments.[7]

Chapter 7, then, concludes my reflections on the system of legalised hegemony/sovereign equality by considering whether the Kosovo intervention was a defection from the system of collective security embodied in the UN Charter and a portent of a new form of (regional) legalised hegemony. I want to compare this potential new hegemony both with the hegemony created at Vienna and with the defection from *that* order by the Holy Alliance in the post-Napoleonic period. I argue that this security action has created a debate not dissimilar to the one conducted throughout the nineteenth century in the international legal academy and that one possible outcome of this debate is a tolerance of the new hegemons. A second possibility is that this usurpation will be seen, not as a foundational constitutional moment, but, as was the case with the Holy Alliance, as an illegitimate 'unilateral' act.[8] So, this chapter assesses these two theses about the Kosovo intervention (I will

---

[6] The possible exception being the establishment of the safe havens in northern and southern Iraq (putatively) under Security Council Resolution 688 and the UK and US bombing raids on Iraq in 1998 and 2000 in support of these zones. These are portents of the more ambiguous fourth period discussed in this chapter. See, e.g. Nigel White and Robert Cryer, 'Unilateral Enforcement of Resolution 678: A Threat Too Far?' (1999) 29 *California Western International Law Journal* 243.

[7] These two positions seem incompatible but, in fact, they were commonly employed in tandem by officials justifying the Nato action. What they share is a refusal to countenance suggestions that the Kosovo intervention inaugurated a new system of international governance.

[8] While the Holy Alliance lost its legitimacy almost immediately, debate continued over the validity in law of the Quadruple Alliance formed at Vienna. See discussions at Chapter 4.

label them the *Verona thesis* and the *Vienna thesis*, after two sites of regime construction in the nineteenth century) and does so primarily through the study of legal scholarship and official statements arising out of the Kosovo crisis.[9] The purpose of this is to complete our story of institution building since 1815 and, in particular, to show how the institution of legalised hegemony might undergo modification in the twenty-first century and indicate the role international lawyers might play in supporting or discrediting that modification. There are a number of important legal debates that I either ignore or touch on only briefly.[10] For example, this is not an analysis of either the legality or morality or desirability of 'humanitarian intervention'.[11] Of course, when scholars seek to defend a norm of humanitarian intervention then that may feed into my arguments about legalised hegemony, too. However, I am less interested in evaluating the norm in its own terms.[12] This chapter is about the role

---

[9] 'Verona' refers to the meeting of the Congress of Great Powers at which there was a split between the Holy Alliance and the British over the nature and limits of intervention. We know, in retrospect, where the meeting of the Holy Alliance at Verona or the Naval Conference in London in 1908 fit in the stream of history. With Kosovo, the situation is murkier because of the inevitable absence of a long perspective.

[10] E.g. the lawfulness of the methods used by Nato in Kosovo (see W. J. Fenwick, 'Targeting and Proportionality During the NATO Bombing Campaign Against Yugoslavia' (2001) 12:3 EJIL 489) and the possible commission of war crimes by the protagonists in Kosovo (see, e.g. *Indictment of Milosevic* IT–99–37 at http://www.un.org/icty/ind-e.htm; P. Benvenuti, 'The ICTY Prosecutor and the Review of the NATO Bombing Campaign Against the Federal Republic of Yugoslavia' (2001) 12:3 EJIL 503).

[11] For a policy debate informed by a keen sense of the moral implications, see M. Ignatieff, 'War of Words' in *Virtual War*, 71–87. There are certainly good policy grounds for doubting the desirability of a doctrine of humanitarian intervention because of its capacity to degrade a more workable norm of international law (that of non-intervention), because its practitioners tend to act in bad faith (supporting mass killings in Central America, intervening 'for humanity' in Haiti), because it draws attention away from the prior (Western) 'interventions' in helping create an environment in which genocide is more likely, because it encourages a belief in military solutions to social problems and because there are many ways in which intervention could take place without the use of military force.

[12] I am not convinced that this debate can be resolved using the material of international law. International law could be employed to support a doctrine of humanitarian intervention in support of an ethnic group (perhaps involving a reference to pre-1945 customary practice or a purposive reading of the Charter). Or the opposite approach could be taken, this time disclosing a different common interest (e.g. state sovereignty). A legal method could then be used to buttress or support this interest (say, a textual reading of the Charter or a reference to post-1945 state practice). One response to the 'social complexity' of this dispute would be a decision in support of humanitarian intervention. Another might insist on the sanctity of state borders. These are legitimate responses but how should we decide which is to be preferred? See Simpson, 'The Situation on the International Legal Theory Front', 439.

arguments surrounding humanitarian intervention play in buttressing or undermining the development of a new hegemony and not about the doctrine of humanitarian intervention itself.[13]

Two theses about the Nato action in Kosovo

In assessing whether Kosovo can be viewed simply as an aberrant departure from the still-dominant norms of the international security order, or whether it heralds a new order altogether, I want to begin by discussing briefly the existing laws on the use of force found in the Charter and in customary international law.[14]

On 24 March 1999, Nato launched a series of air strikes against Serbian targets in Kosovo and in the rest of Serbia.[15] This was a response to reports that Serbian forces had provoked, through violence and threats of violence, an exodus of ethnic Albanians into adjoining Balkan states.[16] The bombing persisted for almost three months and ended when the Serbian Government agreed to allow the deployment of a UN civil and military presence in Kosovo.[17] This intervention by Nato constituted an armed attack by a group of member states against another member-state of the United Nations.[18] The United Nations Charter prohibits

---

[13] For recent views on humanitarian intervention see especially Nicholas Wheeler, *Saving Strangers: Humanitarian Intervention in International Society* and Anne Orford, 'Muscular Humanitarianism: Reading the Narratives of the New Interventionism' (1999) 10:4 EJIL 679. The most productive period, prior to this, followed the Israeli raid on Entebbe (not a humanitarian intervention in the strict sense) and the Tanzanian invasion of Uganda. See Ian Brownlie, 'Humanitarian Intervention' in J. Moore (ed.), *Law and Civil War in the Modern World*, 217–18; A. Verwey, 'Humanitarian Intervention under International Law' (1985) 32 *Netherlands International Law Review* 357; J. P. Fonteyne, 'The Customary International Law Doctrine of Humanitarian Intervention: Its Current Validity Under the UN Charter' (1994) 4 *California Western International Law Journal* 203.

[14] From now on the term 'Kosovo' is used to signify the intervention by Nato in Kosovo in 1999 as well as the term for the region in Serbia.

[15] Around 500 civilians were killed in this action. See *Human Rights Watch Report: Civilian Deaths in the NATO Air Campaign* Vol. 12, No. 1 (February 2000) at www.hrw.org/reports/2000/nato

[16] The bombing was prompted by concerns that President Milosevic would behave towards Kosovo much as he had towards, initially, Croatia and, for a longer period, Bosnia-Herzegovina. For a survey of Nato's involvement in the war in the Balkans see, T. Gazzini, 'NATO Coercive Military Activities in the Yugoslav Crisis (1992–9)' (2001) 12:3 EJIL 391–435. For a broader analysis, see Ignatieff, *Virtual War*.

[17] See Military-Technical Agreement, 9 June 1999; SC Res. 1244, 10 June 1999.

[18] For a discussion of Yugoslavia's status at the time see *Application for Review of Judgement* (2001) submitted by Yugoslavia in *Genocide Case* at http://www.icj-cij.org/icjwww/idocket/ibhy/ibhyframe.htm

the use of force by member states in their relations with one another (Article 2(4)).[19] There are two broad categories of exception to this general prohibition. Member states can use force either in self-defence (Article 51) or as authorised by the Security Council acting under its Chapter VII powers.[20] The right to self-defence encompasses both individual and collective self-defence but its exercise requires an armed attack against a state.[21] Similarly, enforcement measures under Chapter VII can be undertaken either by the Security Council itself, by a coalition of forces authorised by the Security Council or by a single member acting with Security Council authorisation.[22] Though these two exceptions are uncontroversial as categories, there is a great deal of debate about the specific content of the exceptions. It is unclear whether self-defence includes pre-emptive self-defence (sometimes referred to as anticipatory self-defence) or at what point the right to self-defence must cede sole legitimacy to collective security operations.[23] In the case of Security Council actions, there are frequently debates about *what* the Council has authorised in particular cases, and doubts remain over whether there are normative constraints on what the Council can do (Chapter 6).[24]

Alongside these categories is a series of putative exceptions that are controversial in themselves. These include humanitarian intervention, intervention in support of a people's right to self-determination and intervention to protect nationals abroad. Generally, interventions in the post-war era have been justified under a branch of the self-defence norm or by reference to some nexus with Chapter VII authorisation or under

---

[19] This includes action by regional organisations unless authorised under Chapter VIII. B. Simma, 'Nato, the UN and the Use of Force: Legal Aspects' (1999) 10:1 EJIL 1–22 at 3. See UN Charter, Article 53(1). The use of force by the two remaining non-member states is prohibited under customary international law.

[20] See UN Charter, Articles 39–42.

[21] See *Nicaragua Case (Merits)* (1986) ICJ Rep. 14; *Corfu Channel Case (Merits)* (1949) ICJ Rep. 4.

[22] The Security Council has never taken action under Article 42 because no armed forces agreements have been concluded as envisaged by Articles 43 to 50 and no active military staff committee has been established. All action under Chapter VII has been carried out by coalitions of like-minded states acting under general Security Council authorisation. See Higgins, *Problems and Process*, 263–6; Franck, *Fairness*, 298–305. It is generally accepted that the third permissive norm governing the use of force against enemy states under Articles 53 and 107 is defunct.

[23] See, e.g. Don Greig, 'Self-Defence and the Security Council: What Does Article 51 Require?' (1991) 40 ICLQ 366 and Higgins, *Problems and Process*, 260–2.

[24] On the question of interpretation see, e.g. debates about SC Res. 688 and, also, the extent to which SC Res. 678 and 687 provided authority for Anglo-American attacks on Iraq between 1999 and 2001. On the latter point see Franck, *Fairness* at 218–44. See also *Lockerbie Case* (Preliminary Phase).

one or more of the controversial exceptions listed above. The Kosovo intervention was no different.[25]

I want now to relate the cycle of condemnation and justification found in legal commentary and official statements, most of which employed the legal principles found above, to the question of legalised hegemony and, in particular, to the two theses I wish to compare in the remainder of this chapter. The Kosovo action represents a potentially revolutionary moment in the history of the international order and such a moment is likely to be viewed as both illegal usurpation and constitutional reno-vation. This was the case at Vienna, for example.[26] The arguments used by legal scholars reflect, in turn, this ambivalence about revolutionary moments in constitutional design.[27] And in the background to this de-bate is another debate, this time over whether the intervention was an exclusively political or moral action or whether it also had legal or institutional effects. This debate, too, harks back to the disagreements among scholars in the nineteenth century.[28]

The Verona thesis

After 1815, the Eastern powers (Austria, Prussia and Russia) engaged in a regional security effort, disparaged by the other Great Powers of the time, to promote a particular conception of international order.[29] This process reached a peak at Verona, the fourth of the post-Vienna meet-ings of the Concert.[30] The Conference at Verona, 'summoned to decide the fate of two worlds' (the old and the new), took place in 1822.[31] The conservative powers (and in the case of the proposed intervention in

---

[25] To the extent that self-defence arguments were used, it was on the basis that it would be absurd to allow a right of self-defence to states but not to peoples. See Ruth Wedgwood, 'NATO's Campaign in Yugoslavia' (1999) 93:4 AJIL 828.

[26] Chris Reus-Smit, *The Moral Purpose of the State: Culture, Social Identity and Institutional Rationality in International Relations*, chap. 4.

[27] In the following section, I have focused attention on a group of legal scholars writing in the symposium issues of the *American Journal of International Law* and *European Journal of International Law*, publications that might be expected to present the current thinking of the discipline on intervention and hegemony. I do not mean to suggest that these are the best or most precise or most ideologically attractive contributions to the debate. For another view of 'intervention' see Orford, 'Muscular Humanitarianism' and footnotes therein.

[28] See Chapter 4.   [29] See also Chapter 8.

[30] At Verona, the three Eastern powers (with the United Kingdom disapproving from the sidelines) agreed to support interventions in Spain and Italy in order to preserve absolutist governments from the threat of constitutionalism. See F. Mowat, *A History of European Diplomacy 1815–1914*, 39–41.

[31] Phillips, *Confederation of Europe*, 253.

Spain, France as well) intended to put into effect a theory of intervention (already partially realised at the Laibach Conference) whereby constitutional reform and revolution in other states would be met with military reaction and reactionary militancy by the Eastern powers (and, in certain circumstances, France). The idea was to insert 'a salutary fear into the revolutionists of all lands'.[32] This project was to be extended to the Western hemisphere, too, where a revolt against Europe had already resulted in the appearance of several new nations.

The early interventions by the Holy Alliance in Sicily and Piedmont (unwanted but also unopposed by the United Kingdom) were not to be repeated, however. There was a very hostile reaction to Verona on the part of the United Kingdom and the United States. Both Wellington and Canning reiterated the British opposition to meddling in the internal affairs of sovereign states. The problem of Bonapartism was regarded by the British as a problem of territorial aggrandisement and not internal revolution. Canning, in particular, was an advocate of sovereign equality. 'Our business', he said, 'is to preserve the peace of the world and therefore the independence of the several nations which compose it.'[33] The Americans, meanwhile, responded with the Monroe Doctrine, which concluded: 'It is impossible that the Allied Powers should extend their political system, to any portion of our continent, without endangering our peace and happiness.' In the end, the Holy Alliance was short-lived. The constitutionalists of South America and Spain could not be pacified and, ultimately, the conservative regimes of Europe were themselves overthrown by the revolutions of mid-nineteenth-century Europe.[34]

The Verona thesis, then, explains the Nato action as an aberration, a one-off action with limited consequences and little value as a legal precedent. The intervention in Kosovo, like that of the Holy Alliance, represents, according to this perspective, the fruits of a short-lived confluence of ideological affinities (Clinton's and Blair's in 1999; Tsar Alexander's and Metternich's in 1822), a paralysis among potentially obstructive hegemons (China and Russia in 1999; France and Britain in 1822) and an idiosyncratic mysticism among some of the major players (Tony Blair in

---

[32] *Ibid.*, 255.

[33] To Wellesley, 16 September 1823. In Stapelton's *George Canning and his Times: A Political Study*, i. 374 (quoted in *ibid.*, 260).

[34] 'Constitutionalists' is perhaps not quite the right word for the revolutionaries in South America. Most of them established dictatorships following the expulsion of the Spanish.

1999 and Tsar Alexander in 1822). This interventionist effort, embodied in the Holy Alliance, pursued through a sequence of meddlings and undone by the anti-interventionist pressures of the sovereign equality order, might possibly be a template for understanding Nato's intervention in Kosovo. There are certainly good reasons to suppose that Verona could be regarded as a precursor to Kosovo. First, in each case, Great Power interventionism was rationalised from the inside as the logical extension of the already existing international order. Second, the intervention, and the system underlying it, was viewed, from the outside (by, at least, some important actors) as a defection from the old order. Third, among the progenitors of these 'new' orders, there was a Kantian belief in the link between the internal conditions of states and their external behaviour. Fourth, there was a conviction that the moral imperatives of action, grounded in some universal normative order, could be sufficient to outweigh certain 'technical' objections to an interventionist policy.[35] The ultimate test for the Verona thesis's resonance in the Kosovo case lies in whether the new order generates enough opposition to ensure that it is as transient as the Holy Alliance proved (this latter condition represents the key (unknown) variable).

Let me take each of these in turn. The Eastern powers argued that the Holy Alliance was a natural consequence of the adherence of European powers to the Second Treaty of Paris. The pact formed against Napoleon was aimed at destroying the influence of revolutionary politics on international relations. The powers of the Holy Alliance believed that the logical consequence of this war aim was the future suppression of revolutionary practices within domestic contexts. Why fight a future Napoleon on the battlefields of Europe when he could be destroyed *prior* to taking power in one of the states of Europe? Thus, the rhetoric arising out of the Holy Alliance was designed to mollify the other powers and demonstrate the link between the system brought into existence at Vienna and the specific aims of the Alliance itself.[36]

---

[35] This set of justifications contradicts those in the first category. The fact is, though, that both were used in tandem by the Holy Alliance powers in 1822 and by Nato and its supporters in 1999 and 2000.

[36] As Tsar Alexander put it in a letter to his envoy in England, 'The sole and exclusive object of the Alliance can only be the maintenance of peace and the Union of all the moral interests of the people . . .' (quoted in Phillips, *Confederation of Europe*, 143). Phillips, himself, remarked that there was nothing sinister about the Holy Alliance and that its aims were entirely benign and congruent with the Vienna settlement (143).

The Nato powers, too, were at pains to demonstrate that the Kosovo intervention created no new precedents in international law.[37] The member states of Nato employed a straightforward sequence of justifications based principally on humanitarian intervention (derived from a contextual reading of the Charter) and the presence of existing UN Resolutions implicitly authorising the intervention.[38] The British government, for example, spoke of 'exceptional measures' necessary in 'extreme [humanitarian] circumstances' even without express authorisation but in support of the purposes of the Charter.[39] In statements before the International Court of Justice, in the provisional measures phase of *The Legality of Use of Force Case* (*Yugoslavia* v. *United Kingdom*), the United Kingdom emphasised the fact that the Nato action was directed exclusively at the prevention of 'the systematic and intolerable violence being waged against an entire population'.[40] All this was related to an already existing body of law, according to the United Kingdom (which had gradually softened its position on humanitarian intervention throughout the 1990s).[41]

[37] They have argued either that the Security Council did authorise the action in advance under SC Res. 1160 (31 March 1998) and SC Res. 1199 (23 September 1998) or that the bombing was given ex post facto legitimacy by the UN's willingness to create a protectorate over Kosovo after the successful expulsion of the Serbs (SC Res. 1244 (10 June 1999)). Secretary-General Solano came close to such an argument when he said: 'The Allies believe that in the particular circumstances with respect to the present crisis in Kosovo, as described in SC Res. 1199, there are legitimate grounds for the Alliance to threaten and, if necessary, to use force' (quoted in Simma, 'Nato, UN and the Use of Force', 7). The circumstances referred to include the FRY's failure to comply with SC Ress. 1160 and 1199. See discussion and critique of this position in Simma, 'Nato, UN and the Use of Force', 11.

[38] Other (insubstantial) arguments might have been employed, e.g. self-defence on behalf of either a nascent state or a self-determination people or of Nato itself (see Article 5, *North Atlantic Treaty*).

[39] See *Hansard*, HC, vol. 328, cols. 616–17, 25 March 1999. Tony Blair also referred to Security Council resolutions in asserting the legitimacy of the threatened use of force. See *Hansard*, HC, vol. 328, cols. 168–9, 23 March 1999.

[40] UK Attorney-General John Morris, Oral Pleadings, Verbatim Record (uncorrected) para 16, *Legality of the Use of Force* (*Yugoslavia* v. *United Kingdom*) CR 99/23 at http://www.icj-cij.org/icjwww/idocket/iyuk/iyukframe.htm

[41] For a point of comparison, see the *United Kingdom Statement on Humanitarian Intervention*, UK Foreign Policy Doc. 148, UKMIL, 1986, (1986) 57 BYIL, 614. Note that Keith Vaz, the Secretary of State for Foreign and Commonwealth Affairs, denied in 1999 that this was a statement of government policy, stating: 'FCO Policy Document No.148 was a paper prepared by the FCO Policy Planning staff in July 1984 as a basis for discussion. It was not a statement of government policy. As we have stated on many occasions, we are clear that the Nato action in Kosovo was justified in the light of overwhelming humanitarian need' (*Hansard*, HC, vol. 339, col. 18w, 22 November 1999).

United States officials referred to a humanitarian crisis that threatened peace and security and drew support from, 'the resolutions of the Security Council, which have determined that the actions of the Federal Republic of Yugoslavia constitute a threat to peace and security in the region and, pursuant to Chapter VII of the Charter, demanded a halt to such actions'.[42] Nato's former Secretary-General, Javier Solano, justified Operation Allied Force on grounds of humanity ('not to have acted would have meant that the Atlantic community legitimised ethnic cleansing in its immediate neighbourhood'), and because the mass influx of refugees caused by President Milosevic's actions threatened the security of Europe.[43]

Of all Nato member governments, the Belgian government has sought to justify the action in the most forthright and explicit manner. The Belgians, in submissions before the World Court, relied heavily on the existence of several UN Security Council resolutions 'authorising the intervention'.[44] According to the Belgians, Security Council resolutions 1160, 1199 and 1203, 'provide[d] an unchallengeable basis for the armed intervention'. However, the Belgian submissions also invoked the doctrine of humanitarian intervention in cases of humanitarian catastrophes, arguing that states have a right of intervention in order to protect norms with the status of *jus cogens*.[45] Going further, the Belgians suggest that such force can be used to '*prevent* a humanitarian catastrophe' (my italics) and is justified by the doctrine of necessity embodied in Article 33 of the ILC's Draft Articles on State Responsibility.[46] These arguments, and countless others, represent an effort to position the intervention in the

---

[42] Mr David Andrews, State Department Legal Adviser, Oral Pleadings, Verbatim Record (uncorrected) para 1.7, *Legality of the Use of Force (Yugoslavia v. United Kingdom)* CR 99/24 at http://www.icj-cij.org/icjwww/idocket/iyuk/iyukframe.htm

[43] Simma, 'NATO, UN and the Use of Force', 117, 118. This was a way of referring back to the creation of safe havens in northern Iraq under the same principles. See SC Res. 688.

[44] *Legality of Use of Force*, pleadings at 99/15.

[45] *Ibid.* at CR 99/26. See also CR 99/15, 16–17 (arguing that humanitarian intervention was a principle compatible with the UN Charter, Article 2(4)).

[46] Finally, Belgium argued that there are a series of precedents supporting this use of force (Vietnam in Cambodia and West African forces in Sierra Leone and Liberia) and that humanitarian intervention does not imperil Article 2(4) of the Charter because it has no effect on the territorial integrity and political independence of a state. The Belgians also argued for a new norm of international law allowing states to intervene in support of international norms making unlawful the violent repression of minorities (Belgian Pleadings, at CR 99/15).

existing legal framework.[47] The Holy Alliance and Nato, then, share an inclination to justify what, on the face of it might seem a wholly novel procedure, under a set of principles already extant in the international legal order.

In 1822 and 1999, though, there were states outside the Holy Alliance and Nato respectively, as well as scholars, who simply regarded the new interventionism as unlawful. In the case of 1999, the likes of China and Russia condemned the intervention as a breach of the convention of Great Power consensus.[48] The Russians submitted a draft resolution, supported by the Chinese, demanding that air operations cease.[49] And while the Nato powers presented the intervention as an action in further-ance of the aims of the UN Charter and specific UN resolutions, this was not widely accepted by legal commentators or by other states.[50] These commentators regarded the resolutions preceding the intervention as non-committal and lacking in express authorisation. Resolution 1244, meanwhile, was described as producing a, 'happy ending . . . notwith-standing an inextricable (*sic*), contradictory plot'.[51] Some political ana-lysts, too, viewed the action as a clear breach in the existing structure of legalised hegemony.[52] The International Court of Justice, too, in an *obiter*

---

[47] This obsession with maintaining a link to existing practices is seen in the references of various resolutions to Yugoslavia's territorial integrity (in SC Res. 1160 the sovereignty and territorial integrity of Yugoslavia is affirmed in operative para. 5). But this territorial integrity has been subject to renegotiation depending on subsequent events, e.g. SC Res. 713 (25 September 1991) (emphasising territorial integrity of Yugoslavia but imposing certain burdens on the state). Other efforts were made, e.g. there was the argument that the failed Russian resolution, condemning the Nato action, represented a de facto legitimation of the Nato assault on Kosovo. This would require either an imaginative textual reading of the Charter (or a new norm in which majority voting invested an action with legitimacy). The plausibility of these suggestions is not at issue here. What is significant was the length advocates of the bombing went to in order to tie the intervention to the existing framework of international law.

[48] See, e.g. Security Council Statement S/PV/3937, 24 October 1998 at 12 (for Russian doubts about legality of Nato threats) and at 14 (for Chinese concerns).

[49] Draft Russian resolution at S/1999/328.

[50] See Statement of the Movement of the Non-Aligned Countries, 9 April 1999, S/1999/451, Annex; Declaration of the Inter-Parliamentary Assembly of the Commonwealth of Independent States, 3 April 1999, S/1999/461; Communiqué of the Rio Group of Latin American States, 25 March 1999, S1999/347, Annex. Quoted in Gazzini, 'Coercive Activities', fn. 141.

[51] Peter Hipold, 'Humanitarian Intervention: Is There a Need for a Legal Reappraisal?' (2001) 12:3 EJIL 437 at 441.

[52] It was Nato's willingness to use force without achieving 'Great Power consensus' that caused this break with the past. See Robert Skidelsky, 'War of Words' in Ignatieff, *Virtual War*, 82. Skidelsky calls himself a Westphalian but he is really 'Viennese',

dictum, showed a lack of enthusiasm for Nato's action, declaring that it was 'profoundly concerned with the use of force in Yugoslavia'.[53]

The British and the Americans had displayed a similar concern about the ambitions of the Holy Alliance 180 years before. The British, in particular, were fretful about the possible consequences of universalising the strategies of the Alliance. Castlereagh had no time for the interventionist policies of the Eastern powers, regarding them as illegitimate departures from the legalised hegemony of the Vienna Congress. The Congress and the resultant treaties had been designed to prevent a repeat of Napoleonic imperialism in Europe. Like the drafters of the UN Charter in San Francisco, the British, at Vienna, believed they were constructing a post-war system primarily designed to prevent inter-state aggression. It had not been their intention to mould an international system in which the wrong domestic politics might leave a state open to intervention by the 'international community' (at that time, the Concert of Europe). The American response was to warn the Alliance against applying its interventionist strategies in the Western hemisphere.[54] There was little doubt that the British, the Americans and, at least at first, the French, regarded the Alliance as an illegitimate defection from the existing security framework. Like the Russians and Chinese in 1999, they feared that the new interventionism might precipitate a breakdown in that order established with such effort in 1815 and might irreparably harm the European commitment to an important vestige of sovereign equality (non-intervention) and a more limited or constrained form of legalised hegemony (generated at the Congress of Vienna).

The British reluctance to endorse the manoeuvrings of the Holy Alliance was partly a product of its own conservatism (in this case a tendency to support the status quo) in international affairs and liberalism domestically. In the early 1800s, the liberal temper of the British produced, in domestic politics, a faith in Parliamentary institutions and was projected onto the international stage as a preference for the sovereign equality and free choice of nation states. Theirs was a liberalism with a substantive and procedural dimension. The Holy Alliance, on the other hand, was founded on the belief that the internal politics of the state determined the behaviour of that state towards its neighbours.

---

supporting a legitimised form of hegemony rather than a principle of sovereign equality.

[53] See *Legality of Use of Force (Yugoslavia v. Belgium)* (1999) ICJ Rep. para. 17.

[54] In this way, the Holy Alliance led directly to the Cuban Missile Crisis via the Monroe Doctrine.

The Alliance, then, wedded a Kantian belief in the relevance of domestic state orientations to a reactionary substantive politics. The most infamous early example of this vigorous conservatism was the Carlsbad Decrees, which were enacted by the German principalities and provided for a repressive regime of control over universities and private organisations. At Troppau and Laibach, this idea was extended to foreign governments. At Troppau in 1820, the Holy Alliance powers agreed to quash any constitutional innovations 'dangerous to the tranquillity of neighbours', and at Laibach, the constitution of Naples was annulled as a precursor to intervention by the Austrians against the constitutionalists. The intention of the signatories to the Holy Alliance, then, was to create 'a regular European directory for keeping the states of Europe in a fixed political system'.[55] This was to be done by ensuring that all the states of Europe subscribed to Christian principles. This adherence was regarded as purely formal by many of these signatories, and the British, who agreed to conform to these principles, found it difficult to take the Holy Alliance seriously at first.[56] Troppau and Verona, though, proved that the Tsar was very serious in his desire to 'confirm the contracting sovereigns in the principles of political and social conservatism'.[57]

It is not entirely clear to what extent the Nato action was inspired by a similar belief in the relationship of domestic politics to international behaviour.[58] In recent times, the view that domestic political orientation determines the behaviour of states at the international level has certainly been ubiquitous among influential academics and policy makers.[59] More specifically, this now takes the form of a belief in some sort of link between the absence of democracy, the presence of human rights violations and the threat to peace and security. If realism was the handmaiden to Western foreign policy in the immediate post-war era, then theories of democratic governance promise to play that role in contemporary international relations.

In the case of Yugoslavia, it became an article of faith among Western policy-makers that the lack of democracy was a primary cause of Balkan

---

[55] Mowat, *History of European Diplomacy*, 32.
[56] Nicolson, *Congress of Vienna*, 250.   [57] *Ibid.*, 151.
[58] Unlike the Holy Alliance's, the Nato action was taken in pursuit of liberal-humanitarian values.
[59] The literature is voluminous and some of it has taken the form of a disagreement among political scientists about how to interpret data. The accepted classics now seem to be Michael Doyle's pair of articles for *Philosophy and Public Affairs*, 'Kant, Liberal Legacies and Foreign Affairs' (nos. 1 and 2) (1983) 12:3 *Philosophy and Public Affairs* 205–35 and 12:4, 323–53. See, too, Michael Doyle, 'Liberalism and World Politics' (1986) 80:4 *American Political Science Review* 1151–69.

strife. Security Council Resolution 1160 emphasised that 'the way to defeat violence and terrorism in Kosovo is for the authorities in Belgrade to offer the Kosovar Albanian community a genuine political process'.[60] The Nato intervention was aimed at securing peace, not simply by ending human rights violations in Kosovo, but, it was hoped, by precipitating a constitutional crisis in Serbia, the result of which would be the removal of Milosevic and his associates, and the introduction of Western-style democracy in Serbia and Kosovo. The idea was to excise the cancer of authoritarianism from Europe. To fail to take action would have put 'the whole value system on which our policies were built' in jeopardy.[61] Security Council Resolution 1160 made this explicit in a paragraph stating that 'concrete progress to resolve the serious political and human rights issues in Kosovo will improve the international position of the Federal Republic of Yugoslavia and prospects for normalization of its international relationships and *full participation in international institutions*'.[62] This link between democracy and peace, and between constitutionalism at the municipal level and participation at the international level, was reinforced in a variety of policy statements before and after the intervention.[63]

The interventions of 1999 and 1818–22 both then shared a basis in the conviction that internal politics, to some extent, determined international behaviour. This conviction led, in turn, to a belief that the promotion of certain values within the international order was to be (sometimes) preferred to maintaining the integrity of the system. The

---

[60] Para. 3.

[61] Simma, 'Nato, the UN Charter and the Use of Force', 118. Solano, on the other hand, adopted the Simma position in arguing that actions in support of this value system could not 'create new international law'. The action had been 'an exception to the rule' (118). See, too, Javier Solano, 'NATO's Success in Kosovo' (1999) 76:8 *Foreign Affairs* 114–20.

[62] Para. 18, italics mine.

[63] See *Statement of North Atlantic Council* (NATO), 12 April 1999, 'NATO's military action against the FRY supports the political aims of the international community: a peaceful, multi-ethnic and democratic Kosovo . . .', at http://www.nato.int/kosovo/repo2000/aims.htm. See, too, George Robertson, 'Kosovo: One Year On: Achievement and Challenge', 21 March 2000 (stating: 'NATO will remain firm in its resolve to pursue the humanitarian and democratic objectives we all share' at http://www.nato.int/kosovo/repo2000/necessa.htm). See, too, *Statement on Kosovo*, issued by the Heads of State and Government, North Atlantic Council, Washington, DC 23 and 24 April 1999 ('NATO's military action against the Federal Republic of Yugoslavia (FRY) supports the political aims of the international community, which were reaffirmed in recent statements by the UN Secretary-General and the European Union: a peaceful, multi-ethnic and democratic Kosovo'), NATO Press Release SI (99) 62, 23 April 1999. Para. 16 insists that the democratisation of Serbia is a prerequisite to peace in the Balkans.

Holy Alliance was, as the name suggests, an evangelical pact designed to promote a particular version of the good life and buttressed by certain non-negotiable moral beliefs. The Preamble spoke of an international system to be conducted according to the 'sublime truths of the Christian religion'.[64] The resulting policies were grounded in specific ideological commitments (albeit that they were said to be compatible with existing structures of international governance). The Tsar, for example, believed that his massive army ought to be employed in the task of upholding morality whether in Piedmont or Spain.[65] He envisaged it acting as a sort of European police force directed at precisely these ends.[66] Metternich employed language made familiar once again in the West when he spoke of the conflict between civilisation (in 1820, this meant monarchy and absolutism) and evil (democracy, reform, liberalism).[67]

In the Kosovo war, Tony Blair provided much of the pseudo-religious rhetoric designed to seal support for the intervention.[68] When asked whether there was a legal obligation to intervene, Tony Lloyd, the Minister of State for the Foreign and Commonwealth Office, replied: 'A moral obligation'.[69] As Michael Mandlebaum put it: 'The putative doctrine of humanitarian intervention [concerned] the use of force on behalf of universal values rather than narrow national interest. . . .'[70] Bill Clinton confirmed this by saying, 'we need a Europe that shares our values'.[71] This rhapsodic, sentimental style was taking an increasing hold over the public pronouncements of Western leaders.

Academic commentators, too, began to agonise over the distinction between moral imperatives writ global and global rules of intercourse writ legal. Bruno Simma, in one of the first major articles on Kosovo to appear, accepted that Nato action would be illegal as a non-justifiable

---

[64] Mowat, *History of European Diplomacy*, 25.

[65] As Nicolson put it, the Tsar had begun to invoke the assistance of the supernatural in his policy-making. Nicolson, *Congress of Vienna*, 247.

[66] Phillips, *Confederation of Europe*, 255. Phillips describes this as 'a great Republic of Christian states' (142).

[67] C. Metternich, *Memoirs*, 483, 485.

[68] This rhetorical style and moral sensibility have been more fully realised in a series of major policy statements following the war in Afghanistan. See, e.g. 'Let us reorder this world around us . . . only the moral power of a world acting as a community can', Tony Blair, Speech to Labour Party Conference, Brighton, 2 October 2001.

[69] *Hansard*, HC, vol. 328, col. 543, 25 March 1999.

[70] See M. Mandlebaum, 'A Perfect Failure: NATO's War Against Yugoslavia' (1999) 78:5 *Foreign Affairs*, 5: 'NATO waged the war for its values not for its interests'.

[71] Robert Jackson, *The Global Covenant*, 281.

breach of Article 2(4).[72] However, Simma's view was that while the Nato action was illegal, only a thin red line separated the lawful from the unlawful in this case. This left lawyers and policy-makers with a 'terrible dilemma' – do they choose the technically unlawful over the morally imperative? For Simma, the answer was clear. Morality was to prevail. There was, of course, a contradiction in some of these arguments. On the one hand, Nato and its supporters sought to show how closely-tied the action was to the UN Charter.[73] On the other, they wanted to underplay its implications for the future. The division between law and morality was one method by which commentators tried to do this. The 'Oppenheim' approach to sovereign equality/legalised hegemony was also employed by some writers who, in discussing Kosovo, provided a radical separation of moral and political justification on the one hand and legal justification on the other.[74] So, instead of presenting a new norm of international law or deriving legality from existing instruments, these scholars argued for a move from formalism to moral reasoning. Simma wished to minimise the 'precedential significance' of the Nato action in order that it not become a 'general policy'.[75] The point was repeated by the German Foreign Minister, Kinkel, when he said: 'The decision of Nato must not become a precedent.'[76]

The thrust of Simma's article, then, was to demonstrate that no new norm has been created but that instead Nato action represents a one-off use of force justifiable on non-legal grounds but not to be repeated.[77]

---

[72] Simma, 'Nato, the UN and the Use of Force', 1 (Simma was writing prior to the intervention).

[73] One argument in this mode was that in cases where the Security Council is paralysed by the veto it may be permissible for collectives of states to take enforcement action providing that action furthers the purposes and principles of the organisation.

[74] For a discussion of Oppenheim, see Chapter 4.

[75] Simma, 'Nato, the UN and the Use of Force', 1.

[76] Quoted in Simma, 'Nato, the UN and the Use of Force', 13. The problem with this argument is that law and politics cannot be incubated in this way. The precedential value of the Nato action can be minimised but not obliterated. To argue that those illegal actions, 'close to legality', are justifiable in concrete cases under a humanitarian necessity principle is either to state a rule with precedential value or to maintain an unsatisfactory separation between 'justification' and law. Law, in international affairs, though, *is* the realm of justification. For a wider discussion see S. Schieder, 'Pragmatism as a Path towards a Discursive and Open Theory of International Law' (2000) 11:3 EJIL 663.

[77] Though even here there is room for confusion. Simma remarks that the Nato action is as 'a matter of principle' a breach of law but that any '*legal* judgement' will be influenced by an assessment of the balance between 'illegality' and the 'circumstances of a concrete case' (Simma, 'Nato, the UN and the Use of Force', 6).

In line with the other writers he wanted to draw a line (borrowed from Norberto Bobbio) between substantive legality and formal legality.[78] The Kosovo intervention offended only the latter because it was an action 'in accordance with some of the most fundamental principles of international humanitarian law and of human rights'.[79]

Other writers referred to the concept of necessity; a pseudo-legal idea that depended on some moral evaluation of emergency in order to supplement existing law on the use of force.[80] A great many more found themselves unable to view the Nato action as either morally wrong or legally correct.[81] Peter Hipold proposed an awkward rule whereby the law of non-intervention remained intact but future humanitarian intervention might be regarded as legitimate or acceptable.[82] Others marshalled the various human rights instruments established since the war to argue that 'it cannot be *right* (my italics) to tolerate acts which violate widely supported legal norms just because the Charter does not explicitly provide for military action in such circumstances. . . .'[83] The Kosovo Commission, an independent body vested with the task of considering, among other questions, the legality of the Nato intervention, spoke of situating the analysis somewhere between an extension of international law and an emerging international moral consensus.[84] This moral consensus could not, yet, create any precedents but 'the moral imperative' of rescuing oppressed people had to prevail over 'legalistic' arguments and

---

[78] This distinction is unsatisfactory and glib. The UN Charter is the embodiment of certain substantive values. To dismiss it as formal (W. Michael Reisman, 'Unilateral Action and the Transformations of the World Constitutive Process' (2000) 11:1 EJIL 3–18. P. M Dupuy, 'The Place and Role of Unilateralism in Contemporary International Law' (2000) 11:1 EJIL 19–29) is to miss this aspect of the Charter. Conversely, the move to substance is accompanied by numerous formal safeguards (see Cassese, 'A Follow-up: Forcible Humanitarian Countermeasures and Opinio Necessitatis' (1999) 10:4 EJIL 791–800). There is no escape from some degree of formalism in this regard.

[79] Dupuy, 'Unilateralism', 27.

[80] Pseudo-legal in the sense that it was broader than the idea of necessity laid out in general international law. See, e.g. *The Caroline Case* 29 BFSP 1137–8; (1840–1) 30 BFSP 195–6; 2001 *ILC Draft Articles on State Responsibility*, Article 25. Wedgwood, 'NATO's Campaign in Yugoslavia', 833.

[81] One international relations scholar offered the rather muddled thought that 'the legitimacy and legality' of prior UN resolutions was not enough to 'override the fundamental non-intervention norm of international law' (Jackson, *Global Covenant*, 286).

[82] Hipold, 'Humanitarian Intervention', 266–7.

[83] Adam Roberts, 'NATO's "Humanitarian War" over Kosovo', *Survival* (Autumn 1999), 106–7.

[84] International Independent Commission on Kosovo Report at http://www.kosovocommission.org/.

technical 'niceties'.[85] The UK's Select Committee on Foreign Affairs also emphasised the moral issues, concluding its reflections on the ethics of the invasion with the following: 'We conclude that Nato's military action, if of dubious legality in the current state of international law, was justified on moral grounds.'[86]

In one sense, and as with the Gulf War in 1991, the newness of the new world order was, for some purposes, downplayed. Both the coalition governments in 1991 and the Nato states in 1999 emphasised the link between the particular action being undertaken and the existing complex of constitutional rules in the international system. But this concern can be contrasted with another rhetorical tendency; one that accentuated the novelty of such actions in the name of a new human rights order or as part of a process of spreading democracy or in furtherance of some supervening morality.[87] Nato's 'muscular humanitarianism',[88] then, resembled the Holy Alliance in its anti-pluralism, its interventionism, its foundation in moral truth and its apparent defection from an existing political order (but vigorous claim that it was the logical extension of that order).

Will it also resemble the Alliance in its transience? The weight of academic opinion seems finely balanced on the whole. The perceived move to unilateralism has been condemned by a number of commentators. This reluctance to endorse action not explicitly authorised by the UN can be traced back to the response to the US/UK attacks on Iraq both after the Gulf War in 1993 and, much later, in the period 1999–2000.[89] Even the UK Parliament's own Select Committee on Foreign Affairs concluded that '*Operation Allied Force* was contrary to the specific terms of what might be termed the basic law of the international community – the UN Charter, although this might have been avoided if the Allies had attempted to use the Uniting for Peace procedures.'[90] On the other hand,

---

[85] *Ibid.*, para. 176.   [86] *Ibid.*, para. 138.

[87] And this, in turn, is reminiscent of arguments made by realists that (a wholly different set of) moral prescriptions should outweigh any recourse to international law arguments in assessing foreign policy options. The *inter arma silent leges* argument was put by Dean Acheson during the Cuban Missile Crisis. See Chapter 12. See, too, Abram Chayes, *The Cuban Missile Crisis*, i.

[88] A. Orford, 'Muscular Humanitarianism: Reading the Narratives of the New Interventionism' (1999) 10:4 EJIL 679.

[89] See, e.g. White and Cryer, *Unilateral Enforcement*, 243; Christine Gray, 'After the Cease-Fire: Iraq, the Security Council and the Use of Force' (1994) 65 BYIL 135.

[90] United Kingdom Select Committee on Foreign Affairs, Fourth Report, (2000) at http://www.publications.parliament.uk/pa/cm199900/ cmselect/cmfaff/28/2802.htm, para. 128.

there was a large group of international lawyers who supported the intervention. These lawyers were divided between those who regarded the action as legal and those, in the majority, who believed it possessed some form of legitimacy (Simma). Most of these lawyers, though, as I have indicated, tied the legality or legitimacy of the intervention to a complex of existing norms within the international order. I will return to this question again in the conclusion.

Meanwhile, in the following section, I want to consider the counterthesis that Kosovo represents a seismic transformation in world order comparable to the Vienna settlement itself. Here, I focus on the view that the Nato action was neither embedded in the network of pre-existing norms nor justifiable as some morally imperative departure from these norms but was, instead, part of the constitution of a new normative system.

The Vienna thesis

The Vienna thesis argues that the Nato intervention is part of a departure from the Charter model of collective security (and centralised hegemony) and its replacement with a new (regional) legalised hegemony. The early outlines of this new order can be found in British and US unilateralism in Iraq after the Gulf War and in the Nato action in Bosnia. If this thesis is correct, it represents something of a paradox because it may appear in retrospect that the United Nations collective security system has been fatally undermined at the moment of its apotheosis.[91]

At the Congress of Vienna, the Great Powers established a new international regime grounded in the divine right of those powers to rule the international system.[92] This regime persisted formally for half a century but the legalised hegemony that was its basis became a permanent part

---

[91] See Stanley Hoffman, 'Thoughts on the UN at 50' (1995) 6:3 EJIL 317–24 at 317. Simma notes that from 1990 to 1997, Chapter VII was invoked no less than 112 times. The Security Council then is 'functioning in precisely the manner envisaged in 1945' (16). In fact, I trace the roots of the Kosovo action to the increasing assertiveness of the 'West' throughout the 1990s following the initial action taken against Iraq. One would not want to overstate the multilateralism of the original action against Iraq under SC Res. 678 (Chinkin describes it as 'pseudo-multilateralism'. See Christine Chinkin, 'The State that Acts Alone: Bully, Good Samaritan or Iconoclast' (2000) 11:1 EJIL 39). It was very much US-dominated and led in substance but there seems little doubt that it was multilateral in form. See (1992) 63 BYIL 824, 827. See, too, Georges Abi-Saab, 'Whither the International Community?', (1998) 9 EJIL 264 for an optimistic view concerning the functioning of the UN security order.

[92] See, for longer discussion, Chapter 4.

of the international order.[93] If the Kosovo intervention is to be viewed as establishing a new order along these lines then several conditions must be met. First, there must be a realistic possibility of converting the dominance of certain powers within the system into a permanent institutional feature of that system. Second, there would be support for a normatively significant reorientation among the Great Powers (in favour, say, of humanitarianism and away from, say, existential equality). Combined with this would be the presence of some legitimating principle that would, in turn, allow this order to flourish for a substantial period.

The Vienna thesis, then, holds that the Nato action is symptomatic of an incomplete 'normative shift' and institutional adjustment from Charter-based hegemony to regional hegemony.[94] In this first section, I explore the arguments that there is a new institutional framework or a new regional regime. In the second section, I consider the question of normative change.

The diffidence of the Nato powers themselves in proclaiming a new imperial norm of intervention and legalised hegemony has not dampened the enthusiasm of some commentators for (yet another) new world order and it is at least plausible to argue that Kosovo represents a shift from one form of legalised hegemony ('Charter hegemony') to another (the dominance of a small elite of states outside the Charter). The most obvious implication of this thesis is that the United Nations would no longer play the central role in maintaining security it had filled in the decade prior to Kosovo.

There are signs of this process already afoot. The United States, keen to avoid the charge that it is, in Huntingdon's phrase, a 'rogue superpower', has begun co-opting regional organisations into the legitimising role once filled by the UN.[95] At the same time, the United Nations has been downgraded after its 'failures' in Rwanda and Somalia. It seems the failures of multilateralism can be blamed on the UN and the successes of

---

[93] There are varying opinions on how long the Concert persisted. It is undeniably true that a major war was averted for forty years and a general peace was maintained until well into the twentieth century. See Nicolson, *Congress of Vienna*, 243.

[94] The phrase 'normative shift' is Coral Bell's (paper delivered at Research School of Pacific and Asian Studies, ANU, International Relations Seminar 1999, on file with author).

[95] This regionalism was much discussed in policy circles after the Kosovo war, with suggestions being made that even OPEC could solve security issues in Asia. See M. Hirsch, 'The Fall Guy? Washington's Self-Defeating Assault on the United Nations', *Foreign Affairs* (November/December 1999), 4–5.

regionalism attributed to the lack of UN involvement.[96] Michael Hirsch, for example, has spoken of the UN's marginalisation in relation to Nato and, in particular, the United States.[97] This process of marginalisation was foreshadowed in the war in Bosnia where the UN was increasingly sidelined as the war progressed. By 1995 and the advent of Operation Deliberate Force, one commentator, after surveying in detail the relations between the Security Council and Nato in that period, described the 'intentional and complete exclusion of the Security Council from the decision-making process'.[98] This, then, perhaps began the era of collective humanitarian intervention outside the structure of the United Nations.[99]

Official statements around the time of the Kosovo intervention tend to mirror this attitude. Strobe Talbott, Deputy Secretary of State in the Clinton Administration, had said at the beginning of the crisis that 'we must be careful not to subordinate Nato to any other international body or compromise the integrity of its command structure'.[100] Kosovo, then, appears to mark the reinvigoration of Nato as an active self-defence regime.[101] Indeed, the organisation exceeded its original mandate in both Kosovo and Bosnia.[102] The Kosovo action, itself, has emboldened advocates of regionalism and defection. The move from Security Council action in Iraq, to unilateral action in Iraq and under Dayton but with some UN authorisation to full-blown unilateralism in Kosovo indicates a profound shift.[103] As the United Nations Association of North America warns: 'The UN Security Council risks disappearing as a security body

---

[96] Thus, the actions in Iraq and Kosovo can be portrayed as American achievements while images of dead US Rangers in Somalia or inaction in Rwanda are seen as the product of UN incompetence. In fact, as many commentators have pointed out, the fiasco in Somalia was caused by renegade US unilateralism within the context of a UN peace operation (see, e.g. Hirsch, 'Fall Guy', 7).

[97] Ibid., 2–8. Hirsch describes the UN as an organisation 'infected with morbidity' (3).

[98] Gazzini, 'Coercive Activities', 429.

[99] See Tesón, 'Collective Humanitarian Intervention' (1996) 17 *Michigan Journal of International Law* 323 at 368.

[100] Simma, 'Nato, the UN Charter and the Use of Force', 15.

[101] See the invocation of Article 5 of the Nato Treaty in response to the attack on New York and Washington, *The Observer*, 16 September 2001, 1.

[102] 34 UNTS 243.

[103] This is not to suggest that Nato did not operate largely within UN-prescribed boundaries during the Bosnian conflict. See Gazzini, 'Coercive Activities', 397. In the case of the more recent bombings of Iraq, the United States and United Kingdom have tried to justify the actions as implementations of resolutions arising out of the Gulf War in 1991. Here, it was argued that the violation of SC Res. 687 had, in effect, revived the application of SC Res. 678.

as the genuinely powerful prefer to work through a more convenient instrument.'[104]

Pierre-Marie Dupuy describes the increasing tendency towards regional extra-constitutional hegemony built around powerful groups of states and the consequent weakening of 'a system of collective security'.[105] He gives the examples of US and UK action against Iraq in the post-Gulf War era and the bombing of Kosovo and Serbia. For Dupuy, these interventions are cast as dangerous sequels to the more cautious unilateralism seen in Bosnia in 1993/4 and over Iraq in 1999.[106] What is clear is that as the decade progressed the forces of this new regional legalised hegemony became more and more emboldened and the various operations associated with this hegemony became less tied to the organising principles of the UN.

All of this was anticipated in Churchill's early thoughts on post-war reconstruction. The Nato intervention in Kosovo may represent a move back to a more robust European-centred hegemony along the lines of the Concert of Europe or the European Security Order anticipated by Churchill when he spoke of a United Nations made up of several relatively autonomous regional enforcement mechanisms, one of which would be an 'instrument of European government . . . to embody the spirit of the League of Nations'.[107]

This then would be the institutional shift. Vienna marked a turn from a loosely arranged system of states conducting relations through ambassadors and organising themselves in temporary coalitions of interest, to a society of states based around a set of values and structured in a Concert for the maintenance of peace and security in Europe and the world. The Kosovo intervention can then be interpreted as a move from a collective security order based at the United Nations, premised on the agreement of all the Great Powers and compatible with some level of sovereign equality, towards a regional security order based on European hegemony, dismissive of the claims of outsider powers (e.g. the Ottomans in 1815; Russia and China in 1999) and premised on the

---

[104] United Nations Association of the USA, *Words to Deeds: Strengthening the UN's Enforcement Capabilities* (1997), 45 in Simma, 'NATO, the UN and the Use of Force', 21.

[105] Dupuy, 'Unilateralism in Contemporary International Law', 27.

[106] It is unclear whether Dupuy approves of this shift to regional hegemony. Most of the article is an expression of anxiety about this movement generally. On the other hand, the substance/form distinction indicates a level of support for the Kosovo action.

[107] 'Morning Thoughts: A Note on Post-War Security', 2 February 1943 in *The Hinge of Fate*, 710–11.

existence of a very distinct society of states within the larger international state framework.

But how would this change be legitimated and given normative substance? If there is a full-blown normative shift, accompanying the institutional adjustments discussed above, there would seem to be two versions of this shift currently on offer. In the first, a 'new' norm of humanitarian intervention is recruited as an adjunct to some form of regional hegemony. In the second, more radical version, the whole Charter idea is abandoned in favour of a more responsive 'moral' regime based on justice and (Western) values.[108]

In the first category, there is a series of modest proposals for a 'new' norm of humanitarian intervention (based on the idea of regional humanitarian intervention).[109] The most intellectually coherent of these provide the normative resources to argue for the existence of a new regime of (extra-)constitutional legalised hegemony. In the *European Journal of International Law*, for example, Antonio Cassese, makes a frank appeal for the development of such a norm. He asks the familiar question: 'Should respect for the Rule of Law be sacrificed on the altar of human compassion'?[110] Cassese's disagreement with, say, Simma, lies in his willingness to see this moral or ethical justification as, at least, potentially, part of a developing principle of international law, namely the right of humanitarian intervention. This right is rooted in a version of Kant's cosmopolitan insight that violations of human rights in one territory are felt in all others. The contemporary equivalent is the obligation to respect human rights owed *erga omnes*. Cassese's conclusion is that a new norm of international law is evolving permitting the use of force by powerful coalitions of forces outside the parameters of the UN Charter. Accordingly a breach of *lex lata* (in this case, the law on the use of force)

---

[108] These two versions of the normative shift differ from the doctrine of humanitarian intervention articulated by Nato itself and the ethical discourse discussed under the Verona thesis. In the case of the Verona thesis, humanitarian intervention is presented as a Charter-based norm, implied in the existing framework rather than part of a shift away from that system. Meanwhile, the move from legal to moral arguments described in the section on Verona is designed to bring out the unique quality of the Kosovo intervention and the absence of permanent legal consequences. Under the Vienna thesis, I discuss those responses to Kosovo which emphasise morality and justice as aspects of a whole new system of security.

[109] Antonio Cassese, '*Ex iniuria ius oritur*: Are We Moving Towards International Legitimation of Forcible Humanitarian Countermeasures in the World Community?' (1999) 10:1 EJIL 23–30.

[110] *Ibid.*, 25.

can give rise here to a new, highly circumscribed, right to humanitarian intervention.[111]

Other prominent legal scholars have adopted a variation on the Cassesse argument.[112] Michael Reisman distinguishes four systems or 'constitutive regimes'.[113] These are regimes with no centralised decision-making and enforcement capacity such as nineteenth-century Europe (this is the classic picture of anarchy proffered by neo-realists); regimes with hierarchical institutions which are 'manifestly ineffective' (e.g. the League of Nations); regimes which are generally effective but prone to periodic dysfunction, and constitutive processes in which enforcement is consistently achieved through centralised law-making and legitimate vertical coercion.[114] According to Reisman, the international legal system is best characterised as a generally effective regime.[115] In this type of regime, unilateral action on humanitarian grounds will sometimes be justified, indeed compelled, by what Reisman calls 'the international legal process'. The participants in this process include the liberal elites who manage the media, NGOs and inter-governmental organisations as well as states themselves.[116] While the international legal process may mandate or sanction action otherwise illegal under a formal interpretation of the Charter, the actors undertaking such action remain states. Cassese, from the legalist mainstream, and Reisman, from the policy-oriented approach, agree on the desirability and existence (at least in an embryonic form) of a new norm of regional hegemony.[117]

The second set of arguments relates all this to a deeper shift in the operation of international law. More radical variations of the Reisman/Cassese argument refuse to tether the new regime to the old order.

---

[111] See, too, Cassese's supplementary essay, 'A Follow-up', 791–800. Here, Cassese is cautiously equivocal about the generation of this new norm and concludes that regardless of whether the nascent norm fully crystallises the Security Council must remain the core of the collective security system.

[112] See, e.g. C. Greenwood, 'NATO Intervention in Kosovo', and V. Lowe, 'Legal Issues Arising in the Kosovo Crisis', Memoranda submitted to the Foreign Affairs Committee of the House of Commons, reprinted in (2000) 49 ICLQ 926–43.

[113] Reisman, 'World Constitutive Process', 3–18.   [114] Ibid., 7.

[115] The typical Western liberal state is an example of the fourth regime. Arguably, the UN in its collective security mode in the Iraq-Kuwait war operated along the lines of the fourth constitutive regime.

[116] Reisman, 'World Constitutive Process', 17.

[117] For a view favourable to this new hegemony see M. Glennon, 'The New Interventionism: The Search for a Just International Law', Foreign Affairs (May/June 1999), 2 and Reisman, 'World Constitutive Process'. For an ambivalent view see Chinkin, 'Bully, Good Samaritan or Iconoclast', 31–42. For a sceptical view see James Hathaway's 'America: Defender of Democratic Legitimacy?' (2000) 11:1 EJIL 121–34.

Here, the Western powers are said to be articulating a new norm of Great Power interventionism and management in Kosovo uncoupled from the UN Charter and the peculiar circumstances of the Cold War. In Michael Glennon's words: 'The United States and Nato – with little discussion and less fanfare – have effectively abandoned the old UN Charter rules that strictly limit international intervention in local conflicts.'[118] Glennon is not alone. Other academic commentators have rushed to pronounce the death of the old United Nations order. Even those who are diffident (Chinkin, Dupuy) accept that there is a normative shift afoot. Christine Chinkin described Kosovo as 'an icon smashing event in which the UN is marginalised by powerful bullies and private samaritans'.[119] Noam Chomsky, too, fulminated in the following terms: 'Nato's bombing further undermines what remains of the fragile structure of international law.'[120]

However, it is Glennon's contribution to *Foreign Affairs* that reads like a gleeful valediction to the Charter model. The old system is deemed a failure because it could not prevent inter-state war (see Vietnam) and failed to recognise that the new threat is civil war.[121] In the end, 'challenging an unjust law, (as Nato has done with the Charter) can actually reinforce the legal regime'.[122] Offering the same analysis, but more mournfully, was Victor Chernomyrdin who bemoaned an approach that, 'clashes with international law, the Helsinki Agreements and the world order that took shape after World War II'.[123]

But what would ultimately provide the legitimating idea behind this new order? The most frequently voiced legitimating principle has been humanitarianism. Each one of the Nato leaders and officials presented the intervention as a humanitarian necessity.[124] However, in the background, and articulated more transparently in the days following the aerial attacks on New York City and Washington DC, was a further and perhaps deeper idea. The defence of the West, variously described as 'Europe' or 'civilisation' or 'democracy', had become the animating idea behind the move to this new legalised hegemony. This is part of the

---

[118] Glennon, 'New Interventionism', 2.
[119] Chinkin, 'Bully, Good Samaritan or Iconoclast'.
[120] Chomsky, *Rogue States*, 46.   [121] Glennon, 'New Interventionism', 3.
[122] *Ibid.*, 4. This is not to say that the new norm will not face opposition. The new interventionists must reconcile the need for broad acceptance of their regime with the resistance of the defiant (outlaws), the indolent (failed states) and the miscreant (the periphery) (7).
[123] *International Herald Tribune* (28 May 1999).
[124] For examples, see Jackson, *Global Covenant*, 282.

liberal anti-pluralism that I take up in the following chapters, especially Chapter 10. For the present, it is enough to say that the new interventionism present in Kosovo has the potential to disturb radically the foundations of the Charter model. I have described how the assumptions of universal legalised hegemony embodied in the operation of the Security Council are affected by this possible shift.

This normative shift, then, if it exists, is signalled by a rejection of the old norms of international law, a willingness to abandon 'unjust' doctrine and a move from sovereignty to humanitarianism.[125] Glennon makes the implications for sovereign equality explicit: 'The West's new rules of thumb on intervention', he goes on to argue, 'accord less deference to the old idea of sovereign equality – the erstwhile notion that all countries, large or small, are equal in the eyes of the law. The new posture recognises the hollowness of this concept, accepting that states are not in fact the same in power, wealth or commitment to human rights and peace.'[126] This new interventionism, then, is clearly as much a threat to Charter-based legalised hegemony as it is to sovereign equality.[127]

To conclude, at Vienna, the Great Powers formalised their position as constitutional hegemons and underpinned that role with a set of principles based on the need for management of a chaotic international system and preservation of certain Western values (later to be embodied in the 'standard of civilisation'). Have the Nato allies, through the Kosovo intervention, established the conditions for a similar process of constitutional management or permanent regional legalised hegemony? As I suggested in the conclusion to the section on the Verona thesis, the evidence is inconclusive. The durability of the Vienna settlement, like the transience of the Verona scheme, was revealed only in retrospect. What can be said, is that, despite the contextual adjustments to the Nato Treaty and the general tenor of the Washington Conference in 1999, the

---

[125] The ideological shift or legitimating ideas behind this change are many. The underlying normative shift would seem to be from sovereignty to humanitarianism. Promoting the shift from sovereignty to human rights (see Vienna's shift from sovereignty to hegemony), see Tony Blair, 'Speech to the Economic Club of Chicago', 27 April 1999. This idea is now one of the most dog-eared among thinkers in the international system. International lawyers have been repeating this half-truth for at least two decades and now it has acquired currency at the highest echelons of power. See Glennon, 'New Interventionism', 2: 'in Kosovo, justice (as it is now understood) and the UN Charter seemed to collide'.

[126] *Ibid.*, 4.

[127] *Nicaragua Case* (Merits) at para. 202: 'It [non-intervention] has moreover been presented as a corollary of the principle of the sovereign equality of states.'

Kosovo intervention and its normative and institutional accoutrements lack the formalisation and institutional innovation of even the fairly loosely structured Vienna settlement. If regional legalised hegemony is to supersede the Charter system, this process is likely to be incremental rather than the product of a dramatic constitutional moment.

Conclusion

This chapter concludes my reflections about legalised hegemony on a note of ambivalence. I have suggested, though, that a useful way to approach the question is to compare Kosovo with both the new security project outlined and agreed upon at the Congress of Vienna, and the more ephemeral arrangements made by the Holy Alliance at a series of meetings immediately after Vienna.

The Kosovo intervention recalls elements of both these moments of institutional innovation or, in the case of the Holy Alliance, attempted innovation. I have tried to read Kosovo as alternatively part of a new legitimate system of international relations (Vienna) and as an illegitimate usurpation (Verona) of the existing Charter order. This oscillation between Verona and Vienna can be seen in the arrangements under Security Council Resolution 1244. The Council appeared to wrest full control away from Nato and place it under a civil authority whose powers are derived from the Security Council and whose leading figure is the Secretary-General's Special Representative.[128] However, it is equally true that, in Annex 2 to the resolution, it was specified that there was to be an 'international security presence with substantial North Atlantic Treaty Organization participation'.[129] Resolution 1244, then, managed to satisfy a number of different interests. The Russians, for example, were no doubt consoled by their role in the post-war occupation of Kosovo and by the reference to Serbian sovereignty and territorial integrity in 1244 while Nato would have viewed the resolution as an implicit authorisation of its support for Kosovo's autonomy.[130] At a broader level, the resolution seems to embody this split between a return to the official collective security of the UN system and an accommodation with a surgent regional hegemony.

The test will be whether Nato is able to perform the role of 'Great Powers' in the post-Kosovo era. In a key passage in *The Anarchical Society,*

---

[128] UNMIK Regulation No 1/1999 On the Authority of the Interim Administration in Kosovo, 25 July 1999.

[129] Draft Russian resolution S/1999/649.   [130] See Jackson, *Global Covenant,* 281.

Hedley Bull defines Great Powers as those states that 'assert the right, and are accorded the right, to play a part in determining the issues that affect the peace and security of the international system as a whole'.[131] Is Nato capable of performing this task and adopting the managerial responsibilities of international society?[132] The response by other states to the intervention was equivocal and it may be that even the states of Nato remain chary of shouldering the responsibilities required for a new legalised hegemony.

In the end, neither the Verona nor the Vienna thesis can fully explain the implications of the Kosovo action. The UN's authority has eroded under the challenge of a decade of regional hegemony.[133] Successive interventions in Iraq (1992, 1993 and 1998–2003), and in the former Yugoslavia, have boosted the credentials of a post-Charter international order. But has this hegemony been legalised in the way that the Vienna agreements were given constitutional authority in the society of states? Or is this erosion likely to do no lasting damage to the international system inaugurated in 1945? History is unable to provide entirely satisfactory answers to these sorts of questions but the precedents of Vienna and Verona allow us to explore some possible futures for legalised hegemony in the international order.

[131] Bull, *Anarchical Society*, 202.   [132] *Ibid.*, 202.   [133] Gazzini, 'Coercive Activities', 435.

Part IV Histories: Outlaw States

8   Unequal sovereigns: 1815–1939

> The civilised nation is conscious that the rights of the barbarians are
> unequal to its own and treats their autonomy as only a formality.[1]

Introduction

This book is about the changing forms adopted by one particular genus
of sovereignty, juridical sovereignty, in the international legal order
since 1815. In particular, I argue that the principle of sovereign equality
has provided the doctrinal terrain on which different visions of international order and conceptions of sovereignty have clashed. The central argument is the idea that juridical sovereignty has been constituted since 1815 by the interplay of sovereignty as equality (expressed
mainly through non-intervention and equal participation doctrines) and
sovereignty as inequality (expressed through the special position of the
Great Powers and outlaw states in relation to other states in the society).
In Chapters 4 to 7, then, I described and assessed the relationship between sovereign equality (and in particular the idea of legislative equality outlined in Chapter 3) and the special position of the Great Powers
under international law and in international organisations. I showed
how juridical sovereignty accommodates the numerous forms taken by,
what I called, legalised hegemony. In these next three chapters, I focus
on outlaw states. I want to approach the problem of outlaw or outsider
states, indirectly, through the two conceptions of international community developed in Chapter 3 which, in turn, are drawn from two versions of liberal thought. I have called these liberal pluralism and liberal

---

[1] Hegel, *Philosophy of Right* (1952 edn), 219 at para. 351.

anti-pluralism.[2] I argued in Chapter 3 that the tension between these two liberalisms is a defining quality of the inter-state order. The two liberalisms in question also approach the question of international society differently. I want to reintroduce the idea of the outlaw state in these chapters by discussing the theory of international society first developed by Hedley Bull and his associates in order to show how this society can either be inclusive and heterogeneous or exclusive and anti-pluralist. I then link this discussion back to liberal pluralism and liberal anti-pluralism.

I begin, in Chapter 8, by exploring the ways in which some states were thought to be legally inferior to others in nineteenth-century international law and how this inferiority manifested itself (in interventionist doctrines and in the unequal treaties and capitulations). I show how this began as a form of anti-pluralism based on Christianity or civilisation or, in the case of the Holy Alliance, on a conservative anti-liberalism, but ended up as a specifically liberal anti-pluralism. I also indicate here how this unequal status was rarely applied to defeated enemy states in a way that became more prevalent in the twentieth century. (I say a little also about the post-Vienna rehabilitation of France in order to make this point.)

In Chapter 9, I show how institution design in the twentieth century continued to revolve around two competing positions on state equality. According to the egalitarian, pluralist conception, states were regarded as free and equal members of the world community regardless of their internal moral or political characteristics. Under the anti-pluralist conception, the behaviour of states and, in a stronger version of this thesis, their constitutional practices determined their standing in the law of nations. This debate reached its peak in the making of the League of Nations and the United Nations Charter where these conceptions clashed. I describe these clashes in Chapter 9 with particular emphasis on the debates at San Francisco, which were resolved in favour of a universalist orientation for the new UN organisation. This period also marked a rejection of two other forms of anti-pluralism. At Nuremberg, the criminalisation of states and their consignment to outlaw status was rejected in favour of a regime of individual responsibility which proved to be entirely compatible with, and perhaps necessary to, the rehabilitation of

---

[2] By giving them these labels I do not mean to imply any normative claim about the two approaches. It might be good to be anti-pluralist in the sense that I will use it (though anti-pluralism might have bad consequences, too). See Chapter 1 for an elaboration on this theme.

Germany and 'enemy states' generally. Meanwhile, alongside the Nuremberg and San Francisco rejection of the anti-pluralism of democratic governance and state crime regimes was a push towards a full-blooded anti-imperialism (located in New York at the General Assembly). The decolonisation norms produced by this movement were pluralist inasmuch as they insisted on the complete independence and freedom of choice of newly created states in Africa and Asia regardless of the internal politics or democratic credentials of these states.[3]

In Chapter 10, I turn to the contemporary outlaw state and, in particular, the position of such states in current international legal practice and among a group of liberal anti-pluralist theorists.

The idea here is to show that just as legislative equality is compromised or mediated by the practice of legalised hegemony traced through Chapters 4 to 7 so, too, is the norm of existential equality (defined in Chapter 2) redefined by the practice and theories of liberal anti-pluralism.

International society: two conceptions

Though I focus on liberalism, it seems to me that this debate can be recast in a number of different forms or understood through a number of distinct theoretical debates. At a general level, a contrast can be made between pragmatists and legalists in international affairs. Legalism can be understood in a variety of ways.[4] However, one form of legalism manifests itself as a commitment to the foundational norms of international law. According to this sort of legalism, norms of sovereign equality, non-intervention and equal participation make up the very essence of international law and ought to be preserved as such. In contrast with this legalism, there is a form of pragmatism that accentuates the need for compromise with power (legalised hegemony) and repression of dissidence (anti-pluralism). Or, to adopt Martin Wight's categories, the revolutionism of those who would wish to enforce certain ideological preferences on the world of states (anti-pluralists) can be contrasted with a Grotian middle way whose adherents support a tolerant society of differently

---

[3] This is not a major focus of the book. See Robert Jackson, *Quasi-States*.

[4] E.g. signalling a commitment to war crimes trials (Gary Bass, *Stay the Hand of Vengeance: The Politics of War Crimes Trials*; Judith Shklar, *Legalism*) as a programme for ordering the world using legal institutions (Woodrow Wilson's *Fourteen Points*), as a form of utopianism (criticised in George Kennan, *American Diplomacy 1900–1950*; E. H. Carr, *The 20 Years' Crisis*).

configured states.[5] But this is also a dispute *between* two Grotianisms – a Grotianism in the spirit of the first paragraphs of *de jure praedae* (with its emphasis on outlaws and enemies) and the Grotius found in Lauterpacht's study of the Dutchman in 1946; a Grotius dedicated to building a system based on sovereign equality.[6]

In studying the nineteenth century, I have been influenced by the English school approach to international law and relations and, in particular, its focus on the concept of international society. It is clear that my work in this study shares many assumptions with that of the English school approach more generally. Most obviously, the prominent writers in this tradition, for all their realism, take international law seriously. For Bull, the international order was an international legal order, a common enterprise bound together through accepted legal norms.[7] Scholars in this tradition also focused on the operation of norms rather than more narrowly defined rules or doctrines. This study is in that vein because it grapples with the play of fundamental principles and norms of the international legal order (sovereignty, participation) rather than specific legal techniques or rules. More importantly still, the English school emphasis on history and, particularly, historical evolution has been influential on this work. One of the questions Bull and Watson grappled with was: how do international societies develop?[8] This book, too, is about the operation of norms in history or through history. The argument is that international society developed, partly, through a process of institutional innovation and encounter with outsider states that reached a peak in the late nineteenth century and partly by the formation of Great Power directorates in the post-1815 period. Though this work modifies the classical English school account of society, it is inspired, partly, by Hedley Bull's social or institutional understanding of the Great Powers and by Martin Wight's view that the outlaw state in some way defines a particular approach to international order.[9]

Bull and Watson described an international society in the following terms:

---

[5] Wight, 'Anatomy'.

[6] H. Lauterpacht, 'The Grotian Tradition in International Law' (1946) 23 *British Yearbook of International Law*, 1–53.

[7] See H. Bull, B. Kingsbury and A. Roberts, *Hugo Grotius and International Relations*. See also O. Yasuaki (ed.), *A Normative Approach to War*.

[8] See, e.g. Bull and Watson, *Expansion*; Adam Watson, *The Evolution of International Society*.

[9] M. Wight, 'Western Values' in Butterfield and Wight, *Diplomatic Investigations*; M. Wight, *International Theory: The Three Traditions*; Bull, *Anarchical Society*.

a group of states (or, more generally a group of independent political communities) which not merely form a system, in the sense that the behaviour of
each is a necessary factor in the calculations of the others, but also have established by dialogue and common consent rules and institutions for the conduct
of their relations and recognise their common interest in maintaining these
arrangements.[10]

This definition emphasises the state-based nature of the society, the
legal techniques used to hold the society together and the common interests acknowledged by the participants in the society. Later English school
writers emphasised the role played by norms such as non-intervention
(Armstrong) and equality (Stivatchis) in buttressing or defining this society of states.[11] I argue in this book that this is just one possible
(pluralist) view of international society. An alternative definition of society would emphasise the non-consensual aspects of international society
and, most pointedly, its source and continuing operation within a conception of international order that depends on the identification of certain states as outlaws or outsiders. One might say, then, *contra* Stivatchis,
that this international society is founded on certain sovereign inequalities and, *contra* Armstrong, that it inspires highly interventionist doctrines. I argue that this conception of international society accurately
describes a significant anti-pluralist element within the international
legal order.

Indeed, it is my contention that the present international order can
best be understood as a struggle between these two conceptions of international society. The pluralist conception is universalist and egalitarian in orientation. The salient norms are those of non-intervention,
sovereign immunity and state equality. The anti-pluralist conception emphasises the existence of two spheres of order. In one, there is, what Bull
would call, a solidarist international society composed of a core of liberal states that share certain cultural attributes and ideological presup-
positions and whose common values and interests support a deepening
constitutionalism within that society. In the other sphere, are outlaws
and outsiders subject to a repressive international criminal law and denied the benefits of full sovereign equality. Liberal anti-pluralism is the
term I use to describe a series of theories and practices of international

---

[10] Bull and Watson, *Expansion*, 1.
[11] D. Armstrong, *Revolution and World Order: The Revolutionary State in International Society*;
Y. Stivatchis, *The Enlargement of International Society: Culture versus Anarchy and Greece's
Entry into International Society*.

order that promotes this distinction between these two spheres. Liberal pluralism is the term I use to characterise a more conventional way of understanding international legal order as a way of organising relations between all sovereign states on the basis of equality and diversity. International criminal law and the developing norms of democratic governance each represents a challenge to a liberal voluntarist conception of international order based on a system of universal social relations.[12]

To recap, then, I set up an initial tension in Chapter 3 between two forms of international community. The first is a Charter-based liberal international law in its pluralist mode emphasising the sovereign equality of states, their rights to domestic jurisdiction and their right to, what I call, existential equality, a sub-set of sovereign equality that allows states to choose their own form of government and that underpins the heterogeneity of the international legal order. The opposite of this is the anti-pluralism that denies certain states the right to participate fully in international legal life because of some moral or political incapacity such as lack of civilisation, absence of democracy or aggressive tendencies.

Unequal sovereigns

Introduction

I want to begin with the nineteenth century, a period in which there was a clash between these two approaches to structuring the international community. On the one hand were those who advocated the expansion of the international order through a policy of openness and universalism. On the other hand, there was the continuing exclusion of certain sovereign states from the Family of Nations on the grounds that these states lacked civilisation (as well as the support for these practices on the part of a number of late-Victorian international legal scholars).

Hedley Bull and Adam Watson describe the pre-1815 period as one in which:

European states sought to deal with Asian states on the basis of moral and legal equality, until in the 19th century this gave way to notions of European superiority.[13]

---

[12] For the classic statement of this voluntarism, see Weil, 'Relative Normativity', *passim*.
[13] Bull and Watson, *Expansion*, 5.

Prior to 1815, then, international law embraced civilisations of different stripes. True, relations between the European powers and other civilisations were conducted at a different level to those within Europe. Nonetheless, equality appeared to be a mark of these various relationships.[14] This commitment to equality went back at least to Westphalia where, as we have seen in Chapter 2, the problem of difference within Europe itself was resolved by conducting relations among religious, cultural and ideological competitors on an equal basis.[15] For example, Article 5 of the Treaty of Osnabruck called for 'an exact and reciprocal equality amongst all the Electors, princes and States of both religions . . .'. This commitment continued into the late eighteenth century and operated in relation to non-European states, e.g. the Ottomans were enjoying special rights within European capitals such as Amsterdam.[16] There was no sense in which these cultural aliens were to be regarded as legally inferior.

After 1815, this changed. Distinctions were drawn on the basis of ideological credentials or cultural practices. In the early part of the nineteenth century, the then dominant principle of equality was challenged by the idea that the international system could be based on a demarcation between an inner circle of right-thinking European core states and an outer rim of second-class states. This began as a Christian/Non-Christian or European/Non-European distinction but the ideas of liberalism began to play a larger role by the middle to late nineteenth-century period as liberal governance became the norm within Western Europe. New regimes in Europe became more tolerant and less authoritarian in relations with their own citizens. Revolutionary Europe cast aside absolutist monarchies and religious dynasties, and forms of democracy

---

[14] See Alexandrowicz, 'Empirical and Doctrinal Positivism in International Law', 288.

[15] Armstrong, *Revolution*, 34.

[16] H. Theunissen, 'Ottoman-Venetian Diplomatics: the *Ahd-names*. The Historical Background and the Development of a Category of Political-Commercial Instruments together with an Annotated Edition of a Corpus of Relevant Documents' (1998) 1:2 *Electronic Journal of Oriental Studies* 1–698 at 306, fn. 2 (noting the reciprocal nature of the capitulations established between the Ottomans and the Venetians in the 1500s). Compare the assumption of non-reciprocity prevalent in the nineteenth century and recounted by Morgenthau in 1914: 'Enver wished to discuss the capitulations. He added that certainly a country which had fought for its independence as we had would sympathise with Turkey's attempt to shake off these shackles. We had helped Japan free herself from similar burdens and wouldn't we now help Turkey? *Certainly Turkey was as civilized a nation as Japan*', see Henry Morgenthau, *Ambassador Morgenthau's Story*, ch. 10 (my italics).

often took their place.[17] However, at the same time, these liberal states continued to relegate non-liberal, non-European societies such as China, Korea and Japan to second-class status because of a perceived lack of civilisation. In this sense, the behaviour of European powers towards non-European civilisations compared rather poorly to those of their 'illiberal', pre-nineteenth-century predecessors.

Christianity and, later, 'civilisation' were the key terms in this period. One attribute of civilisation was the possession of a liberal or at least pseudo-liberal legal order in which alien (read Western) nationals would be afforded full liberal rights. Those entities excluded from the system were thought incapable of ensuring this level of protection and were thus deprived of certain sovereign rights and jurisdictional immunities in 'unequal treaties' and capitulations.[18] In this period, beginning in the early nineteenth century and extending through to, at least, The Hague Peace Conferences, the international legal order was divided into a European-centred Family of Nations and a non-European zone of semi-sovereign, unequal or uncivilised states. This development has a theoretical and practical component. In international legal theory, nineteenth-century international legal scholars developed and justified a conception of international order in which states were classified according to their capacity to meet certain culturally specific standards. In international legal practice, too, a number of doctrines arose that appeared irreconcilable with sovereign equality. As well as the unequal treaties regime, and the extra-territorial jurisdiction of the European powers, embodied in the system of capitulations, there was the exclusion of peripheral states from the institutions of the international system. The early part of this period also provides a parallel with the increasing

---

[17] E. J. Hobsbawm, *The Age of Revolution: Europe 1789–1848*.

[18] The term 'capitulations' is used to refer to the system of consular jurisdiction operated by the Western powers in Turkey. It refers to the immunities from jurisdiction enjoyed by West European, American and Russian foreigners in Turkey. The phrase 'unequal treaties' is applied to contractual relations between these powers and East Asian states. These unequal treaties contained provisions on the enjoyment of extra-territorial jurisdiction but also included arrangements for the transfer of territories (see, e.g. Hong Kong). This was true only of the Asian civilisations. African nations (apart from peculiarities such as the Orange Free State and Liberia) were denied any sort of recognition at all in the early part of the period. As Hegel put it: 'Africa proper, as far as history goes back, has remained – for all purposes of connection with the rest of the World – shut up; it is the God-land compressed within itself – the land of childhood, which lying beyond the day of self-conscious history, is enveloped in the dark mantle of Night' (Hegel, *Philosophy of Right* (1952), 91). See, too, Anghie, 'Finding the Peripheries'; Gerrit Gong, *Standard of Civilisation*.

interventionism of the present period. The Holy Alliance was formed during the early nineteenth century and its whole ethos was interventionist even though, of course, this interventionism was conducted in the name of conservatism and *against* liberalism and was, in fact, resisted by the dominant liberal power of the day, Great Britain. Nonetheless, unequal sovereigns became prey to the interventionist anti-pluralism of the Eastern powers.

The 'short' nineteenth century, then, was marked by sovereign inequality in relations between the core and periphery. However, its anti-pluralism was different from that of the twentieth century's in one crucial respect. Enemy states were not regarded as criminal states in the same manner as Germany in 1918 and 1945, Iraq in 1991 and Serbia in 1999. For those states already part of the European core, even an expansionist war was insufficient to achieve the sort of outlaw status that defined post-war settlements in the twentieth century. The fate of France in 1815 was quite different from that of, say, Germany in 1918.

The publicists of anti-pluralism

In the nineteenth century, international lawyers were obliged to respond to John Westlake's challenge when he demanded that the principle of sovereign equality 'furnish a test showing to what states it applies'.[19]

During this period, the international legal order operated not as a universal system but as an international or regional society of states embedded into a wider system of inter-state relations. An international system can be reinterpreted as the set of processes and institutions through which a society accommodates its relationships with entities outside the core.[20] The international order, then, worked on two levels. At one level, were the full members of the society of states enjoying all the rights and benefits of such membership. At the other level, were the relations between these full members and other entities within the wider system. Lassa Oppenheim, in his third edition, makes this distinction explicit: 'Statehood [the system] alone does not include membership of the Family of Nations [the society].'[21] According to Oppenheim there were states which, not being members of the Family, were not able to avail themselves of the full protection of international law.[22] Statehood thus enabled a state to enjoy membership of the *system* but this did not guarantee membership of the *society* of states.

---

[19] J. Westlake, *Collected Papers*, 87.   [20] See Wight, *Systems of States*.
[21] Oppenheim, *International Law* (3rd edn), 34.   [22] *Ibid.*, 108.

By the nineteenth century, then, Europe had begun to view itself as an entity ('Europe') and as a special society situated within the broader international system. The international legal order thus followed Leopold Ranke's famous classification dividing nations into two types: those that made history and those that lack history.[23] The nations that made history believed that they belonged to a unique society but one that would eventually become a world society of states embracing the peripheries and converting them. As Peter Fitzpatrick puts it: 'The Universal as project is, however, particularly located.'[24] In this instance, the universal was located in Europe. Europe was the locus for the society of states and, 'as the sense grew of the specifically European character of the society of states, so also did the sense of its cultural differentiation from what lay outside: the sense that European powers in their dealings with one another were bound by a code of conduct that did not apply to them in their dealings with other and lesser societies'.[25] European international law then had two ambitions, to be realised consecutively. First, Europe was to establish itself as a unique and superior legal and cultural order. Second, it was to export this order through the adoption of universalist forms. International law became more closely associated with the law of nations in Europe at the very moment when Europe embarked on its universalist strategy. The initial step involved transforming Europe into a society of states underpinned by a combination of legalised hegemony and liberal exceptionalism and embedding that society in a wider system of state entities. For the anti-pluralists, this society/system separation was to be replaced eventually by an international society of civilised states along European lines. In the meantime, European states were to create an international society for export. For the pluralist, the idea was to embrace difference at the periphery and create an international system of states with many different cultural and social forms represented in this system. This pluralism, however, did not re-acquire influence until the early twentieth century (and reached its peak with the UN Charter).

As I have shown, nineteenth-century publicists endlessly wrestled with the contradictions inherent in a theory of sovereign equality forced to accommodate the principle of legalised hegemony. The preponderance of the Great Powers and the equality of states proved difficult to

---

[23] See Alexandrowicz, 'Empirical and Doctrinal Positivism', 286.

[24] P. Fitzpatrick, 'Nationalism as Racism' in Fitzpatrick (ed.), *Nationalism, Racism and the Rule of Law*, 15.

[25] Bull, *Anarchical Society*, 33.

reconcile. However, initially at least, scholars displayed more confidence in justifying the division of humanity into those entities entitled to full sovereignty (European states) and groups possessing some lesser form of sovereignty.

At first, Christianity was the test of 'good breeding'. Wheaton's *Elements of International Law*, published in 1836 and translated into Chinese in 1864, characterised international law as Christian, civilised and European and marked out the standard to which the Asian empires had to aspire if they were to be admitted to the international legal community.[26] Later, civilisation became the key term. W. E. Hall's *International Law* is typical:

> It is scarcely necessary to point out that as international law is a product of the special civilisation of modern Europe, and forms a highly artificial system of which the principles cannot be supposed to be understood or recognised by countries differently civilised, such states only can be presumed to be subject to it as are inheritors of that civilization.[27]

In another text by the same author, the word 'civilised' appears five times in the first five pages.[28] In this sort of work, there is a good deal of overlap between the criteria for full standing in the Family of Nations and that of civilisation.[29] In this way, civilisation became a key idea in international law in the nineteenth century and early twentieth century.[30]

[26] Wheaton's *Elements* was regarded by the Chinese and Japanese as an authoritative source of international law doctrine and standards. See Gong, *Standard of Civilisation*, 18, 26. So, it had direct and traceable consequences for the practice of international law. The first edition characterised international law as Christian, civilised and European (Gong, 18), marking out the standard to which the Asian empires had to aspire if they were to be admitted (Gong, 26). Material power did not seem relevant to this evaluation.

[27] William Edward Hall, *A Treatise on International Law* (6th edn), 39.

[28] Hall, *International Law* (1880).

[29] For Hall, civilisation is associated with the capacity to understand legal rules and the possession of a fixed territory (*ibid.*, 15).

[30] There are numerous examples where the term is used in the laws of war, too, e.g. 1868 St Petersburg Declaration (1867–8) 58 BFSP 16–17 (Fr.) ('forbidding the use of certain projectiles in time of war among civilised nations . . .') and in the projects of colonialism (the Berlin Conference spoke of 'instructing the natives and bringing home to them the blessing of civilisation'). Like Christianity and the enlightenment, 'civilisation' was defined according to its opposite. The nineteenth-century colonisers spoke of republican principles 'unknown in other parts of the world' (Gong, *Standard of Civilisation*, 46). The concept of civilisation has been important in establishing the criteria for statehood. See, e.g. discussion in Crawford, *Creation of States*, 73.

Yet, significantly, these uncivilised entities were regarded as 'sovereign' states. The likes of China, Turkey and Japan were not colonies of the Western powers nor were they peoples claiming self-determination or unrecognised nations. They were sovereigns but unequal ones. They were like the European powers in a functional sense (effective government, territory) but dissimilar in a cultural sense (lack of democracy/civilisation/Christianity). John Westlake made the point colloquially when he compared the late-nineteenth-century society of states to a group of persons simply 'interested in maintaining the rules of good breeding'.[31]

What was interesting about some of this work, then, was the recognition that states could be part of the international law society while at the same time excluded from the inner circle or family.[32] Westlake seems to envisage a sort of staggered admission policy: 'Our international society exercises the right of admitting outside states to parts of its international law without necessarily admitting them to the whole of it.'[33] Oppenheim, as I have indicated, saw statehood and membership as two separate categories.[34]

The Scottish jurist James Lorimer took this idea furthest in his portrayal of an international order organised around the relations between an inner circle composed of civilised European states and an outer circle consisting of the 'barbarian Turks' and savages.[35] The problem of defining an inner circle and outer circumference, though, was only a preliminary issue for Lorimer, who wanted to show the many different ways in which states could be unequal. In this, he anticipated some of the

---

[31] Westlake, *Collected Papers*, 6.

[32] Oppenheim, for example, noted that: 'There are states in existence, although their number decreases gradually, which are not, or not fully, members of that family' (Oppenheim, *International Law*, 3rd edn, 33). The distinctions between statehood, membership and sovereignty are hazy in all this. The Victorian publicists accepted that the entities on the periphery were states and possessed some sort of unequal sovereignty but did not concede that statehood entitled them to full participation in the international system.

[33] Westlake, *Collected Papers*, 82.

[34] *Ibid.* So, relations with China and Japan were more or less normal apart from the extra-territorial jurisdiction enjoyed by the civilised powers and Turkey was admitted to the public law of Europe and membership of the European political system in 1854 but did not yet enjoy full jurisdictional sovereignty.

[35] James Lorimer, *Institutes*, 101–3. Whatever the standard of civilisation and however systematised, it remained the case that colonised peoples (or savages) could not reach it. These peoples were the same and different. They wanted what the core already had. There was the same 'yearning for freedom' but they would not get it or were not ready for it. See Fitzpatrick, 'Nationalism as Racism', 11.

writings referred to in Chapter 10 when he divided outsider states into different categories: criminal, unchristian and imbecilic/immature. He also argued that the recognition of these entities could either be partial or merely human as opposed to the plenary recognition bestowed on each other by the Christian states of Europe.

According to Lorimer, international legal institutions ought to have resembled a shareholders' meeting where voting is weighted according to power and influence. Lorimer agonised over the appropriate posture civilised states were to adopt towards uncivilised humanity.[36] He recognised that there had to be relations but he thought these could not operate at the same level of intensity, or be of the same jural status, as those among civilised states.[37] How, then, in periods of expansion by the civilised states, were non-civilised states to be included within the range of jural relations without according them full membership?[38] Much of the discussion related to the impossibility of reconciling universalistic notions of international law with 'intolerant creeds', whether religious (e.g. Judaism, Islam) or secular.[39]

In Chapter 10, I elaborate on the idea of regimes of outlawry and, in particular, the criminal state regime and the democratic governance regime. These regimes have nineteenth-century antecedents that come through strongly in Lorimer's work. Lorimer's criminal states were divided into three types. First, there were those states that threatened the international order with revolutionary or Jacobin programmes of transformation. These 'intolerant anarchies' ceased to be fully equal sovereign states in Lorimer's view.[40] Surrounding states could decide freely whether to intervene in the vacuum created by the extinguishment

---

[36] Having said that, James Lorimer was also committed to an 'ethnological' approach that warned against imposing alien constitutional structures on sovereign states (*Institutes*, 95). His tolerance, though, had limits.

[37] *Ibid.*, 101. Lorimer went further by dividing the savage states into those of progressive and non-progressive races though confusingly he described the barbarian Turks as a non-progressive race. *Ibid.*, 102.

[38] *Ibid.*, 102. Lorimer thought about the appropriate forms of recognition to accord different religious creeds as well. It was the contrast between the core Christian nations and the rest which most concerned him but he also felt the need to justify relations with Roman Catholic states on the grounds that while the religion was clearly based on a series of superstitious rituals it was nevertheless 'moribund' and, therefore, harmless (117). Judaism, by contrast, was of much greater concern (118).

[39] Thomas Franck makes a similar point in *Fairness* where he speaks of the need to find agreement on procedural matters, agreement excluded by states that profess fealty to a supreme being or idea (16–17).

[40] Lorimer, *Institutes*, 132.

of the reciprocating will.[41] What was most interesting about this category were the examples Lorimer gave of 'Intolerant Anarchies', i.e. the Paris Commune and a hypothetical nihilist or communist Russia. These were states whose organising principle was the political theory of anarchism i.e. they possessed the wrong ideology. The point for Lorimer was to defend a particular vision of international law rather than accede to what Martin Wight calls 'catastrophic revolutionism' and 'contemplate the final triumph of the first Napoleon, of the French Commune, of Russian Nihilism, or of the Koran . . .'.[42] These states were the very negation of legality and they possessed, what he called, a non-reciprocating creed. Lorimer also associated monarchies with this group.[43] International law required the consent of the state or 'the contracting will of the community as an organic whole'.[44] Personal governments were unable to meet this standard.[45]

The second type of criminal state was the intolerant religious state. Lorimer included Judaism, Catholicism and Islam among these religious creeds incapable of forming a reciprocal will because incapable of modifying their religious practices in accordance with the norms of international society. Piratical Barbary states constituted the third type of criminal state. These were characterised by Grotius as bands of robbers. Criminality on this scale permits concerted police action on behalf of the civilised states. In each of these three instances, Lorimer suggested that the commission of crimes results in a loss of certain aspects of a legal personality. The states in this category were different, of course. The Barbary states posed a direct threat to the external peace of the European society of states while the other two types merely possess ideologies that were incompatible with the dominant norms of that society. Nevertheless, in each case a repressive criminal law was to be applied to these unequal sovereigns.

For Lorimer, as with later scholars such as Thomas Franck and John Rawls, there was a group of states that did not conform to the ideal picture of what an international good citizen should be but could nevertheless have relations with the society of states. These states were not criminal and such entities were entitled to partial recognition.

---

[41] *Ibid.*, 133.
[42] *Ibid.* How little the periphery has changed! See, e.g. Franck, *Fairness*, 86 (condemning the 'dictatorship of the proletariat' and 'modernization').
[43] Lorimer, *Institutes*, 129.   [44] *Ibid.*, 163.
[45] *Ibid.*, 133. Lorimer suggested that this was true of elective personal governments also, on the grounds that the act of the rational will on the part of the electorate represents this will only for one period or one instance (the election itself) (*ibid.*, 164).

These states were not Christian but they engaged in a form of ethical monotheism that presented no direct threat to the Christian ideal.[46] For Lorimer, the absence of negation made relations possible.[47] These states resemble Rawls's category of states that are well-ordered but not quite democratic.[48]

Alongside the three forms of criminal States and the decent but flawed states were states that had not reached the requisite level of civilisation or development. Lorimer gave two examples: nonage and imbecility. Nonage is a concept that has had a surprising amount of influence in international law. Lorimer acknowledged that 'the most barbarous communities are probably as old as the most civilised'.[49] However, these communities had not yet reached a level of political maturity – they were in a state of, what Lorimer described as, 'political nonage'.[50] Political nonage, of course, and the correlative fact of guardianship, are both integral aspects of the way international law has managed the doctrines of inequality through mandates, trusteeships and protectorates. The revival of nonage can be seen in the proposals to dust off the trusteeship itself in the case of failed states. The other reason states 'failed', according to Lorimer, was because of insanity. Like human beings, mature nations go mad. This madness consisted of an attempt to impose social or political institutions which, 'assume the existence of impossible facts'.[51]

All of this had implications for recognition (a topic I intend only to touch upon). Lorimer argued for something called partial recognition in the relations between the civilised and semi-barbarous states.[52] Diplomatic relations were established but there was no recognition of the municipal law of the partially recognised entity. This permitted the

---

[46] *Ibid.*, 114.

[47] Lorimer appeared to accept that China, Japan and Siam belong in this category but confusingly also placed Turkey among states entitled to partial recognition.

[48] Lorimer, unlike Rawls, disliked democracy quite profoundly and saw it as a threat to international order. Lorimer spoke of intolerant republics, i.e. democracies based upon forms of despotism. Here, in a series of Burkean pronouncements, Lorimer decries the excesses of democracy found in France at the Proclamation of the French Convention in 1793 (*Institutes*, 131–2).

[49] Lorimer, *Institutes*, 157.   [50] *Ibid.*

[51] *Ibid.*, 159. Other entities, meanwhile, simply did not possess the requisite intellectual potential to reach the level of statehood. Imbecility in international law had, for Lorimer, three aspects: congenital imbecility, insanity and dotage. In the first case, the relationship was one of 'perpetual pupillarity' (the race is simply incapable of sovereign statehood). International law's attitude toward indigenous peoples contains traces of both nonage and congenital imbecility doctrines though neither is prevalent in any obvious sense today.

[52] *Ibid.*, 217.

extra-territorial application of laws in the entity (as relating to citizens of the civilised state). Savage states, meanwhile, were consigned to the state of nature.

There are obvious traces of this in much contemporary work by the new anti-pluralists. Singer and Wildavsky, for example, premise their 1993 book, *Real World Order*, on the idea of spheres of democracy and civilisation and spheres of anarchy, and the democratic peace literature bears some affinity to the pioneering nineteenth-century texts.[53] The interventionist approach of some of this earlier work also reverberates in contemporary treatments of failed states or humanitarian intervention. Lorimer, for example, remarked that 'the conquest of Algeria by France was not regarded as a violation of international law' because Algeria was a barbarian state not entitled to the typical immunities from intervention enjoyed by other states.[54] In Chapter 10, I consider an analogous scheme for international order drawn up by John Rawls.[55]

Among Lorimer's contemporaries, it was John Westlake who offered the most sophisticated understanding of sovereign inequality and anti-pluralism. For Westlake, the sort of extra-territoriality that was a feature of unequal relations with the likes of Japan and Siam could not operate in the absence of some forms of civilisation in the peripheral state (so these states are civilised but not 'equally civilised').[56] The Europeans exercise jurisdiction in, say, China but this requires the support of the local jurisdiction. This support, in turn, depended on the existence of some sort of civilised order, 'complex enough for the leading minds of the country to be able to appreciate the necessities of an order different from theirs'.[57] Turkey was, as ever, 'anomalous'.[58]

So this inequality of jurisdictional power was based on an individual equality. In order for Western citizens to be treated equally, they must come under the protection of Western law.[59] If natives and foreigners were treated equally badly, the right of interference revived.

---

[53] See M. Singer and A. Wildavsky, *The Real World Order: Zones of Peace/Zones of Turmoil*, (1993).

[54] Lorimer, *Institutes*, 161.

[55] See passages in John Rawls, *A Theory of Justice*, e.g. at 377–82.

[56] Westlake, *Collected Papers*, 102.   [57] *Ibid.*, 102.   [58] *Ibid.*, 103.

[59] The example Westlake gives involves a citizen of the United States who is imprisoned for failure to pay a debt in Haiti. The laws of Haiti allow release providing there is an assignment of property to the creditors. This was impossible for a foreigner (Westlake does not indicate why). Therefore, in order to give the US citizen the same rights as Haitians, US interference was necessary. Westlake, *Collected Papers*, 104. See, too, J. Westlake, *International Law*, 318–19.

Practices of anti-pluralism: capitulations and unequal treaties

The writings of Westlake and Lorimer gelled with the preoccupations of European states at this time. By the end of the nineteenth century, the mark of distinction was no longer Christianity but, as I have indicated, the more neutral characteristic, 'civilisation'. A standard of civilisation was applied to those peripheral entities claiming full membership. But what was 'civilisation'? Civilisation was a usefully elusive term. As one writer put it, 'it is difficult to indicate with precision the circumstances under which such admission takes place in the case of a nation formerly barbarous'.[60] According to Gerrit Gong, a civilised state was one that accorded basic rights to its citizens and, in particular, to foreign traders and diplomats. The capitulations or unequal treaties of this period, partly, were attempts to apply liberal standards of law to the internal affairs of sovereign states.[61] To this extent, the standard of civilisation can be perceived as an early example of liberal anti-pluralism since the result was the exclusion from the system of those states that failed to meet the (liberal) standard. Of course, there are significant differences, too. The imposition of liberal standards by the core on the periphery extended only to the treatment of Western aliens in these nineteenth-century cases. There was no attempt to widen the application of the standard of civilisation as there is in the case, say, of contemporary democratic governance theory. It is also true that the Western powers were more concerned with the protection of commercial and diplomatic interests than with the export of human rights.[62] Nevertheless, the standard of civilisation was a way of imposing a particular set of values on the international legal order. Failure to meet these values meant

---

[60] F. E. Smith, *International Law* (5th edn), 35.

[61] The Sublime Porte (Turkey) is a curious case. On the one hand, Turkey was admitted to the Family of Nations in 1856 under the terms of the Treaty of Paris. However, on the other, it was this treaty that converted the capitulations from unilateral privileges given by the Ottoman rulers to Western citizens into international obligations (see, e.g. Article 32). Thus, it was precisely in the Victorian period that Turkey's second-class status within the Family of Nations was confirmed. A. D. F. Hamlin's explanation is revealing. He claimed that Turkey's admission into the European Family of Nations was a favour. Turkey had been admitted to 'a quasi-equality with the nations about her . . .' and now possessed what Hamlin described as 'qualified membership in the political family of nations . . .' ((July 1897) 23 *The Forum*, July 523, 530 quoted in Nasim Sousa, *The Capitulatory Regime of Turkey*, 168). These extra-territorial powers held by the Western states in Turkey had existed for centuries (Sousa, 3–12). For an early example of an unequal treaty see, e.g. The Treaty of Nanking (1842) at www.isop.ucla.edu/eas/documents/nanjing.htm

[62] See generally Gilbert, *Unequal Treaties*.

exclusion or unequal sovereignty and at least some of these values can be viewed as inherently liberal.

The Ottoman Empire was the classic unequal sovereign of the nineteenth century. Indeed, it filled the role of outlaw almost perfectly. Here was an entity culturally strange, politically powerful and yet, crucially, not strong enough to impose itself in the councils of the Great Powers. The treatment of the Ottomans throughout the long nineteenth century is almost a model for the way in which outlaw states and unequal sovereigns have been treated ever since. The Ottoman Empire was one of the most successful and powerful political actors of the post-mediaeval period. Its territory embraced southern and eastern Europe, central Asia and some Arab lands. It was a major, if not the major, source of religious competition to European Christianity in the seventeenth and eighteenth centuries and its armies were powerful and well organised. Though it became an unequal (inferior) sovereign in the nineteenth century, the Sublime Porte had long regarded itself as the superior to European civilisation. Relations between the Ottomans and the rest of Europe were carried out on the basis of a presumed inequality between the Sultan and leaders from the rest of Europe. One of the earliest capitulations was granted to the Ottomans in Amsterdam by the government of the Netherlands and the extra-territorial privileges enjoyed by the Western powers in Constantinople were just that, privileges granted at the sufferance of the Sultan and capable of being withdrawn unilaterally by the Sultan in his personal capacity.

This relationship of equality was transformed in the nineteenth century and replaced by one in which the Ottomans were excluded from the new European society of states and, increasingly, treated as a second-class social group. One of the starkest manifestations of this was the apparent admission of Turkey into the society of states in 1856 at the Congress of Berlin, an act that implicitly acknowledged its exclusion up to that point and, anyway, conferred no substantive rights on the Ottomans who were still excluded from decision-making in the late nineteenth century as they had been in 1815 from the Congress of Vienna.[63] Indeed, the 1856 admission coincided with the newly minted image of Turkey as the sick man of Europe and, as the Tsar put it: 'It would be a pity if

---

[63] For example, in 1878 at the Congress of Berlin to settle claims to the Balkans, the Ottoman Empire remained on the outer rim of the important decision-making elites. Krasner, *Organised Hypocrisy*, 159.

he were to pass away without the necessary arrangements having been made.'[64] From then on the debilitating effect of the capitulations, the Balkanisation of the Empire by the 1878 Congress and the general attenuation of Ottoman territorial integrity and existential equality meant that Turkey was slowly becoming an unequal sovereign par excellence.[65] So much so that Hans Wehberg, in discussing proposals to exclude Turkey from the proposed court of justice in 1907, remarked: 'It is interesting to note how this idea of the exclusion of the Turks from the European Family is constantly recurring.'[66]

Those states that emerged from the ruins of the Ottomans' European Empire fared no better. As Stephen Krasner puts it, 'the internal autonomy of every state that emerged from the Ottoman Empire in Europe was compromised by the major European powers . . .'.[67] The Berlin Treaty, which assigned sovereign rights to the Balkan newcomers, created a complex network of semi-sovereign entities that each corresponded in some way to Lorimer's category of nonage. They were regarded as incapable of exercising full sovereignty and, in the case of Bosnia, reverted to being part of the Austro-Hungarian Empire at the beginning of the twentieth century (an act which in turn precipitated the Great War). In the 1876 Treaty of Berlin (Article 15), the Great Powers decided that: 'The provinces of Bosnia-Herzegovina shall be occupied and administered by Austria-Hungary.' Radical title remained with Turkey and there was some limited local autonomy. Meanwhile, the Great Powers had attached a secret codicil to the Congress of Berlin giving Austria rights to acquire full sovereignty by annexing Bosnia. In 1908, by an Austro-Hungarian Imperial Rescript (7 October), the Hapsburgs assumed full sovereignty over Bosnia, saying,

we deem the moment come to give the inhabitants of the two lands a new proof of our trust in their political maturity . . . for this reason . . . we extend the rights of sovereignty to Bosnia . . .[68]

Of course, China was perhaps the greatest of the unequal sovereigns at this time. It was subject to unequal treaties and the Boxer rebellion precipitated an intervention on behalf of the international community to protect diplomats. As Watson noted, 'it may be compared with similar

---

[64] Watson, *Evolution of International Society*, 269.   [65] *Ibid.*, 271.
[66] Wehberg, *The Problem of an International Court of Justice*, 79, fn. 3.
[67] Krasner, *Organised Hypocrisy*, 155.
[68] Lawrence, *Documents Illustrative of International Law*, 73.

interventions in the Congo, and other chaotic areas'.[69] The standard of civilisation introduced and reflected a series of technical innovations and subversions of the sovereign equality ideal as applied to China.[70] The unequal treaties introduced a system of extra-territorial jurisdiction based on consular rights for foreigners on Chinese territory and China was partially excluded from the society or Family of Nations.[71] Foreigners were given consular protection in Chinese ports and certain economic and trading rights. Chinese and British officials were to be treated equally *within* China.[72] In this way, China was 'compelled to abandon its inveterate anti-commercial and anti-social principles'.[73]

Ultimately, these late-Victorian practices, whether in relation to Turkey or China, can be viewed as precursors to the current liberal anti-pluralist movement in international law. There was a shared willingness to apply standards of political and legal practice universally as well as a readiness to deny admission to the international community to those states that fail to meet the required standards. The early part of the nineteenth century introduced a formal distinction between sovereign entities that were not quite part of the society of states and those, mostly European, states at the centre of this society.[74] These non-European or outsider states possessed a form of sovereignty but they exercised it very much on the margins. There was a core of states within a right-thinking international society regulated by European public law and a periphery of states to which different rules applied.[75] Those civilisations and empires on the periphery were denied full membership on account of a lack of civilisation. International lawyers played their part in developing

---

[69] Watson, *Evolution of International Society*, 273.   [70] Nussbaum, *Concise History*, 204.

[71] Unequal treaties are defined here as treaties which impose unequal obligations, and/or are imposed through the use or threat of force and/or impair the sovereignty of one of the parties in an unjust manner (Gong, *Standard of Civilisation*, 67).

[72] F. E. Smith, *International Law* 4th edn (revised J. Wylie), 35.

[73] Gong, *Standard of Civilisation*, 27 (quoting Wheaton).

[74] The idea of partial sovereignty may not make sense to contemporary international lawyers who have a tendency to see juridical sovereignty as an all or nothing concept. However, the Victorians had no such doubts about packaging sovereignty in this manner. See Oppenheim, *International Law*, above. Statehood at that time did not automatically bring with it the various benefits that might accrue now.

[75] This is not to suggest that all these early writers believed that the division ought to be maintained. In fact, the rhetoric of colonialism in the period was often couched in the language of equality and universality, e.g. P. Reinsch, *Colonial Government: An Introduction to the Study of Colonial Institutions* ('To foster the cohesion and self-realization of native societies, while at the same time providing the economic base for a higher form of organisation – that should be the substructure of an enlightened colonial policy' (109)).

justifications for the imposition of this policy and in elaborating it. And this academic writing had a curious two-way relationship with the doctrines and practices I discuss. On the one hand, the scholars of the period purported to describe the diminution in sovereign status caused by the imposition and acceptance of a series of intrusive practices and doctrines (e.g. capitulations). The result of these practices was inequality. On the other hand, the continual labelling of entities as 'uncivilised' or peripheral or dangerous led to a belief that these groups were not entitled to the protections and privileges of sovereignty that render unlawful the sorts of extra-territorial intrusions occurring throughout the nineteenth century.

The scholars of the nineteenth century, then, constructed an elaborate system of inequality while purporting to ground a new scientific conception of international law on sovereign equality. At the same time, they brought into relief the European essence of the society of states; a society that was confined initially to a few European and, latterly, North American powers, but which was designed to spread across the civilising globe. At this stage, though, it remained a society of unequal sovereigns.

The practices of anti-pluralism: intervention and the Holy Alliance

The principle of sovereign equality was challenged from a different direction in the early nineteenth century. As I indicated in Chapter 2, sovereign equality contains at least three separate elements. In the chapters on legalised hegemony, I was most concerned with departures from one of these elements, i.e. legislative equality and its variants. This chapter has begun an analysis of those doctrines and theories that challenge two principles central to what I call existential equality.[76] One is the right to exist and be recognised as a state with the full attributes of sovereignty. The other is concerned with the right to political independence. This commitment to pluralism and territorial and political stability in the international system has been a feature of the international order since Westphalia. At the time of the Vienna Congress, the Great Powers, apart from Great Britain, were absolutist monarchies but they did not, initially, require that other states be legitimated in this way. Britain was a parliamentary monarchy but had no interest in exporting its liberal constitution. Religion, meanwhile, had receded in

---

[76] See Georg Schwarzenberger on the difference between existential equality, ('small nations have a right to unhampered existence and should be protected against arbitrary decisions . . .') and legislative equality (*Power Politics*, 303).

importance and nationalism was yet to be the force it became from the mid-nineteenth century onwards.

However, after Vienna, and as a result of the French Revolution and the Napoleonic expansionism it spawned, sovereign equality came to be challenged by the growing sense, on the part of the large Eastern powers (especially Austria), that security was threatened as much from within by revolutionaries and nationalists as it was externally by re-vanchist European powers in the Napoleonic mode.[77] Metternich, for example, was concerned to promote equilibrium both internally and externally. The balance of power was to co-exist alongside the right to intervene to prevent revolution and Jacobinism. The post-Congress period thus witnessed two conflicting approaches to existential equal-ity/pluralism and hierarchy. The British view was that internal politics were an internal matter. Britain had no intention of becoming involved in messy domestic political affairs and, unlike its liberal-democratic suc-cessors (e.g. US), it was entirely uninterested in making the world safe for democracy.[78] Great Britain was content enough to make Europe safe for the British. In this sense, the British supported sovereign equality if it meant the equal right of nations to 'choose' the government of their own preference.

According to Castlereagh, the Quadruple Alliance was created for:

The Liberation of a great proportion of the Continent of Europe from the military dominion of France . . . It never was, however, intended as an Union for the Government of the World or for the Superintendence of the Internal Affairs of other States.[79]

---

[77] This is reflected in the preamble to the Second Treaty of Paris concluded after Napoleon's 'late enterprise' when he escaped from Elba (on 25 February 1815) in which the Allied powers impose much more punitive conditions on France than were present in the First Treaty. In the Second Treaty, the Allies speak of the threat from Bonaparte and from 'the revolutionary system reproduced in France' (Hertslet, *Map of Europe*, 342).

[78] See Letter from Lord Castlereagh to Lord William Bentick, Paris, 7 May 1814, *Correspondence of Viscount Castlereagh*, Ser. 3, 10: 'It is impossible not to perceive a great moral change coming on in Europe, and that the principles of freedom are in full operation. The danger is, that the change may be too sudden to ripen into anything likely to make the world better or happier . . . The attempts may be made, *and we must abide the consequences*, but I am sure it is better to retard than accelerate the operation of this most hazardous principle which is abroad . . .' (19). See also Kissinger, *Diplomacy*, 98–100.

[79] Quoted in Kissinger, *Diplomacy*, 91. Of course, Britain continued to intervene and interfere but as a matter of policy and strategy not principle. See, e.g. the support for the French in Crimea.

The British had been prepared to enter France in order to destroy Napoleon, 'in the destruction of whose power all mankind had a common interest', but they could never consent to ongoing meddling in the internal affairs of France.[80] The Prussians took a different view. In Houssaye's words, Prussia,

resounded with the press's barking: 'We were wrong to be merciful with the French. We should have exterminated them all. Yes, we must exterminate this bunch of 500,000 robbers. We must do more than that: we must outlaw the French people'.[81]

The British view, and the eventual policy of the Allies, was that France ought not to be treated as an enemy state but a potential ally fit for rehabilitation. Indeed, the treatment of France following the Napoleonic wars suggests that, in some respects, the fallen power was to remain an equal rather than an outlaw. The idea that enemies were automatically outlaws can be seen in hindsight as a twentieth-century invention, the effects of which can be seen at Versailles, at Nuremberg and in Iraq.[82]

At the same time, a more anti-pluralist view was being expressed by the Austrians, who wanted the Quadruple Alliance to act against domestic rebellions when those rebellions threatened the international order. This was combined with Tsar Alexander's belief in a Christian brotherhood of Great Powers prepared to act collectively against infidels and revolutionaries. Metternich and Alexander, thus, adopted a Wilsonian approach to international politics. The resultant Holy Alliance can be characterised as a precursor to some of the liberal anti-pluralisms discussed in the following two chapters though this might strike modern readers as odd.[83] The Holy Alliance is anti-pluralist because anti-pluralism in international law can best be understood as a pattern of

---

[80] Letter from Lord Castlereagh to Lord Stewart, 19 April 1815, *Correspondence of Viscount Castlereagh*, Ser. 3, 10, 318.

[81] See Henry Houssaye, *1815: La Première restauration, le retour de l'île d'Elbe, les cent jours*, vol. I, 458–9 (quoted in Bass, *Politics of War Crimes Trials*, 55).

[82] For a discussion of the debates over what to do about France in 1814–15 see Bass, *Politics of War Crimes Trials*; G. Simpson, 'The Balance between Forgetting and Remembering' (2001) 72:4 *The Political Quarterly*, 503.

[83] As Holbraad points out, the Holy Alliance 'adopted a cosmopolitan view of European society . . .' (casting aside what Holbraad calls the traditional view). This cosmopolitan view emphasised 'the solidarity of the monarchs on one side and the universal character of the revolutionary pressure on the other'. The method was armed intervention. This was how Holbraad was able to speak of the 'cosmopolitan doctrines of the legitimists' (Holbraad, *Concert of Europe*, 23).

thought that takes domestic structures seriously and seeks to promote a particular form of domestic political order through intervention.[84]

Of course, anti-pluralists adopt a range of substantive politics. In Wight's analogous category of revolutionism everyone from Kant to Hitler to Marx is included.[85] The distinguishing mark of anti-pluralism is a missionary quality and a desire to universalise a particular form of political order. Wilson's liberalism and Metternich's conservatism are poles apart in many respects but they share a concern to export an approved political system in order to make the international order more stable (safe for democracy or safe from nationalism). The result, in 1815, was the Holy Alliance between Austria, Prussia and Russia.[86] These powers did not recognise a zone of domestic jurisdiction. Not every state was entitled to exercise its political independence by choosing any form of government it wished. Only some forms of government were regarded as legitimate.

The large Central Powers tried to build into Vienna the permanence of a particular type of reactionary conservative regime within each state.[87] This failed but the subsequent Holy Alliance represented a *revolutionist* (in Wight's terminology) or anti-pluralist twist to international affairs including a right to intervene to protect the system and individual states from succumbing to *revolutionary* and nationalistic tendencies.[88] This was a clear attack on the strong conception of sovereign equality (in the form we now see in the Charter) and was hierarchical to the extent that it preferred and gave legitimacy to states based on a particular,

---

[84] So, cosmopolitans or anti-pluralists reject two popular conceptions of international order: the realist and the legalist/classical liberal. Realists tend to accept a radical disjuncture between domestic institutions and international behaviour while legalists, whatever their views on national political order, have long preferred an international order in which states are prohibited from intervening in one another's affairs.

[85] Wight, 'Anatomy of International Thought', 221–5.

[86] The Holy Alliance was signed by the three Eastern powers, Prussia, Russia and Austria on 26 September 1815 (Treaty between Austria, Prussia and Russia in Hertslet, *Map of Europe*, 317).

[87] The Tsar claimed that the Treaty of Alliance signed at Vienna had committed the signatory powers (including the British) to common action against 'the same revolutionary principles that caused the recent usurpation in France' (W. P. Cresson, *The Holy Alliance*, 38).

[88] It was on this issue that the British and the rest of the Concert were at loggerheads, with the British adopting a more straightforwardly liberal position of non-intervention resembling the later Charter model. The Prince Regent's Reply to the three Central Powers following their invitation to accede to the Holy Alliance refers to none of this but merely regrets that the British Constitution cannot allow accession to such a treaty (Hertslet, *Map of Europe*, 320).

reactionary political theory and deprived revolutionary governments of the same legitimacy. In this case, the values were those of the Christian religion.[89] The Holy Alliance was naturalist and cosmopolitan. It derived certain truths about human affairs from 'divine providence' and intended to base the system of international relations on these truths.[90] The Treaty creating the Alliance makes explicit the movement of these 'truths' from the private world of religion to the public world of interstate relations: 'The precepts of Justice, Christian Charity, and Peace were to have an immediate influence on the councils of Princes, and guide all their steps . . .'.[91] In this way, the Holy Alliance challenged both constitutional liberalism and the liberal-pluralist idea of international law and relations. There is a double movement from the private (the internal conscience and values of human beings, the internal public values and constitution of the state) to a public law of Europe based on religion.[92] This was interpreted as an intention to intervene to prevent revolution and reform.[93] The Holy Alliance was, of course, explicitly hierarchical. Austria, Prussia and Russia were said to be part of the same Christian nation with powers delegated from God to lead these three branches of that nation. The promise made as a consequence of this declaration was that these three states would 'on all occasions and in all places lend each other aid'.[94]

---

[89] Kissinger describes this Holy Alliance as 'a document [not seen] since Ferdinand II had left the throne of the Holy Roman Empire' (*Diplomacy*, 83).

[90] Holy Alliance Treaty.

[91] Christian precepts, 'far from being applicable only to private life, ought, on the contrary, to have direct influence on the resolve of princes' (*ibid.*).

[92] Tsar Alexander makes this idea explicit in a letter he sent to his Ambassador in London, Lieven, where he describes the Alliance as 'a means of associating ourselves with the very essence of the saving precepts – rules of conduct which have been too long confined to the sphere of private relationships' (Cresson, *Holy Alliance*, 41).

[93] Reactionary cosmopolitans can believe one of two things about internal disturbance or revolution. Either they believe that revolutionary governments will disturb the balance of power by embarking on revisionist and radical foreign policies or they might believe that revolutionary success can lead to imitation. The Soviet Union was feared for both those reasons. In one case, revolution is viewed as a direct threat to order, in the second case, the revolutions leave the international order untouched but radically transform the domestic systems. Metternich *et al.* were afraid of both. Von Gentz, initially concerned about the horizontal relations between states because of the possibility of aggression, then turned to the possible effects of revolution on the foreign policy of states, then the possibility of the spread of revolutionary ideas. The Alliance intervened against revolution in Spain and Naples but was prevented from going further by the British (in Europe) and the Americans (in South and Central America, the Monroe Doctrine).

[94] Hertslet, *Map of Europe*, 318, Article 1, Holy Alliance Treaty.

The first test of this interventionist doctrine arose with the revolutions in Spain (March 1820) and Naples (July 1820). The Holy Alliance, in a circular issued to foreign courts, saw a direct link between Napoleon's external military threat and what it called 'a force no less tyrannical and no less detestable, that of revolution and crime'.[95] At Troppau, the Alliance further elaborated its anti-pluralist *raison d'être*, arguing that there was an 'undeniable' right of intervention in cases where revolution had taken place. The circular gives three grounds for supporting this right. First, the overthrow of legitimate governments created a dangerous precedent and example. Second, the governments formed by revolution tended to adopt subsequently a hostile attitude towards surrounding states. Third, revolution tended to cause chaos in surrounding states. The three Central Powers argued forcefully that this interventionist doctrine was at the heart of the system created at Vienna.

The Alliance, therefore, refused recognition to revolutionary governments and requested that the King of Naples act as a mediator between the Alliance and his 'erring peoples'.[96] While the Holy Alliance was proclaiming this new interventionist doctrine in the name of international law, the British Government denied its existence on the same grounds.[97] In a circular from Castlereagh issued to British Missions on the 19 January 1821, the British distanced themselves from the Holy Alliance, claiming that anti-revolutionary intervention had no basis in international law, being irreconcilable with the equality of states or the general interest.[98] Interestingly, the British felt such a right to be compatible only with a federative Europe 'leading to many serious inconveniences'.[99]

The Alliance's reply came at Laybach in 1821 following the suppression of a later revolt in Piedmont by the Austrian armies. In the Declaration of Laybach 1821 (Prussia, Austria, Russia), the Holy Alliance shifted position slightly. Instead of speaking of erring peoples, these same peoples became the possessors of a sovereignty that itself had been subverted by criminal tendencies within the body politic. The Allied powers had come

---

[95] *Ibid.*, 659.   [96] *Ibid.*, 660.

[97] The UK Parliament feared that the Alliance might be directed against democracies. See Cresson, *Holy Alliance*, 42–3.

[98] Hertslet, *Map of Europe*, 664.

[99] Circular Dispatch to British Missions at Foreign Courts, London, 19 January 1821. The British did not deny that the Austrian or Italian powers might have some justification for intervention but this required evidence of serious direct danger to these powers.

to the assistance of a subdued Peoples, and they considered it as coming in support of their liberty, and not as an attack against their independence . . . the object of that policy will always be the preservation of the Independence and of the rights of each State.[100]

The Holy Alliance could not in the end be sustained. It lacked the support of the British and French, who were not always sympathetic to its anti-pluralist ambitions and, in the end, squabbles among the Eastern powers and the rise of liberalism within Germany and Austria led to its unravelling. More importantly, the Alliance was viewed as an effort to impose a particular political idea on the states of Europe. This was incompatible with the growing liberalism and openness of the international order itself and intolerable to the increasingly influential liberal elites within European states.

This movement between equality and hierarchy and pluralism and anti-pluralism is captured in the transformation of Tsar Alexander I who begins as a realist, proposing an extreme form of bilateral hegemony between Russia and the United Kingdom, as Europe's only true, impartial powers, before calling for a General Congress, at Vienna (his legalist phase). Following Napoleon's final defeat, Alexander embraces the equality of all *Christian* nations in the Holy Alliance and thus adopts a more interventionist, anti-pluralist position.[101] The Tsar's various apostasies capture the movement of international law itself through the modern period, in perpetual compromise between the functionality of hegemony, the democratic appeal of equality and the demand of ideology.

By the end of the nineteenth century, sovereign equality was becoming ascendant. Anti-pluralist interventionism in Europe receded early in the century with the demise of the Holy Alliance. Meanwhile, the unequal sovereigns were asserting their full sovereignty from the periphery, demanding the rights and immunities commensurate with this sovereignty and entering the widening society of civilised nations in large numbers.

---

[100] Declaration of the Allied Sovereigns of Austria, Prussia and Russia (Laybach), 12 May 1821 in Hertslet, *Map of Europe*, 667–9.
[101] Klein, *Sovereign Equality*, 15; Hertslet, *Map of Europe*, 317–18; Kissinger, *Diplomacy*, 189.

9 Peace-loving nations: 1945

Introduction

The immediate effects of the San Francisco conference in 1945 had made themselves felt, it seemed, in the culmination of the impulses found in the nineteenth century, away from exclusion on the basis of ideology or civilisation or, even, 'democracy', away from the idea of state crime and away from using intervention as a means of creating homogeneity among states. The United Nations Charter and the International Military Tribunal Charter together were suggestive of a world in which states of different character would be equal, intervention to promote particular versions of the good life would be illegal, and enemy states would be rehabilitated through selective criminal trial rather than subject to mass punishment through 'reparations'.

In 1815, the Prussian press had demanded that: 'We outlaw the French people' but what prevailed was a sober British preference for re-engaging with a defeated enemy after selective purging. When the Holy Alliance demanded a right to intervene to prevent the fomentation and spread of revolutionary liberalism, the Western powers made their lack of enthusiasm very clear and the right came to nought. And, most importantly, the tendency to distinguish a civilised, and predominantly European, core from a non-Western fringe was slowly reversed as the nineteenth century played itself out. The overall effect was to buttress the idea of sovereign equality and pluralism. San Francisco and Nuremberg seemed, then, simply to continue these egalitarian trends in relations among states.

The regimes of state delinquency (abandoned after Versailles and revived in the case of Iraq), and democratic governance/standard of civilisation (applied to the Ottomans, pervasive in the nineteenth century, residually applied to the Bolsheviks, defeated at San Francisco but ascendant again in the late twentieth century), were both in abeyance during the period under discussion in this chapter. The San Francisco Conference produced an (eventually) inclusive and largely non-interventionist international legal order. The UN was given no explicit mandate to promote particular ideological forms through military intervention and the admissions policy of the UN was pluralistic.

This chapter is about these trends but it is also about a countervailing anti-pluralism present in the discussions about how to punish Germany after the Second World War and in the debates over membership foreshadowed at Versailles and rehearsed at San Francisco. Outlaw states, then, continued to be a feature of the international legal landscape throughout the early twentieth century and this period to an extent prefigured the post-cold war anti-pluralisms discussed in Chapter 10. In particular, amidst all the apparent tolerance and inclusiveness of Wilsonian liberalism, two early anti-pluralist notes were struck in relation to Germany and the USSR respectively. In the first case, the Versailles Peace Treaty imposed a highly punitive series of sanctions on a defeated Germany. While it became increasingly unacceptable to distinguish civilised from uncivilised states, the idea that some states were outlaws intensified in its effects.[1] Germany was largely excluded from the councils of Europe and the world as a result of its crime of aggression and its suspect revisionist, militaristic 'character'. As this book has argued, states are outlawed not always or generally because of what they do but because of what they are perceived to be. This is, partly, true of Iraq

---

[1] The standard of civilisation continued to influence both the way non-state actors were treated and, in particular, the operation of the mandate territories established under Article 22 of the Covenant (envisaging independence or continuing dependence according to judgements about the varying levels of development among the mandate territories and peoples). The League of Nations Covenant introduced, in Article 22, the idea of a mandate to be applied to colonies not yet ready for independence. The notion that backward peoples could, through the benevolence and wisdom of their colonial masters, become more civilised and better prepared to exercise forms of self-government was an important aspect of international society from at least 1918 through to 1960 (the trust idea was derived ultimately from principles of domestic law and was first applied by the British in their colonial practices. See, e.g. Martin Wight, *British Colonial Constitutions 1947* (1952) for examples. See, too, General Act of the Berlin Conference on Africa 1888 at Article 6). A belief in the progressive effects of modified colonialism under international supervision was reiterated in Chapters XII and XIII of the Charter of the United Nations. These regimes were, of course, applied to non-state actors so the principle of sovereign equality is not directly implicated. Nonetheless, the mandate and trusteeship system has become an inspiration for the expanding zone of international competence over unequal sovereigns or failed states.

today and was certainly the case in relation to Bolshevik Russia whose propensity to spread revolution and revolutionary-bearing towards the international community marked it out as another outlaw. The story of these two outlaws, Germany and the USSR, will be taken up briefly in this chapter.

The turn of the century

By the turn of the century, the international system was undergoing a dramatic change. The division of humanity into a family of mostly European and North American on one side and an uncivilised periphery on the other was impossible to sustain. Pressure to modify this demarcated system came from two sides.

First, states such as Japan and the South American states embraced the standard of civilisation and could no longer be legitimately excluded from the society of states.[2] Civilised states were those entities that accorded basic rights to their citizens and aliens, boasted an organised bureaucracy, adhered to international law and possessed capacity to enter into diplomatic relations.[3] For example, following the significant changes wrought by the Meiji Restoration, Japan met these conditions and became the first Asian state to be admitted into the Family of Nations.[4]

It had become a fully fledged member of the international community by adopting the European standards implicit in international law. But in being admitted it also effected a shift in the way these standards were perceived. International law was now open to non-Christian, non-Western states. Civilisation remained important (e.g. see Turkey)[5] but

---

[2] Gong, *Standard of Civilisation*, 14–15. Uncivilised behaviour included polygamy, slavery and suttee.

[3] The Japanese formally entered the Family of Nations under the terms of the Aoki-Kimberley Treaty (1894) (see Gong, *Standard of Civilisation*, 31). The Ottomans had been admitted by Article 7 of the 1856 Treaty of Paris but whether this Treaty had the effect of making the Sublime Porte a full member of the Family of Nations is open to question (see Gong, *Standard of Civilisation*, 29; F. E. Smith, *International Law*, 5th edn, 36).

[4] Gong also suggests that one of these was the Japanese display of military power in the Sino-Japanese War of 1895 and the Russo-Japanese War of 1905. Of the latter, he implies civilisation is a standard reached when a nation or ancient empire defeats a Western state. See Gong, *Standard of Civilisation*, 184.

[5] According to Oppenheim, even as late as 1912, Turkey was still not a member of the society of states or the Family of Nations because it was only semi-civilised. See *International Law* (3rd edn), 34.

the special European ingredient in international law was already being diluted and the system became increasingly ecumenical.[6] This secularisation and de-Europeanisation of difference resulted in definitions of civilisation such as Oppenheim's 'civilisation of such a kind only is conditional so as to enable the respective State and its subjects to understand and to act in conformity with the principles of the laws of Nations'.[7]

There was, as Bull and Watson put it, a 'revolt against exclusion'. This took many forms.[8] Usually, it was prompted by the claims of the semi-periphery (Turkey, China and Japan) to membership of the Family of Nations.[9] However, the word 'revolt' suggests a wholesale assault on the exclusionary idea. In fact, in many of these cases, accommodation or co-option rather than revolt proved the dominant practice. The Persian delegate, disturbed at Persia's relegation to a fourth rank power in the discussions involving the Permanent Court at The Hague, was obliged to plead for greater representation on the basis of Persia's ancient civilisation and the calmness of contemporary Persia as 'a friend of progress' willing to 'enter into the ways of Western civilisation'.[10]

Second, the scholars of the early twentieth century, in their eagerness to place international law on a scientific basis, were keen to present themselves as open-minded and cosmopolitan in comparison with more backward contemporaries. Lawrence, for example, embraced a form of secularism:

We have therefore in our definition, spoken of it [international law] as, 'the rules which determine the conduct of the general body of *civilised* states'. But we have not thought fit to follow the example of some writers, and limit still further to *Christian* states (his emphasis).[11]

---

[6] There was still no place for China (despite it having been invited to The Hague) and it was still subject to unequal treaties and extraterritoriality. See Gong, *Standard of Civilisation*, 28.

[7] *Ibid.*, 59 (quoting Oppenheim, *International Law*, 31).

[8] Bull and Watson, *Expansion*, 220.

[9] *Ibid.*, 220–4. This revolt adopted many different forms through a number of phases. The second and third phases coincide with the liberation struggles in the Charter era and revolve around claims to racial equality and self-determination (racial and political phase). Finally there were the more recent economic (the New International Economic Order) and cultural phases of the revolt where Western values and economic dominance came under attack.

[10] J. B. Scott, *The Hague Peace Conferences*, 632.

[11] Lawrence, *Principles of International Law* (3rd edn), 5.

Later, Lawrence, writing in 1910, and after noting wryly that entry to the Family of Nations required 'a certain or rather uncertain amount of civilisation', accepted that states could be 'civilised after the European model'.[12] Some began to present the 'standard' as a functional test rather than one based on civilisation. What is clear is that international lawyers, writing in the late Victorian era, were by now rejecting the idea of international law as a closed system. Writers such as Lawrence favoured a liberal international order in which states were admitted on the basis of some formal capacity rather than internal political organisation.

By the end of the nineteenth century, then, the standard of civilisation could no longer be simply modified and refined to accommodate the aspirant states. The stress of imposing cultural and political homogeneity on a radically diverse group of states proved too much for the European powers and they eventually came to reject the standard altogether and embrace a different egalitarian liberalism. The European ideas of sovereign equality and political independence were adapted to fit the needs of these new entities just as these principles later supported the post-decolonisation development of new nation-states in Africa and Asia.[13] The practice of international organisations and at international conferences mirrored this. There was a general widening of participation in response to these claims from the periphery and doubts at the centre. For example, at the first Geneva Convention Conference in 1864 there were fourteen states present whereas at the 1908 equivalent there were thirty-five states. Similarly, in the short time between the First and Second Hague Peace Conferences, the number of delegations expanded from twenty-six to forty-four. The story was similar in the constitution of technical bodies. Fourteen states attended the 1863 Postal Conference in Paris, twenty-two were present at the Congress of Berne in 1874 and by 1914 there was universal membership of the Universal Postal Union.[14] More and more states were being brought in from the periphery.[15]

So, by the time Versailles approaches there was a general tendency in the direction of universal participation and existential sovereign equality. Of course, the interventionist elements of anti-pluralism did not

---

[12] Lawrence, *Principles of International Law* (4th edn), 58, 84.
[13] Adam Watson, *Evolution of International Society*, 280.
[14] Lande, 'Revindication', 401.
[15] This process had begun, tentatively, in the late nineteenth century with the recognition of Liberia (in 1847), the Congo (in 1884) and Transvaal (in 1877) though each of these states had a chequered, and in two cases, short, life-span.

disappear entirely. More states than ever participated in international society but many of these states remained subject to the dictates of one or more of the Great Powers. President Roosevelt, for example, in his annual message of 1904, made it clear that: 'Chronic wrong-doing, or an impotence which results in a general loosening of the ties of civilised society, may in America, as elsewhere, ultimately require intervention by some civilized nation . . . may force the United States . . . to the exercise of an international police power'.[16] Nor was the system entirely inclusive. Korea was excluded from the Second Hague Peace Conference and, as I shall go on to discuss, the response to the Communist Revolution in Russia was hardly accommodating.[17]

It is equally true that while an increasing number of entities gained full sovereignty, the equality extended to states was not thereby automatically devolved to the colonised peoples of Africa and Asia. Whatever the standard of civilisation, it remained the case that colonised peoples could not reach it. As Peter Fitzpatrick puts it, the colonies were 'called to be the same yet repelled as different, bound in an infinite transition which perpetually requires to attain what is intrinsically denied to it'.[18] So, that in the period between 1918 and 1960, the idea of trusteeship was regarded as a legitimate way to deal with uncivilised or immature peoples *who were not yet sovereign states.*[19]

Nonetheless, by the time of Versailles:

The doctrine of positivism finally broke down the distinction between civilised and uncivilised States, which had been the last remaining barrier to heterogeneity.[20]

The state system was embracing pluralism.

---

[16] Annual Message of the President, 1904.

[17] See *Luthor v. Sagor (James) and Co* [1921] 3 KB 532 (for discussion of the attitude of the UK towards recognition of the Soviet Union immediately following the revolution). The Soviet Union, of course, was in a state of self-imposed exile, declaiming the liberal order from the sidelines. The Soviets responded to the debate about their membership of the League of Nations by suggesting that they would participate providing the Covenant incorporated 'the expropriation of the capitalists of all countries as another of the basic principles of the League of Nations'. See Kathyrn Davis, *The Soviets at Geneva*, 16.

[18] P. Fitzpatrick, 'Nationalism as Racism', 11.

[19] Italics mine. Colonised peoples were not regarded as possessing any sovereignty at all. See Chapter 10.

[20] Schwarzenberger, *Power Politics*, 41. For an entirely different view of the relationship between positivism and the standard of civilisation see Anghie, 'Finding the Peripheries'.

Versailles

By the time of the Versailles Conference, then, there were two clearly competing positions. These are summarised in Georg Schwarzenberger's fine book on the League of Nations.[21] For Schwarzenberger, one of the key debates at Versailles concerned the future structure and membership of the new international organisation. He organised these debates around two poles, describing them as *homogeneous universality*: 'a collective system [comprising] communities of a certain constitutional structure only' and *heterogeneous universality* where the system or organisation 'does not apply such standards'.[22] These two theories of community draw on the debates of the late Victorian age and anticipated the discussions held at San Francisco. They, also, derive from the two liberalisms I discuss in Chapter 8, liberal pluralism (the liberalism of inclusion) and liberal anti-pluralism. On one side, Schwarzenberger's heterogeneous universality was favoured by states' representatives who believed that 'sovereignty' ought to be the sole test of membership.[23] Entities that were sovereign and independent were entitled to the same rights as other similarly situated states in the international system. The core liberal ideals of liberty and equality were bound up in this idea of sovereignty. States, like individuals, were entitled to full status regardless of constitutional structure or political belief. On the other side were the anti-pluralists who wished to impose, sometimes quite stringent, standards on membership in order to enforce liberalism *within* states.

The debates revolved around, mainly, the question of admission of ordinary members of the international community or the application of what is now known as the democratic governance norm. However, the other regime discussed in more detail in the next chapter, the criminal state regime, was also a feature of the Versailles discussions. I now want to consider the post-Versailles period in relation to a defeated Germany and a resurgent Bolshevik Soviet Union.

The Versailles Peace Treaties marked a profound shift from the nineteenth-century sensibility of forgiveness and rehabilitation of fallen enemies to a much more vindictive, anti-pluralist approach towards the defeated powers. In 1815, the other Allied powers' refusal to countenance a Carthaginian peace prevailed over the vengefulness of the victorious

---

[21] Schwarzenberger, *League of Nations and World Order.*   [22] *Ibid.,* 4.
[23] See, e.g. The Argentine Proposal, First Assembly, Plenary Meetings at 261–2, in Schwarzenberger, *League of Nations and World Order, ibid.,* 62–3.

Prussians. The Prussians had wanted territorial amputation, reparations and permanent occupation (anticipating the Versailles and, later, the Iraq model).[24] This solution was regarded with horror by the British, in particular. It was the British, after all, who had sent Napoleon to a very gentle initial exile on Elba and who eventually managed to engineer France's return to the Great Power camp informally at Vienna and officially at Aix-la-Chapelle.[25] Later in the century, there were signs of a more punitive peace-making approach after the Franco-Prussian war of 1871 where large-scale reparations were imposed on France.[26] At Versailles, the Allies adopted a policy based on what the former UK ambassador to Germany called, the 'Mad Dog of Europe' theory.[27] Germany was regarded as a criminal state, i.e. one that posed 'a *permanent* danger and a *constant* military menace' (my italics).[28] In this way, Versailles provided the template for the punitive peace imposed on Iraq and now seems to be established as a respectable model for dealing with enemies.

Meanwhile, the USSR had, in effect, outlawed itself. In 1918, the Soviet state was not thought capable of contributing to the existence or non-existence of a rule of Public International Law. Indeed, the Nazis themselves were later to declare the USSR an 'anti-state'.[29]

However, even this level of antipathy could not be maintained and by 1925, there was a shift in attitudes towards Germany and the Soviet Union. Much of this was related to the inevitable consequences of the passage of time but the decision to admit Germany in 1926 was an important development in a long-running debate within the League about whether the institution should be developed along pluralist or anti-pluralist lines. Even the German Government understood this, describing its admission as 'an appreciable step towards the establishment of the universality of the League'.[30] Certainly, universal membership was regarded as a very positive goal by many of the League's founders. As Schwarzenberger argued, 'the Peace Conference intended to create a

---

[24] Bass, *Politics of War Crimes Trials*, 55.

[25] See Note Addressed by the Plenipotentiaries of Great Britain, Austria, Prussia and Russia to the Duke of Richelieu, 4 November, 1818 in Hertslet, *Map of Europe*.

[26] Indeed, France's vindictiveness in 1918 might be explained as an act of retribution for 1871.

[27] Schwarzenberger, *League of Nations and World Order*, 75.

[28] *Ibid.* (quoting Lord D'Abernon).

[29] See Georg Schwarzenberger, *International Law and Totalitarian Lawlessness*, at 26, 103–6.

[30] Letter of the German Government to the Secretary-General of the League, 12 December 1924 (1925) *League of Nations, Official Journal* 325.

League of Nations based on the principle of universality which was only restricted by moderate qualifications of constitutional homogeneity'.[31] Many delegates supported a League based on universal membership and a pluralist attitude towards difference. In all this there was a fear of the anti-pluralism of previous schemes, whether Napoleonic Jacobinism or the Holy Alliance's interventionist response to the vestiges of that Jacobinism. Lord Robert Cecil, in a letter to Colonel House, put the case for pluralism:

Prussian militarism is indeed a portentous evil, but if, misled by our fear of it, we try to impose on all the nations of the world a form of government which has been indeed admirably successful in America, and this country, but is not necessarily suited for all others, I am convinced we shall plant the seeds of very serious international trouble.[32]

Prior to the admission of Germany, though, a liberalism of tolerance and inclusion had been challenged at Versailles by those delegates to the Peace Conference who sought to enforce liberal standards *within* states.[33] Prominent writers, too, supported the idea of an homogeneous and, therefore, efficient League.[34] These anti-pluralists included those, like Carl Schmitt, who worried that ideological discrepancy would result in paralysis and others such as M. Viviani, the French representative at the First Assembly, who argued that: 'A nation desirous of entering here must have a free and responsible government; it must be a democracy.'[35] Philip Marshall Brown took the view that some states lost their right to exist either because they were in a hopeless state of anarchy (such as Persia, Morocco) or because the Great Powers had ruled by decree that they were henceforth non-existent (e.g. Congress of Vienna). Equality, then, was a provisional right to be recognised and respected when a state possessed an appropriate political personality and was readily forfeited by anarchic government and bad behaviour, e.g. aggression.

---

[31] Schwarzenberger, *League of Nations and World Order*, 44.

[32] *Ibid.*, 28. Though Lord Robert Cecil also insisted that the admission of new states should be made conditional on these states abiding by certain standards in relation to minorities, Records, First Assembly (1920), Plenary Meetings, 406–7 in Schwarzenberger, *League of Nations and World Order*, 60.

[33] There were also proposals from groups who wanted to see a League made up of only the nineteenth-century Family of Nations. See the Bryce Scheme (in the UK) and an early American proposal (both referred to in A. Zimmern, *The League of Nations and the Rule of Law*, 162 and 169).

[34] See Philip Marshall Brown, *International Realities*, 14.

[35] *Records, First Assembly* (1920), Plenary Meetings, 575, in Schwarzenberger, *League of Nations and World Order*, 88.

The result of the jostling between these positions was not entirely clear.[36] The League of Nations Covenant at Article 1(2) implies that the League was to be a closed system of like-minded states. A central qualification of membership was to be 'self-government' meaning democratic government. However, the practice of the League tells a different tale. In the two decades of its existence, the organisation embraced a more pluralistic approach to membership with the admission of Abyssinia, the toleration of an authoritarian Italy and the decision to include Bolshevik Russia.[37] As Schwarzenberger puts it, 'the practice of the League tended away from the principle of homogeneous universality . . . as it was envisaged by the authors of the Covenant, towards that of heterogeneous universality'.[38] By 1939, Alfred Zimmern, the great chronicler of the League, began his defining text by saying that the term 'League' was a misnomer implying exclusiveness and adversarialism whereas the League itself was 'inclusive and universal'.[39] By the time of the Second World War, the standard of civilisation was largely discredited but the idea of drawing distinctions of a different sort was not entirely rejected.[40]

San Francisco

In the negotiations at San Francisco two liberalisms clashed again. Once more there was the liberalism of inclusion and universality, a liberalism that sought to extend the benefits of international law to all peoples and

---

[36] Indeed, quite often, the position of individual delegates was unclear. At the Third Meeting of the Commission, there was a debate about President Wilson's draft Article 6 of the Covenant in which he proposed that 'only self-governing states shall be admitted to membership in the League'. Lord Robert Cecil believed this would be hard to define, M. Bourgeois preferred the phrase 'responsible government' while Wilson himself remarked that 'we ought not to pass an act of oblivion by putting up standards that we have not always lived up to ourselves' (see D. Miller, *The Drafting of the Covenant*, vol. I, 164–7).

[37] Each of these was controversial. The admission of the Soviets, for example, was resisted by the Vatican and by powerful lobbies within the host state's government. See *British Documents on Foreign Affairs* Part II, Ser. I, vol. II (ed. K. Bourne and D. Cameron-Watt), 23 and 304.

[38] Schwarzenberger, *League of Nations and World Order*, 94.

[39] Zimmern, *League of Nations*, 183–91.

[40] 'In practice we no longer insist that States shall conform to any common standards of justice, religious toleration and internal government . . . this means that, in effect, we have now abandoned the old distinction between civilised and uncivilised States', H. A. Smith, Radio Address, 'Where the League Failed', *The Listener*, London (1938), 183 (quoted in Schwarzenberger, *Power Politics*, 42).

all states. This project emphasised the civilising effect of an international liberal legal order. Merely to participate in such an order was to be subject to positive influences. It was imperative, according to advocates of this view, that all states be admitted to the new international organisation. At the same time, there was another liberalism, a more forthright anti-pluralism that sought to exclude enemy states and undemocratic states from the brave new world of a United Democratic Nations.[41] This early liberal anti-pluralism had its roots in a reluctance to accord UN membership to certain categories of illiberal states (these included the enemy states (Japan, Germany), states who had failed to embrace democracy in the post-war era (notably Spain) and even, in some cases, states who had remained ambivalent during the war (e.g. Argentina)). These instincts were developed into a conception of international society that wished to make democracy a condition of entry into the system.

Perhaps naturally, in 1941, a clear distinction was being drawn between enemy states and allied states. To this extent, these early proposals were engineered in an atmosphere of moral and political differentiation rather than sovereign equality and pluralism. The Washington Declaration, for example, adopted this adversarial, wartime rhetoric in its reference to 'savage and brutal forces' and 'enemies'.[42]

In preparations for the meeting that produced the Atlantic Charter, Roosevelt continued to take up this theme but this time gave it a liberal-democratic twist. He claimed that the meeting between him and Churchill would instil hope in the peoples of the world that 'the English-speaking democracies' would construct a new world order based on freedom and equality.[43] This was repeated (but with the (diplomatic) deletion of the term 'English-speaking') at Teheran on 1 December 1943 when the Three Powers agreed to welcome all nations 'into a world family of Democratic Nations'.[44] The Moscow Declaration underwent several

---

[41] It is not always clear which of these liberalisms was being favoured in the various statements made around this time. Clearly, an optimistic democratic liberal would argue that if the extension of liberal democracy around the world is inevitable then there is no choice to make between the liberalism of accommodation and the liberalism of certainty. Liberalism can be both insistent on certain internal standards being met and aspire to universality and inclusion.

[42] Declaration by the United Nations, 1 January 1942 (Washington Conference) (1941), *A Decade of American Foreign Policy: Basic Documents, 1941–9* (1950). The Washington Declaration was signed by twenty-six belligerents (twenty-one more states signed the Declaration prior to San Francisco).

[43] Russell, *A History of the United Nations*, 34.

[44] Department of State Bulletin IX, 409. The Berlin Conference 1945 reiterated this position by calling for admission of those erstwhile enemy states who had become

re-drafts in order to avoid the impression that 'sovereign equality' was to apply to the defeated enemy states.[45] The Russians themselves had surprisingly little to say on the question of pluralism at this early stage though at Dumbarton Oaks they called for the exclusion of fascist states from the organisation.[46]

A more pluralistic orientation was present in a number of the pre-San Francisco statements. In Moscow, Anthony Eden, the British Foreign Minister, was already warning against establishing an international organisation in which ideology determined membership. He wanted included in the Charter a general principle that there would be 'no great power interference with forms of government'.[47] The Chinese, no doubt remembering their experience with the standard of civilisation, went further and in the Dumbarton Oaks conversations called for equality of races in the UN Charter.[48] A number of NGOs in North America also took the position that universal membership was desirable.[49] The American-Canadian Technical Plan, for example, argued against a democracy requirement because of its fear that 'a union of democratic states might

democracies: L. M. Goodrich and E. Hambro, *Charter of the United Nations* 2nd edn), 57. Churchill, too, lacked enthusiasm for the idea of universality though his worries were directed at Britain's Great Power allies. He was secretly fearful of the potential 'disaster' if a 'Russian barbarism overlaid the culture and independence of the great ancient states of Europe' (see Churchill, *Hinge of Fate, The Second World War*, 561). Churchill was more interested in regional security organisations than in any ideal of a universal international organisation believing that 'it is upon the creation of the Council of Europe and the settlement of Europe that the first practical tasks will be centred' (E. L. Woodward, *British Foreign Policy in the Second World War*, 433–4, 437, and ff. (quoted in A. B. W. Simpson, *Human Rights and the End of Empire, Britain and the Genesis of the European Convention*, 227–8)). This view, however, was not shared by the likes of Anthony Eden, who believed that a focus on regional organisations would compromise the operation of the new world organisation. See Simpson, *Human Rights and the End of Empire*, 223, 226–7. Eventually, what prevailed in UK policy circles was a compromise, engineered by Eden, whereby regional groupings could exist providing they were secondary to the world organisation (226). This was to be the inspiration for the way in which collective security was structured in the UN Charter with Chapter VIII giving regional organisations a role in ensuring security but providing in Article 53(1) that 'no enforcement action shall be taken under regional arrangements . . . without the authorisation of the Security Council'. This debate about the proper role of regional organisations was revived during the Kosovo intervention (see Chapter 7).

[45] Russell, *History of the United Nations*, 134. Article 4 refers to 'the principle of sovereign equality' as the basis for the new organisation.

[46] *Ibid.*, 424.

[47] *Ibid.*, 138. It is likely that this was directed at the fear of Soviet interference within the liberated states of Eastern and Central Europe.

[48] *Ibid.*, 424.

[49] See American-Canadian Technical Plan, United States Technical Plan, UNCIO vol. 3 at 79, doc. 2 6/7, 23 April 1945.

find itself confronted by a union of non-democratic states; and recent history has shown that a union of like-minded states of a certain mind may lead to union of like-minded states of another mind'.[50] This was mirrored in a statement made at the Inter-American Conference on Problems of War and Peace held in Mexico City in 1945 where the principle of universality was unanimously adopted as an aspiration of the new international organisation.[51]

It was inevitable, then, that these two conceptions of international organisation would result in a measure of equivocation in the lead-up to the San Francisco Conference itself. The Uruguayan Government, for example, produced a statement in 1944 that anticipated the ambivalence of many of the delegations at San Francisco. The anti-pluralism of statements such as 'in the democratisation of international society it would recognise the most perfect system of maintenance of peace and security' is tempered by a more pragmatic position on membership calling for a universal system in which 'a specific form of government' would not be required.[52]

Early drafts of the UN Charter at the US State Department also tried to have it both ways, envisaging a distinction between membership and participation, with the latter being reserved for 'properly *qualified* states' (my italics).[53] Article 1 of the Draft Constitution stated that the new organisation would 'reflect the universal character of the international community' but Article 1(2) went on to say that 'all qualified states . . . shall be members of the International Organisation'.[54] This ambiguous formulation was a condensed version of the tension between the two modes described above and set the scene for a debate between the anti-pluralists and the pluralists during the drafting of the Charter at San Francisco and in the 'Admissions' period. It also resembled the formulae of Oppenheim and Westlake and their distinctions between statehood and 'full' membership of the international community.

At the beginning of the San Francisco Conference itself, M. Rolin, the Belgian delegate, set out two of the questions to be resolved by the committee on membership:[55] 'Does the Committee consider that

---

[50] *Ibid.*, 80.   [51] N. Bentwich and A. Martin, *Commentary*, xix.

[52] The Position of The Government of Uruguay Respecting the Plans of Postwar International Organisation for the Maintenance of Peace and Security in the World, UNCIO vol. 3 at 32, doc. 2 G/7 28 September 1944. A democracy principle might, they argued, be 'abusively applied' and result in an 'indirect form of intervention'.

[53] Russell, *History of the United Nations*, 351.   [54] *Ibid.*, 352.

[55] There were other questions to consider here but these are the two that matter most from the point of view of this study. Interestingly, one of the other questions turned

the Organisation should eventually be universal . . .?' and 'If the Committee considers that members to be admitted are states, does it wish to mention the nature of their institutions?'[56] By the end of the conference, Rolin commented that the questions facing Committee I/2 on membership were the profoundest difficulties of substance facing the Commission.[57]

Delegations were divided on these questions at first. States that supported universality did so on several grounds. The Venezuelans took it for granted that universality was to be preferred, 'in view of the actual interdependence of all countries in the modern world'.[58] The Uruguayans spoke forcefully in favour of the *obligation* to become a member of the United Nations[59] while the Brazilians preferred a system in which membership was open to 'all sovereign states that now exist'.[60] The Guatemalans called for 'absolute universality'[61] and the Egyptians spoke against the exclusionary technique.[62]

The West European states adopted a less inclusive position at first, drawing inspiration from the early meetings of Churchill and Roosevelt. The Netherlands, for example, argued that new states should have 'political institutions which insure [sic] that the state is the servant of its citizens . . .'. Adopting a democratic peace perspective, the Dutch delegate saw democratic government as proof of a state's likely international behaviour.[63] The French were concerned to promote a measure of solidarity among member states of the United Nations. New states, they asserted, should meet certain conditions 'in order to guarantee the existence of certain common ideals and a community of political principles shared by members of the organisation'.[64] Indeed, the French wanted 'proof'

---

on the use of the word 'state' in the term 'peace-loving states'. Some delegations worried that this usage failed to foresee 'the further incorporation of other communities', UNCIO vol. 7 at 288, doc 1074, I/2/76, 18 June 1945.

[56] UNCIO vol. 7 at 15, doc. 195, I/2/8 10 May 1945. The word 'political' was inserted in the subsequent meeting of the Committee, UNCIO vol. 7 at 19, doc. 202 I/2/9 10 May 1945.

[57] UNCIO vol. 6 at 114, doc. 1167 I/10, 23 June 1945.

[58] UNCIO vol. 7 at 19, doc. 202 I/2/9, 10 May 1945.

[59] UNCIO vol. 7 at 288, doc. 1074 I/2/76, 18 June, 10 May 1945.

[60] Brazilian Comment on DO at UNCIO vol. 3 at 236, doc. 2 g/7 (e) (1), 2 May 1945.

[61] Guatemalan Observations on International Organisation, UNCIO vol. 3 at 257, doc. 2 G/7 (f), 23 April 1944.

[62] Egyptian Tentative Proposals on DO, UNCIO vol. 3 at 447, doc. 2 g/7 (q), 16 April 1945.

[63] UNCIO vol. 7 at 19, doc. 202 I/2/9, 10 May 1945.

[64] *Ibid.*, See, too, Norway's Proposals, UNCIO vol. 3 at 359, doc. 2 G/7 (n), 16 April 1945 calling for admission of governments harmonious with the aims and purposes of the organisation.

of 'peace-lovingness' in the institutions of a state. This view was shared by other delegates from the developing world, though the criteria were often modified. The Haitians, for example, proposed an amendment to Article 2(1) which required states to 'exclude from their relations racial or religious discrimination'.[65] The Chileans thought that 'membership should be open to all states that love peace and the democratic system' because 'democratic principles are essential to peace'.[66] The *Spanish Case* gave the delegates a concrete case to debate. This issue arose in the First Commission at San Francisco where a number of states used Franco's Spain as an example of the sort of entity that would not gain admission to the organisation at least until the entity had 'stripped itself of Fascism'.[67] The Ukrainian representative, advocating an even more searching test for Spanish membership, asked: 'Can we admit among us representatives of Franco's government . . . which violated the basic principles of constitutional freedom?'[68] Spain was not in the end one of the founding members of the United Nations though the Security Council later resisted imposing any further sanction on the Franco regime.

The Drafting Sub-Committee dealing with the general issue of membership rejected the anti-pluralist approach on two, potentially contradictory, grounds. The Committee's ambiguous final statement was to haunt the UN in its early years. The Sub-Committee was against referring to a requirement that states have 'democratic institutions' on the grounds that, 'this would imply an undue interference with internal arrangements'.[69] This view was adopted by the full Committee on membership.

[65] UNCIO vol. 3 at 52, doc. 2 G/7(b)(1), 5 May 1945.

[66] Comments of the Chilean Government on IO, UNCIO vol. 3 at 284, 294, doc. 2 G/7 (i), 2 May 1945. A third group of states thought the question was somewhat moot given that universality was not to be achieved until much later. A selective organisation was eventually to give way to one based on true universality but it was thought to be precipitate to claim universality so early in the organisation's life.

[67] French delegate M. Paul-Boncour. UNCIO vol. 6 at 129, doc. 1167 I/10, 23 June 1945.

[68] UNCIO vol. 7 at 19, doc. 202 I/2/9, 10 May 1945. The Polish Government asked the Security Council in 1946 to declare Franco's regime a threat to the peace and to call upon all states to sever diplomatic relations with Spain. A UN sub-committee found that the Franco regime represented only a distant threat to the peace, capable of bringing the matter within the Council's Article 34 powers but not permitting Chapter VII enforcement (*Report of the Sub-Committee on the Spanish Question*, SCOR, 1st Year, 1st series, Special Supplement, 5). At that point a decision had already been taken to refuse Spain admission to the UN (for discussion see SCOR 1st year, 1st series, 4th mtg, 317–19) but no further sanctions were imposed. Spain was eventually admitted to the United Nations in 1955.

[69] UNCIO vol. 7 at 37, doc. 314 I/2/17, 15 May 1945.

On the other hand, the absence of any specific provision to this effect also meant an element of elasticity in the adjective 'peace-loving'. This was thought to be a positive feature since it allowed greater discretion to the member-states in assessing membership claims.[70] Unfortunately, this proposal did not anticipate that the very flexibility of the provision would permit states to incorporate highly intrusive and ideological criteria into their assessments of prospective members in the early life of the organisation.

The universalist, pluralist position prevailed in the end. The dominant principles arising from the San Francisco discussions were universality and equality.[71] Delegates were concerned not to place too much emphasis on the internal politics of a state.[72] The Report of the Rapporteur in Committee is important here.

The Committee did not feel that it should recommend the enumeration of the elements which were to be taken into consideration. It considered the difficulties which would arise in evaluating the political institutions of States and feared that the mention in the Charter of a study of such nature would be a breach of the principle of non-intervention, or, if preferred, of non-interference.[73]

This was a rejection of Holy Alliance interventionism and, less explicitly, the standard of civilisation, discussed in Chapter 8.

The UN system was not, however, entirely inhospitable to the liberal anti-pluralism I am about to discuss. After all, there were provisions relating to expulsion and suspension included in the Charter (Articles 5

---

[70] *Ibid.*

[71] Some vestiges remained of the wartime anti-pluralism. First, at San Francisco, a decision was made to distinguish the original from elected members. This was not merely a procedural distinction because only elected members were subject to a potentially qualitative admission process. The original members were those states who had declared war on one of the two remaining Axis Powers (Germany and Japan) and who had signed the 1942 Declaration by the United Nations as well as those states who had participated in the San Francisco Conference and subsequently signed and ratified the Charter (see Articles 3 and 110). Prospective members were obliged to seek recommendation from the Security Council followed by admission by the General Assembly. Admission was then subject to the state meeting certain requirements laid out in Article 4(1) (see later discussion). In addition to this, the Charter embodies a distinction between enemy states and allied or neutral states. These enemy states are subject to the provisions of Article 107 permitting UN members to 'take action' against those states providing such action is 'taken or authorized as a result of that war by the Governments having responsibility for such action'. Article 53 makes it clear that such action does not require the prior authorisation of the Security Council. Bentwich and Martin, *Commentary*, 19.

[72] UNCIO vol. 7 at 288 (doc. 1074 I/2/76, 18 June 1945).

[73] UNCIO, Report of the Rapporteur of Committee 1/2 on Chapter III (membership), vol. 7 at 326, doc. 1178, I/2/76 (2), para. 3.

and 6).[74] It is also true that though the delegates at San Francisco rejected an anti-pluralist model for international organisations, their governments, initially, did not embrace the idea of the UN as a universal, non-discriminating body. Individual states in the late 1940s and early 1950s continued to make decisions about membership on ideological grounds though this anti-pluralism was not accompanied by any conceptual justifications.[75] As a consequence of this politicisation of the admissions process, in 1946, five applications were rejected either by the Soviet Union (Eire, Transjordan and Portugal) or by the Western majorities on the Security Council (Albania and Mongolia). This was repeated in 1947 when applications from Austria, Italy, Hungary, Finland, Bulgaria and Romania were rejected.[76]

The pluralist conception, though, reasserted itself in the *Admissions Case* in 1948.[77] In the opinion of the Court handed down on 28 May 1948, the nine majority judges began by restating the two competing approaches to membership in international organisations articulated in the San Francisco discussions:

two principal tendencies were manifested in the discussions. On the one hand, there were some that declared themselves in favour of inserting in the Charter specific conditions which new members should be required to fulfil especially

---

[74] A provision on withdrawal was not included. The delegations at San Francisco tended to divide on the reasons for omitting a mechanism for withdrawal. The Americans, for example, believed that such a provision would be otiose since the right to withdraw from an international organisation was an incident of sovereignty. Other states were more concerned to ensure that the organisation remained universal to avoid the mistakes of the League of Nations. There was a real fear at this time that the experience of the League of Nations might be repeated with mass withdrawals eventually crippling the organisation or states forming competing organisations. Securing a universal basis for membership became vitally important to this group and it was only with some reluctance that they accepted the need for Articles on expulsion and suspension. For a general discussion of withdrawal, see Goodrich and Hambro, *Charter of the United Nations*, 142–4.

[75] For discussion see Bentwich and Martin, *Commentary*, 3. The United States, for example, was still fully committed, on paper at least, to the idea of universality. See the Remarks of the Deputy US Representative on Security Council (Johnson), 28 August 1946, Documents on Foreign Relations, vol. 8 at 524–6 (American Peace Foundation 1948): '[The UN], should in its first year, seek as great a universality as possible'.

[76] See for British practice, FO Document 371/57165: 'On the question of recognition of the governments of Bulgaria and Roumania' (File 95); Goodrich and Hambro, *Charter of the United Nations*, 129. The Americans and British opposed the Bulgaria, Hungary and Romania applications because of 'alleged flagrant violations of human rights'.

[77] *Admission of a State to the United Nations* (Charter, Article 4), Advisory Opinion: (1948) ICJ Rep. at 57. Six judges dissented.

in matters concerning the character and policies of government. On the other hand, others maintain that the Charter should not needlessly limit the Organisation in its decisions concerning requests for admission . . .'[78]

The Court favoured the second tendency, holding that member-states were 'not juridically entitled to make . . . consent to the admission dependent on conditions not expressly provided by paragraph 1 [of Article 4]'.[79] In the Court's reasoning, this commitment to pluralism was tied to the scope of a state's domestic jurisdiction under Article 2(7). In some ways, Article 2(7) is the very expression of pluralism. States are not to be judged by their internal practices and this zone of immunity can be breached only if the Security Council acts under Chapter VII or in cases where matters previously thought to occupy this zone are transferred into the international sphere. Article 2(7) on its face is quite unhelpful as a piece of legal draughtsmanship. It does not precisely demarcate the international from the national and it does not provide any guidance as to what might be thought to be essentially within the domestic jurisdiction of a state. Nonetheless, it signals that there is an aspect of a state's internal affairs that remains untouchable by the United Nations in its non-enforcement modes. In this sense at least, Article 2(7) can be read as an endorsement of ideological pluralism in the organisation.[80]

In the *Admissions Case* the World Court preferred universalism to ideology. This was to be the spirit behind future admission decisions and the United Nations' image of itself over the next forty years. I do not mean to suggest that ideology was left behind. Of course, actual decision-making authority was left in the hands of states and, as Goodrich and Hambro remarked, while those states were restricted in the criteria they could employ in coming to decisions (i.e. they had to meet the

---

[78] *Ibid.*, 45.

[79] The Court suggests that the conditions are exhaustive but that these are wide and allow for a great deal of latitude ('these conditions constitute an exhaustive enumeration and are not merely stated by way of guidance or example. The provision would lose its significance and weight, if other conditions, unconnected with those laid down, could be demanded . . . The conditions [are] . . . not merely necessary conditions, but also the conditions which suffice' (*ibid.*, 62)).

[80] The Court admits that the internal politics of an aspiring member may motivate other states in their decision to refuse support for an application but these motivations can never be stated as reasons. As the Court puts it: 'Although the Members are bound to conform to the requirements of Article 4 in giving their votes, the question does not relate to the actual vote, the reasons for which are a matter of individual judgment and are clearly subject to no control, but to the statements made by a Member concerning the vote it proposes to give.' The point is that these internal motivations can have no normative significance (being unstated).

conditions set forth in Article 4(1)), 'there is no such limitation . . . on the considerations that may be taken into account and the evaluation of them in determining whether these conditions have been fulfilled'.[81] Sporadically, states continued to do just that in ensuring the exclusion of unfriendly states.[82] Nonetheless, the Court confirmed in the *Admissions Case* that the prevailing norm of membership was to be an inclusive, pluralistic one. In the absence of any possibility of agreement concerning the sorts of qualifications that states might be required to meet, the UN's approach to ideology and membership became both functional (could new states meet their formal international obligations?) and agnostic (was the government in effective control regardless of legitimacy or representativeness?).[83] This reflected at least one powerful strand of thought at San Francisco and was threatened only intermittently until the rise of the new liberal anti-pluralism fifty years later.

The UN, then, though it began as an association of the victor states in the Second World War, quickly aspired to universality. As Inis Claude wrote: 'The adjectival qualification, peace-loving, was not taken seriously except as a basis for excluding the defeated Axis states and Franco's Spain.'[84] It is possible to see the period 1945 to 1989 as one marked by a rejection of standards of civilisation, culture and democracy as criteria for membership of the international community.[85] Even as early as 1945 Josef Kunz could claim, plausibly, that: 'Since 1920 positive international law has recognised the pluralism of the legal and value systems of the world.'[86] This pluralism is reflected both in the UN Charter in its modest classical liberal incarnation and in various cosmopolitan projects

---

[81] Goodrich and Hambro, *Charter of the United Nations*, 132.

[82] See e.g. US refusal to support Vietnam's application for membership in 1975.

[83] See the 'effective control' test applied to statehood criteria under the Montevideo Convention (1933).

[84] Inis Claude, *Swords into Ploughshares*, 88.

[85] But see the continuing duty to accord minimum standards of civilisation to foreign nationals. See the Ahmadou Diallo Case, *Republic of Guinea v. Democratic Republic of the Congo*. www.icj-cij.org/icjwww/idocket/igc/igcframe.

[86] Josef Kunz, 'Pluralism of Legal and Value Systems of the World' (1955) 49 AJIL 370 at 372. Kunz dates this movement from 1856 when Turkey joins the European Family of Nations. The key moment may well have been the First World War, after which it made little sense to divide the world into barbarians and civilised peoples. The savagery of the war in Europe, as well as the accompanying propaganda, made the distinction between European civilisation and non-European barbarism untenable. Norms such as the persistent objector principle are derived from this idea of tolerance. For a criticism of this idea and a call for 'universality' see Jonathan I. Charney, 'Universal International Law' (1993) 87 AJIL 529.

suggested in the post-war era.[87] The UN Charter itself makes no reference to any ideological requirements for membership. The founders of the UN swapped ideological exclusivity for normative universalism.

The treatment of the enemy powers also to an extent reflected this pluralism or quest for universalism. The admission of Germany and the Soviet Union to the League of Nations had already pointed to a more accommodating attitude towards enemy powers.[88] At the end of the Second World War, the Versailles model was rejected in favour of a regime of individual responsibility. The Nuremberg Trials, then, were important as a method of punishing the major Nazi war criminals but they served another function by deflecting attention away from the criminal conduct of the state of Germany. So Kellog-Briand and the Covenant were used at Nuremberg to show that the Nazi High Command had committed crimes against peace but their application to Germany as a whole was thereby avoided.

However, like the vengeful Prussians at Vienna, there were those who preferred the Carthaginian, state crime model.[89] Henry Morgenthau, the US Treasury Secretary, called for the pastoralisation of Germany. The Morgenthau Plan called for mass deportation of Germans, the de-industrialisation of the Ruhr and an array of reparations.[90] Roosevelt was initially sympathetic to this state crime model, warning that:

---

[87] Kunz, 'Pluralism', 375. See, also, F. S. C. Northrop's 'Contemporary Jurisprudence and International Law' (1956) 61 *Yale Law Journal* 636; *Ideological Differences and World Order*; and his *The Taming of Nations*. Northrop, for example, recommended a UN Charter with only two main articles, one of which would 'declare the pluralism of the ideologies as a basic principle'.

[88] Article 16 of the League of Nations Covenant stated: 'Should any Member of the League resort to war in disregard of its covenants under Articles 12, 13, or 15, it shall ipso facto be deemed to have committed an act of war against all other Members of the League, which hereby undertake immediately to subject it to the severance of all trade or financial relations, the prohibition of all intercourse between their nationals and the nationals of the covenant-breaking State, and the prevention of all financial, commercial, or personal intercourse between the nationals of the covenant-breaking State and the nationals of any other State . . . Any Member of the League which has violated any covenant of the League may be declared to be no longer a Member of the League by a vote of the Council concurred in by the Representatives of all the other Members of the League represented thereon.'

[89] Not all of this was revenge. Some, like Cordell Hull, wanted collective punishment because he believed Nazism was a 'thousand miles deep' in the German people and could only be eradicated through radical measures. See Bass, *Politics of War Crimes Trials*, 162.

[90] *Ibid.*, 153–5.

The German people as a whole must have it driven home to them that the whole nation has been engaged in a lawless conspiracy against the decencies of modern civilisation.[91]

Even as late as the Quebec Conference, the meeting in 1944 of Roosevelt and Churchill, an official document was released stating that Germany was to become 'a country primarily agricultural and pastoral in character'.[92] However, this model was not adopted partly because of the fear of provoking a new war and partly because it offended the American ideal of individual guilt and responsibility.[93] In the end, as Gary Bass put it, legalism prevailed. The effect of this was to allow for the prosecution of the German war criminals and the rehabilitation of Germany. In this way, San Francisco and Nuremberg worked in tandem. At San Francisco, a new standard of civilisation based on democratic governance was rejected in favour of a pluralist approach to membership while Nuremberg was an implicit repudiation of the criminal state regime and permitted the re-entry of Germany into international society.[94]

So, the classical liberal approach to membership, then, is based on a pluralist-functionalist reading of international order. Entities meeting certain neutral criteria based on effectiveness and a purely formal promise to comply with international norms are admitted to the system. The diversity of states is to be celebrated. International law is liberal, then, in the same way that a modern industrial state is said to be liberal, it tolerates highly illiberal, even 'criminal', elements within its membership. Following the *Admissions Case* most applications for membership were processed in a routine manner.[95] This applied to aspirant colonial peoples too. The idea behind the UN's admissions policy after

---

[91] Letter from Roosevelt to Stimson, 26 August 1944, *Morgenthau Diary* vol. I, 443–5, quoted in Bass, *ibid.*, 154.

[92] Morgenthau Plan, 5 September, 1944, in B. F. Smith (ed.), *The American Road to Nuremberg*, 27–9.

[93] Of Morgenthau's various plans, partition was the only one that survived and this was because of the geo-political nature of the occupation rather than any desire to punish Germany.

[94] A similar story can be told about Tokyo and the Japanese.

[95] There were cases where the General Assembly affected some analysis of the criteria under Article 4(1), e.g. SC Res. 167 (on Mauritania). See Karel Wellens, *Resolutions and Statements of the United Nations Security Council (1946–1989): A Thematic Guide* (1990) 597. On 23 June 1976 the Security Council failed to recommend Angola because of US doubts about the presence of Cuban troops. Angola was subsequently recommended for admission in SC Res. 397 of 22 November 1976. On 15 November 1976 the Security

about 1960 was to welcome as many decolonised entities into the ranks of states as possible. Self-determination, during the period in which the Afro-Asian voice in the United Nations and world affairs had most resonance, was defined as the right held by the majority within a colonially defined territory to external independence from colonial domination by metropolitan powers alien to the continent.[96] It did not apply to ethnic groups within these territories nor to majorities who were being oppressed by indigenous 'alien' elites. Neither secession nor democratic representation was regarded as part of this novel right of self-determination.[97] In this period, 'anti-colonial results [were] deemed more important than genuine self-determination methods'.[98] The idea was to treat these new states equally, not to apply standards of democracy or constitutional viability to them. Sovereignty (now accorded the majority of former colonies), full membership and statehood were regarded as co-extensive rights of former colonial peoples. All states, rich or poor, were fully sovereign.[99] The decolonisation story, then tells of a shift from hierarchical and oppressive empires to free and independent sovereigns. A relative few see this as an essentially uplifting tale, the end of empire. Others are concerned not to deprecate the great achievement of decolonisation but view it as merely an initial step towards the abolition of economic inequalities between nations (or among individuals in world society). The pessimists among this group see the structure of the international capitalist order as divisive (world systems and dependency theorists). A smaller number again worry that decolonisation

Council failed to adopt a draft resolution on Vietnam's admission because of US doubts concerning Vietnam's ability to carry out 'obligations of the Charter'.

[96] In virtually all cases this meant European. But see the right to self-determination held by the South African and Rhodesian non-white majorities and the Palestinians in the Israeli-occupied territories.

[97] See, generally, M. Pomerance, 'Self-Determination Today: The Metamorphosis of an Ideal' (1984) 19 *Israel Law Review* 310.

[98] *Ibid.*, 329.

[99] However, the representation enjoyed by states on certain key institutions depends on levels of development and wealth (e.g. IMF, World Bank). In addition, there are international organisations, membership in which is restricted according to economic capacity. To an extent, these organisations maintain and manage economic hierarchy. These are economic associations based on inequality not on region or culture see, e.g. the composition of the G7 (now G8 since Russia's admission in 1994) which issues communiqués and takes positions on various political and economic situations. See, also Robert Jackson's distinction between positive sovereignty (possessed by the industrialised states) and negative sovereignty (possessed by the developing states), (Jackson, *Quasi-States*, 26–31).

has retarded a long term improvement in the economic conditions of 'the South' by creating a large number of helpless, corrupt, damaged and, most of all, premature states.[100] The division then becomes one between states enjoying positive sovereignty or international capacity (in the non-legal sense) and those with merely negative sovereignty (territorial integrity, political sovereignty).[101] Quasi-states and states are juridical equals but not substantive equals.[102]

The Charter era, then, was marked by a commitment to a formally non-hierarchical international order. This is certainly true of a period between 1960 (the Declaration on the Granting of Independence) and 1989. Scores of African-American states entered the UN and the Family of Nations. What was for so long denied even to states (sovereign equality) was now granted to peoples (external self-determination). The distinction between civilised and non-civilised peoples had been finally abandoned, previously criminal states were returned to the fold and democracy was left as a desideratum rather than a genuine prerequisite of admission to the society of states.

In a way, then, the nineteenth century can be seen in retrospect as a time of great innovation as far as forms of legitimate social organisation are concerned. Since 1945, or at least 1960, international law, in one sense, had become *more* statist, not less as is commonly asserted. The state became the dominant, perhaps sole, form of organisation among territorially based entities. Compare this with the nineteenth century when states were arranged hierarchically according to their levels of civilisation and when there was a practice of sub-dividing or attenuating sovereignty itself. The half-sovereign, or part-sovereign, entity may have presented a jurisprudential conundrum but it, nevertheless, existed in reality. Statesmen along with legal advisers had created suzerainties, protectorates, confederations, guaranteed states and various levels of civilisation. In the nineteenth century, it fell to legal scholars to explain the relationship between sovereign equality and these novel social formations.

---

[100] See, for a highly sophisticated version of this position, Jackson, *Quasi-States, passim.*
[101] 'Self-determination gave independence without either power or liberty.' *Ibid.*, 190.
[102] Jackson calls this the negative sovereignty game. Two innovations change the nature of the game. First, states are created lacking in positive sovereignty (IR) or effectiveness (IL). Second, there are nonreciprocal obligations to aid and prop up these negative sovereigns. The international regime is committed to their survival as a matter of regime ethics. *Ibid.*

By the time of San Francisco, much of this had disappeared along with the Versailles model of state crime. States were to be regarded as equals and, within fifteen years, even the trusteeship concept was in disrepute as an offence to sovereign equality and self-determination. This phase in the life of the sovereign equality norm, however, was to last less than half a century.

10   Outlaw states: 1999

The terrors of lawlessness must be responded to . . . if need be, by the
terrors of the law.[1]

the moment of victory of a political force is the very moment of its
splitting: the triumphant liberal-democratic "new world order" is more
and more marked by a frontier separating its inside from its outside.[2]

Introduction: the shift to anti-pluralism

On 23 April 1999, in Washington DC, Nato celebrated its fiftieth anniversary. The organisation had been created in 1949 with the purpose
of defending western Europe from the threat of Soviet invasion.[3] At a
dinner held that evening, the leaders of Nato states gave speeches outlining their agenda for the future of the institution.[4] It was clear from
these speeches that both the ambit of Nato's activities and the range of
its self-images had expanded quite considerably since 1949. For some,
Nato had, like the Concert of Europe, come to embody a particular set
of values. British Prime Minister Tony Blair, reflecting the comments
made by European leaders at Chaumont and Langres 185 years before,
trumpeted: 'The shared values of democracy, the rule of law, and human
rights make Nato more than a military alliance. They are the practical
embodiment of trans-Atlantic unity.'[5] Others in Washington emphasised

---

[1] Lorimer, *Institutes,* 93.   [2] Quoted in Fitzpatrick, 'Nationalism as Racism', 18.
[3] The Soviet Union claimed the Warsaw Pact had been established to defend Eastern
    Europe from invasion by the Americans and their allies.
[4] Nato at this time was engaged, in Kosovo, in its first military action. See Chapter 7.
[5] Speech of Prime Minister Tony Blair at Nato Anniversary Ceremonies, Washington DC,
    23 April 1999 (quoted in *New York Times,* 24 April 1999, A21). Though the rhetoric is
    similar, the states of Nato possess an ideological common purpose lacking in the states
    that made up the Congress of Vienna. See Chapter 4.

278

the idea of Europe as a zone of peace.[6] Vaclav Havel characterised Europe as an expanding, universalising sphere whose enlargement 'signifies the real and definitive end of the imposed division of Europe and the world'.[7] For others, the repudiation of practices endorsed in the periphery gave this European sphere its meaning. Antonio Gutteres, the Prime Minister of Portugal, asked:

Have we got an enemy? Our enemy is the rejection by so many in the world of the values of the Enlightenment, of reason, as the fundament of behaviour in politics. Our enemy is extreme nationalism, religious fundamentalism, racism, xenophobia . . . .[8]

In the vivid imagery circulating at this meeting, the western European and North American core was projected as ordered, unified, lawful(l); a place where human rights flourished, while the rest of the world was variously portrayed as lawless, anarchic, chaotic, backward and dangerous. The central argument of this chapter is that the rhetoric heard in Washington was mirroring a shift in the basis of international legal order and the theories employed to describe that new order. In this chapter, I want to consider these theories and, in particular, the international legal regimes that reflect and inspire such manifestos.

I have described the broad outlines of anti-pluralist thought in international studies in Chapters 2 and 8. Here I want to examine in more detail the precise ramifications of such thinking for the international legal order. The argument made here is that twenty-first-century international lawyers are faced with, at least, two alternatives when it comes to constructing political community among states. These alternatives were contested in the nineteenth century at Versailles, and at San Francisco and have been a feature of international legal life since, at least, the beginning of the nineteenth century (Chapters 8 and 9). The first alternative is grounded in sovereign equality and, in particular, what I have called existential equality. Existential equality has two elements. First, it incorporates a commitment to pluralism. The principle of existential equality ensures that states are at liberty to pursue a number of different political programmes without fear of sanction from the international community (Chapter 3). But existential equality also qualifies the extent to which sanctions can be imposed on states for breaches

---

[6] Suleyman Demirel, the Turkish Prime Minister, referred to 'the peace-loving democracies of the Euro-Atlantic area', *New York Times*, 24 April 1999, A8.
[7] *New York Times*, 24 April 1999, A8.   [8] *Ibid.*

of international legal obligations. In this sense, it is a doctrine of constraint. The principle of existential equality embedded in the principle of sovereign equality, then, embodies a number of different norms (political independence, dignity, territorial integrity) that place limits on the intrusiveness of international legal regimes and ensures a degree of tolerance for different political orders.

These commitments have been challenged and threatened by competing norms within the international legal order. In particular, two regimes are developing, each of which undermines the system of equal sovereigns. Each of these regimes is based on an implicit distinction between two categories of states: states in good standing and outlaw or pariah states. Importantly, I believe these new regimes can be understood as components of a revived conception of international order that I have called anti-pluralism.[9] In this chapter, then, I describe and assess the major contributions to anti-pluralist theory in the late twentieth century and weave this assessment into an analysis of two regimes of anti-pluralism, each of which attempts to construct a separate identity for the outsider or pariah state.

The first regime, the *criminal law regime*, assigns criminal liability to violator states for gross breaches of international law. Elements of the debate over the International Law Commission's Draft Articles on State Responsibility can be viewed as a disagreement about whether states that breach fundamental norms of international law should be subject to a special punitive regime of responsibility that results in outlaw status. Paralleling this idea of the criminal state is the image of the terrorist (Sudan, Afghanistan) or outlaw (Iraq, Serbia) state and the new rules of intervention applied to these states. The Security Council has adopted increasingly intrusive mechanisms of enforcement against states adjudged to have defied basic principles of the international community (e.g. Iraq). A particular focus here will be on the developing legal norms that deprive such states of the traditional privileges of sovereignty (e.g. territorial integrity and sovereign immunity). Alongside this consideration of the criminal regime I will discuss two anti-pluralists who set out a theory of criminality or outlawry for those states consigned to the moral and legal peripheries (Tesón and Rawls).

---

[9] And this has coincided with a return to the language of the nineteenth century also. The concept of civilisation, thought to have disappeared altogether from international law, apart from an anachronistic reference to 'civilised nations' in Article 38 of the Statute of the International Court of Justice, has now become an integral part of the rhetorical armoury of the Western statesman.

The second regime of control is the *democratic governance regime*. This is applied to undemocratic or illiberal or uncivilised states and threatens them with exile from the inner core of international society. This regime remains incipient but it is a feature of some liberal anti-pluralist theory and it is present in the practices or attitudes of the European Union towards both outsiders (Turkey) and insiders (Austria) who breach the democratic norm. These states are not necessarily criminal and they might well be capable of meeting their basic conventional obligations to the international community. However, like their predecessors in the nineteenth century, they have not conformed to a contemporary 'standard of civilisation'. In this section, I begin by tracing the portents of the contemporary theory and practice of anti-pluralism in the post-Charter expansion of the human rights system before illustrating a recent deepening of this process with an examination of both anti-pluralist writings and democratic governance practices.[10]

There is a tendency to use terms such as recalcitrant or outlaw or illiberal interchangeably. At this point, I want to make some preliminary distinctions. Outsider states (to use a neutral category) fall into at least two categories (these are obviously not mutually exclusive), which, in turn, refer back to the regimes of anti-pluralism I mentioned before. In the first category are those *criminal states* that fail to play by the rules of the international system. They are illiberal in their external relations or pathological in their domestic affairs. These states include aggressive states (states that threaten the liberal-democratic core, in particular) and, in a more benign variant, states that reject the dominant norms of procedural justice. These states repudiate the international legal order altogether because of its alleged incompatibility with that state's core

---

[10] There may be a third regime related to inequality: the failed states regime. The existence of the failed state inverts the classic Hobbesian picture of a serene domestic society located within an international state of nature (Jackson, *Global Covenant*, 295). Failed states are not regarded as full members of the Family of Nations 'in good standing' because they are unable to bear the responsibilities and obligations of international personhood. These states are also unequal sovereigns or quasi-states (Jackson, *Quasi-States*, *passim*). These are unequal sovereigns not because of what they do but rather by virtue of what they are unable to do. The increasing interventionism found in relation to Liberia and Somalia can be seen as part of this regime of disablement but it is found, also, in John Rawls's *Law of Peoples*. The failure of these states is more literal than normative. Indeed, in some cases, it may be that, rather than being unequal sovereigns, they cease to be states at all. See Lorimer's idea of 'imbecility' discussed in Chapter 8.

values.[11] Also included in this category are states that are worse than merely illiberal but are, in addition, genocidal or gross violators of core security rights such as the right to life.

In the second category are those states that are constitutionally illiberal. I call these *undemocratic states*. The theorists under discussion use the term 'illiberal' to describe a state that fails to offer its citizens a typical range of civil and political rights (including market rights), lacks a system of government in which authority is dispersed and does not hold free periodic elections in which the government is elected by the citizens of that state.[12] Undemocratic states might have no foreign policy designs on neighbours and might well abide by the classical inter-state norms of the international order. However, their treatment of their population or embrace of intolerable ideologies makes them offensive to significant elements of the inter-state elite and brings them into conflict with the democratic governance norm.[13]

The debate about pluralism is a debate about how the society of states should be configured. As Ian Clark suggested in 1988, 'the very basis of international society, its criterion of eligibility for membership, may be in the process of modification'.[14] Anti-pluralism seeks to confirm this change by incorporating political and behavioural criteria into the conditions of membership for the international community. This is clearly a shift from the Charter liberalism that prevailed, in the end, at San Francisco (see Chapter 9). The *Admissions Case* seemed to signal a waning of anti-pluralism for the time being, and in the immediate post-war era, Charter liberalism (or liberal pluralism) dominated the way that membership in the international community was structured. In the absence of agreement on what might constitute an ideal substantive politics of the state, there was, at least, a grudging consensus on the state (in any form) as the legitimate form of representation.[15] Article 2(1) came to embody a truth about international relations. States were entitled to

---

[11] In other words, a state can adopt illiberal or undemocratic practices internally and/or they can refuse to comply with the rules of the liberal international legal order, i.e. they can be illiberal towards other states.

[12] These criteria are inevitably the subject of much debate. See, e.g. J. F. Metzl and F. Zakaria, 'Information Intervention; When Switching Channels Isn't Enough: The Rise of Illiberal Democracy' (1997) 76 *Foreign Affairs* 22.

[13] In at least one significant case, Tesón's, the absence of democracy places a state within the criminal regime rather than the democratic governance regime.

[14] I. Clark, 'Making Sense of Sovereignty' (1998) 14 *Review of International Studies* 306.

[15] See M. Koskenniemi, 'Future of Statehood' (1991) 32 *Harvard International Law Journal* 397.

sovereign equality whether they were republics, centrally planned socialist states, kleptocracies or modernising post-colonial territories. The
moral qualities of aspiring members or, indeed, states already admitted
to the club, were not on the agenda.

This sovereign equality assumption has been rethought. In popular
writing on international affairs by the likes of Francis Fukayama and
Samuel Huntingdon there has been an emphasis on the differences
between groups of states, cultural blocs or civilisations.[16] Theorising
around this idea has become ubiquitous, too, in recent international law
scholarship. Either implicitly or explicitly, a new liberal anti-pluralism
has been drawn to the idea of separating the globe into zones – the
democratic-liberal or decent society of states operating in a sphere of
cosmopolitan law and the failed state/outlaw state subsisting in the state
of nature.[17] Alongside the pluralistic, procedural attitude of Charter liberalism, there is now a more judgemental, substantive liberalism. The
core norms of the old egalitarian liberalism based on sovereign equality,
it is argued, no longer capture the reality of the new transnational order
(Slaughter), are morally bankrupt (Tesón) or are in the process of radical
modification (Franck).

There is, of course, much that could be said about this new liberal theory.[18] Questions abound. Where do the new norms come from? How can
they best be implemented? Should undemocratic groups within states
be tolerated? Is democracy contagious? Is democracy a universally valid
value?[19] How is political community physically constituted? Who is admitted into the society? Who is excluded? What are the consequences
of exclusion for those states confined to the state of nature or the zone
of war?

It is these final three questions that interest me here. I am particularly
concerned with the two most obvious and provocative consequences of

[16] See F. Fukuyama, 'The End of History' (1989) 16 *The National Interest*, 3 and S.
Huntingdon, *The Clash of Civilisations and the Remaking of World Order*. See, too, Singer
and Wildavsky, *The Real World Order*. These ideas have been heavily contested. See, e.g.
After history?: Francis Fukuyama and his Critics (ed. Timothy Burns); D. Sneghaas, 'A Clash
of Civilisations' (1998) 35:1 *Journal of Peace Research*, 127–33 (arguing that Huntingdon
overemphasises cultural factors at the cost of socio-economic determinants); S. Marks,
'The End of History? Reflections on Some International Legal Theses' (1997) 8:3 EJIL
449–77 (arguing that the Fukayama vision of democracy, and its international law
derivatives, are impoverished).

[17] Zicek quoted in Fitzpatrick, 'Nationalism as Racism', 18.

[18] For a description and empirical critique see Alvarez, 'Liberal States'.

[19] These questions are taken up in some of the essays contained in G. Fox and B. Roth,
Democratic Governance and International Law (2000).

the regime for outlaws developed by anti-pluralists: exclusion and intervention. Some of the milder anti-pluralists regard the differences between states as significant for analytic purposes but do not believe it provides an automatic ground for exclusion of that state from the international community or intervention in that state's affairs (Slaughter, Franck). Strong anti-pluralists, on the other hand, tend to favour forms of exclusion and are less constrained about recommending military action against illiberal or outlaw or recalcitrant states (Reisman, Rawls, Tesón).

Exclusion encompasses either denial of admission to membership to a state on the basis of its internal or external behaviour or the expulsion of a member state because of its failure to meet certain conditions. The hope in these cases is that a spell in the wilderness will make the pariah state come to its senses and re-enter international society as a reformed character. Intervention can be seen as either an alternative or a supplement to exclusion. In this case, the international community or the democratic alliance takes military action either to suppress a threat from the outlaw state against the democratic community or, in a variant of humanitarian intervention, to enforce democracy or human rights or good governance within a state. The intervention, itself, can be either unilateral or UN-sanctioned. Liberal anti-pluralists diverge quite sharply on the legality of the former.

Regimes of anti-pluralism

Criminal states

The concept of state 'crime' is one of the most contentious in international law. In this section, I want to adopt a broad definition of crime in order to illustrate the increasing tendency of the international community to place, or contemplate placing, states under a quasi-penal regime of responsibility or constraint. I focus on two areas of regulation here: state crime (as envisaged by the International Law Commission in its, now superseded, 1996 Draft Articles) and threats to the peace (as defined and regulated by the Security Council). These categories overlap a great deal though both the legal position and the rhetoric are distinguishable in important respects.

Before saying something about crime as it relates to states, though, I want to show why the idea of state crime remains so controversial in international law because this controversy, in turn, arises from prior commitments to the idea of sovereign equality under international law.

The traditional view of international law was that the responsibility of states towards each other was regulated by a private law of obligations.[20] The injuries done by one state to another operate at the level of tort or delict.[21] So, on one view, state responsibility can be understood as a scheme of accountability and redress analogous to that which might exist between individuals in the absence of sovereign authority. All of this makes the idea of state crime appear anomalous.[22] When a state commits a wrong, that wrong, no matter what its magnitude or moral seriousness, is punishable at the level of inter-state relations.[23] It makes no sense to speak of crime because there is no body to adjudicate in international criminal proceedings and there is no agency capable of enforcing penal sanctions.[24] This absence of 'defined procedures' makes international state crime a category error.[25] States are equal and the concept of crime requires some degree of hierarchy.

There is powerful resistance to the idea of crime or supernorm for other additional reasons. Prosper Weil has argued that such a category threatens the system with relative normativity and is likely to undermine the foundations of the international legal order by blurring the boundaries between types of law or levels of legality. The legitimacy of the international legal order will suffer as mere delicts come to be viewed as unenforceable while crime remains indefinable. Alongside all this is the argument made by some political scientists that criminalising states and individuals is bad policy either because all states are 'cold-hearted monsters' (Aron) or because states make mistakes but do not commit crimes (A. J. P. Taylor).[26] For many political scientists, the rehabilitation of France in 1815, following Waterloo, is the model for dealing with adversaries and enemies, not some half-baked notion of criminality.

---

[20] G. Gilbert, 'The Criminal Responsibility of States' (1990) 39 ICLQ 345 at 356.

[21] See Nina Jorgenson, *The International Criminal Responsibility of States* (2000); *International Crimes of State: A Critical Analysis of the ILC's Draft Article 19 on State Responsibility* (ed. J. H. H. Weiler, A. Cassese, M. Spinedi); Malcolm Shaw, *International Law*.

[22] See, e.g. Prosper Weil, 'Relative Normativity'.

[23] See, e.g. the *Nicaragua Case* (Merits), (1986) ICJ Rep. 14.

[24] James Crawford, *Fourth Report on State Responsibility*, UN Doc. A/CN.4/517 (2001) at para. 43 at http://www.un.org/law/ilc/index.htm.

[25] See *Report of the International Law Commission on the Work of Fiftieth Session*, UNGAOR, 53rd Sess., Supp. No. 10 para. 245 at http://www.unorg/law/ilc/index/htm. This is not the case with the laws of individual responsibility under international law.

[26] See Raymond Aron, *De Gaulle, Israel and the Jews* (trans. John Sturrock), 27; A. J. P. Taylor, *The Origins of the Second World War*, xxviii (quoted in Bass, *Politics of War Crimes Trials*, 10).

Despite these objections, the International Law Commission spent a number of years developing the idea of state crime.[27] This body, established by the UN General Assembly under Article 16 of the Charter and essentially a Law Reform Commission for the international legal order, tried to answer two questions. What is a state deemed to have done, beyond the everyday delictual, to acquire the label 'criminal'? What are the consequences of criminal acts under the law of state responsibility?

Article 19 of the 1996 Draft Articles on State Responsibility has been set aside for the time being but nonetheless it represents the most labour-intensive attempt to define the meaning of crime in the international system.[28] Article 19(2) defines crime as a breach of an obligation 'so essential for the protection of fundamental interests of the international community that its breach is recognised as a crime'. So, criminal states are those states that at some point or another breach a super-norm of the international order. The commission of a crime strikes at the heart of the international legal order and such a violation creates a legal interest on the part of all members of that order that the violation cease and some manner of reparation be paid.[29]

Is there anything in the 1996 Draft Articles that envisages an inequality subsisting between 'criminal states' and other states in the system? Article 52 is critical in this regard. It spells out the consequences arising out of the commission of international crime. Most notably, it deprives the criminal state of a series of protections found elsewhere in the Draft. For example, under Draft Article 43, restitution in kind is limited in ordinary delictual circumstances by the requirement that such restitution

---

[27] The term first appeared in 1976. See *Yearbook of the International Law Commission* (1976) II, Part 2, 95–112.

[28] The idea seemed to be that the category of 'crime' would be substituted by a fuller re-working of concepts such as *jus cogens* and *erga omnes* (see *Report of the International Law Commission on the Work of its Fiftieth Session*, UNGAOR, 53rd Sess. Supp. No. 10, paras. 241–331, UN Doc. A/53/10 (1998), para. 33). The articles referred to here have been deleted from the ILC Articles on Responsibility of States for Internationally Wrongful Acts (2001). See, also, Drafting Committee Report, UN Doc. A/CN.4/2662 (2000).

[29] Compare, say, an unwarranted assertion of extra-territorial jurisdiction or a failure to recognise a new state with, say, the commission of genocide or the execution of diplomats. The first pair represent violations of international law but they do not threaten the existence of the society of states nor do they implicate the moral core of the legal order. The prohibition of genocide and the norms protecting diplomats are norms that form the basis of international society. For a comparison of society and system see Wight, *Systems of States*. See 1996 Draft Article 40(3). See, too, G. Abi-Saab, 'The Uses of Article 19' (1999) 10:2 EJIL 349.

does not 'seriously jeopardise the political independence or economic stability of the State which has committed the internationally wrongful act . . .' Article 45, meanwhile, states that, in the case of crime: 'The right of the injured state to obtain satisfaction does not justify demands which would impair the dignity of the State which has committed the internationally wrongful act.'[30]

So, Draft Article 52, by depriving certain wrong-doers of the protections expressed in Articles 43 and 45, sought to establish a category of criminal state beyond the parameters of ordinary international law. This state forfeited some aspects of its existential equality when it committed certain acts (though its territorial integrity was not one of them since the 1996 Draft Articles expressly forbade the use of force as a means to vindicate claims). As the ILC stated in its commentary to Draft Article 52: 'The Commission would exclude this limitation in relation to satisfaction for a crime simply because, by reason of its crime, the wrongdoing State has itself forfeited its dignity.'[31]

It is unclear to what extent the ILC's most recent amendments to the Draft Articles transform this picture. Certainly, the category 'crime' has been removed. Has the idea of crime survived? The categories created by Article 52 no longer exist in that form. However, there are still important distinctions drawn between serious breaches and other breaches. In the case of serious breaches, the Commission allows for a more punitive regime of reparation (Article 42) and permits states not directly affected by the breach to initiate claims for damages and to adopt countermeasures, 'in response to serious and manifest breaches of obligations to the international community'.[32] The push to substitute, for the idea of 'crime', another set of ideas, thus 'avoiding the penal implications of the term', has led a number of scholars, and, now, the ILC itself, to embrace the notion of obligations to the community as a whole (obligations *erga omnes*, peremptory norms).[33] These 'serious breaches of obligations essential to the whole international community' in the 2001 Articles 41 and 42 are undoubtedly analogous to the category crime, involving as they do 'gross or systematic failure' or 'serious breach' of 'fundamental

---

[30] Article 40 (making the duty not to commit a crime an obligation *erga omnes*) is also important to the definition of international crime though less relevant to the idea of sovereign equality.

[31] http://www.law.cam.ac.uk/rcil/ILCSR/Arts.htm

[32] See James Crawford *et al.*, 'The ILC's Draft Articles on State Responsibility: Towards Completion of a Second Reading' (2000) 94:4 AJIL 660–74 at 674.

[33] G. Gaja, 'Should all References to Article 19 Disappear from the ILC Draft Articles on State Responsibility?' (1999) 10:2 EJIL 366.

interests'. The consequences of such breaches differ from those envisaged by the 1996 Draft Articles but what has remained unchanged is the conviction that these breaches ought to have different consequences from ordinary or less serious breaches of international law.[34] According to James Crawford, this allows the law of state responsibility to develop in such a way that certain grave breaches can attract 'special consequences' without those breaches becoming crimes (a term suggestive of a 'full-scale criminal regime').[35] This criminal regime would be deeply flawed in the absence of any institutional machinery to apply it.[36]

Yet, perhaps this is too narrow a view of criminality. Inevitably, the term crime is likely to have a different meaning in international law to the one found in domestic law. A penal regime involving incarceration is an impossibility but there are ways in which criminality and outlawry operate that do not depend on imprisonment or even punishment but rather on stigma, repression and representation. It is this sort of criminal regime that, I believe, can and does operate in international law.[37] True, the ILC's early Draft Articles on the implications of crime are tautological and inadequately expressed but they point to a system of repression that already exists in the way the international order approaches the problem of the outlaw state. The regime of responsibility encapsulated by the now-deleted Article 52 anticipates and tracks the regimes of repression established in recent times by the Security Council in relation to Iraq and imposed on the Germans by the Treaty of Versailles. It is at least

---

[34] In the case of the 2001 Articles on State Responsibility, any damages awarded may reflect the gravity of the breach (opening the way for the imposition of punitive sanctions, perhaps), obligations of non-assistance are imposed on third parties and any state may impose counter-measures in the interests of the directly affected victim state.

[35] Though it seems unlikely that even this compromise will entirely satisfy those states that dislike the lack of precision in this area of the law. See, e.g. *Comments by United Kingdom on ILC Draft Articles on State Responsibility*, 28 February 2001 (on file with author), 1–3.

[36] James Crawford, 'Revising the Draft Articles on State Responsibility' (1999) 10:2 EJIL 443. Robert Rosenstock, the US member of the ILC, remarked recently that 'there is no comparable institution for denominating certain actions as criminal' (R. Rosenstock, 'An International Criminal Responsibility of States?' in *International Law on the Eve of the Twenty-First Century – Views from the International Law Commission* (1997), 272). As Pierre-Marie Dupuy points out, some members of the ILC have been lobbying for this for some time. See P.-M. Dupuy, 'Reviewing the Difficulties of Codification' (1999) 10:2 EJIL 371.

[37] International law is often compared unfavourably to domestic law in discussions of enforcement. However, in England and Wales, for example, 4 million of the 5.3 million offences reported are unsolved. See 'Revealed: Three out of Four Crimes are Unsolved', *The Observer*, 13 May 2001, 3.

arguable that there is an imperfect machinery of criminalisation as well as an international community in which the notion of state crime is implicitly accepted.

In what sense does the Security Council adopt penal measures? There is a real risk in drawing too facile a link between the potential criminal responsibility of states under the law of state responsibility and the imposition of collective measures by the Security Council. Rosalyn Higgins, for example, has argued that there is no connection between the UN's security system with its emphasis on terminating threatening situations and the law of state responsibility with its emphasis on the assignation of fault and responsibility.[38] Chapter VII provisions, according to Pierre-Marie Dupuy, are 'measure(s) of constraint and not of responsibility'.[39]

Outlaws, though, are created by both police and courts. Even if the Security Council was simply an instrument of constraint, it would be part of a regime of criminal repression. An array of sanctions imposed under Article 41 is likely to have the same repressive effects as laws enacted by Parliaments or norms created under treaties.[40]

In any event, the Council has become more than an institution of constraint. Martti Koskenniemi has alerted us to the increasing presence of the police in the temple, i.e. a Security Council over keen to supplement its policing function with a quasi-judicial allocation of rights and responsibilities.[41] Security Council Resolution 687, as I will go on to demonstrate in more detail, contains several legal or judicial determinations concerning Iraq's obligations and responsibilities.[42] James Crawford has spoken of the 'de facto criminalisation of Iraq, Libya and Yugoslavia in recent practice'.[43] The ILC noted in its Fiftieth Report that the 'unsuccessful experiment of the war-guilt clause in the Treaty of Versailles . . . was

---

[38] Higgins, *Problems and Process*, 166.

[39] Dupuy, 'The Institutionalisation of International Crimes of State' in Weiler *et al.* (eds.) *Crimes of State*, 170 at 176, quoted in R. Higgins, *Problems and Process*, 166.

[40] Security Council resolutions cannot create legal obligations under this view but they can enforce them and action taken to enforce these norms is binding on other states under Article 25.

[41] M. Koskenniemi, 'The Police in the Temple: Order, Justice and the UN: A Dialectical View' (1995) 6:3 EJIL 325–48. See, too, Franck, *Fairness*, 232–3.

[42] And in SC Res. 674 of 29 October 1990, the Security Council found that the Iraqis were 'liable for any loss, damage or injury arising in regard to Kuwait or third states'. Rosalyn Higgins has noted: 'That is an assertion that an international tribunal might want to make in more qualified terms' (*Problems and Process*, 183).

[43] Crawford, 'Revising the Draft Articles', 443.

the nearest that the international community had come to the criminalisation of a State'.[44] With the sanctions in Iraq resembling those at Versailles so strongly, it is plausible to argue that the international community has, again, embraced criminalisation.[45] Certainly, the Security Council has displayed an increasing tendency both to expand its jurisdiction physically and, at the same time, adopt quasi-judicial practices. It is no longer acceptable to see Chapter VII action as exclusively 'political' or solely as an instrument of constraint. Security Council determinations refer to breaches of important norms, they impose reparations and suspend rights.[46]

A number of prominent scholars have linked the idea of state crime to Security Council action.[47] Even those that do not do so explicitly cannot avoid associating the protection of common interests, and the criminalisation of conduct violative of those interests, with the Charter approach to peace and security.[48] The ILC made the connection in its 1996 commentary:

Article 53 is drafted so as to express this minimum requirement, as well as to reinforce and support any more extensive measures which may be taken by States through international organizations in response to a crime.[49]

So, when the ICTY recently stated in *Blaskic* that 'under international law States could not be subject to sanctions akin to those provided for in national criminal justice systems', it was expressing only a half-truth.[50] The criminalisation of the state is not identical to that of the individual in domestic legal orders. However, this does not render the idea of state crime null. There are many customary systems of crime that

---

[44] *Report of the International Law Commission on the Work of its Fiftieth Session*, chap. 7: State Responsibility, para. 248.

[45] 'Nazi Germany and Saddam Hussein's Iraq can be called "criminal states" and have been treated as such by the international community' (Pellet, 'Can a State Commit a Crime? Definitely, Yes!' (1999) 10:2 EJIL 425 at 433). For a cautious analysis of the parallels between 1919 and 1991 see David Bederman, 'Collective Security, Demilitarization and "Pariah States"' (2002) 13:1 EJIL 121–38.

[46] Vera Gowlland-Debbas, 'The Limits of Unilateral Enforcement of Community Objectives in the Framework of UN Peace Maintenance', (2000) 11:2 EJIL 361–84, 365.

[47] *Ibid.*, 364–6; R. Ago, *Fifth Report, Yearbook of the International Law Commission* (1976), ii. Pt I, p. 3, 26–57; and his comments at *ibid.*, i. PP. 7, 8, 56–61; B. Graefrath, 'International Crimes: A Specific Regime of International Responsibility of States and its Legal Consequences', in J. Weiler *et al.* (eds.), *Crimes of State*, 160, 161.

[48] G. Abi-Saab, 'The Uses of Article 19', 339–40.

[49] http://www.law.cam.ac.uk/rcil/ILCSR/Arts.htm

[50] *Prosecutor v. Tihomir Blaskic*, Case no. IT-95-14-T, Decision of 3 March 2000. See, too, *ILC Second Reading* (1999), para. 250.

do not adopt the same form as the classic crime control model, and yet they still represent criminal sanction of some sort. In addition, and *contra Blaskic*, states *are* subject to criminal sanction 'akin' to that found at the domestic level. The criminalisation of Iraq has featured a number of the techniques of repression found in a domestic criminal legal order including stigmatisation, deprivation of rights and immunities, a change in status, the application of sanctions and ongoing surveillance.

Of course, the regime imposed on Iraq did not occur in an historical vacuum. Indeed, it can be characterised as one of the three great international law projects of criminalisation after aggressive wars. The other two occurred after the First and Second World Wars. In each instance there was a debate about the appropriate mode of criminalisation (or indeed if criminalisation was an appropriate remedy at all). There were, in each case, statesmen who wanted to return quietly to 'diplomacy as usual' after the conflict. For such individuals, the notion of criminal responsibility for states or individuals was the solution of the naive, the dangerous and the idealistic. These pragmatists believed that the difference between a criminal state and a triumphant coalition is a matter of luck not morality. As Göering once said, 'we will go down in history either as the world's greatest statesmen or its worst villains'. But pragmatists are not always simply cynical about the application of justice to international affairs. Buttressing their dislike of legalistic solutions is the belief that criminalisation creates martyrs out of the accused or retards the rehabilitation of outlaw states or paralyses those governments (such as the Weimar Republic) who succeed criminal or aggressive governments and who then become prey to revisionist nationalism.[51] Those who *do* embrace legal solutions, of course, can adopt, what might be called, a Nicaragua model, whereby disputes over aggression are settled bilaterally in a civil court.[52] This is the idea of aggression as a civil wrong or tort giving rise to a right of private action by one 'citizen' (Nicaragua) against another (United States).

However, neither tort nor diplomacy was favoured in the three cases under discussion. In the case of Germany, after the two world wars, and Iraq following the invasion of Kuwait, the idea of crime played a

---

[51] Hitler and Göering met at a rally to protest against the post-First World War trials of German war criminals.

[52] Though given the US withdrawal from proceedings, this is hardly a perfect example of bilateral judicial dispute resolution. See *Nicaragua Case* at 14. See US Statement, (1985) 24 ILM 246.

prominent part in discussions over how to deal with the fallen power.[53] In each instance, there was a debate between those who favoured the imposition of individual responsibility on enemy soldiers and statesmen and those who wanted to punish the state itself for the crime of aggression. As I indicated in the previous chapter, Versailles resulted in the criminalisation of Germany through a highly punitive reparations programme. At Nuremberg, the Allies, inoculated against state crime after their experiences in the inter-war period, preferred the individual responsibility model. The Nuremberg Trials represented both a landmark for the idea of individual punishment and the beginning of a process of state rehabilitation. However, the lessons of Versailles and Nuremberg were not carried over to the treatment of Iraq. As with Versailles, the main protagonist was tantalisingly out of reach so the possibility of war crimes trials along the lines of Nuremberg receded quite rapidly after the conclusion of the war.[54] On the other hand, the recent experience with sanctions (South Africa and Rhodesia) was equivocal rather than disastrous (Versailles) and so the model of state criminality and outlawry was imposed on Iraq.

The repression of Iraq was conducted in a manner that mirrors the structure of reparation announced in the 1996 Draft Articles. Simple delicts on the part of Iraq would have given rise to reparation and restitution at a primarily bilateral level. The crime of aggression, however, provoked, what George Abi-Saab describes as, an aggravated regime of international crimes whereby the injurious or wrongful act requires, not simply reparation but 'guarantees against its repetition as well as the uprooting of its continuous effects'.[55] Thus Draft Articles 42 and 45 in effect describe the legal regime imposed on Iraq after the Gulf War.[56]

The consequences of Iraq's loss of sovereign equality or existential equality and its ensuing criminal status were numerous. The imposition of sanctions under Security Council Resolution 687 resulted in

---

[53] There also were those who believed that the enemy was criminal but that any sort of criminal procedure would be inappropriate. Henry Morgenthau, Roosevelt's Treasury Secretary, worried that the Nuremberg Trials might end in acquittals or endless procedural debates. For him, the punishment for sin was death not indictment. Lord Liverpool, too, was frustrated in 1815 by Castlereagh's bloodless shuttle diplomacy and Wellington's chivalric distaste for extra-judicial killings. See Bass, *The Politics of War Crimes Trials*, 37–57.

[54] Two years elapsed before international tribunals were established in more auspicious circumstances at The Hague and at Arusha.

[55] Abi-Saab, 'The Uses of Article 19', 350.

[56] Gowlland-Debbas, 'The Limits of Enforcement', 365.

'a burden out of all proportion to the benefit which the injured state would gain' (Article 43(c)).[57] Such a burden would, of course, be permissible according to the terms of Draft Article 52.[58]

Similarly, the political independence and economic stability of Iraq have been seriously compromised by the sanctions regime (Draft Article 43(d)). Another attribute of existential equality, territorial integrity, has been attenuated by a number of legal innovations. In the most obvious case, Security Council Resolution 687 ordered the deployment of UN military observers ten miles inside Iraq (paragraph 5), demanded that Iraq allow international teams to oversee the destruction of its chemical and biological weapons and its ballistic missile production facilities (paragraphs 8 and 9), approved on-site inspections of nuclear capabilities (paragraph 13) and applied classic economic sanctions (paragraph 19).[59]

These policing actions had the full authority of the UN Security Council. Criminalisation can also occur, of course, when the 'police' act beyond their official duties or within the spirit, if not the letter, of the law. This seems to be the case with the Anglo-American attacks on Iraq during the 1996/7 period and in 1998 and 2001. Security Council Resolution 688 condemned the repression of the Iraqi civilian population and this was interpreted as an implicit authorisation of the no-fly zone policy undertaken in the north and south of Iraq by the Allies.[60] The sporadic bombing of Iraq since then has been variously justified as an

---

[57] The benefit presumably involves some measure of security for Kuwait and interests in the maintenance of peace and stability enjoyed by other members of the international community.

[58] It would not have been permissible if the reparations 'result in depriving the population of a State of its own means of subsistence' (Article 42(3)), even where that state has committed a crime. It seems likely, then, that the 'persistent deprivation, chronic hunger, endemic under-nutrition . . . widespread human suffering', partially caused by the sanctions, go further, and may even violate the terms of ILC 1996 Draft Articles. For various reports outlining the effects of sanctions on the Iraqi population see Garfield, Zaidi and Lennock, 'Medical Care in Iraq after Six Years of Sanctions', *British Medical Journal*, 29 November 1997, 1474–5 and Committee on the Elimination of Racial Discrimination, Summary Record, 1023rd Meeting, UN Geneva, 14 March 1997, CERD/C/SR.1203, 25 April 1997.

[59] The physical effects of all this on Iraq's territorial integrity ought not to be dismissed. This sovereign state (its integrity reaffirmed in successive UN resolutions) was subjected to the indignity of thousands of monitors accessing its most sensitive national defence sites while attacks on its territory by Turkey were ignored (see Geoff Simons, *Iraq – Primus Inter Pariahs*, 79, 101).

[60] The resolution in question stated that the *consequences* of the repression of Iraqi Kurds 'threatened international peace and security'. Fixed wing and helicopter flights over Iraq were also permitted as part of the surveillance operation (see, e.g. SC Res. 1134, 23 October 1997).

enforcement of the no-fly zone (authorised by a reading of Resolutions 678 and 688) and an enforcement of the terms of the cease-fire under Resolution 687.[61] This mixed informal and formal criminal regime imposed on Iraq has made it the paradigmatic case of outlawry at the beginning of the twenty-first century.

In other cases, the Security Council has shown an increasing tendency to label states as terrorist as a precursor to depriving them of certain basic sovereign rights. In the wake of the Lockerbie bombing, several Western governments assigned blame to the Libyan Government. This led to a sequence of Security Council resolutions in which Libya was denounced as a terrorist state, at first implicitly in Security Council Resolution 731, and then, more openly, in Resolution 748.[62] The Security Council, without making any judicial finding that terrorist activity has been linked to Libya, then imposed a highly repressive regime of sanctions on the outlaw state.[63] In the case of Afghanistan, meanwhile, Security Council Resolution 1333 condemned the use of Taliban areas for sheltering and training terrorists.[64] This prefigured, amongst other measures, an arms embargo and the closure of Taliban offices and airlines offices. Similar patterns with certain variations can be seen in the case of other outlaws.[65] These states are subject to an innovative form of regulation that possesses some of the characteristics of a penal regime.

Ultimately, then, it might be said that the now defunct 1996 Draft Articles on State Responsibility invented a category of 'criminal states' but failed to give it any substance while the Security Council treats certain states as criminal without explicitly establishing a category of crime.

These institutional and normative developments mesh well with the preoccupations of two recent contributions to the philosophy of international law by Fernando Tesón and John Rawls. In both cases, there is a clear distinction to be drawn between the lawful state and the criminal state though each draws the line in a different place.[66] For Tesón,

---

[61] For a general analysis see Higgins, *Problems and Process*, 259. SC Res. 1154 (2 March 1998) warns Iraq that failure to accord access to the UN's monitoring teams would 'have the *severest* consequences for Iraq' (my italics).

[62] See SC Res. 731 (21 January 1992) (referring to documents implicating the Libyan Government and condemning terrorism) and SC Res. 748 (31 March 1992) para. 2 (stating that Libya must 'cease all forms of terrorist action').

[63] SC Res. 883 (11 November 1993), SC Res. 1192 (27 August 1998) all at http://www.un.org/Docs/sc/committees/LibyanArabJamahiriya/LibyaResEng.htm

[64] SC Res. 1333 (19 December 2000).   [65] *Ibid.*

[66] Tesón ('Kantian Theory') departs from the typology I have adopted in this chapter by placing undemocratic states in the criminal category.

the status of states such as Iraq and Libya is obvious: 'Tyrannical governments are outlaws.'[67] These states are outlaw because they abuse human
rights and/or are aggressive and/or are illiberal in some way. The resulting constitutional arrangements of this neo-Kantian international law
are simple. 'States observe human rights as a precondition for joining
the alliance.'[68] Outlaw states that do not observe human rights become
vulnerable to exclusion and intervention. They are excluded from the
United Nations (either through an amendment to Articles 4 and 6 of
the Charter or through a re-interpretation of the phrase 'peace-loving'),
their governments are disenfranchised from representing a state for the
purpose of entering into treaties, and representatives of these entities
are denied diplomatic immunity.[69]

As for intervention and the use of force, liberal states are vested with
responsibility for seeking peace and upholding it. As Tesón puts it, 'illegitimate governments are no more than a gang of outlaws, usurpers'.[70]
Such governments become automatically susceptible to criminal sanction. The particularities of this sanction would vary but it seems likely
that a serious degradation in existential equality would ensue.[71] Later
he admits that, in the case of human rights abuses, only 'in rare cases
[is] intervention acceptable'.[72]

This criminal regime is developed further by John Rawls in his
Law of Peoples.[73] Rawls divides states into three categories: the liberal,
the illiberal but well ordered and the outlaw. He constructs an ideal
theory to arrange relations between liberal and well-ordered illiberal

---

[67] *Ibid.*, 89.   [68] *Ibid.*, 87.

[69] See VCLT Article 7, (1969) 8 ILM 683; Vienna Convention on Diplomatic Rights and
Immunities 18 April 1961, UNTS 95. The San Francisco delegates did accept the need
for provisions dealing with suspension and expulsion. Suspension can only occur
where the Security Council has taken enforcement action against a state under
Chapter VII. Expulsion is an option where a state, 'has persistently violated the
Principles contained in the present Charter' (Article 6). The language seems to
encompass only a pattern of outlawry.

[70] Tesón, *The Philosophy of International Law*, 63.

[71] Tesón, 'Kantian Theory', 90. It is not entirely clear to what extent and for what
purposes they are entitled to use force in inter-state affairs. Tesón accepts that force
can be used as 'a last resort . . . in self-defence or in defence of human rights', *ibid.*, 93.
Is intervention equally legitimate in cases of self-defence, in action against gross
violators of human rights and as a way of establishing republican democracy in
illiberal states?

[72] Tesón, 'Kantian Theory', 90.

[73] I have drawn from his essay 'The Law of Peoples' found in the book *The Law of Peoples*.
This essay is an expanded and refined version of the original work found in Rawls's
1993 Amnesty Lectures, 'Law of Peoples' in S. Shute and S. Hurley (eds.), *On Human
Rights*, 41–82. See also J. Rawls, *Collected Works* (ed. S. Freeman).

peoples and a nonideal theory to regulate relations between these 'decent' states and the outlaw or burdened (failed) states.[74] For Rawls, a form of reasonable intercourse is possible between liberal states and the decent illiberal states and he describes one hypothetical decent illiberal state, Kazanistan, in order to show how this would work.[75] On the other hand, the outlaw or failed states are simply subject to the dictates of those states in the zone of law.[76] Rawls's nonideal theory dictates the appropriate policies to be adopted by decent peoples in their relations with those regimes that 'refuse to acknowledge a reasonable law of peoples'.[77] Here, Rawls is embracing a distinction made earlier but one not followed by Tesón. A state is outlaw not because it is undemocratic or internally illiberal but because it is illiberal in its dealings with other states or because it is a gross violator of human rights.[78] Unlike Tesón, Rawls wants to distinguish decent illiberal states (states that respect human rights and, more importantly, harbour no designs on the territory of other states) and outlaw states (states that are not only illiberal but also aggressive, states that are rational but unreasonable and states that consistently violate core human rights).[79] If a state is undemocratic but decent and abides by the dominant norms of procedural justice operational in the international legal order then it remains part of that society.[80]

For Rawls, the outlaw state is worse than merely illiberal, it is aggressive externally or vicious internally. So, the model outlaw states are

---

[74] See Brilmayer for criticisms of Rawls that his work is statist and unsystematic, 'What Use is Rawls' Theory of Justice?' at 5–6.

[75] A number of commentators has argued that the world contains no Kazinistans; that the decent hierarchical state of Rawls's imaginings does not exist. I think an equally large problem for Rawls is that his liberal state represents an idealised version, too.

[76] There is nothing new in this tripartite distinction either. James Lorimer was distinguishing between civilised states (Western Europe, North Americas), barbarians (the Turks) and savages ('criminal states' such as Algeria and Egypt) in the late nineteenth century. It is even mirrored in the ABC mandate system. See Chapter 8 for discussion.

[77] Rawls, *Collected Works* at 555.

[78] In this way, Rawls is distinguishing between 'the fact of reasonable pluralism' (Slaughter's 'zone of legitimate difference', perhaps) and the fact of unreasonable pluralism (the differences between outlaw states and others).

[79] In other words, the possibility of liberalism exists in three spheres. First, the international order can be either illiberal or liberal. Second, states are either constitutionally liberal or illiberal and third, states, in their posture towards the international, can adopt either a liberal mode of behaviour or an illiberal attitude.

[80] I am not certain that even this would be sustainable but at least it accommodates the insight that so many illiberal states continue to embrace judicial or multilateral forms and liberal-democracies often adopt a recalcitrant attitude to liberal international law.

those that fought wars of world or regional domination and were willing to sacrifice their own populations in doing so. These states were often highly advanced and economically powerful.[81] Rawls advocates a system in which such states are denied the benefits of the international economic order (through sanctions) and censured for breaches of human rights. Most importantly, the outlaw states should be refused admission 'as members in good standing into their mutually beneficial cooperative practices'.[82] John Rawls regards the defence of the decent core of states as the primary justification for the use of force by states in that group. In grave cases, force may also be used to protect the victims of these outlaw states. On Rawls's conception of the international order, it is possible to imagine a case where illiberal states (Tesón's outlaws) and liberal states combine to intervene in those states that Rawls regards as outlaws. Indeed, Rawls's view of the international order resembles the current operation of the UN Security Council where illiberal states such as China and Russia are accorded high institutional status in actions taken against outlaw states such as Iraq (it is precisely this order that Tesón finds objectionable).

In his *Fairness in International Law and Institutions*, Thomas Franck sheds more light on this Rawlsian conception of international order when he distinguishes, not between democratic and non-democratic states, but, instead, between those states, whether liberal or illiberal domestically, who are willing to embrace a liberal notion of multilateralism, or as Chris Reus-Smit puts it, 'a norm of procedural justice', in their external relations (i.e. most of the non-democratic states in the UN) and those illiberal states whose 'particular ideology becomes the sole valid norm for judging disputes between nations'.[83] This second group of states has included the Soviet Union (at various times), Napoleonic France and Hitler's Germany, and it is in relation to this second group that Franck's anti-pluralism kicks in: "a global community of fairness could not include any group which believes in an 'automatic trumping entitlement'".[84] The illiberal state becomes a criminal only if it rejects the rules of the game altogether in its external relations. The merely undemocratic state is not (yet) an outlaw (though its government lacks the validation it may need to survive).

---

[81] Rawls, *Law of Peoples*, 106.
[82] Note that nonideal theory also applies to failed states or states burdened by unfavourable conditions. Rawls, *Collected Works*, 557.
[83] Franck, *Fairness*, 15.   [84] *Ibid.*, 16.

In contrast to Tesón, both Rawls and Franck accept that states that are illiberal in their domestic relations can nevertheless adopt liberal practices in their international dealings. It is equally possible, too, of course, that a liberal state might act in a highly illiberal manner internationally (realists, of course, built a whole theory of international politics on this supposition). Imperial Germany in 1914 arguably possessed a liberal constitution and yet adopted a chauvinistic posture in its foreign affairs.[85] Similarly, the Reagan Administration was no great respecter of the system of multilateralism and non-aggression.[86]

In a sense, then, Franck and Rawls are not Kantians in that they do not claim a direct link between oppression at home and aggression in international affairs. What Tesón, Franck and Rawls do share, however, is a willingness to describe some states as outlaws. For Rawls and Tesón, at least, this could justify the imposition of a system of criminal repression on the outlaw.

So, the writers discussed in the preceding paragraphs are important because they provide the theoretical underpinning for the project of criminalisation the international community appears to be embarked upon. Each of them nominates certain states as candidates for the periphery and these states are then to be subject to an array of sanctions, enforcement measures and exclusions that strongly resembles criminalisation and reflects the efforts on the part of both the International Law Commission and the Security Council to establish a criminal law regime based on the inequality of states.

These regimes, and the theories that have buttressed their application, violate the principle of existential equality as I have characterised it in this study. The Westphalian idea of sovereign equality married a normative commitment to a prohibition. The normative commitment was directed at supporting the equality of states regardless of religious affiliation and ensuring that they retained certain basic immunities within an order of equal sovereigns. This was designed to discourage future wars between Protestant and Catholic Kingdoms over the question of religious truth. The prohibition was directed against the idea that intervention was legitimated by some moral or religious or political superiority. The international community (Security Council) and its private enforcers

---

[85] See Doyle, 'Liberal Legacies', 216–17 fn 8. See also Mortimer Sellers, 'Republican Principles in International Law' (1996) 11:3 *Connecticut Journal of International Law* 403–32; Michael Doyle, 'Liberalism and World Politics' (1986) 80:4 *American Political Science Review* 1151–69.

[86] See B. Weston, 'The Reagan Administration versus International Law' in A. D'Amato *et al.* (eds.), *International Law and World Order*, 1141–7.

(e.g. Nato, see Chapter 7) have abandoned this structure in favour of a return to hierarchy through criminal repression.

The democratic governance regime

While the proponents and enforcers of the state crime model have tended to focus on either aggressive or genocidal states, the theory and practice of democratic governance represents an attempt to impose upon undemocratic states a regime of constraint and inequality.

The advent of the international human rights machinery modified the view that a state's internal affairs were just that, matters for the state alone and not subject to international supervision or surveillance. The domestic jurisdiction of states underwent shrinkage as the human rights regime became more and more intrusive. Human rights instruments began to create an expectation that states would conform to certain human rights standards in their domestic practices. The Universal Declaration on Human Rights and the two Human Rights Covenants of 1966 each enumerated a number of standards and rights that had the aim of severely circumscribing states' latitude in their behaviour towards their citizens.[87]

However, the human rights system did little to change the practice of universal international organisations in their admissions policies. So, while human rights law seemed to insist on adherence to certain values, the practice of international organisations remained pluralistic. There was no serious attempt made to fix human rights obligations, routinely, to entry requirements into the international community during the Charter era.[88] Notice that this is not an argument that human rights during this period were wilfully violated or that there is a gap between reality and rhetoric in the area of human rights or that there is no such thing as human rights law.[89] The argument is simply that, on the whole, the behaviour of a state was not regarded as

---

[87] See the Universal Declaration on Human Rights (1948) at http://www.un.org/Overview/rights.html; the International Covenant on Civil and Political Rights and the International Covenant on Economic, Cultural and Social Rights (1966) at http://www.unhchr.ch/html/intlinst.htm

[88] The Council of Europe is an obvious exception to this norm. However, my primary concern in this book is with international or universal organisations rather than regional organisations. The Council experience was only taken seriously as a possible model for international organisation by the liberal internationalists in the post-cold war era.

[89] James Shand Watson, *Theory and Reality in the International Protection of Human Rights*. For an interesting constructivist position at odds with Watson's methodology see T. Risse, S. Roppe and K. Sikkink, *The Power of Human Rights*.

significant for the purposes of that state's engagement in multilateral organisations.[90] This remained the case in the period up to 1966 (or during, what David Forsythe called, the standard setting and promotional phases of the human rights regime[91]). It was the UN's response to apartheid in South Africa and white rule in Rhodesia (now Zimbabwe) beginning in 1966 that first saw a link made between internal practices and status in the international community.[92] Here are found the portents of the anti-pluralism that was to flourish in the post-cold war era.[93] The forerunners of today's pariah states were South Africa and, to a lesser extent, Rhodesia.[94] For example, as a response to Ian Smith's Unilateral Declaration of Independence in 1965, the Security Council called on states to break off relations with Rhodesia and applied a sanctions regime that became increasingly punitive.[95] In South Africa, the same process occurred.[96] These legal processes, partly, were about imposing liberal values on states but they were ultimately directed at ending apartheid, deemed the most egregious and offensive form of racism in existence at that time. In the absence of this special quality (apartheid), the internal politics of a state continued to be regarded as irrelevant to a state's or government's status in the international order.[97] The failure to expel, or even to sanction seriously, the likes of Kampuchea, Idi Amin's Uganda or Guatemala spoke volumes for the continuing commitment to inter-state pluralism.[98] As Alan James put it in 1986, 'constitutional

---

[90] Perhaps the most egregious example of this was the continued membership of the Khmer Rouge in the General Assembly long after it had been shown that the organisation was implicated in a human rights holocaust and after it had been replaced by the Hun Sen Government with the aid of Vietnamese intervention.

[91] See David Forsythe, *The Internationalisation of Human Rights*.

[92] In 1946 there was the ambiguous case of Spain (see Chapter 9).

[93] For a discussion of the sanctions regime as applied to South Africa see A. Klotz and N. Crawford, *How Sanctions Work: Lessons from South Africa*.

[94] There is some doubt as to whether Rhodesia ever became a state. The weight of legal opinion is against the conclusion that Rhodesia's declaration had legal effect. See James Crawford, 'The Criteria for Statehood' (1977–8) 48 *British Yearbook of International Law* 93–182 at 163; R. Higgins, 'International Law, Rhodesia and the UN' (1967) 23:3 *The World Today* 98. For an important case supporting this view see *Madzimbamuto* v. *Lardner-Burke* [1967] AC 645, 39 ILR 61. For a contrary view from the international relations side, see Alan James, *Sovereign Statehood: The Basis of International Society*, 157.

[95] SC Res. 221 (9 April 1966); SC Res. 232 (16 December 1966); SC Res. 277 (15 March 1970).

[96] See, e.g. SC Res. 418 (4 November 1977).   [97] See James, *Sovereign Statehood*, 160–1.

[98] Inter-state pluralism at this stage was also an indispensable end for those newly independent states that were reluctant to have their own domestic practices investigated.

independence . . . is applied as it stands, with no further questions asked or requirements imposed'.[99]

All of this began to change in the late 1980s with the development of norms and practices designed to promote democratic governance. On the normative front, various human rights organs within and outside the UN system articulated new democratic standards.[100] In practice, the United Nations entered the business of election-monitoring through its Electoral Assistance Division and, in several prominent instances, acted forcibly to restore democratic governance through the use of force.[101] In addition, Western commentaries began to adopt a celebratory air in discussing the spread of democracy.[102] Accompanying this body of practice and rhetoric was early jurisprudential work by scholars proposing a wider link between the internal political arrangements of states and their rights to enjoy full sovereign rights within the international community.[103]

In 1990, Michael Reisman argued that undemocratic governments lacked the sovereignty that was a prerequisite to the enjoyment of full status in the international community.[104] The government could derive authority and thus exercise sovereignty at the bidding or sufferance of the people but governments could not displace that sovereignty with a sovereignty founded on effectiveness alone. The intended effect of all this was the de-legitimisation of undemocratic states and governments and the development of a right of unilateral intervention, in certain cases where, for example, elected leaders had been deposed in a military

---

[99] See James, *Sovereign Statehood*, 161.

[100] See, e.g. Human Rights Committee, General Comment 25(57), UN Doc. CCPR/C/21/Rev.1/Add.7 (1996), OSCE Copenhagen Declaration, www.osce.org/inst/oscepa/copenhagen.htm. For an overview see C. M. Cerna, 'Universal Democracy: An International Legal Right or the Pipe Dream of the West?' (1995) 27 NYUJILP 289.

[101] For example in Haiti, SC Res. 940 (1994); Sierra Leone, SC Res. 1270 (1999); Liberia, SC Res. 866 (1993); Angola, SC Res. 747 (1992) (supporting elections in 1992); and, lately, in Kosovo, SC Res. 1244 (1999) and in East Timor, SC Res. 1246 (1999). But see George W. Bush, prior to his election, arguing 'against extensive US engagement in nation-building, in democracy promotion . . .', *Guardian Weekly*, 12–18 October 1999, 35.

[102] Most obviously in Francis Fukuyama's *The End of History and the Last Man*. Some of this enthusiasm remains today. Following the fall of Milosevic, Alexander Lukashenko, the President of Belarus, was described as 'the last unelected leader in Europe', *Washington Post Weekly*, Editorial, 12–18 October 1999, 35.

[103] H. Steiner, 'Political Participation as a Human Right' (1988) 1 *Harvard Human Rights Yearbook* 77.

[104] W. M. Reisman, 'Sovereignty and Human Rights in Contemporary International Law' (1990) 84 AJIL 866.

putsch. The legitimacy of such an action, it was true, would depend on the particular context but in no case would the sovereignty of the state operate as an automatic bar to intervention. This was a departure from the standard assumptions about sovereignty found in international law where sovereignty was a quality of statehood encompassing internal effectiveness and external status. This democratic governance perspective was then taken up and embroidered by others until it became something of an orthodoxy.

Some developed full-blown Kantian theories of international law based on a normative individualism that saw liberal-democratic states or republican governments as the sole means by which justice and human rights could be secured at the international level.[105] These 'Kantians' also believed that a society of republican states could be nothing but pacific because it would be founded on the consent of rational, free and peaceable individuals. When governments are despotic, autocratic or authoritarian, the state will display contempt for individual autonomy in the domestic sphere and will act in an irrational manner internationally. State behaviour in the international sphere is subject to the moderating influence of public opinion (supplemented by a separation of powers that ensures a system of checks and balances). This institutional repertoire mitigates the tendency of executive government to act rashly, unilaterally or belligerently. Self-governing states are disinclined to go to war because the effects of war are felt by the people who, when represented in the decision-making process, will seek to avoid the privations associated with their role in the war. Finally, liberal states, in favouring a global free market, have invested too much in peace to risk it all in war. The free exchange of goods and persons has the dual effect of spreading common ideas and pacifying the international culture through rational communication.[106]

Kantian theory is an explicit rejection of the sovereign equality inherent in liberal pluralism.[107] The individual's democratic and human

---

[105] According to Tesón, the protection of human rights is the central aspiration of a just, normative order ('Kantian Theory', 54). For Tesón, as for Kant, the liberal-democratic state is the only political unit capable of advancing this conception of justice (see, e.g. *To Perpetual Peace: A Philosophical Sketch* [1795] in H. Reiss (ed.), *Kant: Political Writings*. In this study, Kant outlines the conditions for a liberal-cosmopolitan world community dedicated to peace and underwritten by a commitment to individual liberty).

[106] For a critique of these views see G. Simpson, 'Imagined Consent', (1994) 15 *Australian Yearbook of International Law* 103–28.

[107] Tesón, 'Kantian Theory', 54. He says at one point: 'A liberal theory of international law can hardly be reconciled with the statist approach.' Needless to say, this whole book denies that claim. Statism is a liberal theory of international law. Liberalism is

rights prevail over the state's claims to territorial integrity or political sovereignty. The state's sovereignty, such as it is, is derived from the consent of the people. In this way, domestic legitimacy rather than effectiveness or recognition determines international status.[108] Fernando Tesón's Kantian Society, for example, is thus guaranteed to produce justice at two mutually supportive levels. Just municipal institutions are good in themselves but they also reproduce justice and peace at the international level. Liberal states establish liberal international relations. Equally, a just, liberal international order will support, promote and, occasionally, enforce a just, democratic domestic order.

Others, of a less obviously Kantian persuasion, focused on realising the fruits of the democratic peace and this idea was further elaborated in the suggestion that there existed in international law a right to democracy. Behind all this was a belief in the link between 'arbitrary government at home and aggressive behaviour abroad' and a symbiosis between the international and the domestic. Free citizens will insist on a just foreign policy while just (international) institutions will insist that citizens are free. The ideal, then, is 'a federation of free states' where the domestic and the international become parasitic on each other. The result of all this is a distinction between democratic or liberal or republican states in good standing and outlaw states variously referred to as 'hard-core abstainers' or illiberal states.[109] The liberal states possess and the illiberal regimes lack

some form of representative government secured by the separation of powers, constitutional guarantees of civil and political rights, juridical equality, and a functioning judicial system dedicated to the rule of law.[110]

as much about non-intervention and self-determination as it is about justice. What Tesón means is that the Kantian theory of international law is irreconcilable with statism though even this claim is dubious given Kant's own willingness to accommodate the state in *Perpetual Peace*.

[108] *Ibid.*, 54.

[109] Franck, 'Legitimacy and the Democratic Entitlement', in G. Fox and B. Roth (eds.), *Democratic Governance*, 40. Franck seems to associate them with two bankrupt theories of the state: the dictatorship of the proletariat and forced modernisation ('Democratic Entitlement' at 48–9). These abstainers appear to number about sixty. This figure is derived from subtracting Franck's list of 130 democratic states from the 190 or so states in the international system. These states are not even interested in acquiring external validation from the international community. The figure of 130 is, of course, highly contentious. As Franck admits, while these 130 states hold elections not all of them are fair. Franck, 'Democratic Entitlement', 27–8, fn. 2. Louis Hartz referred to the 'impulse [in American liberalism] which inspires it to define dubious regimes elsewhere as "liberal"', *Liberal Tradition*, 285.

[110] Slaughter, 'Liberal States', 511, fn. 18. But see also the important work of Harold Koh, e.g. 'Why Do Nations Obey International Law?' (1995) 106 YLJ 2599; 'Transnational

This capacity to distinguish is the key to success in understanding international society and in ordering it; by building on the different behavioural patterns exhibited by liberal and illiberal states to create the basis for an international law of democratic peace.[111] This can be contrasted with the old Charter liberal or liberal pluralist view of the international community which, it is argued, refuses to take seriously the differences between states for the purposes of norm creation and institutional design.[112]

It is worth distinguishing two forms of anti-pluralist thought at this point. In the case of strong anti-pluralism, intervention, exclusion and exile are regarded as feasible and principled responses to the problem of outlawry. So, the work of Tesón and Reisman dovetails rather neatly with current US foreign policy on this issue. Mild anti-pluralists reject both exclusion and unilateral intervention as methods by which states that are merely undemocratic might be brought to heel. In some cases, at least for the present, an illiberal state that plays by the norms of multilateralism suffers no exile even if it treats its citizens rather poorly and/or refuses to embrace democratic governance. For the present, there is a preference for engagement over exclusion or pro-democratic unilateral intervention. For example, Anne-Marie Slaughter believes some form of dialogue is possible between liberal and non-liberal states.[113] To this extent, Slaughter's liberalism is a theory of international relations, not a conception of law in a world of exclusively liberal states.

> Liberal international relations theory applies to all States. Totalitarian governments, authoritarian dictatorships, and theocracies can all be depicted as representatives of some subset of actors in domestic and transnational society, even if it is a very small or particularistic slice.[114]

Presumably, liberal states could engage with their illiberal counterparts using the (outmoded) techniques of classical international law. In

---

Legal Process' (1996) 75 *Nebraska Law Review* 181. For a more detailed description of Slaughter's oeuvre see Alvarez, 'Liberal States'.

[111] See, e.g. M. Brown *et al.* (eds.), *Debating the Democratic Peace*. Liberal international lawyers, such as Slaughter, want to take the insights found in this work and transform it into a wider and more comprehensive theory not only about why liberal states avoid war with each other but about why, and the different ways in which, they get on so well together.

[112] Slaughter, 'Liberal Theory', (2000) 1 (paper on file with author).

[113] Slaughter also discusses, albeit briefly, law in a world composed exclusively of illiberal states. This would resemble the realist view of international relations, a world dominated by state actors ('Liberal States', 530).

[114] *Ibid.*, 509.

addition, though, non-state actors within the liberal state could influence policy and conditions within the non-liberal state by seeking to open up that state's economy and by targeting humanitarian aid.[115] The aim appears to be the promotion of liberalism by non-forcible stealth. For this to occur, engagement is necessary and desirable. Slaughter's anti-pluralism is mild because instead of expelling states from the system (Tesón, Rawls) or using military intervention to impose democratic governance from the outside (Reisman), it seeks to engage with outlaw states using a combination of old-fashioned classical international law combined with an ambitious private and public transnationalism of networks.[116]

Indeed, Slaughter appears less and less comfortable with the distinction between liberal and non-liberal states. In the most recent refinement of her Liberal Theory, she has recanted the strong anti-pluralist position, stating that, for the time being at least, 'we should not explicitly limit global institutions to liberal states or develop domestic and international doctrines that explicitly categorise entire states as such' (though she does accept that regional organisations may and do adopt such practices). However, Slaughter continues to ascribe a descriptive role to the distinction between liberal and non-liberal states. Indeed, her general theory of international behaviour mandates her to do this. Thus, the distinction will operate, she claims, 'as a positive predictor of how [states] are likely to behave in a wide variety of circumstances, including within or toward international institutions'.[117] I wonder if Slaughter can escape so readily the normative implications of this descriptive theory.[118] If the difference between liberal and illiberal states is so critical to the success and failure of international institutions and processes then does it

---

[115] Slaughter, 'Government Networks' in Fox and Roth (eds.), *Democratic Governance*, 199–235, *passim*.

[116] In Slaughter's work, the central distinction is not between liberal and illiberal states but between one-level statist conceptions of international order and those, like her own multi-level liberal theory, which focus on the role of other international and domestic actors acting through and beyond the state.

[117] Slaughter, 'Liberal Theory', 11.

[118] In an essay on 'Government Networks', she believes that ' "enlargement" through embracing specific institutions in transgovernmental networks can sidestep the often thorny problem of labeling countries wholesale as democracies or non-democracies', 202. This, perhaps, underestimates the extent to which the form of government in a state will condition the extent to which it will permit such transgovernmental networks to flourish. It may be that the distinction between democratic and non-democratic states is fundamental to the success of such networks rather than rendered irrelevant in the face of them.

not, for example, behove designers of institutions to take the distinction into account in modelling membership criteria and organisational principles? As she puts it elsewhere:

The most distinctive aspect of Liberal international relations theory is that it permits, indeed mandates, a distinction among different types of states, based on their domestic political structure and ideology.[119]

One subtle suggestion about how a distinction between liberal and illiberal states might be reflected in norm-development is made by James Crawford in his essay on 'Democracy and the Body of International Law', in which he weaves a path between outright exclusion and full engagement, between the Charter liberal ideal where no distinctions are permitted and the liberal anti-pluralist approach where they are mandated.[120] Crawford recommends that a more tempered legal norm be developed that permits engagement with unrepresentative states and governments but requires that parties entering into either contracts or treaties with that state do so at their own risk. Crawford describes these treaties as 'unconscionable transactions with wholly undemocratic regimes'.[121] Successor governments, democratically elected, might then decide to review the transactions of the previous regime. The international system would presumably look upon such review with a degree of tolerance *pace* the classic *Tinoco* approach.[122]

Whichever techniques are preferred, the group of writers I have characterised as mild anti-pluralists accepts the central point that democracy is good for international law. They also, however, reject both outright exclusion (for the time being) and unilateral forms of intervention as options for confronting the phenomenon of the undemocratic state.[123]

---

[119] Slaughter, 'Liberal States', 504.

[120] James Crawford, 'Democracy and the Body of International Law', in Fox and Roth, *Democratic Governance*, 108–9.

[121] *Ibid.*, 110.   [122] See *Tinoco Arbitration, Great Britain* v. *Costa Rica* 1923 1 RIAA 369.

[123] Some political theorists are, like Fernando Tesón, less cautious in their approach to exclusion and intervention, e.g. David Held has created a blueprint for an effort to create a society of like-minded states (David Held, *Democracy and the Global Order*). He calls for the establishment of an independent assembly of democratic peoples. 'To begin with at least such an assembly is unlikely to be an assembly of all nations; for it would be an assembly of democratic nations, which would in principle, draw in others over time' (274). In some cases, the imposition of rights in 'zones of development' might be deferred for a period of negotiation (276). He lists a number of principles that might undergird such an order, e.g. the principle that: 'Cosmopolitan democracy might justify the deployment of force . . . in the context of a threat to international democracy and a denial of democratic rights and obligations

The practice of international law is as equivocal as the theory on the question of what to do about undemocratic states. There have, of course, been unilateral interventions justified on pro-democratic grounds.[124] The US invasions of Panama and Grenada were defended as pro-democratic exceptions to Article 2(4) but approval for this sort of practice remains lacking despite the enthusiasm of some scholars.[125] Equally, UN sponsored democratic enforcement has been patchy and tentative. Security Council enforcement actions against Haiti in 1994 and Sierra Leone in 1998 point to a very cautious expansion of the Council's activities as opposed to a wholesale extension of the grounds on which the Council might legitimately intervene. In each case, the key resolutions were careful not to adduce democratic rehabilitation as the sole or even most prominent basis for the intervention. While Resolution 940 (1994) emphasises the humanitarian crises afflicting Haiti and the approval for the intervention on the part of the exiled President Aristide, Resolution 1132 (1998) operates as a retroactive justification of an intervention by a coalition of (undemocratic) African states. It is difficult to extract from these actions a norm that permits such interventions by private actors (i.e. in the absence of UN approval) or a UN practice that would lead us to expect a pattern of such interventions in the future.

The idea of intervening to promote democracy through the use of force, then, has struck most observers as self-contradictory and, in the case of unilateral intervention, as contrary to basic norms of international law. However, liberal anti-pluralists have embraced the possibility of *exclusion* either implicitly (Slaughter), as a future possibility (Franck) or partially (Rawls), as an alternative to intervention.

This seems a much more plausible future for the democratic governance norm. I want to consider two case studies very briefly in order to assess the likelihood of a democratic governance regime developing

by tyrannical regimes, or by circumstances which spiral beyond the control of particular peoples and agents (such as the disintegration of a state)' (272–3).

[124] Though the relatively small number of unilateral interventions since 1945 has tended to be justified as extensions of the right to self-defence (the US invasion of Panama) or actions in support of pre-existing Security Council resolutions (the attacks on Iraq by British and US warplanes in 2000) or various forms of humanitarian intervention (the Israeli raid on Entebbe, the Indian support for the Bangladeshi secessionists). The Soviet anti-counter-revolutionary interventions in Hungary and Czechoslovakia are the closest in form to pro-democratic interventions and they were condemned by large sections of the international community.

[125] E.g. A. D'Amato, 'The Invasion of Panama was a Lawful Response to Tyranny' (1990) 84 AJIL 520. In the case of Grenada, the US offered three justifications and only one of these was tangentially related to promoting democracy.

whereby undemocratic states might be expelled from the international order or, at least, from a coalition of like-minded states.

In early February 2000, the Austrian Freedom Party was invited to become part of the governing coalition in Austria.[126] The previous October the Party, led by Jorge Haider, had won 27 per cent of the vote in a national election. Haider was known throughout Europe for his sympathies with Hitler and his virulent speeches about immigration.[127] The new coalition was immediately condemned by the US Government and European Union states began to downgrade diplomatic relations and cancel official visits to Austria, with the President of the EU, Jorge Sampaio, saying that the Freedom Party was 'not suitable' to be in the EU.[128] Meanwhile the Chancellor of Austria, Wolfgang Schussel, pleaded that Austria was 'not a pariah state'.[129] Austria was 'quarantined' in the months following the election.[130] The most common idea expressed at this time was that Austria had violated certain criteria for membership in Europe[131] or in the 'Western democratic community of nations'.[132]

---

[126] The coalition was formed between the conservative People's Party and the Freedom Party. The deal gave the Freedom Party half the seats in the cabinet and several of the key posts. See 'Backlash Boosts Austrian Far Right', *The Australian*, 4 February 2000, 8.

[127] Haider had described the Waffen SS as 'men of honour' ten years before the election and had praised Hitler's policies in speeches at that time.

[128] Madeline Albright recalled the US Ambassador for consultation and stated that no European government should include a party that 'doesn't distance itself clearly from the atrocities of the Nazi era and the politics of hate', 'Riots as Far-Right Takes Power in Austria', *Guardian Weekly* 10 February 2000, 1.

[129] *Ibid.*

[130] The fourteen European Heads of State in the EU agreed to break off bilateral official contacts with the Austrian Government, cease supporting any Austrians seeking positions in international organisations and receive Austrian ambassadors only at the technical level if Haider's party was included in the government.

[131] Italy's Prime Minister Massimo D'Alema noted that 'Europe has certain criteria and values that unite it' (*Guardian Weekly*, 10 February 2000, 14). Guterres called the whole issue 'a question of principles and values' (14) and argued that 'a whole range of values which underpin our civilisation are at stake' ('EU Launches Anti-Haider Campaign', *Sydney Morning Herald*, 5 February 2000, 19). On the other hand, when the premier of Bavaria had invited President Klestel of Austria to defend Austria's commitment to 'Europe's Values' he was speaking of a different tradition – one of conservatism and exclusion (*Guardian Weekly*, 17 February 2000, 1).

[132] Editorial comment, *Guardian Weekly*, 10 February 2000, 14. The editorial went on to state that the coalition, 'threatens the identity and cohesion of the EU and other Pan-European institutions that arose from the ashes of Europe's fascist era'. It could also be argued that Austria had been condemned not for failing to meet the democratic threshold or because it was not 'republican' but because democracy in Austria had produced a leader thought to be despicable. Haider's associations with fascism were the catalyst for the exclusion, not any lack of democracy. Technically,

There were those who exercised some caution on this matter. The German Chancellor, Gerhard Schroeder, was keen to point out that the EU's actions did not interfere with Austria's sovereignty and political independence while the European Commission decided to take no action unless there were specific human rights violations.[133] The EU did not move to suspend Austria's membership under the provisions of Article 7 of the Treaty of the European Union.[134] Indeed, it may be that such suspension would violate provisions of the Treaty of Rome. Ilias Bantekas, though, has suggested that, 'at an EU level, we are witnessing the emergence of a customary obligation of democratic governance'.[135] However, one would have to be careful in endorsing such a proposition. First, the Austrian case marks the first time the EU has even considered such sanctions against one of its members. Second, the developing norm would be a regional one at best.[136] Third, the EU was unable or reluctant to ostracise Austria and, indeed, there is now a sense that the episode was mishandled.[137]

Perhaps the best that can be said here is that the Austrian case, coupled with the democratic governance criteria included in the membership norms of the Union, signals that the democracy governance norm may be taken seriously in Europe, at least.[138]

The position is even less clear in international law, generally. Since the collective sanctions against Rhodesia and South Africa, the internal or undemocratic nature of a state has not tended to leave it vulnerable to sanctions. But even here there are signs of an embryonic norm of democratic governance being applied to the admissions and expulsions policy of the UN. The Yugoslav case, perhaps, best illustrates how this might occur. When, in 1992, Yugoslavia dissolved into its constituent

---

Austria may have violated Article 6(1) of the Amsterdam Treaty of 1992 which states that the European Union is to be based on 'principles of liberty, democracy . . . and the rule of law' (1778 UNTS 1 November 1993).

[133] Ilias Bantekas, 'Austria, the European Union and Article 2(7) of the UN Charter', *ASIL Insight*, February 2000, 1.

[134] Permitting suspension of rights in cases of serious and persistent breach.

[135] Bantekas, 'Austria', 3.

[136] Though, see, too, the actions of the Commonwealth vis-à-vis Fiji, Nigeria and Pakistan discussed in Alison Duxbury, 'Austria and the European Union: The Report of the Three Wise Men' (2000) 1 *Melbourne Journal of International Law*, 173, fn 35.

[137] See the *Report of Martti Ahtisaari, Jochen Frowein and Marelino Oreja* adopted 8 September 2000 at www.virtual-institute.de/en/BerichtEU/index/cfm recommending that measures against Austria be lifted, partly because of fear of nationalist sentiments.

[138] *Summary and Conclusions of the Opinion of the Commission concerning Application for Membership to the European Union* at www.eurunion.org/legislat/agd2000/opinsumm.htm

units following the civil war there, a question arose as to whether Serbia and Montenegro had succeeded to the international personality of the old Yugoslavia. The Serbs themselves did not apply for membership of the UN because they regarded the issue as one of succession rather than commencement or recognition.[139] The international community, through its various organs, decided that a new state had been created.[140] The General Assembly and the Security Council refused to admit this new state as a member of the United Nations.[141] The EC guidelines of 16 December 1991 made it clear that recognition by EC states would depend on compliance with certain conditions, among them a duty to protect minorities. These conditions were imposed on the other aspiring states of the former Yugoslavia as well as the states of the former USSR.[142] The failure to follow these democratic standards proved costly to the FRY. At the unilateral level, the United States, for example, had imposed a series of sanctions on the FRY following the wars in Bosnia and the attack on Kosovo.

More significantly for our purposes, the elections in 2000 precipitated a sea change in the attitude of the international community towards Yugoslavia. In October 2000, the Congress included, in its annual Foreign Operations legislation, a section approving financial aid to the former Yugoslavia on condition that the new government led by President Kostunica cooperated with the ICTY, ceased support of the Republika Srpska and implemented polices 'which reflect a respect for minority rights and the rule of law'.[143] In the same month, the FRY applied for

---

[139] See *Case Concerning Application of the Convention on the Prevention and Punishment of the Crime of Genocide (Bosnia v. Yugoslavia)*, Application for Revision of Judgement of 11 July 1996, 23 April 2001 (on file with author).

[140] *Arbitration Commission, EC Conference on Yugoslavia*: Opinions No 8 and 10, 92 ILR 199 and 206.

[141] GA Res., 46/1 (22 September 1992); SC Res. 777 (19 September 1992) (recommending to the General Assembly that Yugoslavia 'shall not participate in the work of the General Assembly'). On the other hand, the Yugoslav flag continued to fly at the UN Headquarters and Yugoslavia continued to pay its dues.

[142] See, e.g. Badinter Opinions Nos. 4–7, (1992) 92 ILR 173. Croatia was initially refused recognition for failure to comply with certain minority guarantees. See Observations on Croatian Constitutional Law, Arbitration Commission, Conference on Yugoslavia (1992) 92 ILR 209. On the states of the former USSR, see EC Guidelines on the Recognition of New States in Eastern Europe and in the Soviet Union, 16 December 1991, UKMIL 1991, (1991) 62 BYIL 559 (requiring among other things, 'respect for the provisions of the . . . Charter of Paris especially with regard to the rule of law, democracy and human rights').

[143] *Foreign Operations, Export Financing and Related Programs*, 2001 Pub. L. No. 106-429, s594(a) (c), 114 Stat. 1900, 1900A-60 (2000).

membership of the UN as a new state, i.e. under Article 4(1) of the UN Charter and according to Article 134 of the Rules of Procedure of the General Assembly governing new members.[144] The 'new state' was given membership of the United Nations after a Security Council recommendation and a General Assembly vote.[145] This example does not, in itself, indicate the development of some rule of democratic governance. The situation involving the former Yugoslavia is muddied by the fact that the FRY's status was so uncertain in the first place and because it is not always clear whether the former Yugoslavia was deprived of membership because of its lack of democracy or because of its involvement in a sequence of aggressive wars in the Balkans.

Nonetheless, the Austrian and Yugoslav examples are suggestive of a growing tendency to distinguish between the democratic core and the undemocratic or illiberal periphery. The increasing significance of the EU itself, the OECD and the free trade pacts may give the impression that the UN's old-fashioned commitment to sovereign equality is a universalist hangover from the twentieth century. Certainly, much of the impetus for the new democratic norm seems to have come from the European experience. Whether it be censure (Austria) or conditional admission (Badinter in the former Yugoslavia),[146] the Europeans have led the way in developing a principle of democratic governance which has the potential to create an inside/outside world that displaces the pluralist assumptions behind the Charter.[147]

Conclusion: a bifurcated legal order

In this chapter, I have considered two regimes of anti-pluralism, each of which is a threat to existential equality in international law. These anti-pluralist regimes create (or recreate) categories of states perhaps alien to international lawyers immersed in the atmosphere of post-war

---

[144] See President Kostunica, Letter to the Secretary-General Requesting Admission to the UN, 27 October 2000, Annex 23, to Application for Revision of Judgement.

[145] SC Res. 1326 (31 October 2000); GA Res. 55/12 (1 November 2000).

[146] A. Pellet, 'The Opinions of the Badinter Arbitration Committee: A Second Breath for the Self-Determination of Peoples' (178) and 'Appendix: Opinions No. 1, 2 and 3 of the Arbitration Committee of the International Conference on Yugoslavia' (1992) 3:1 EJIL 178–85.

[147] See other re-statements of the democratic governance norm in the OSCE's *Charter of Paris for a New Europe* (19–21 November, 1990) and Copenhagen Document on the Human Dimension (5 June–29 July, 1990). See, too, Krasner, *Organised Hypocrisy*, 98–104.

Charter pluralism. Criminal states and undemocratic states have always existed in a sociological sense but, at least since 1945 and until recently, these categories had relatively little jurisprudential purchase. The system of law introduced at Nuremberg, San Francisco and in the 1960 Declaration on Colonial Peoples disparaged the idea that states could be consigned to the margins because of criminality, illiberalism or incapacity. Nuremberg asserted the principle that men and not abstract entities committed crimes, thereby confining the idea of criminal responsibility to individuals.[148] The San Francisco Conference delegates preferred a system in which states of various persuasions became members of the United Nations. The 1960 Declaration on Colonial Peoples, meanwhile, made it clear that 'inadequacy of political, economic, social or educational preparedness should never serve as a pretext for delaying independence'.[149] The two regimes of anti-pluralism described in this chapter have each, to varying degrees, undone this skein of Charter pluralism. What does this mean, though, for the international system?

Anne-Marie Slaughter has said that: 'Non-liberal states . . . are freer now than at any time since 1945 to pursue their ambitions, however defined, and when frustrated, to settle their grievances by force'.[150] This view of the outlaw state was advanced as early as 1945 in San Francisco during discussions at Committee I/2, where delegates argued against a provision allowing expulsion of 'rogue' states on the grounds that it would create two zones of international order; a zone of peace (the remaining members of the United Nations) and a zone of lawlessness in which 'expelled members would be free of their obligations' and where the UN Security Council's writ would no longer run.[151] In debates at the same time, there were concerns that a right of withdrawal from the United Nations, too, might allow recalcitrant states to 'menace' the organisation from outside and free those states from the obligations

---

[148] See 1 *Trial of the Major War Criminals Before the International Military Tribunal Nuremberg* (1947) Judgement at 223. But see Nuremberg's treatment of organisations at Volume 22.

[149] GA Resolution 1514 (14 December 1960), para 5.

[150] Anne-Marie Burley, 'Toward an Age of Liberal Nations', 33 *Harvard International Law Journal* (1992) at 393.

[151] UNCIO Vol VII at 113; Doc 604 I/2/42 26 May 1945. See, too, Observations of the Government of Venezuela on the Dumbarton Oaks Proposals Doc 2, G/7d 31 October 1944, UNCIO III at 193.

imposed by the Charter.[152] A variation on this fear is reprised in José Alvarez's anxiety that:

the liberals' 'badge of alienage,' once imposed, tends to put the target outside of reach or leaves the question to be resolved outside the constraints of law. This kind of liberal theory shrinks, rather than expands, the domain of law (footnotes omitted).[153]

The argument in this chapter, however, is that while the law shrinks in some regards it expands in others. In the case of criminal states, there is control through exclusion followed by a mixture of surveillance and community-sanctioned violence when these states are declared sovereign *non grata*.[154] The practice in recent years, as I have shown, has been to subject such states to quite intrusive forms of regulation coupled with a loss of state immunities and rights. The highly intrusive regimes established in Iraq and Libya under Security Council Resolutions 687 and 748 are examples of this tendency.[155] These 'outlaw' states were certainly not 'freed' of their obligations. Indeed, the peace imposed on Iraq in New York and Serbia at Dayton extended the duties of these states well beyond their normal responsibilities as states in international law.[156] Tesón explains their position as analogous to common criminals. These states remain subject to law or, at least, 'elementary principles' of criminal law.[157] Pushing this metaphor further, one might argue that the outlaw state is incarcerated within a separate legal regime without

[152] See Report of the Rapporteur of Committee I/2, San Francisco Doc. 606 I/2/43, 26 May 1945 at UNCIO VII at 120. The Belgians worried that provisions on expulsion would create a 'cleavage' and that expulsion was not the best way to deal with 'dissident states' (UNCIO Volume 3 at 331, Doc. 2 G/7 (k) 5 February 1945).

[153] Alvarez, 'Do Liberal States Behave Better?'. Alvarez regards this as an unfortunate development in theorising about the international order. The body of his essay is an argument against the proposition that international law currently makes these sorts of distinctions or that international law works better among liberal states. Note that my argument is that the liberal theorists themselves do not envisage placing outlaws beyond the law. See also C. Hillgruber, 'The Admission of New States to the International Community' (1998) 9:3 EJIL 491–509 (for the argument that excluding states would reduce the universality of international law and minimise the chances of the international community fettering outlaw states).

[154] John Rawls, too, favours this sort of response though, as I indicated, his definition of the outlaw state is narrower than, say, Tesón's.

[155] SC Res. 687 (1991), SC Res. 1244 (1999).

[156] See Franck's analysis of the Iraq ceasefire and peace agreement, *Fairness*, 204–11.

[157] Tesón, 'Kantian Theory', 89.

rights and subject to continual surveillance and occasional disciplinary violence.

In the case of undemocratic states, the idea is not to give these illiberal states a 'freer rein' but instead to enmesh them in a system of transnational networks designed to ease them into the liberal-democratic legal order. This combination of engagement for illiberal states and repression for criminal states is mirrored in recent international legal practice. In some cases, outlaw or illiberal states are lured into the society of states with a series of incentives (North Korea) or through the operation of private networks and institutional processes (China). The mere presence of undemocratic government will rarely lead to intervention (collective or otherwise) but illiberal states are targets for a mixture of engagement (China) and, if engagement fails, semi-exclusion (FRY).

The effect of all this is that a thin and fragile system of universal law applicable to all (liberal pluralism) is replaced by two highly developed legal domains. In one domain, the sphere of liberal transgovernmentalism or democratic peace, international law is more pervasive and has more bite than in the classical model. In the other domain, an incipient international criminal law is the mark of what will be a highly regulated sphere of intervention and intrusion. The 'criminal' outlaw state's fate is much more likely to resemble that of the criminal or deviant in the contemporary state (subject to constant monitoring and occasionally arbitrary violence) than the traditional image of the outlaw cut loose from society. In the case of undemocratic states, engagement and exclusion (or a withdrawal of some of the benefits of law) will tend to alternate.

. . . .

In Chapters 8, 9 and 10, I suggest that the constitution of political community in international law can be viewed as a dialogue between two traditions. I describe these as liberal pluralism (or Charter liberalism) and liberal anti-pluralism. These international law liberalisms are derived, in turn, from deeper currents in liberal thought and are reflected in long-standing debates in international law (e.g. between Grotians and realists or among Grotians). I describe these traditions and their philosophical roots in Chapters 2 and 8.

I trace this dialogue through two time periods: the late-Victorian era (Chapter 8) and the Conference at San Francisco in 1945 (Chapter 9). In each case, international lawyers argued about the appropriate membership norms in the international community. Throughout most of the nineteenth century, international lawyers supported the idea that there were unequal sovereigns, i.e. entities that possessed some attributes of sovereignty but lacked the capacity to exercise jurisdiction over aliens on their territory. In a period running from around the end of the nineteenth century to the late twentieth century, a liberalism of inclusion (liberal pluralism) prevailed over the idea that states could be arranged according to some hierarchy. The late twentieth century, however, saw the revival of liberal anti-pluralism in the work of several prominent academics and in the practice of states and, to a lesser extent, international institutions. This new liberal anti-pluralism is a powerful force in academic work and increasingly, too, seems to animate the behaviour of the international community towards states on the margins (Chapter 10).[158]

These liberal anti-pluralists embrace the empirical and normative distinctions either between liberal and illiberal states or between legitimate and outlaw states. However, the consequences of this distinction vary among the liberal anti-pluralists. While mild anti-pluralists (Slaughter, Franck) are hesitant about either excluding outlaw states from the international system or permitting unilateral intervention in the affairs of these states, the strong anti-pluralists (Reisman, Tesón) have fewer qualms.

So, what I have called anti-pluralism varies in its intensity. Some liberal anti-pluralists embrace 'an impulse to impose Locke [or Kant] everywhere'.[159] Where there is a reluctance to accept Locke, diminished status, if not outlaw status, follows.[160] In other cases, liberal anti-pluralism is more tolerant in its acceptance of the illiberal. For Rawls, it is, 'human rights . . . [that] . . . set a limit on pluralism among peoples' and not the presence or absence of republicanism or liberalism.[161] In both cases, I argue, the outlaw state is enclosed in a highly developed legal regime.

However it is conceived, I have tried to show in these chapters that inter-state hierarchy or anti-pluralism has a long pedigree in international law. Exclusion, civilisation, culture and difference are as deeply embedded in the system as universality, legality and equality. So, it

---

[158] The treatment of illiberal or undemocratic states varies quite dramatically. In Haiti, the repression of democratic forces led to a full-scale military operation. In the case of China, even mild trade sanctions have been ruled out of the question by powerful trade interests. Most cases fall somewhere in the middle where the response to a suspended election, a fraudulent poll or a disqualified opposition candidate is a combination of threat and promise. See, e.g. the threat of 'strained relations' in the UN official response to the electoral skullduggery in the Ivory Coast. 'Candidates Excluded in Ivory Coast Elections Join Forces' *Guardian Weekly* 12–18 October 2000, 36.

[159] Hartz, *Liberal Tradition*, 13.

[160] In fact, Franck is equivocal on this point.   [161] Rawls, *Collected Works*, 555.

should not seem surprising that the new liberal scholarship and practice described here resonate with some of international law's historical projects. There is a line of development in international law that relies on formal distinctions between the core and periphery of sovereign states in the manner of new liberal anti-pluralism. Against this has been a more inclusive, perhaps over-inclusive, liberal pluralism reflected best in the practice of the United Nations in relation to membership but present as a driving force in the late-Victorian expansion of international society and the efforts to ensure that the League of Nations would be a universal body.

I have argued in this book, and more specifically in the preceding three chapters, that this tension between these pluralist and anti-pluralist traditions has been, and continues to be, a defining quality of the international legal order.

Part V Conclusion

11 Arguing about Afghanistan: Great Powers and outlaw states redux

"[P]osses" of such allies should be coalesced according to the requirements of specific situations rather than necessarily through existing international institutions.[1]

Every nation has a choice to make . . . . If any government sponsors the outlaws and killers of innocents, they have become outlaws and murderers, themselves.[2]

Every political regime has its foes or in due course creates them.[3]

Introduction: juridical sovereignty and the war in Afghanistan

This book has been about the ways in which the sovereign equality of states has been qualified by the existence of legalised hegemony and anti-pluralism. I have characterised this combination of sovereign equality and these two legalised hierarchies as *juridical sovereignty*. As I concluded the writing of the main body of the text in early 2002, the United States and its allies were engaged in military action in Afghanistan against the remnants of the al-Qa'ida group, having successfully prosecuted a war against the Taliban regime which resulted in that government falling and being replaced by a temporary administration of national reconciliation. In a sense this conflict, though not, of course, its immediate cause, was foreshadowed by the analysis in the preceding pages. After

---

[1] Select Committee on Foreign Affairs, *Foreign Policy Aspects of the War Against Terrorism*, HC 384 (20 June 2002) (paraphrasing views of Richard Haass, Director of Policy Planning in the State Department), para. 219.

[2] George Bush, *Address to the Nation Announcing Strikes Against Al Qaida Training Camps and Taliban Military Installations*, 37 *Weekly Compilation of Presidential Documents*, OC 1432, (7 October 2001).

[3] Otto Kirchheimer, *Political Justice: The Use of Legal Procedure for Political Ends*, 1.

all, this was a war fought by a coalition of Great Powers in the territory of an outlaw state.[4] As a result, the norms and practices of legalised hegemony and anti-pluralism were, again, brought into relief.

Yet, much of the debate surrounding the lawfulness of the intervention in Afghanistan has assumed a rough juridical parity among the various protagonists in that war. In particular, scholars have been concerned to elaborate norms with universalisable potential, i.e. principles and rules that can be applied equally to all states within the international legal order. This has generated positions that manage to appear either intuitively implausible or jurisprudentially incomplete. Much of this discussion has been structured along the same formalist/pragmatist axis found in the debates among late-nineteenth-century scholars and discussed in Chapter 4. Formalists have applied textual readings of the UN Charter to the US-led intervention in Afghanistan and have found that intervention wanting. Has there been an 'armed attack' against the United States within the terms of Article 51? Was Afghanistan responsible? Was the response to that attack 'proportionate'? In each case the question could be answered, very readily and honestly, in the negative. Ultimately, though, this formalism seems detached, cold-blooded and too easily neutralised by reference to 'necessity' or 'common sense' or 'politics'. The scholasticism of these international lawyers appears puny when set against the emotivism of 'war and vengeance' rhetoric or the powerful moralism of successive new world order projects. Nor does this analysis seem to capture developments in customary law where the response of states to interventions is central to assessing the legality or otherwise of such interventions. The dizzying pace of change in the world of customary international law has left some international lawyers asking: How can states acquiesce in operations that appear to stretch the law on self-defence to breaking point?

The pragmatist retort emerges as initially more satisfactory, sonorously proclaiming its basis in the new 'realities'. Public international law is presented here as flexible, responsive and dynamic. The law on self-defence, the pragmatists argue, is broad enough to accommodate a delayed response to aggression or an anticipatory action against terrorism

---

[4] It may be that the phrase 'Great Powers' seems no longer quite appropriate given the material superiority of one of these powers (the United States) over the others. However, such dominance does not preclude the formation of Great Power groupings under legalised hegemony. See my earlier analysis of the San Francisco settlement (when the US was as dominant as it is now) and the Vienna settlement (where, for example, the British and Russians were distinctly more powerful than the Hapsburgs).

or a cumulative reading of the term 'armed attack'. In short, the law would look ridiculous if it failed to characterise the al-Qa'ida terror as an 'armed attack' or objected to the response on the ground that the state of Afghanistan was not the perpetrator. Like the formalists, though, the pragmatists are tied to a view of international law that requires them to apply their expansive and politically attentive reading of the self-defence norms to all states equally. But can pragmatists do this without forfeiting the very plausibility or 'realism' that makes theirs a politically attractive interpretation or modification of international law? Probably not if the expanded right to self-defence enjoyed by the United States and its Great Power allies is applied equally to India and Pakistan. Universalising a new, more liberal norm of self-defence would increase the likelihood of nuclear conflagration in such a case. More likely, the norms of international law emphasised in the Kashmir conflict will be based on the peaceful resolution of disputes and the imperatives of restraint, i.e. the very language dismissed as naive in the context of the US attack on Afghanistan. The largely negative response to Australian Prime Minister John Howard's newly articulated doctrine of anticipatory self-defence (a more modest and constrained version of the Bush Doctrine) indicates that these new norms are far from universalisable.[5] Similarly, can Pakistan's or Saudi Arabia's immunity from intervention be cast aside quite as readily as that of the outlaw state, Afghanistan? Again, the permissive 'norms' applied to Afghanistan turn out not to be universal norms at all but rather specific legal privileges enjoyed by the Great Powers to act on the territory of outlaw states.

The whole formalist/pragmatist debate lacks purchase because it occurs on the terrain of sovereign equality. In this final chapter, I advance an alternative interpretation of the Afghan intervention based on a juridical sovereignty that emphasises the prerogatives of Great Powers and the vulnerability of outlaw states. The international legal order continues to be structured around the idea of juridical sovereignty, a sovereignty regime in which the rights and duties of states can vary. As a consequence, the new rules generated by the action in Afghanistan may not have quite the universal applicability implied in the use of

---

[5] Prime Minister Howard's comments in a TV interview on the *Sunday* show earned rebukes from the governments in the Philippines and Indonesia. Malaysia's Prime Minister, Mahathir Mohammad, said: 'If they used rockets or pilotless aircraft to carry out assassination, then we will consider this as an act of war.' See D. Fickling, 'Australia's New "Hairy-Chested" Attitude Riles its East Asian Neighbours', *The Guardian*, 4 December 2002.

phrases such as 'customary international law'. Indeed, the new principles of international law applying to self-defence outside the Charter are likely to operate in ways rather similar to the operation of collective security under the terms of the Charter. The putative legitimacy of a use of force in each case may become conditional on the status of the actors employing such force and the status of those who are subject to such attacks. Tentatively in Kosovo and, more confidently, in Afghanistan, the Great Powers have redefined the limits of legalised hegemony and antipluralism.[6] The intervention in Afghanistan, indeed the whole response to the attack on the Twin Towers, can only be understood fully in the context of an international legal order composed of unequal sovereigns. Having said this, however, and before I continue, I want to emphasise that this book has been about the operation of legal norms. One of the assumptions behind the central thesis is that the Great Powers are constrained by law and outlaws enjoy *some* of the protections of law. This is not a realist analysis that seeks to deprecate the effects of law altogether but it is one in which inequality is taken seriously.[7]

Hegemons

In the foregoing pages, I have first described a tendency on the part of the Great Powers to will into existence, at pivotal moments of international legal history, a new legal order shaped by the particular security imperatives of the age. At Vienna, the five Great Powers forged a post-Napoleonic order based on a loose form of legalised hegemony designed to maintain peace and security in Europe. A brief interregnum of resistance on the part of the middle and small powers at The Hague gave way to progressively more institutionalised forms of legalised hegemony at Versailles and, then, most formatively, at San Francisco. In Chapter 7, I queried whether the centralised hegemony found at Vienna, Versailles and San Francisco was fragmenting and giving way to regionalised or localised legalised hegemony and I used the intervention in Kosovo as the primary basis for my investigations. Was it the case there that an alliance of North Atlantic powers was preparing to usurp constitutionally the Charter regime (based around a balance between Great Power prerogatives and sovereign equality) in favour of an ideologically focused

---

[6] T. Mills-Allen, 'US Plans Anti-Terror Raids', *Sunday Times*, 4 August 2002, 1 (paraphrasing Washington 'insiders').

[7] See discussion in Chapter 1.

hegemony dedicated to the promotion of values more concrete than those of peace and security and one in which the use of force was to be much less constrained by Charter principles?

In that chapter, I discussed two possible futures for the international legal order and for the practice of legalised hegemony within it. I argued that these two futures could be derived from two models of the past. I described these as the Vienna thesis and the Verona thesis. At the Congress of Vienna, a new European order was inaugurated in which the right of collective action was conditioned upon agreement between the five Great Powers of the time: Russia, Prussia, Great Britain, Austria and France. The latitude for intervention under this form of legalised hegemony was constrained by a number of factors including the need to get the agreement of all five parties before any action could be taken, by the widely differing ideological dispositions of the five states and by the terms of the Vienna settlement, which, like that at San Francisco, emphasised the threat to international order from revisionist large powers as opposed to internal strife.

I contrasted this form of legalised hegemony with the efforts of the Holy Alliance at Verona to make Europe safe from democracy by creating an alternative regime in which intervention by a smaller coalition of Great Powers was to be permitted in cases where internal conditions within a state (provoked by the activities of revolutionaries and constitutionalists) threatened the Alliance or European peace as defined by the Alliance.

Following the Kosovo intervention, the international order was poised between these two futures (or pasts). On one hand, Nato had broken free of the UN Charter to intervene in Kosovo against a backdrop of Security Council paralysis. On the other hand, the UN very quickly came to play a prominent role in the interim administration established in the wake of the Nato action.[8] Of course, both sides benefited from this appearance of collaboration. Nato seemed to have secured some form of *ex post facto* recognition for an attack of dubious legality while the UN found itself with a central role in an enforcement action that had begun with its marginalisation.[9] But both sides lost something as well. The UN sacrificed a measure of credibility by acquiescing in an intervention that had

---

[8] See, for example, SC Res. 1244 (10 June 1999), SC Res. 1345 (21 March 2001) (welcoming the efforts of KFOR to implement 1244 and calling on it to continue its efforts to prevent unauthorised movement and illegal arms shipments).

[9] Ruth Wedgwood, 'Unilateral Action in the UN System', (2002) 11 EJIL 349, 356–9.

been undertaken without its authority and in apparent contravention of its Charter while Nato had laid itself open to accusations that it was using the UN opportunistically to lend a veneer of multilateralism to an operation that was marked by a move to unilateralism.[10]

In a number of respects, the attack on Afghanistan was quite different from the intervention in Kosovo. In Kosovo, the outlines of a new unilateralism or localised legalised hegemony, were drawn on a doctrine of humanitarian intervention that is, at the very least, controversial under international law. Notwithstanding the arguments concerning the doctrine's acceptability, it is at least plausible to argue that the intervention fitted the category of humanitarian intervention. In the case of Afghanistan, the converse applied; the US relied on the better-established doctrine of self-defence in justifying the action. However, in this case, the controversy arose around the question of whether this was a legitimate exercise of that particular right in the first place and what the boundaries of the right were.

In the end, the US articulated an expansive doctrine of self-defence and this doctrine was accepted by a number of states within the system and endorsed by the majority of international lawyers. Once again, a coalition of Great Powers had redeveloped the idea of legalised hegemony, this time basing a highly interventionist doctrine on anti-terrorist rhetoric and self-defence law.

At first blush, the coalition action in Afghanistan, like that in Kosovo, resembled the actions of the Holy Alliance and, indeed, I think that regime offers a useful comparison. Like the Holy Alliance, the new coalition pursued a specific ideological agenda while adopting the language of universality. This was a war fought for specific Western interests but in the name of a universal struggle against terrorism. The Great Powers again 'invoked humanity' but this time it was humanity's war against terror rather than its struggle with human rights abusers. It may also be the case that the post-Charter interventionism of the Western powers will prove as short-lived as the Holy Alliance. On the other hand, the United States and its allies may be in the process of forging a new 'Concert' system: a semi-permanent structure of relations designed to re-order international affairs by breaking with elements of the existing order. This alternative regime was anticipated by Winston Churchill when he spoke of a United Nations made up of several relatively

---

[10] I use the term 'unilateral' to indicate a mode of action undertaken outside the Charter system as opposed to action taken by a single state.

autonomous regional enforcement mechanisms, one of which would be an 'instrument of European government . . . to embody the spirit of the League of Nations'.[11]

Outlaws

In the preceding pages I have also shown how, in successive periods of international ordering since 1815, outlaw states, or what British Prime Minster Tony Blair described as 'irresponsible and repressive states', have been the subject of separate legal regimes.[12] I have described the tension between two conceptions of international community, an inclusive conception (pluralism) and a more selective conception (anti-pluralism), and the ways in which that tension has shaped the international legal order. The anti-pluralist tendency allocates the benefits of sovereignty on the basis of conformity to some standard of behaviour or moral characteristic. In Chapter 10, I focused on the position of Iraq in (or outside) international society. In the second section of this final chapter, I describe two relatively new developments in the treatment of outlaw regimes. The first is the creation of a bureaucracy of oversight and monitoring to regulate the interaction between the international community at large and the outlaw state, with a view to ensuring that outlaw states remain outside the society of commerce, diplomacy and sovereign equality. The second development relates to the treatment of personnel associated with outlaw states. The US detention of Taliban personnel and the labelling of these individuals as 'illegal combatants' purports to place them outside the full protection of the law (i.e. the law of the Geneva Conventions as it applies to POWs) while their place of detention can be viewed as a metaphor for the treatment of outlaws generally. Guantanamo Bay is a place outside the law: an extra-territorial, extra-constitutional locale where the rules of domestic law and international law are suspended and yet where the suspects or detainees (lacking the rights of both soldiers and common criminals) are closely monitored and controlled. Like the outlaw states from which they hail, outlaw personnel are both outside the law and at the same time entangled in its terrors and violence.[13]

---

[11] 'Morning Thoughts: A Note on Post-War Security', 2 February 1943 in *The Hinge of Fate*, 710–11.

[12] PM Blair's Speech to Foreign Office Conference, *The Guardian*, 8 January 2003, 4.

[13] The Taliban was recognised by only two other states. It was, however, the effective government of Afghanistan. The Security Council imposed obligations on it and demands were made of it in its governmental capacity. Afghanistan's outlaw status is

Unequal sovereigns I: legalised hegemony modified

The war in Afghanistan was part of the response by one of the Great Powers (indeed, the *greatest* power) to a direct attack on its own territory.[14] The international legal order was partially defined in the final half of the twentieth century by the cold war. It is not impossible that the first half of the twenty-first century will be defined by the 'war on terrorism' that grew out of this attack. In both cases, the state of Afghanistan has provided the territory on which various adversaries have clashed. The Soviet invasion of Afghanistan, itself a response to 'terrorism', can be viewed retrospectively as the final external adventure of an overextended empire committed to rooting out Western-sponsored counter-reaction. Now, in 2002, Afghanistan is again the site of imperial violence in response, this time, to cognate networks operating within the territory of that state.

The background to all this is complex but, as with the Balkans, it is primarily marked by a sequence of Great Power interventions. Afghanistan has long been a strategic source of access to the Indian Ocean and a vulnerable southern frontier for various Russian empires. The major Great Power rivalry of the modern era was that of Great Britain and Russia, who fought a number of wars, proxy and otherwise, in Afghan territory.[15] By 1979, the Soviet Union had managed to install a friendly Communist regime in Kabul. This government survived throughout the 1980s with the help of a very substantial Red Army presence. By 1988, Gorbachev was keen to extricate the Soviets from their 'Vietnam' and the Russians finally departed in 1989 under the terms of the Geneva Accords.[16] The Communist regime then fell in 1992 and, after a long civil war, the Taliban took control of the majority of Afghan territory. This regime became notorious for its imposition of a punitive and harsh Islamic theology.

---

thus derived from the Taliban's status as an outlaw regime. See, for example, *Tinoco Arbitration (Great Britain v. Costa Rica)* (1923) 1 RIAA 369: 'non-recognition . . . cannot outweigh the evidence disclosed by this record before me as to the de facto character of Tinoco's government according to the standard set by international law . . .' (Taft CJ).

[14] President Bush gained the approval of Congress to use all necessary and appropriate means to combat terrorism (Authorisation For Use of Military Force, Pub. L. No. 107–40, 115 Stat. 224 (2001) (stating, 'the President is authorised to use all necessary and appropriate force against those nations, organisations or persons . . . he determines planned, authorized, committed or aided the terrorist attacks . . . or harboured such organisations or persons . . .')).

[15] See Musa Khan Jalalzai, *Taliban and the Great Game in Afghanistan* (1999), 19–20.

[16] Geneva Accords, (1998) 27 ILM 77.

The intervention in Afghanistan in 2001 was provoked by the events of 11 September 2001 when four US civilian airliners were hijacked by members of the al-Qa'ida network. Two of the aircraft were flown into the World Trade Centre in New York, one into the Pentagon in Washington DC and the other crashed in Pennsylvania en route to Washington DC.[17] By now, these events have been described and analysed perhaps more than any single incident in world history. In response, the US-led coalition attacked Kabul and Kandahar on 7 October using cruise missiles. Bombing from the air using B-52 bombers and low-flying gunships continued throughout October and, on 12 November 2001, Kabul fell to the Northern Alliance (a coalition of forces hostile to the Taliban). At the beginning of December 2001 an agreement to establish a provisional interim government was reached in Bonn and at around the same time, the Taliban was expelled from Kandahar.[18] At the time of writing, the United States is maintaining a military presence in Afghanistan intent on destroying any remaining Taliban and al-Qa'ida forces.

In the following discussion, I argue that the debates about the applicability of the law, and the legality or illegality of the response by the US and its allies, have missed an important aspect of this war, namely the way in which the Great Powers can develop new law to meet their own security needs and the manner in which these modified legal regimes are permissive in relation to the Great Powers but remain restrictive in relation to other states. I want to begin by describing the two 'classic' positions on the use of force in Afghanistan: one arguing that this was an act of lawful violence (the pragmatist position); the other doubting the legality of the action (the formalist position) but both relying on an image of international law as general and universalisable. I contrast these classic formulations with a conception of the international order that acknowledges the potential emergence of special regimes in which the Great Powers possess exceptional rights.

Lawful violence: pragmatists

The majority of international law scholars has defended the US-led response to the 11 September violence as a lawful counter-measure permitted under the terms of the UN Charter. There are two limbs to this

---

[17] See 'Thousands Die in Terrorist Assault', *Guardian Weekly*, 20 September 2001, 2.
[18] See Agreement on Provisional Arrangement in Afghanistan Pending the Re-Establishment of Permanent Government Institutions, 5 December 2001 (UN Doc. S/2001/1154) ('The Bonn Agreement').

argument: collective security and self-defence. The self-defence case is more relevant to the argument pursued here because advocates of the legality of the response have, in some cases, significantly broadened the limits of self-defence.[19]

The Charter contains, alongside its robust collective security mechanisms, a procedure for exercising the 'inherent' right of self-defence. Article 51 preserves this right of self-defence in cases where a state is the object of an armed attack. This right of self-defence requires three conditions to be met before it can be exercised lawfully.[20] First, there has to have been an armed attack. Second, the response must be directed at the state or party responsible for the armed attack. Third, the response must be necessary and proportionate (under the terms of the famous *Caroline* dictum there must be a 'necessity of self-defence, instant, overwhelming, leaving no choice of means and no moment for deliberation').[21]

The argument for the legality of the US use of force in terms of self-defence was relatively straightforward and ran as follows: the United States had been subject to an armed attack because the scale and intensity of the destruction was akin to the cross-border attack the San Francisco drafters had in mind.[22] There was no contradiction between the Security Council's determination that the events of September 2001 were a threat to the peace and the characterisation of these events as an armed attack.[23] The attack was, in effect, ongoing, since the September

---

[19] The use of force under international law is undoubtedly permitted in cases where the Security Council has authorised or requested such action acting under Chapter VII. The more difficult question, then, is not whether the Security Council can authorise force but rather whether it has done so in a particular case. The sometimes necessarily opaque language of Security Council resolutions renders them open to differing interpretations. This problem arose in relation to the resolutions preceding the Nato intervention in Kosovo and has arisen again here. See SC Res. 1160 (31 March 1998) and SC Res. 1199 (23 September 1998).

[20] There is, in addition, a reporting requirement in Article 51. This requirement was satisfied by the United States.

[21] 29 BFSP 1137–8 and 30 BFSP 195–6.

[22] See, also, Secretary General Lord Robertson, Statement at Nato Headquarters, 2 October 2001 at http://www.nato.int and the OAS Meeting of Ministers of Foreign Affairs (describing the attacks on the US as attacks on all American states) in Terrorist Threat to the Americas, Res. 1, Twenty-Fourth Meeting of Consultation of Ministers of Foreign Affairs Acting as Organ of Consultation in Application of the Inter-American Treaty of Reciprocal Assistance, OAS Doc. OEA/Ser.F/II.24/RC.24/RES.1/01 (21 September 2001), at http://www.oas.org. See Karen DeYoung, 'OAS Nations Activate Mutual Defence Treaty', *Washington Post*, 20 Sept 2001, A18.

[23] Indeed, for some, the two are mutually enhancing: 'By characterising the attacks as "a threat to international peace and security" and by implying that the Security

2001 attacks were merely part of a sequence stretching back to 1993 and the original World Trade Centre bombings and included the 1996 attack on the US military accommodations in Dharhan, the 1998 embassy bombings in Africa and the bombing of USS Cole in Aden in 2000. The United States was thus in the midst of an assault whose next individual element could take place at any time.[24]

The response was directed at an eligible target according to those who support the intervention. Though the Taliban did not itself attack the United States, it was responsible for harbouring those who did. The Draft Articles on State Responsibility make responsible those states that allow their territory to be used for terrorist attacks.[25] In *Tadic*, the Appeals Chamber reiterated the rule that the requirement of international law for attribution is control but went on to say that: 'The degree of control may . . . vary.'[26] In that case, concerning individual responsibility, the ICTY found that Serbia had 'overall control' over the activities of the Bosnian Serb irregulars sufficient to internationalise the conflict. This, according to those who argue for the legality of the war, was precisely the level of control exercised by the Taliban. In any event, the United Nations acknowledged the inherent right to self-defence in the two resolutions immediately following the action.[27]

Council was acting under Article 51 of the UN Charter, Resolution 1368 also gave immediate legal authorisation for military action by the United States and its allies, provided that such action was demonstrably one of self-defence against "armed attack", and provided that the action was immediately reported to the Security Council.' Select Committee on Foreign Affairs, Foreign Policy Aspects of the War Against Terrorism, HC 384, para. 63.

[24] 'The attacks on 11 September 2001 and the ongoing threat to the United States and its nationals posed by the Al-Qaeda organization have been made possible by the decision of the Taliban regime to allow the parts of Afghanistan that it controls to be used by this organization as a base of operation . . . In response to these attacks, and in accordance with the inherent right of individual and collective self-defence, United States armed forces have initiated actions designed to prevent and deter further attacks on the United States.' Letter dated 7 October 2001 from the Permanent Representative of the United States of America to the United Nations Addressed to the President of the Security Council, UN Doc. S/2001/946 (7 October 2001), at http://www.un.int./usa/s-2001-946.htm. The United Kingdom provided a similar notification.

[25] For evidence of al-Qa'ida responsibility, see UK Government publication, 10 Downing Street Newsroom, *Responsibility for the Terrorist Atrocities in the United States*, 4 October 2001 (extracts in *London Evening Standard*, 5 October 2001, 1, at http://www.number-10.gov.uk/output/page3554.asp). See, too, ICJ (Australian Section) Position Paper, para. 5.

[26] *Tadic* (Appeals Judgement) at para. 117.

[27] T. Franck, 'Terrorism and the Right of Self-Defence', (2001) 95 AJIL 841.

Advocates of legality also insisted that the intervention met the requirements of immediacy, necessity and proportionality. The existence of the prior attacks discussed above meant that this attack was merely one part of a sequence of events constituting an ongoing armed attack. Thus, the United States, while it was bombing Afghanistan, was under attack.[28] Alternatively, the threat of future attacks, in the light of these past attacks, meant that, even if the United States was not presently under attack, it was entitled to take action in anticipatory self-defence.[29] The intervention in Afghanistan was proportionate to the threat of future attacks (as seen in the light of the scale of prior attacks).

Shortly after the attacks on the United States in 2001, John Negroponte, the US Ambassador to the UN, reminded the Security Council that self-defence was the justification for using force in Afghanistan and that the US might find 'our self-defence requires further actions with respect to other organisations and states'.[30] Several years prior to this, George Shultz had remarked on the absurdity of saying

that international law prohibits us from . . . attacking them [terrorists] on the soil of other nations . . . or from using force against states that support, train and harbor terrorists or guerrillas.[31]

The important point, for the purpose of this study, is that these justifications widen considerably the potential scope of self-defence and have gained a measure of approval from other states and international organisations within the legal order. The rule articulated here would permit the use of force against states that harbour terrorists suspected of having committed an armed attack on another state's territory even if the level of control exercised by the harbouring state is relatively weak. In the stronger version of this norm, states would be able to take action against such states in anticipation of such attacks or because those states were a threat to international order.[32] The fruits of this conception are, of course, being felt in the US-UK inclination to depose Saddam Hussein.

---

[28] See Yoram Dinstein, *War, Aggression and Self-Defence*, 203 (elaborating the accumulation of events thesis).

[29] C. Greenwood, 'International Law and the "War Against Terrorism"' (2002) 78:2 *International Affairs* 301, 312.

[30] UN Doc. /2001/946, 7 October 2001.   [31] See (1986) 25 ILM 204, 206.

[32] See, too, George W. Bush's recently articulated doctrine of self-defence that disposes of the requirement of imminence altogether (F. Kirgis, 'Pre-Emptive Action to Forestall Terrorism' (June 2002) ASIL *Insights* 1).

Unlawful violence

Those who argue that the war was illegal or, at least, not clearly legal, have tended to dwell on two aspects of the operation. First, they argued that the Security Council had failed to authorise a use of force in this case. The Council had neither authorised a collective security operation nor had it given its approval for a use of force in self-defence. Second, they argued that the conditions for a free standing use of force in self-defence (i.e. one that requires no Council mandate) had not been met.

According to the first argument, neither of the two critical resolutions (1368 and 1373) expressly authorised force.[33] Nor did these resolutions make it clear that the US is entitled to use force in self-defence. Thus, the reference to the inherent right to self-defence did not constitute a direct signal to the US that such force is permitted, partly because, while the authorisations referred to threats to the peace, they did not characterise the Twin Towers attack as an armed attack.[34] More broadly, the reference to threats to the peace and various measures mandated by the Security Council represent a strong indication that there is to be a UN-led multilateral approach to the repression of terrorism.[35] Indeed, in SC Resolution 1373, the Council had begun to 'legislate' for the international community as a whole. Nowhere in these resolutions is it anticipated that the US would take unilateral measures in its own defence.[36] Indeed, the whole thrust of the Security Council's response has been in the direction of a criminal justice approach and not a collective security approach.[37]

[33] Greenwood, 'International Law and the "War Against Terrorism"', 309 (comparing these resolutions to SC Res. 678 (29 November 1990).

[34] See E. Myjer and N. White, 'The Twin Towers Attack: An Unlimited Right to Self-Defence?' (2002) 7:1 *Journal of Conflict and Security Law* 5, 10. See, also, arguing against the authorisation view: Kirgis, 'Addendum: Security Council Adopts Resolution on Combating International Terrorism' (October 2001) ASIL *Insights* (noting that SC Res. 1373 (28 September 2001) says the Council is ready to take all necessary steps and not that it authorises states to take all necessary steps and comparing SC Res. 678 (29 November 1990)); Carsten Stahn, 'Addendum: Security Council Resolutions 1377 (2001) and 1378 (2001)' (December 2001) ASIL *Insights*; Dupuy, 'The Law After the Destruction of the Towers'.

[35] See, too, A. Pellet, 'No, This is not War!' (2001) EJIL Discussion Forum – The Attack on the World Trade Center: Legal Responses' at http://www.ejil.org/forum_WTC/ny-pellet.html.

[36] This is leaving aside the argument that the SC has extinguished the US right to self-defence by virtue of the measures undertaken in SC Res. 1373 (28 September 2001) and elsewhere.

[37] See, too, GA Res. 56/1 (18 September 2001) calling for 'international cooperation to bring to justice the perpetrators'.

Of course, no Security Council resolutions are required if the US has a right to use force in self-defence. However, those concerned about the legality of the US action believe that the US has stretched the law on self-defence in three respects: by claiming that it has been subject to an 'armed attack'; by holding Afghanistan (or, at least, the Taliban) responsible for this attack; and by failing to establish that the US use of force was necessary and proportionate.

There is no definition of 'armed attack' in the UN Charter. It is probably the case that the drafters of the Charter simply did not have in mind the sort of violence seen on 11 September 2001.[38] Indeed, as a text, it has offered very little guidance on four major sources of bloodshed in the post-war era, i.e. inter-ethnic violence, terrorism, rebellion and state terror.[39] In customary law and in international jurisprudence, though, an armed attack has been understood as a large-scale military cross-border violation by one state of another state's territorial integrity or an attack analogous to this. In *Nicaragua*, the Court stated that it 'did not believe that the concept of "armed attack" included assistance to rebels in the form of the provision of weapons or logistical or other support'.[40] Those who argue against the characterisation of the September killings as an 'armed attack' point to this definition and the one found in the General Assembly's Definition of Aggression from 1974, both of which require activity analogous to large-scale cross-border attacks undertaken by or on behalf of states.[41]

---

[38] There was a Turkish proposal to the effect that 'it would be useful to insert in the Charter a provision justifying legitimate defense against a surprise attack *by another state*' (my emphasis). See Suggestions of the Turkish Government, UNCIO Doc. 2 G/14(e), 1 May 1945, as reproduced in *United Nations Conference on International Organisation* (1945) vol. III, 483. 'Self-defence, traditionally speaking, applies to an armed response to an attack by a state' (Myjer and White, 'The Twin Towers Attack', 7).

[39] Nor, of course, does the UN Charter provide for the case where a Great Power uses force. Article 2(4) and Article 39, then, are really directly relevant only to cases of cross-border aggression by medium or small powers. This is why the Iraqi invasion of Kuwait was the paradigm case for the United Nations. The drafters at San Francisco had in mind the League of Nation's failure to deal with aggression by Japan (in Manchuria) and Italy (in Abyssinia) when the Charter was drafted. It was thought that these failures had emboldened Hitler. Thus, the Charter is directed towards preventing war by discouraging such interventions on the part of middle powers.

[40] *Nicaragua* v. *USA (Merits)* at para. 195. Interestingly, the *Caroline Case*, which introduced into custom the ideas of proportionality and necessity, did feature a cross-border attack against the British in Canada by a group of Americans acting as private citizens.

[41] See Resolution on the Declaration of Aggression (1974), GA Res. 3314 (14 December 1974) (but see, too, Article 4). Note that President Bush, at least initially, referred to an act of 'mass murder' rather than an armed attack, Bush, Address to the Nation, 11 September 2001. Nine days later this was described as 'an act of war', Address to Congress, 37 *Weekly Compilation of Presidential Documents* 1347 (20 September 2001).

Those who are sceptical of the justifications offered for using force also question Afghanistan's responsibility for the attack. Under the authoritative International Law Commission's Draft Articles on State Responsibility, a state is responsible for conduct breaching international law when that conduct is 'attributable to the state'.[42] Importantly, this conduct can encompass 'omissions' as well as positive action, i.e. failure to take appropriate steps to prevent a breach. Were the activities of the al-Qa'ida network imputable to the state of Afghanistan? Article 8 of the Draft Articles states:

The conduct of a person or group of persons shall be considered an act of a State under international law if the person or group of persons is in fact acting on the instructions of, or under the direction or control of, that State in carrying out the conduct.[43]

In normal circumstances, a State is not responsible for the action of private individuals. Were the al-Qa'ida operatives found to be acting autonomously, then Afghanistan could not have been responsible for the attack on the United States. Those who argue against the legality of the US intervention in Afghanistan tend to assert a lack of control or direction on the part of the Taliban. In *Nicaragua*, the World Court held that the United States was not responsible for the breaches of international humanitarian law committed by the 'Contras' in the state of Nicaragua since it had not directed and controlled the individual operations giving rise to these breaches. A relationship of support and dependence was insufficient to establish responsibility in that instance.[44] Here, the Taliban regime and al-Qa'ida were in precisely this sort of loose relationship of dependence. Accordingly, the argument goes, Afghanistan's involvement in the 11 September bombing was simply too remote for it to be held responsible for that attack.[45] In *Nicaragua* it was held that 'organising or encouraging the organisation of irregular forces or armed bands . . . for incursion into the territory of another state, whilst illegal under international law, does not constitute an armed attack sufficient to give rise to a right to exercise self-defence'.[46]

---

[42] ILC Draft Articles (2001), Article 2(a). Note that the Draft Articles do not authorise force when such breaches occur.

[43] *Ibid.*

[44] James Crawford, *The International Law Commission's Articles on State Responsibility*, 111.

[45] See Myjer and White, 'Twin Towers', 7.

[46] For a discussion of the possible application of others of the Draft Articles on State Responsibility see G. Gaja, 'In What Sense was There an "Armed Attack"?' (2002) EJIL Discussion Forum.

According to this view, the third set of requirements for self-defence had not been met either. In order to be a lawful use of force in self-defence the US action would have had to have been immediate, necessary and proportionate. The doubters assert that the US response, made long after the attack, was in fact an illegal reprisal rather than a lawful use of force in self-defence.[47] The action was unnecessary because the attack had already taken place and could not therefore be affected by what would become essentially anticipatory measures. Furthermore, the element of proportionality was missing. As Myjer and White put it: 'Does an attack against a small part of the United States . . . justify an armed response against a whole country . . .?'[48]

The analysis described above seeks to maintain the integrity of the Charter regime by constraining the use of force as much as possible and by disallowing creative interpretations of the law on self-defence. The result is a legal regime in which the US and her allies are not entitled to use force against those sovereign states even where those sovereign states have harboured terrorists guilty of inflicting terrible loss of life on the United States' mainland or where those states pose a plausible threat to the security of the US and her allies. This textual reading of the Charter results in a position that lacks correspondence with the realities of international politics and, more importantly, cannot explain states' overwhelming approval of the US action in Afghanistan.

Legalised hegemony revisited

There is something unsatisfactory about the debate between pragmatists and formalists. Those who argue for the illegality of the war are faced with the problem that law dissolves into empty prescription when it ceases to produce a reasonable fit with international politics and, instead, embraces an abstract formalism. The debates about the responsibility of Afghanistan or the 'characterisation' of the Twin Towers attack take on an unreal aspect when set against the imperatives of response and the power of the US. Sir Robert Jennings made a similar point in his dissenting opinion in *Nicaragua* when he discussed the majority's judgement that the provision of arms and other support by one state to rebel armies operating in another could not rise to the level of an armed attack:

---

[47] On the illegality of reprisals see Harib Fort Incident (SC Res. 188 (9 April 1964)) and the 1970 Declaration on Friendly Relations.
[48] Myjer and White, 'The Twin Towers Attack', 8.

This looks to me neither realistic nor just . . . The original scheme of the United Nations Charter, whereby force would be deployed by the United Nations itself, in accordance with the provisions of Chapter VII of the Charter, has never come into effect. Therefore an essential element in the Charter design is totally missing. In this situation it seems dangerous to define unnecessarily strictly the conditions for lawful self-defence, so as to leave a large area where . . . a forcible response to force is forbidden.[49]

The illegality thesis also has a difficult job explaining why, if the US action in Afghanistan was so obviously unlawful, the vast majority of states supported it.[50]

On the other hand, pragmatists who are convinced of the war's lawfulness cannot quite come to terms with the *tu quoque* question. If this expanded norm of self-defence is extended to all states then clearly a greater potential for violence is present. India's right to invade Pakistan, Nicaragua's right to strike at the US in 1984 and the United Kingdom's right to use force against IRA bases in the Republic of Ireland in the 1970s become less implausible in the light of this new rule (some are or would have been politically and militarily impossible, of course). The problem for proponents of the legality thesis is that most of them would, rightly, have reservations before supporting a universal right to strike at terrorist bases in states and, much more importantly, so would the states currently articulating or supporting this rule. This newly minted norm of self-defence might be superficially compelling as part of the post-11 September mood but has not been voiced a great deal in the debate about the Pakistan–India conflict where the language of force, vengeance and unilateralism has been displaced by a call to negotiate in the shadow of reminders that international law is dedicated to peaceful resolution of disputes. The suspicion remains that this 'instant custom' will dissolve as quickly as it appeared when an expansive right to self-defence

---

[49] *Nicaragua v. USA* (Merits), 543–4.

[50] 'Military action was taken with a remarkably high level of international endorsement. Islamic countries at the Asia-Pacific Economic Co-operation forum in October were generally supportive of the US-led campaign. The Chinese Foreign Minister Tang Jiaxhuan referred to the anti-terrorism campaign as a 'fight between justice and evil', and Russia issued strong statements of support, encouraged Central Asian states to offer the US use of military bases and reportedly co-operated with the US on intelligence to aid the campaign in Afghanistan, Select Committee on Foreign Affairs, *Foreign Policy Aspects of the War Against Terrorism*, HC 384 at para 76. See, too, Greenwood, 'International Law and the "War Against Terrorism"', 308: 'It is noticeable that this claim did not meet the resistance from other states which might have been expected . . . if there had been real doubts whether the conditions for the exercise of that right existed' (312).

is claimed by, say, India or Indonesia. The difference between the international response to Vietnam's invasion of Cambodia and the instal-
lation of a more sympathetic regime in Phnom Penh (following mass
cross-border killings by the Khmer Rouge in Vietnam) and the reaction
to US claims to be exercising a right to self-defence is not found in
the historical development of the norm or the changing technologies
of terror. Instead, as this book has argued in relation to a number of
norms, it is a question of status. In 1979, Vietnam was an outlaw state
vilified as a threat to order in Southeast Asia. Its right to self-defence was
simply more constrained than that of the US today. The expanded doctrine of self-defence may then be an aspect of legalised hegemony and
not a generalisable rule of conduct in international relations. The overwhelmingly negative response to the relatively unambitious and modest
Howard doctrine is clear evidence that this new doctrine of self-defence
does not apply to middle powers.

Ultimately, these debates over legality and illegality take place on the
terrain of sovereign equality and it is their basis in this equality that
makes them flawed. Without a frank acknowledgement of the claims
of a modified form of legalised hegemony and an appreciation of the
operation of anti-pluralism, it is not possible to understand the way in
which law adapts to the imperatives of the hegemons. In an encounter
between a Great Power and an outlaw state, the sovereignty norms associated with a traditional conception of international law are suspended.
The legal scope for the use of force by Great Powers is widened while
the territorial integrity and political independence of the outlaw state
shrinks. The result is a highly permissive environment in which the use
of force can be more readily employed. In the case of Afghanistan, and
possibly in future cases, the United States will be operating within an
international legal culture that is weakly anchored to the text of the UN
Charter. International lawyers are already participating in this process
through the anti-formalist endorsement of more permissive norms of
self-defence, assessments of international law that demand a more politically responsive approach and the threat that unilateralism will be
the default position if international law remains too 'utopian'.

This book has argued for the recognition of legalised hegemony as
a primary determinant of normative innovation in international law.[51]
Thus, an analysis of the actions of the US-led coalition in Afghanistan
can only be understood in the context of the special position of the

---

[51] This should not be confused with an argument in favour of legalised hegemony.

Great Powers. The two classic models of analysis I have described above are flawed but each contains certain insights. The formalist position, arguing against the legality of the war, is unable to explain the absence of protest at what may appear to be straightforward cases of non-compliance by the Great Powers in Afghanistan but it remains an accurate account of the self-defence norms (or authoritative interpretations of those norms) applicable on the plane of sovereign equality. The pragmatist reading of public international law that would re-conceive the laws on state responsibility and self-defence to allow for such interventions by the United States and its allies is faithful to the 'realities' of international order but misses the vital insight that such reformulations are likely to resist universal application as 'new custom'.

Afghanistan, like San Francisco, Versailles, Vienna and, more ambiguously, Kosovo, is an example of regime change where the legalised hegemony of the Great Powers is modified to meet the current exigencies. It is not that a new universalisable rule of self-defence has come into operation. Rather, the legalised hegemony of the Great Powers found in the UN Charter has become freshly embedded in an extra-curricular and unwritten norm of international law.[52] Just as the Permanent Five have special prerogatives under the terms of the Charter, so it is that they have come to possess them outside the Charter framework. The right to self-defence must now be understood as a norm that applies unequally (just as collective security applies unequally). The United States and India are unequal sovereigns in this sense: the United States' right to use force in self-defence is wider and more inflated than that of India's.[53] Of course, initially at least, this new norm will not be recognised as such. Indeed, the language of legitimacy will displace the language of legality when these practices and norms are being discussed. The ICJ, for example, will continue to apply the generalisable law of force in its determinations.

---

[52] This, it is said, could result in a situation where self-defence takes place 'outside the context and thereby outside the limits of the Charter of the UN', Myjer and White, 'Twin Towers', 16.

[53] Or, for that matter Israel's. The Security Council condemned the Israeli attack on Tunis in 1985 by 14-0 (US abstention) in SC Res. 573 (4 October 1985). Israel argued that it had been attacking the PLO Headquarters in Tunis, stating: 'Tunisia, then, actually provided a base for murderous activity against another State and, in fact, the nationals of many States who are the objects and victims of this terrorist organization. The protection of sovereignty cannot be claimed by any government when it makes available such facilities, especially against the State that must protect itself' (UN Doc. S/PV.2615, 86–7 (4 October 1985) (statement of Mr Netanyahu)). There is no guarantee that a similar action by a small or middle power would not be condemned again in exactly the same way.

Yet, if the international legal process is constituted more broadly than this, then my analysis begins to look more compelling.[54]

There have been hints of this mode of analysis in some of the writing on both the formalist and pragmatist side of the international law debate. White and Myjer, for example, worried that 'the US is dealing with a situation, which threatens international peace, *in lieu* of the Security Council' and seem bemused that, in spite of what they see as the unlawful nature of the US response, it 'Nevertheless . . . quickly found broad support'.[55] What they are witnessing is a usurpation similar to that seen at Vienna. Michael Byers refers to support for 'the modification of customary law' inherent in the claim to be acting in self-defence against the state of Afghanistan and suggests that the lack of condemnation of the Negroponte letter (asserting a more generalisable right to use force in anticipatory self-defence against terrorists) might come to be regarded as 'acquiescence in yet another change to customary law'.[56] Kirgis, too, has noted that it might be possible to argue that conditions have changed since *Caroline* and Nuremberg such that this sort of action might be permissible.[57] Meanwhile, Antonio Cassese remarked:

> It would thus seem that in a matter of a few days, practically all states have come to *assimilate* a terrorist attack by a terrorist organization to an armed aggression *by a state*, entitling the victim state to resort to individual self-defence and third states to act in collective self-defence (at the request of the former state). The magnitude of the terrorist attack on New York and Washington may perhaps warrant this *broadening of the notion of self-defence*.[58]

What these states have assimilated, though, is a modified version of legalised hegemony and not a universalisable norm of self-defence. There is some agonising over the Security Council's failure to clarify for international lawyers whether the US was within its rights to use force but it is precisely this ambiguity which allows for the operation of legalised hegemony.[59] These 'changes in customary law' may simply turn out to be modifications to a localised customary law as it applies to the Great

---

[54] See Reisman, 'World Constitutive Process', 3

[55] Myjer and White, 'Twin Towers', 11 and 8.

[56] Byers, 'Terrorism, the Use of Force and International Law after 11 September' (2002) 51:2 ICLQ 401–14.

[57] Kirgis also raises the possibility that provisions of the UN Charter regulating the use of force in self-defence are subject to suspension given the radical nature of the change in the basis of the obligation: 'Pre-Emptive Action to Forestall Terrorism'.

[58] Cassese, 'Terrorism is Also Disrupting Some Crucial Legal Categories of International Law' (2001) 12:5 EJIL 993, 996–7.

[59] Myjer and White, 'Twin Towers', 13.

Powers. As Dickinson put it almost a century ago, equality 'is not inconsistent with the grouping of persons into classes, each of which the law regards differently'.[60]

Arthur Watts states that:

There is room for the view that all that States need for the general purposes of conducting their international relations is to be able to advance a legal justification for their conduct that is not demonstrably rubbish. Thereafter, political factors take over.[61]

Or, as Byers states, 'a tenable argument may well be good enough'.[62] But good enough for whom? It seems likely that a great range of arguments about the use of force in self-defence is tenable or, at least, not demonstrably rubbish. Indeed, in all the numerous articles written about public international law and the war on terrorism, I have yet to come across an argument that is 'demonstrably rubbish'. So, Watts's 'political factors' are liable to play a fairly large role in deciding the lawfulness or unlawfulness of a particular action. But this does not result in indeterminacy. Indeed, this whole book is an argument for the ways in which the rules have been and are determined – according to the imperatives of legalised hegemony.

Unequal sovereigns in the Afghanistan war: out of law

In assessing the legality of the response to the attacks on the United States, I have emphasised the need to move beyond an analysis of legal rules divorced from the special constitutional status of the Great Powers. These powers have both explicitly stated legal privileges and immunities (see the status of the permanent five members of the Security Council) and more implicit legal powers in the sphere of law making (e.g. through the doctrine of specially affected states) and law application (e.g. Great Power prerogatives in relation to self-defence). In the analysis above, I have shown how the special position of the United States has given it the opportunity to develop the law on self-defence through the acquiescence of influential allies and the support of scholars and how an expanded version of that law is likely to operate as a localised form of customary law.

---

[60] Dickinson, *Equality of States*, 2.

[61] A. Watts, 'The Role of Law in International Relations', in Byers (ed.), *The Role of Law in International Politics*, 8.

[62] Byers, 'Terrorism, the Use of Force and International Law after 11 September', in *The Role of Law in International Politics*, 412.

I now want to turn to Afghanistan under the Taliban regime in order to show how outlaw status made that state particularly susceptible to armed attack by a coalition acting in the name of the international community. Certain states, pre-designated as outlaws, lack the immunities available to other states in warding off the possibility of armed intervention. So, regardless of any evidence showing links between, say, Pakistan or Saudi Arabia and the attacks on Western interests, it is improbable that these states could find themselves on the peripheries and subject to attack in the near future.[63] In contrast, Iraq, Serbia (until recently) and Libya are continually vulnerable to such interventions. This difference is not simply one of politics. The breaches of international law committed by these states contribute to outlaw status and this outlaw status determines the legality of measures taken against these states (combined with a concomitant loss of immunities).

Afghanistan's outlaw status was exemplified by two processes which are part of the repertory of regulation (to be discussed in more detail later in this chapter) arising out of the war on terrorism. The first involved the establishment, by the Security Council, of executive committees to scrutinise relations between the outlaw and the international community. The second demonstration of the reduced status of the outlaw state was seen in the treatment by the United States authorities of Taliban POWs. In the normal circumstances of sovereign equality, enemies are accorded the mutual protection of the laws of war. This has tended to be the case even when the Western powers have been confronted with extraordinarily venal regimes.[64] However, following the US-led intervention in Afghanistan, the enemy soldier was treated as an 'illegal combatant' (something significantly less than an equal).

. . . .

In Chapter 10, I discussed how, in a sequence of Security Council resolutions, the status of Afghanistan and the Taliban regime had been modified. The Security Council had made it clear in Resolution 1193 that the Taliban's offensive against rebel movements within its own territory was 'causing a serious threat . . . to regional and international peace and security'.[65] A later resolution called on all factions within Afghanistan to cease support for terrorism and demanded that 'the Taliban stop

---

[63] E.g. S. Henderson, 'The West Must Stop Kidding Itself about Saudi Arabia', *Daily Telegraph*, 11 July 2001, 24.

[64] See, for example, the ways in which German and Japanese POWs were, quite properly, accorded POW status during the Second World War.

[65] Preambular para. 4.

providing sanctuary and training for international terrorists'.[66] In October 1999, the Council finally determined that the Taliban's continued support for terrorist organisations on its soil 'constitutes a threat to the peace' and acting under Chapter VII imposed a series of sanctions on the Taliban, the effect of which was to isolate Afghanistan and subject it to the various forms of monitoring and surveillance identified in previous Chapters.[67] Two months later, the Council began to focus on the role of the Taliban in the drug trade and to make specific demands on the regime that it surrender Osama bin Laden. In the same resolutions, a host of additional measures were imposed on the Taliban, 'as designated by the Committee'.[68] Interestingly, the language of these resolutions did not strengthen appreciably after the attack on the United States. However, by 14 November 2001, the Council condemned the Taliban regime and supported 'the efforts of the Afghan people to replace the Taliban regime'.[69]

Before considering the rhetoric accompanying these resolutions, one relatively new technique employed by the Security Council in regulating the boundaries between the international community and outlaw states ought to be mentioned. This involves the establishment of committees to oversee sanctions and the behaviour of the outlaw state (or regime).[70] These committees essentially monitor the relationship between the international community at large and the outsider state. States then have a duty to report to the committee on their efforts to punish and constrain the outlaw state. The situation in Afghanistan provoked the creation of two such committees. Security Council Resolution 1267 brought into being a committee with the task of securing compliance with a range of measures designed to isolate the Taliban regime. Meanwhile, the Anti-Terrorism Committee established under Resolution 1373 was vested with the task of ensuring the implementation of an extensive list of measures imposed by that resolution. These committees have considerable power.

---

[66] SC Res. 1214 (8 December 1998), para. 13. The Council also 'deplores' the failure of the Taliban leadership to conclude a ceasefire (para. 15).

[67] Preambular para. 8. Apart from freezing funds and denying permission to land Taliban aircraft, the Resolution also establishes a committee to oversee these sanctions (para. 6).

[68] SC Res. 1333 (19 December 2000).   [69] SC Res. 1378 (14 November 2001).

[70] The Security Council's methods of surveillance used in Afghanistan and in the war on terror are being employed elsewhere, too. In the case of Liberia there is currently investigation and monitoring by a Panel of Experts established pursuant to SC Res. 1343 (2001), para. 19, and SC Res. 1395 (2002), para. 4. The first Sanctions Committee was established in SC Res. 661 (6 August 1990) to implement the measures imposed on Iraq after its invasion of Kuwait.

Resolution 1373, for example, requires states to report, within ninety days, on the measures they have adopted to implement the resolution. These committees then are becoming an integral aspect of the creation, regulation and surveillance of outlawry.

The bureaucratic segued into the political when the image of the outlaw state was further refined in the accompanying language and officialese of the second Bush administration.[71] Most famously President George W. Bush referred to the 'axis of evil': a group of states who stand accused of exporting terrorism and constituting a threat to the international order.[72] The United States also warned that it was prepared to attack such states when they harbour terrorists.[73] The blunt language used to describe these states operates to set them apart from the existing legal order. These are not simply states that fail to comply with international law. They are delinquent states deprived of the full benefits of international legal personhood on account of their moral traits or associability. The Director of Policy Planning in the State Department, Richard Haass, has spoken of a

body of ideas ... about what you might call the limits to sovereignty. Sovereignty entails obligations. One is not to massacre your own people. Another is not to support terrorism in any way. If a government fails to meet these obligations, *then it forfeits some of the advantages of sovereignty.*[74]

It is clear from this that the United States (and this rhetoric is also present if muted in the language of Prime Minister Blair) has adopted an anti-pluralist view of the international legal order in which good and evil are demarcated (with the sovereignty or existential equality of the latter

---

[71] The term outlaw state has not been used much. The preferred term now appears to be 'states of concern'. See, for example, Select Committee Seventh Report, para. 3 at http://www.publications.parliament.uk/pa/cm200102/cmselect/cmfaff/384/38404.htm.

[72] State of the Union address, 29 January 2002: http://www.whitehouse.gov/news/releases/2002/01.

[73] President George W. Bush's Address to the Nation. Under Secretary of State John Bolton clarified the scope of this label when he included Cuba, Libya and Syria as enemy states in a Speech to the Heritage Foundation, Washington DC, 6 May 2002. See 'Beyond the Axis of Evil: Additional Threats from Weapons of Mass Destruction'.

[74] Foreign Affairs Select Committee, para. 218, italics mine. The Committee went on to state: 'Our discussions with a number of US officials in Washington and New York in March 2002 confirmed that the views articulated by Richard Haass have wide currency.' See, too, the following response to the Committee from the US Embassy: 'When governments violate the rights of their people on a large scale – be it as an act of conscious policy or the byproduct of a loss of control – the international community has the right, and sometimes even the obligation, to act . . .' (para. 217).

being severely compromised).[75] The Foreign Affairs Select Committee of the British House of Commons gave a strong indication as to the effects of this reconceptualisation on the sovereignty of one outlaw state:

> in the case of Iraq we gained the impression that established international legal standards would be of secondary importance compared with the need to take action in a world which has seen an evolution in how the international community views sovereignty.[76]

As this book has demonstrated, this 'new' sovereignty is nothing new. Outlaws have been with us, periodically, since at least the early nineteenth century. However, as I have shown in the rest of the book, at each constitutional moment there has been a debate about whether to include or exclude the outsider states and whether to apply a specially tailored legal regime to them.

At these constitutional moments, there has often been, also, a debate about how to treat outlaw personnel. The book has traced a sequence of events from Napoleon's, initially, gentle exile to the decision to abandon trials of the defeated Germans after the Great War and then, finally, to the trials at Nuremberg and The Hague. The treatment of the Taliban prisoners captured in Afghanistan marks a further development in the study of outlaws in the international legal order because it reverses a movement in the direction of proceduralism and trial for outlaw personnel.[77] After the war had ended a number of Taliban and al-Qa'ida prisoners were detained by the American authorities at Guantanamo Bay in Cuba from January 2002 onwards. Traditionally, the POWs of a regular army are entitled to certain protections under the laws of war. During the ground war, various statements made by, amongst others, Donald Rumsfeld, the US Defense Secretary, suggested that the Taliban fell outside some of the protections of the laws of war.[78] These comments and the associated legislative moves created a legal environment in which

---

[75] See e.g. 'Look for a diplomatic solution. There is no diplomacy with Bin Laden or the Taliban regime', PM's Speech to Labour Party Conference, 3 October 2001 at http://www.number-10.gov.uk/news.asp? NewsId=2680&SectionId=32.

[76] The quotes are from Richard Haass, Foreign Affairs Select Committee at para. 221.

[77] See, too, recent comments by Tony Blair and Donald Rumsfeld indicating that the outlaw states are to be deprived of the benefits of the global public order, *Sunday Times*, 4 August 2002, 1.

[78] See, for example, Adam Roberts, 'Crisis at Kunduz', *Guardian*, 24 November 2001, 13, and US Secretary of Defense Donald H. Rumsfeld, United States Department of Defense News Transcript, 8 February 2002 at http://www.defenselink.mil/news/Feb2002/t02082002_t0208sd.html.

members of the Taliban were placed outside the standard protections of the law and this general picture was, of course, further enhanced by the detention of Taliban and al-Qa'ida prisoners on Guantanamo Bay.[79] These prisoners were described, subsequently, as 'illegal combatants'.[80] This purported to place them beyond the full protection of the Geneva Conventions. In addition, while Guantanamo Bay came within the jurisdiction of the United States under a 1903 treaty in which Cuba leased the Bay and other territory in Cuba to the United States, the Bay remained under Cuban territorial sovereignty. It was this latter fact that proved decisive in *Coalition of Clergy, et al.* v *George Walker Bush* where petitioners filed a petition for a writ of habeas corpus in relation to the detainees held by US forces in Cuba. The Court held that no federal court had jurisdiction over the detainees and that these detainees possessed no constitutional rights within the US since their place of detention fell outside the territorial jurisdiction of the United States.[81] In addition, the US has rejected calls for the detainees to be placed before an international criminal court in order to assess guilt, or an independent, impartial tribunal in order to assess status.[82] Finally, the United States has also argued that the law of human rights has no applicability in

[79] See Military Order of 13 November 2001, 'Detention, Treatment and Trial of Certain Non-Citizens in the War Against Terrorism', 66 FR 57833, and Department of Defense Military Commission Order No. 1, 21 March 2002, 'Procedures for Trials by Military Commission of Certain Non-United States Citizens in the War Against Terrorism' at http://www.defenselink.mil/news/Mar2002/d20020321ord.pdf. 'Under the terms of the Geneva Convention, however, the Taliban detainees do not qualify as POWs. Therefore, neither the Taliban nor al-Qa'ida detainees are entitled to POW status [although] they are being provided many POW privileges as a matter of policy.' Statement of US Embassy at Ev 104 (US reply), para. 29. Note that the UK Foreign Minister had described the detainees as 'POWs'; see Foreign Affairs Select Committee, 139.

[80] See *R on the Application of Ferroz Al Abbasi* v. *Secretary of State for the Foreign and Commonwealth Office and Secretary of State for the Home Department (Unreported Judgement)*, Queen's Bench Division (Administrative Court) (hereinafter, *Abbasi No. 1*) at para. 5 (US description of POWs as 'illegal combatants'). For an earlier Supreme Court precedent employing this language see *Ex Parte Quirin* 317 US 1 (1942).

[81] Case No. CV02-570 AHM (JTLx), United States District Court – Central District of California at http://www.cacd.uscourts.gov. The Court also held that the petitioners had no standing to bring the claim. See, too, *Shafiq Rasul et al* v. *Bush*, Case No. No 02-CV 0299 (D., DC), 2002 (19 February) and *Faha Al Odah et al* v. *USA*, United States District Court, District of California Case No. No 02-828 (CKK) (though in *Rasul*, Judge Kollar-Kotelly noted in her conclusion that 'this opinion, too, should not be read as stating that these aliens do not have some form of rights under international law' (at 30)).

[82] See Wedgwood, 'Tribunals and the Events of September 11th', ASIL *Insights*, December 2001'; A. Neier, 'The Military Tribunals on Trial', *New York Review of Books*, 14 February 2002, 11–15.

this matter.[83] As a consequence of this, the detainees with allegiance to the outlaw state find themselves at the same time outside law but subject to a highly disciplinary regime of incarceration and surveillance.[84] These detainees are within the jurisdiction of the United States for the purposes of detention and interrogation but are not held within the sovereign territory of the United States (for the purposes of exercising rights).[85] This, of course, reflects in microcosm the status of the outlaw state itself.[86] These individuals, according to Slavoj Žižek, were 'the political Enemy excluded from the political arena'.[87] They now found themselves placed also outside at least two legal regimes – the laws of war and the laws of the United States. The Taliban prisoners were both outlaws and outside the law. As the petitioners in *Rasul* argued, these prisoners were 'incommunicado from the rest of the world'.[88]

The Great Powers have entered into agreements to disapply the laws of war to their own military personnel as well but this time producing the opposite effect. Under the terms of the Military Assistance Agreement concluded between the International Security Assistance Force (ISAF) and the Interim Government in Afghanistan, the UK military forces

---

[83] It was a matter of public record, the United States argued, that the Guantanamo detainees were not prisoners of war ('POWs') because they 'do not meet the criteria applicable to lawful combatants'. *United States: Response of the United States to Request for Precautionary Measures – Detainees in Guantanamo Bay, Cuba* (12 April 2002).

[84] Though the United States exercises jurisdiction over Guantanamo Bay under international law and according to the terms of the 1903 Lease Agreement between Cuba and the US ('Lease to the United States by the Government of Cuba of Certain Areas of Land and Water for Naval or Coaling Stations in Guantanamo and Bahia Honda', 2 July 1903).

[85] In *Abassi No. 1* (para. 22), it was held that Guantanamo Bay was outside a 'consular district' for the purposes of making a claim under the UK–US Bilateral Treaty (1951) (United States of America and United Kingdom of Great Britain and Northern Ireland, 'Convention (with Protocol of Signature) Relating to Consular Officers', 165 UNTS 121).

[86] In *Bankovic (Admissibility)* (2002) ECHR at http://hudoc.echr.coe.int, the European Court of Human Rights found that the protective jurisdiction of the European Convention on Human Rights did not extend to the victims of the bombing of the Belgrade Television Station (RTS). The Court held that, while the Convention extended to territories under the jurisdiction of the signatory states, and while that jurisdiction itself extended to territories over which the states exercised some form of authority, the European powers did not have jurisdiction over Belgrade at the time of the attacks even though they controlled the territorial airspace above Belgrade. This, in some respects, parallels the situation of the Guantanamo Bay detainees: at the mercy of the Great Powers but not within their territorial sovereignty; under their control but not entitled to the exercise of legal rights.

[87] S. Žižek, 'Are we in a War? Do we Have an Enemy?' *London Review of Books*, 23 May 2000, 3.

[88] See *Rasul*, at 2.

operating in Afghanistan became immune from prosecution in Afghanistan for grave breaches of the Geneva Conventions.[89] The United States, too, has secured an immunity (renewable by the Security Council every twelve months) from commencement of proceedings against 'current or former officials or personnel from a contributing State not a Party to the Rome Statute over acts or omissions relating to a [UN] established or authorized operation'.[90]

These separate legal regimes illustrate a general tendency in the international order to distinguish between a liberal or civilised core and an uncivilised illiberal periphery. Indeed, President Bush made this quite explicit when he described the coming world order in familiar, Old Testament terms:

> Every nation in every region now has a decision to make. Either you are with us or you are with the terrorists. From this day forward any nation that continues to harbor or support terrorism will be regarded by the United States as a hostile regime.[91]

As I have said, this is not the first time such a doctrine has been enunciated.[92] This book has demonstrated that the existential equality of states has been heavily compromised and mediated since at least 1815. In previous chapters I have described the ways in which generations of anti-pluralists have zoned the international order by distinguishing a society of insiders from the uncivilised or undemocratic 'outlaw' states. This process is now at its most explicit, for decades, in the language of the Bush and Blair governments. E. H. Carr spoke about the appeals made to concepts of universality and community in the name of narrowly focused ideological projects of this ilk.[93] Carl Schmitt warned of a

---

[89] Military Technical Agreement Between the International Security Assistance Force (ISAF) and the Interim Administration of Afghanistan ('Interim Administration'). Para. 2: 'All ISAF and supporting personnel, including associated liaison personnel, enjoying privileges and immunities under this Arrangement will respect the laws of Afghanistan, insofar as it is compatible with the UNSCR (1386) and will refrain from activities not compatible with the nature of the Mission' at http://www.operations.mod.uk/fingal/index.htm.

[90] See SC Res. 1422 (12 July 2002).   [91] Bush, Address to Congress, 1349.

[92] See, for example, the Brezhnev Doctrine and the Nixon Doctrine. However, as the Court in *Nicaragua* stated: 'The United States authorities have on some occasions clearly stated their grounds for intervening in the affairs of a foreign State for reasons connected with, for example, the domestic policies of that country, its ideology, the level of its armaments, or the direction of its foreign policy. But these were statements of international policy, and not an assertion of rules of existing international law' (para. 208).

[93] E. H. Carr, *The Twenty Years' Crisis*.

coming order in which a state would 'fight its political enemy in the name of humanity' and thereby 'usurp a universal concept against its military opponent'.[94] After the September attacks international lawyers made precisely these sorts of appeals as they sought to distinguish mere 'breaches of international law' from attacks on the international legal order from outside that order. Michael Reisman, for example, distinguished previous 'crimes' of terrorism (by, for example, the IRA or Basque separatists) from the attack on the Twin Towers. The activities of the IRA were directed at particular political ends whereas, according to Reisman, the terrorist attack on the United States was an 'aggression' against the 'values of the system of world public order'.[95] As a result of the attack, 'all peoples who value freedom and human rights' have been forced into a war of self-defence.[96] Thus the attack on the United States was not simply a hideous breach of international law and an attack on a particular set of values (say, capitalism or US foreign policy in the Middle East) but an assault on international society by those outside this society aimed at its destruction.[97]

The intense debates among people who value human rights and freedom about whether this is a war or not are brushed aside.[98] Instead, Reisman speaks of 'executive committees' of states using 'new methods of response' to attack 'the enemy'.[99] These new methods are validated by the executive committees themselves, by appeals to universal values, and operate through an expanded doctrine of self-defence articulated by Prime Minister Blair when he said, 'what we should learn . . . is that if there is a gathering threat or danger, let us deal with it before it materialises rather than afterwards'.[100]

This is a stark turn from the detached liberalism that seeks a peaceful resolution of disputes and, indeed, from the less assertive legalised hegemony of the likes of Castlereagh who deprecated an earlier Holy Alliance in the following terms:

---

[94] C. Schmitt, *Concept of the Political*, 54.
[95] Reisman, 'In Defence of Public Order' (2001) 95:4 AJIL 833–5.   [96] *Ibid.*, 833.
[97] To this extent, some terrorists (but not all) become pirates. In *Republic of Bolivia*, Pickford J. at the first level, noted that the leader of an insurgent group could not be a pirate since he was: 'Not only not the enemy of the human race but he is the enemy of a particular state', *Republic of Bolivia v. Indemnity Mutual Marine Assurance Co.*, (1909) 1 KB 785.
[98] See, generally, 'Letters and Comments on 11 September' in *London Review of Books*, 29 November 2001, 3.
[99] Reisman, 'In Defence of Public Order', 835.
[100] M. White, 'Blair Survives Landmark Grilling', *Guardian*, 17 July 2002, 2.

What is intended to be combatted . . . is, the notion . . . that whenever any great Political Event shall occur . . . pregnant perhaps with future danger, it is to be regarded almost as a matter of course, that it belongs to the Allies to charge themselves collectively with the responsibility of exercising some Jurisdiction concerning such possible eventual danger . . . We must admit ourselves to be . . . a Power that must take our Principle of action, and our scale of acting, not merely from the Expediency of the Case, but from those Maxims which a System of Government strongly popular and national in its Character, has imposed upon us: – We shall be found in our place when actual Danger menaces the System of Europe, but this Country cannot and will not act upon abstract and speculative Principles of Precaution.[101]

This attitude will not entirely disappear. In confrontations between equal sovereigns, the old liberal language will re-appear. The terrorist attacks in Kashmir, for example, are unlikely to inspire the same strident language in the pages of the *American Journal of International Law*.[102] Instead, there will be return to the language of equivalence, of pacific resolution and of caution. Of the two liberal modes, of course, a muscular anti-pluralism now finds itself in the ascendant but there is likely to be a continued movement between the two in the future and this movement will partially define juridical sovereignty.

Conclusion

The international legal order is composed of unequal sovereigns. This insight requires little modification in the light of 11 September. Indeed, the conflict in Afghanistan and the detention of the Taliban detainees in Guantanamo Bay have merely confirmed and strengthened the underlying argument. When Great Powers meet outlaws, the rules of the equal sovereignty regime are suspended. In the present crisis, the Great Powers (led by *the* Great Power) have detached themselves a little more from the Charter-based legalised hegemony brought into existence at San Francisco. The interventions in Kosovo and Afghanistan have each signalled a shift away from the centralised hegemony of Chapter VII to a looser, regional, more ad hoc and more flexible hegemony outside

---

[101] *Castlereagh's State Paper of 1820*, Minute of Cabinet, 5 May 1820, in H. Temperely and L. Penson (eds.), *Foundations of British Foreign Policy, 1792–1902*.

[102] We need only imagine how we might read an article from an Indian academic in the pages of the *Indian Journal of International Law* that adopted the same language as Reisman's. Would it be dismissed as too transparently local and culturally freighted to stand as a piece of objective legal scholarship?

the framework of the Charter.[103] That the United States and its allies (semi-permanent and temporary) have done this at a time when their dominance of the Security Council is at its peak tends to confirm the threat to the Charter order posed by the new hegemons. This threat to the Charter is not a direct threat to international law, at least not the international law described in this book, i.e. one that is responsive to power and capable of justifying and legalising inequality. Indeed, the elastic nature of customary international law has permitted scholars to argue for a modified law on the use of force that would expand the realm of justified force quite considerably. The argument pursued in this chapter is that this new custom is, in effect, a 'localised' custom brought into being by the Great Powers (with the support of many other states) and with an applicability limited to the activities of those Powers.

This legalised hegemony finds part of its justification in a return to a form of pre-positivism in which the legitimacy of wars could be distinguished depending on the nature of the adversaries. It is useful to compare two alternative just war theories here. In one, the justness of a use of force depended on its conformity with some pre-existing social or legal norm. Thus, Grotius was able to describe wars of self-defence as just. A wholly different just war theory holds that the justness of the struggle will depend on the religious character of the warring state, e.g. wars by Christian states against heathen entities would always be lawful. This latter version of just war theory was abandoned in the nineteenth century in favour of a positivistic treatment that approached war by refusing to enquire into 'the justice of its origin'.[104] As Phillimore put it in discussing intervention in the Ottoman areas: 'The converse of this, viz., Mahometan Intervention with Christian States, has, it is believed, never yet arisen in practice, but it would be subject on principle to the same law.'[105] This is a liberal pluralist conception of intervention where states are treated equally and intervention is determined by the application of consistent legal norms rather than being dependent on a categorisation of certain states as 'unequal sovereigns' or outlaws.

---

[103] I do not want to suggest that the Council or Charter enforcement has been abandoned. See measures undertaken in SC Res. 1390 (16 January 2002). As of the time of writing the United Nations is now, of course, taking a leading role in the transitional arrangements for Afghanistan even as it is frozen out of the enforcement efforts. Under SC Res. 1413 (23 May 2002), the ISAF mandate is extended by six months. The ISAF was established by SC Res. 1386 (20 December 2001).

[104] W. E. Hall, *A Treatise on International Law* (8th edn), 82.

[105] Phillimore's *Commentaries* (3rd edn), 624.

The UN Charter represented a partial return to the Grotian just war model in that Chapter VII set out a normative framework in which the nature or purpose of a use of force would determine its legitimacy. The Holy Alliance framework, however, would apply to a world where the status of the war-makers is a determining factor in the legitimacy or lawfulness of the war.

Alongside the Great Powers are, of course, the outlaw states. The post-11 September order represents a deepening of anti-pluralist trends set out and identified in Chapter 10.[106] Certain states continue to be consigned to the margins of the international legal order by virtue of their nature or because of some threat they are said to pose to that order. The war in Afghanistan exemplifies this trend. Afghanistan was an outlaw state impliedly designated as such in a number of Security Council resolutions discussed above and deprived of any meaningful territorial immunities or political prerogatives through that process. Two consequences of this characterisation bear repetition. First, Afghanistan, as well as the relationship of other states to it, was subject to quite intensive scrutiny under the UN Security Council's Committee system. Second, the combatants of the outlaw state were themselves subject to treatment as outlaws. In 1945, the major German war criminals were put on trial for various offences against international law. In 2002, the Taliban prisoners were denied POW status under the laws of war and, it was claimed, fell outside the jurisdiction of both US law and international human rights law. They were outlaws in a more aggravated sense than even the German High Command. The Taliban prisoners found themselves outside of the law but subject to highly coercive legal control; their status mirroring that of the state to whom they owed allegiance. According to Martti Koskenniemi, Carl Schmitt argued that one of the achievements of classical international law was its treatment of war as a 'duel' between formally equal sovereigns and its humanisation by conceptualising the enemy as *justus hostis*.[107] It seems that this is no longer the appropriate metaphor.

In this chapter I have argued that while the classic or traditional norms of collective security and self-defence will continue to operate on the plane of sovereign equality, the unequal sovereignty regime will predominate wherever there are either Great Powers or outlaw states

---

[106] This is a book about statehood so my attention has not been directed towards the treatment of al-Qa'ida, for example.

[107] Koskenniemi, *Gentle Civilizer*, 416.

involved. In the latter case, many of the normative modifications identified by scholars post-11 September will apply only selectively.[108] In such instances, the legal hegemons operating in a bifurcated international order do not even 'perceive themselves as one of the warring sides, but as a mediating agent of peace and global order, crushing rebellion . . .'.[109] And outlawry.[110]

[108] This has always been the case. The Security Council would be unlikely to vote for action against one of its permanent members.

[109] Žižek, 'Are we in a War? Do we have an Enemy?', 3.

[110] C. Schmitt, *Concept of the Political*: 'To confiscate the word humanity, to invoke and monopolize such a term has certain incalculable effects, such as denying the enemy the quality of being human and declaring him to be an outlaw of humanity: and a war can thereby be driven to the most extreme inhumanity', 54.

12   The puzzle of sovereignty

This book has been written as a sustained engagement with the enigma of sovereignty. In it I have explored a particular aspect of sovereignty, namely juridical sovereignty, in a particular context, namely that of the international legal order. At the same time, I have offered an episodic account of institutional or regime innovation in the two centuries since 1815. I have argued that juridical sovereignty can be best understood as an interplay between conventional international legal conceptions of sovereign equality and two, often obscured, categories of sovereignty inhabited by the Great Powers and outlaw states. I use the term 'legalised hegemony' to capture the special position of the Great Powers in international society since 1815 and I focus on the institutional prerogatives they have enjoyed in this period and the manner in which this hegemony is accommodated within the system of 'sovereign equals'. Meanwhile, 'anti-pluralism' (and, in particular, its ascendant form, liberal anti-pluralism) is a way of organising inter-state relations according to hierarchies based on the internal politics, moral characteristics or temperament of nation-states. Anti-pluralism, then, suspends the conventional rights and immunities of certain sovereign states and characterises them as outlaw states or uncivilised nations. The combination of legalised hegemony and anti-pluralism produces a society in which, to some degree, all states are 'unequal sovereigns'.

James Lorimer once said of Grotius that, 'after having laid down his principles he left them there without making any use of them . . .'.[1] I have used as my point of departure for this book a paragraph at the beginning of Grotius's first book, *De jure praedae*. In this paragraph he refers explicitly to outlaw states ('exceedingly cruel enemies') and

---

[1] Lorimer, *Institutes*, 73.

implicitly to Great Powers (acting 'with public authorisation'). The idea of outlaw states and Great Powers, though, remains underdeveloped in the later Grotius. Elsewhere in his work, he develops a conception of international law that is partly founded on sovereign equality. Indeed, his name is often used in association with a period in international relations during which a strong conception of sovereign equality was in the ascendant (the 'Grotian' period, 1648–1815). In this book, I have taken up Lorimer's challenge by adopting two Grotian principles in trying to answer the puzzle of sovereign equality, i.e. how it is able to accommodate legalised hegemony and anti-pluralism.

At various points since 1815 there have been struggles for the soul of international law. The crises concerning Iraq, weapons of mass destruction and terrorism have exaggerated trends largely discernible but sometimes dormant since 1815. Is the global legal order made up of freely transacting equal sovereigns operating within an essentially non-interventionist environment (Castlereagh in 1822) in which state diversity (Kunz in 1945) and equality (Barbosa in 1907) are preserved? Or is it an order in which Great Powers and outlaw states clash within a highly interventionist normative system (Tsar Alexander in 1822, Prime Minister Blair in 1999) in which some states are subject to intrusive principles, occasionally leading to their criminalisation (Security Council Resolution 687, Tesón in 1994, Lorimer in 1888) while other states possess special prerogatives related to law creation and enforcement (Metternich in 1814–15, Scott in 1907, Bush in 2002)?

The present crisis appears particularly acute. What is the role of sovereign equality in a world where some leading Western politicians talk about the revival of 'Christian clubs' while others openly deprecate the restraining power of normativity?[2] But perhaps it has ever been thus. When the Tsar showed Wellington and Castlereagh the draft agreement to establish a Holy Alliance of Great Powers to supervise the internal arrangements of European states, by force if necessary, when revolutionary currents within those states became a danger to Europe, Castlereagh revealed that: 'It was not without some difficulty that we went through the interview with becoming gravity.'[3] But laughter is not always an option. The Holy Alliance dissolved but future holy alliances may prove more robust.

---

[2] 'EU is not a Christian Club, says Turkey Victor', *The Times*, 12 November 2002 (responses to President of EU Convention on Europe and former French President Valéry Giscard D'Estaing's views that the admission of Turkey to the EU would mean the end of Europe).

[3] H. Nicolson, *Congress of Vienna*, 250.

Select bibliography

Abdy, J. T. (ed.), *Kent's Commentaries on International Law* (2nd edn), Cambridge: Deighton, Bell, and Co. 1878.

Abi-Saab, G., 'The Uses of Article 19' (1999) 10:2 *European Journal of International Law* 339.

'Whither the International Community?' (1998) 9 *European Journal of International Law* 264.

Acheson, D., 'The Arrogance of International Lawyers' (1963) 57 *American Society of International Law Proceedings*.

Akehurst, M., 'The Hierarchy of the Sources of International Law' (1977) 47 *British Yearbook of International Law, 1974–75* 273.

Albrecht-Carrié, R., *A Diplomatic History of Europe Since the Congress of Vienna*, London: Methuen, 1958.

The Concert of Europe, New York: Harper, 1968.

Alexandrowicz, C. H., *An Introduction to the History of the Law of Nations in the East Indies*, Oxford: Clarendon, 1967.

'Empirical and Doctrinal Positivism in International Law' (1977) 47 *British Yearbook of International Law, 1974–75* 286.

Alvarez, J., 'Do Liberal States Behave Better? A Critique of Slaughter's Liberal Theory' (2001) 12:2 *European Journal of International Law* 183–6.

'Judging the Security Council' (1996) 90 *American Journal of International Law* 1.

Anghie, A., 'Finding the Peripheries: Sovereignty and Colonialism in Nineteenth-Century International Law' (1999) 40:1 *Harvard International Law Journal* 1.

Armstrong, D., *Revolution and World Order: The Revolutionary State in International Society*, Oxford: Clarendon, 1993.

'Law, Justice and the Idea of World Society' (1999) 75:3 *International Affairs* 547.

Aron, R., *De Gaulle, Israel and the Jews* (trans. John Sturrock), London: André Deutsch, 1969.

Austin, J., *Lectures on Jurisprudence*, London: John Murray, 1911.

354

Baker, P. J., 'The Doctrine of Legal Equality of States' (1923–4) 4 *British Yearbook of International Law* 1.

Baker, R. S., *Woodrow Wilson and World Settlement: Written from his Unpublished and Personal Material*, vol. III, New York: Doubleday, 1923.

Bantekas, I., 'Austria, the European Union and Article 2(7) of the UN Charter' *ASIL Insight*, February 2000, 1.

Bass, G., *Stay the Hand of Vengeance: The Politics of War Crimes Trials*, Princeton University Press, 2000.

Bassiouni, M. Cherif, 'From Versailles to Rwanda in Seventy-Five Years: The Need to Establish a Permanent International Criminal Court' (1997) 10 *Harvard Human Rights Journal* 11.

Bell, C., *The Debatable Alliance: An Essay in Anglo-American Relations*, Chatham House Essays, London: Oxford University Press, 1964.

Bentwich, N. and Martin, A., *A Commentary on the Charter of the United Nations*, London: Routledge and Kegan Paul, 1950.

Benvenuti, P., 'The ICTY Prosecutor and the Review of the NATO Bombing Campaign Against the Federal Republic of Yugoslavia' (2000) 12:3 *European Journal of International Law* 503.

Bernard, M., *Four Lectures in Subjects Connected with Diplomacy*, London: Macmillan, 1868.

Biersteker, T. and Weber, C. (eds.), *State Sovereignty as Social Construct*, Cambridge University Press, 1996.

Bodin, J., *The Six Bookes of a Commonweale* (trans. R. Knolles), London: 1606.

Bohman, J. and Lutz-Bachmann, M. (eds.), *Perpetual Peace: Essays on Kant's Cosmopolitan Ideal*, Cambridge, MA: MIT Press, 1997.

Bourne, K. and Cameron-Walls, D. (eds.), *British Documents on Foreign Affairs*, Part III, Series I, vol. 2, Frederick, MD: University Publications of America, 1989–91, 1975.

Brierly, J., *The Charter and the Covenant*, Cambridge University Press, 1946.

Broms, B., *The Doctrine of Equality of States as Applied in International Organisations*, Helsinki: Vammala, 1959.

Brown, L. (ed.), *The New Shorter Oxford English Dictionary*, Oxford University Press, 1993.

Brown, M. *et al.* (eds.), *Debating the Democratic Peace*, Boston: MIT Press, 1996.

Brown, P. M., *International Realities*, New York: Scribner, 1917.

   International Society, New York: Macmillan, 1923.

   'The Theory of the Independence and Equality of States' (1915) 9:1 *American Journal of International Law* 305.

Brownlie, I., *Principles of Public International Law* (5th edn), Oxford: Clarendon, 1990.

   'Humanitarian Intervention' in J. Moore, *Law and Civil War in the Modern World*, Baltimore, 1974.

   'The United Nations as a Form of Government' (1972) 13 *Harvard Journal of International Law* 421.

Bull, H., *The Anarchical Society: A Study of Order in World Politics*, London: Macmillan, 1977.

Bull, H. and Watson, A., *The Expansion of International Society*, Oxford: Clarendon, 1984.

Bull, H., Kingsbury, B. and Roberts, A., *Hugo Grotius and International Relations*, Oxford University Press, 1990.

Burley, A.-M., 'Toward an Age of Liberal Nations' (1992) 33 *Harvard International Law Journal* 393.

Butterfield, H. and Wight, M., *Diplomatic Investigations: Essays on the Theory of International Politics*, London: George Allen and Unwin, 1966.

Byers, M., *Custom, Power and the Power of Rules: International Relations and Customary International Law*, Cambridge University Press, 1999.

   The Role of Law in International Politics: Essays in International Relations and International Law, Oxford University Press, 2000.

Carr, E. H., *The 20 Years' Crisis 1919–1939: An Introduction to the Study of International Relations* (2nd edn), London: Macmillan, 1948.

Cassese, A., *International Criminal Law: A Commentary on the Rome Statute for an International Criminal Court*, ed. Judge Antonio Cassese, Oxford University Press, 2001.

   'A Follow-up: Forcible Humanitarian Countermeasures and Opinio Necessitas' (1999) 10:4 *European Journal of International Law* 791.

Castlereagh, Viscount, *Correspondence*, London: John Murray, 1853.

Cerna, C. M., 'Universal Democracy: An International Legal Right or the Pipe Dream of the West?' (1995) 27 *New York University Journal of International Law and Politics* 289.

Charlesworth, H., 'Transforming The United Men's Club: Feminist Futures for the United Nations' (1994) 4 *Transnational Law and Contemporary Problems* 421.

Charney, J., 'Anticipatory Humanitarian Intervention in Kosovo' (1999) 93 *American Journal of International Law* 834.

   'Universal International Law' (1993) 87 *American Journal of International Law* 529.

Chayes, A., *The Cuban Missile Crisis*, London: Oxford University Press, 1974.

Chinkin, C., 'The State that Acts Alone: Bully, Good Samaritan or Iconoclast' (2000) 11:1 *European Journal of International Law* 39.

Choate, J. H., *The Two Hague Conferences*, Princeton University Press, 1913.

Chomsky, N., *Rogue States*, London: Pluto Press, 2000.

Churchill, W., *Hinge of Fate, The Second World War*, Boston: Houghton-Mifflin Co, 1948–53.

Clark, I., *The Hierarchy of States: Reform and Resistance in the International Order*, Cambridge University Press, 1989.

   'Making Sense of Sovereignty' (1988) 14 *Review of International Studies* 306.

Claude, I., *Swords into Ploughshares*, New York: Random House, 1956.

Cobbett, *Cases and Opinions on International Law and Various Points of English Law Connected Therewith* (3rd edn), London: 1909–13.

Corbett, P. E., *Law and Society in the Relations of States*, New York: Harcourt, Brace, 1951.

Cox, R. W., 'Social Forces, States and World Orders: Beyond International Relations Theory' (1981) 10:2 *Millennium* 126.

Craig, G. A., *Europe Since 1815* (3rd edn), New York: Holt Rinehart and Winston, 1971.

Crawford, J., 'The Criteria for Statehood' (1977–8) 48 *British Yearbook of International Law* 93.

  The Creation of States in International Law, Oxford: Clarendon, 1979.

  'Democracy and International Law' (1993) 64 *British Yearbook of International Law* 113.

  'Revising the Draft Article on State Responsibility' (1999) 10:2 *European Journal of International Law* 433.

  The International Law Commission's Articles on State Responsibility, Cambridge University Press, 2002.

Crawford, J. et al., 'The ILC's Draft Articles on State Responsibility: Towards Completion of a Second Reading' (2000) 94:4 *American Journal of International Law*, 660.

Crawford, J., Peel, J. and Olleson, S., 'The ILC's Articles on Responsibility of States for Wrongful Acts: Completion of the Second Reading' (2000) 12:5 *European Journal of International Law*, 963.

Cresson, W. P., *The Holy Alliance*, Oxford University Press, 1922.

Cullet, P., 'Differential Treatment in International Law: Towards a New Paradigm of Inter-State Relations' (1999) 10:3 *European Journal of International Law* 549.

D'Amato, A., 'The Invasion of Panama was a Lawful Response to Tyranny' (1990) 84 *American Journal of International Law* 516.

D'Amato, A., Falk, R. A. and Weston, B. H., *International Law and World Order: An Introductory Problem-Oriented Coursebook*, St Paul, MN: West, 1980.

Davis, C. D., *The United States and the Second Hague Peace Conference*, Durham, NC: Duke University Press, 1975.

Davis, K., *The Soviets at Geneva*, Chambry: Imprimeries Réunies, 1934.

Dickinson, E., 'The Equality of States in International Law', Cambridge, MA: Harvard PhD Thesis, 1918.

  The Equality of States in International Law, Cambridge, MA: Harvard University Press, 1920.

Dinstein, Y., *War, Aggression and Self-Defence*, New York: Cambridge University Press, 2001.

Dixon, M., *Textbook on International Law*, London: Blackstone, 1996.

Doyle, M., 'Kant, Liberal Legacies and Foreign Affairs' (No 1) (1983) 12:3 *Philosophy and Public Affairs* 205.

  'Liberalism and World Politics' (1986) 80:4 *American Political Science Review* 1151.

Drew, C., 'The East Timor Story: International Law on Trial' (2001) 12:4 *European Journal of International Law* 651.

Dunbabin, J., ' "The League of Nations" ' Place in the International System', (1993) 78 *History* 421.

Dupuy, P.-M., 'The Place and Role of Unilateralism in Contemporary International Law' (2000) 11:1 *European Journal of International Law* 19.
'Reviewing the Difficulties of Codification' (1999) 10:2 *European Journal of International Law* 371.

Duxbury, A., 'Austria and the European Union: The Report of the Three Wise Men' (2000) 1 *Melbourne Journal of International Law* 169.

Dworkin, R., *Taking Rights Seriously*, London: Duckworth, 1977.

Eagleton, C., 'The Charter Adopted at San Francisco' (1945) 39 *The American Political Science Review* 934.

Eden, F., *An Historical Sketch of the International Policy of Modern Europe As Connected with the Principles of the Law of Nature and of Nations Concluding with some Remarks on the Holy Alliance*, London: J. Murray, 1823.

Efraim, A. D., *Sovereign (In)equality in International Organisations*, The Hague: Kluwer, 1999.

Evans, R., 'All states are equal, but . . .' (1981) *Review of International Studies* 59.

Evatt, H. V., *The United Nations*, London: Oxford University Press, 1948.

Eyffinger, A., 'Europe in the Balance: An Appraisal of the Westphalian System' (1998) 45 *Netherlands International Law Review* 161.

Falk, R. (ed), *The Vietnam War and International Law*, Princeton University Press, 1968–76.
Revitalizing International Law, Amos: Iowa State University Press, 1994.
A Study of Future Worlds, New York: Free Press, 1975.
'The Pursuit of International Justice: Present Dilemmas and An Imagined Future' (1992) 52:2 *Journal of International Affairs* 409.

Falk, R. and Black, C., *The Future of the International Legal Order: Trends and Patterns*, vol. i, Princeton University Press, 1967.

Fassbender, B., *UN Security Council Reform and the Right of Veto: A Constitutional Perspective*, The Hague: Kluwer, 1998.

Fellmeth, A. X., 'Feminism and International Law: Theory, Methodology and Substantive Reform' (2000) 22 *Human Rights Quarterly* 658.

Fenwick, C. J., *International Law* (2nd edn), New York: D. Appleton-Century, 1934.

Fenwick, W. J., 'Targeting and Proportionality during the NATO Bombing Campaign against Yugoslavia' (2001) 12:3 *European Journal of International Law* 489.

Ferrero, G., *The Reconstruction of Europe: Talleyrand and the Congress of Vienna 1814–1815*, New York: Putnam's, 1941.

Fichte, J. C., *The Vocation of Man* (ed. and trans. W. Smith), Lassalle, IL: Open Court, 1887.

Figgis, J. N., *Studies of Political Thought: From Gerson to Grotius 1414–1635* (2nd edn), Cambridge University Press, 1916.

Fitzpatrick, P., 'Nationalism as Racism' in P. Fitzpatrick (ed.), *Nationalism, Racism and the Rule of Law*, Brookfield, VT: Dartmouth Publishers 1995.

Fonteyne, J. P., 'The Customary International Law Doctrine of Humanitarian Intervention: Its Current Validity Under the UN Charter' (1974) 4 *California Western International Law Journal* 203.

Forsythe, D., *The Internationalisation of Human Rights*, Lexington, MA: Lexington Books, 1991.

Fox, G. and Roth, B. (eds.), *Democratic Governance and International Law*, Cambridge University Press, 2000.

Fox, G., 'The Right to Political Participation in International Law' (1992) 17 *Yale Journal of International Law* 539.

Franck, T., *Fairness in International Law and Institutions*, New York: Clarendon, 1995.

   The Power of Legitimacy Among Nations, New York: Oxford University Press, 1990.

   'Fairness in the International Legal and Institutional System: General Course on Public International Law' (1993) 240 *Collected Courses of The Hague Academy* 189.

   'Legitimacy in the International System' (1988) 82(4) *American Journal of International Law* 705.

   'Is Justice Relevant to the International Legal System?' (1989) 64:5 *Notre Dame Law Review* 945.

Fukuyama, F., *The End of History and the Last Man*, New York: Free Press, 1992.

   'The End of History' (1989) 16 *The National Interest* 3.

Gaddis, J. L., *We Now Know: Rethinking Cold War History*, Oxford: Clarendon, 1997.

Gainaris, W., 'Weighted Voting in the International Monetary Fund and the World Bank' (1990–1) 14 *Fordham International Law Journal* 910.

Gaja, G., 'Should all References to Article 19 Disappear from the ILC Draft Articles on State Responsibility?' (1999) 10(2) *European Journal of International Law* 366.

Galanter, M., 'Why the Haves come out ahead: Speculations on the Limits of Social Change' (1994) 9 *Law and Society Review* 95.

Garner, *Recent Developments in International Law*, Calcutta University Press, 1925.

Gazzini, T., 'NATO Coercive Military Activities in the Yugoslav Crisis (1992–99)' (2001) 12(3) *European Journal of International Law* 391.

Ghathi, J. T., 'International Law and Eurocentricity' (1998) 9(1) *European Journal of International Law* 184.

Gilbert, G., 'The Criminal Responsibility of States' (1990) *International and Comparative Law Quarterly* 345.

Gilbert, R., *The Unequal Treaties: China and the Foreigner*, London: Murray, 1929.

Gilpin, R., *The Political Economy of International Relations*, Princeton University Press, 1987.

Gilson, B., *The Conceptual System of Sovereign Equality*, Leuven: Peeters, 1984.

Glennon, M., 'The New Interventionism: The Search for a Just International Law', May/June (1999) *Foreign Affairs* 2.

Glenny, M., *The Balkans 1804–1999: Nationalism, War and the Great Powers*, London: Granta, 1999.

Goebel, J., *The Equality of States: A Study in the History of Law*, New York: Columbia University Press, 1925.

Gold, J., *Voting and Decision in the International Monetary Fund: An Essay on the Law and Practice of the Fund*, Washington: IMF, 1972.

'Developments in the Law and Institutions of International Economic Relations' (1974) 68 *American Journal of International Law* 687.

Gong, G., *The Standard of Civilisation in International Society*, Oxford: Clarendon, 1984.

Gooch, B., *Europe in the Nineteenth Century: A History*, London: Macmillan, 1970.

Goodrich, L. M., 'Pacific Settlement of Disputes' (1945) 39 *American Political Science Review* 956.

Goodrich, L. M. and Hambro, E., *Charter of the United Nations: Commentary and Documents* (2nd edn), Boston: World Peace Foundation, 1949.

Goodrich, L. M., Hambro, E. and Simons, A. M., *Charter of the United Nations Commentary and Documents* (3rd edn), New York, London: Columbia University Press, 1969.

Gowan, P., *The Global Gamble*, London: Verso, 2000.

'Neoliberal Cosmopolitanism' (2001) 11 *New Left Review* 79.

Gowlland-Debbas, V., 'The Limits of Unilateral Enforcement of Community Objectives in the Framework of UN Peace Maintenance' (2000) 11:2 *European Journal of International Law* 361.

Gramsci, A., *Selections from Prison Notebooks* (ed. and trans. Q. Hoare and G. N. Smith), 1971.

Grant, A. J. *et al.*, *An Introduction to the Study of International Relations*, London: Macmillan, 1916.

Gray, J., *The Two Faces of Liberalism*, Cambridge: Polity, 2000.

Gray, C., 'After the Ceasefire: Iraq, The Security Council and the Use of Force' (1999) 65 *British Yearbook of International Law* 135.

Greenwood, C., 'NATO Intervention in Kosovo' (Memorandum submitted to the Foreign Affairs Committee of the House of Commons) (2000) 49 *International and Comparative Law Quarterly* 926.

Greig, D., *International Law* (2nd edn), 1976.

'Self-Defence and the Security Council: What Does Article 51 Require?' (1991) 40 *International and Comparative Law Quarterly* 366.

Grotius, H., *De Jure Praedae Commentarius* (1605), *The Classics of International Law* (ed. J. B. Scott), Oxford: Clarendon, 1950.

Halberstam, M., 'The Copenhagen Document: Intervention in Support of Democracy' (1993) 34:1 *Harvard Journal of International Law* 163.

Hall, W. E., *International Law* (1st edn), Oxford: Clarendon, 1880.

International Law (6th edn), Oxford: Clarendon, 1909.

A Treatise on International Law (8th edn), 1924.

Halleck, G., *International Law*, New York: D. Van Nostrand, 1861.

Halperin, M. H., 'Guaranteeing Democracy' (1993) 91 *Foreign Policy* 105.

Hannum, H., 'Rethinking Self-Determination' (1993) 34:1 *Virginia Journal of International Law* 1.

Hardt, M. and Negri, A., *Empire*, Cambridge, MA: Harvard University Press, 2000.

Harris, D. J., *Cases and Materials on International Law* (4th edn), London: Sweet & Maxwell, 1991.

Hart, H. L. A., *The Concept of Law* (1st edn), Oxford: Clarendon, 1961.

The Concept of Law (2nd edn), Oxford: Clarendon, 1994.

Hartz, L., *The Liberal Tradition in America*, New York: Harcourt, Brace, 1955.

Hathaway, J., 'America: Defender of Democratic Legitimacy?' (2000) 11:1 *European Journal of International Law* 121.

Hayek, F., *The Constitution of Liberty*, London: Routledge and Kegan Paul, 1960.

Hegel, G. W. F., *Philosophy of Right*, Oxford: Clarendon, 1952.

Philosophy of Right (ed. S. W. Dyde), London: G. Bell & Sons, 1896.

Held, D., *Democracy and the Global Order*, Cambridge: Polity Press, 1995.

Henkin, L., Pugh, R. and Schachter, O., *International Law: Cases and Materials* (4th edn), St Paul, MN: West, 1987.

Herrera, R., 'The Evolution of Equality of States in the Inter-American System' (1946) 60:1 *Political Science Quarterly* 90.

Hershey, A., *The Essentials of International Public Law*, New York: Macmillan, 1930.

Hertslet, E., *The Map of Europe by Treaty: Showing the Various Political and Territorial Changes Which have Taken Place Since the General Peace of 1814*, London: Butterworths, 1875–91.

Hicks, F. C., *The New World Order, International Organization, International Law, International Cooperation*, New York: Doubleday, 1920.

Higgins, A. P., *The Hague Peace Conferences*, Cambridge: Cambridge University Press, 1909.

Studies in International Law and Relations, Cambridge: Cambridge University Press, 1928.

Higgins, R., *Problems and Process: International Law and How We Use It*, Oxford: Clarendon Press, 1994.

The Development of International Law through the Political Organs of the United Nations, New York: Oxford University Press, 1963.

'International Law, Rhodesia and the U.N.' (1967) 23:3 *The World Today* 98.

'The United Nations and Law-Making: the Political Organs' (1970) 64 *Proceedings of the American Society of International Law* 37.

Hillgruber, C., 'The Admission of States to the International Community' (1999) 19:3 *European Journal of International Law* 491.

Hipold, P., 'Humanitarian Intervention: Is There a Need for a Legal Reappraisal?' (2001) 12:3 *European Journal of International Law* 437.

Hirsch, M., 'The Fall Guy, Washington's Self-Defeating Assault on the United Nations' (November/December 1999) *Foreign Affairs* 4.

Hirst, P., 'The Global Economy – Myths and Realities' (1997) 73:3 *International Affairs*.

Hobbes, T., *De cive*, Oxford: Clarendon Press, 1983.

Hobsbawm, E. J., *The Age of Revolution: Europe 1789–1848*, London: Weidenfeld and Nicholson, 1962.

Hoffman, S., 'Thoughts on the UN at 50' (1995) 6:3 *European Journal of International Law* 317.

Holbraad, C., *The Concert of Europe*, Harlow: Longman, 1970.
  Middle Powers in International Politics, London: Macmillan Press, 1984.
  Superpowers and International Conflict, Basingstoke: Macmillan, 1979.
  Superpowers and World Order, Canberra: Australian National University Press, 1971.

Hull, W., *The Two Hague Conferences and their Contribution to International Law*, Boston: 1908.

Huntingdon, S., *The Clash of Civilisations and the Remaking of World Order*, New York: Simon and Schuster, 1997.

Hurrell, A. and Woods, N., *Inequality, Globalization and World Politics*, Oxford University Press, 1999.

Hurst, C., 'The Nature of International Law and the Reason it is Binding on States' (1944) 30 *Transactions*.

Ignatieff, M., *Virtual War*, London: Vintage, 2001.

Jackson, R. H., *Quasi-States: Sovereignty, International Relations, and the Third World*, Cambridge University Press, 1993.
  The Global Covenant, Oxford University Press, 1999.

Jackson, V. and Tushnet, M., *Comparative Constitutional Law*, New York: Foundation Press, 1999.

Jalalzai, M. K., *Taliban and the Great Game in Afghanistan*, Lahore: Vanguard, 1999.

James, A., *Sovereign Statehood: The Basis of International Society*, London: Allen and Unwin, 1986.

Janis, M., *International Courts for the 21st Century*, Boston and Dordrecht: Martinus Nijhoff, 1999.

Jenks, W., 'The Scope of International Law' (1954) 31 *British Yearbook of International Law* 1.

Jessup, P., *A Modern Law of Nations: An Introduction*, New York: Macmillan, 1948.

Jorgenson, N., *The International Criminal Responsibility of States*, Oxford University Press, 2000.

Kant, I., *Perpetual Peace, and Other Essays on Politics, History and Morals* (trans. T. Murphy), Indianapolis: Hackett Publishing Company, 1983.

Kant, I., *To Perpetual Peace: A Philosophical Sketch* [1795] in *Kant: Political Writings* (ed. H. Reiss), Cambridge University Press, 1970.

Keal, P., *Unspoken Rules and Superpower Dominance*, London: Macmillan, 1983.

Kelsen, H., 'The Principle of Sovereign Equality of States as a Basis for International Organisation' (1944) 53 *Yale Law Journal* 207.
  The Law of the United Nations: A Critical Analysis of its Fundamental Problems, London: Stevens, 1951.
  Principles of International Law (1952).

Kennan, G., *American Diplomacy 1900–1950*, University of Chicago, 1951.
  Memoirs 1925–1950, Random House USA Inc., 1988.

Kennedy, D., 'A New Stream of International Law Scholarship' (1988) 7:10 *Wisconsin International Law Journal* 1.

'A New World Order: Yesterday, Today and Tomorrow' (1994) 4 *Transnational Law and Contemporary Problems* 329.

'Theses about International Law Discourse' (1980) 23 *German Yearbook of International Law* 353.

Kennedy, P., *The Rise and Fall of the Great Powers: Economic Change and Military Conflict from 1500–2000*, London: Fontana, 1989.

Kenny, M., 'Engaging Gramsci: International Relations Theory and the New Gramscians' (1983) 24:1 *Review of International Studies* 3.

Kingsbury, B., 'Sovereignty and Inequality' (1998) 9:4 *European Journal of International Law* 599.

Kirchheimer, O., *Political Justice: The Use of Legal Procedure for Political Ends*, Princeton University Press, 1961.

Kissinger, H., *Diplomacy*, New York: Simon and Schuster, 1995.

Klein, P. and Sands, P., *Bowett's The Law of International Institutions*, London: Sweet & Maxwell, 2001.

Klein, R., *Sovereign Equality Among States: The History of an Idea*, University of Toronto Press, 1974.

Klotz, A. and Crawford, N., *How Sanctions Work: Lessons from South Africa*, Cambridge University Press, 1999.

Knop, K., 'Feminist Re/Statements' (1993) 3:2 *Transnational Law and Contemporary Problems* 293.

Koh, H., 'Transnational Legal Process' (1996) 75:1 *Nebraska Law Review* 181.

'Why Do Nations Obey International Law?' (1995) 106 *Yale Law Journal* 2599.

Knutsen, T., *A History of International Relations Theory*, Manchester University Press, 1992.

Kooijmans, P., *The Doctrine of the Legal Equality of States*, Leiden: A. W. Sythoff, 1964.

Koskenniemi, M., *From Apology to Utopia: The Structure of International Legal Argument*, Helsinki: Finnish Lawyers Publishing Company, 1989.

The Gentle Civiliser of Nations: The Rise and Fall of International Law 1870–1960, Cambridge University Press, 2001.

'The Future of Statehood' (1991) 32:2 *Harvard International Law Journal* 397.

'The Normative Force of Habit: International Custom and Social Theory' (1990) 1 *Finnish Yearbook of International Law* 77.

'The Politics of International Law' (1990) 1:1/2 *European Journal of International Law* 1.

(ed.), *Sources of International Law*, Aldershot: Ashgate, 2000.

Krasner, S., *Sovereignty: Organised Hypocrisy*, Princeton University Press, 1999.

Kunz, J., 'Pluralism of Legal and Value Systems of the World' (1955) 49 *American Journal of International Law* 370.

Lacey, N., 'Legislation Against Sex Discrimination: Questions from a Feminist Perspective' (1987) 14 *Journal of Law and Society* 413.

'Punishment and the Liberal World' (1987) 11 *Australian Journal of Legal Philosophy* 70.

Lall, K. B., 'Economic Inequality and International Law' (1974) 14 *Indian Journal of International Law* 7.

Lande, A., 'Revindication of the Principle of Legal Equality of States 1871–1914' (1947) 62 *Political Science Quarterly* 401.

Lauterpacht, H., 'The Grotian Tradition in International Law' (1946) 23 *British Yearbook of International Law* 53.

Lawrence, T. J., *Documents Illustrative of International Law*, Boston: D. C. Heath, 1914.

Essays on Some Disputed Questions of International Law, Cambridge: Deighton Bell, 1884.

International Problems and the Hague Conferences, London: J. M. Dent, 1908.

Principles of International Law (3rd edn), Boston: Heath, 1905.

Principles of International Law (4th edn), Boston: Heath, 1910.

Lenin, V., *Imperialism, The Highest Stage of Capitalism*, Moscow: Progress Publishers, 1883.

Levi, W., *Law and Politics in the International Society*, Beverley Hills: Sage Publications, 1976.

Locke, J., *Two Treatises of Government*, London: Dent & Son., 1924 (Everyman, 1990, reprint).

Lorimer, J., *Institutes of International Law: A Treatise of the Jural Relations of Separate Political Communities*, Edinburgh: Blackwood, 1883.

Lowe, V., 'Legal Issues Arising in the Kosovo Crisis' (2000) 49 *International and Comparative Law Quarterly* 934.

Lowe, V. and Warbrick, C., *The United Nations and the Principles of International Law: Essays in Honour of Michael Akehurst*, London: Routledge, 1994.

MacDonald, R. St. J., 'Fundamental Norms in Contemporary International Law' (1987) 25 *Canadian Yearbook of International Law* 115.

Mackinnon, C., *Towards a Feminist Theory of the State*, Cambridge, MA: Harvard University Press, 1989.

Malanczuk, P., *Akehurst's Modern Introduction to International Law* (8th edn), London and New York: Routledge, 2001.

Manning, Wm. Oke., *Commentaries on the Law of Nations*, London: S. Sweet, 1839.

Marek, 'Criminalising State Responsibility' (1978–9) 14 *Rev. Belge Droit Int. L.* 460.

Marks, S., 'The End of History? Reflections on Some International Legal Theses' (1998) 8:3 *European Journal of International Law* 449.

The Riddle of all Constitutions, Oxford University Press, 2000.

McIntyre, E., 'Weighted Voting in International Organizations' (1954) 8 *International Organization* 484.

McNair, Lord, 'Equality in International Law' (1927) 26 *Michigan Law Review* 13.

Melvern, L., 'Dispatching Lumumba' (2001) 11 *New Left Review* 147.

Mendelson, M., 'Diminutive States in the United Nations' (1972) 21 *International and Comparative Law Quarterly* 609.

Metternich, C., *Memoirs*, New York: Harper, 1881.

Metzl, J. F. and Zakaria, F., 'Information Intervention; When Switching Channels Isn't Enough: The Rise of Illiberal Democracy' (1997) 76 *Foreign Affairs* 22.

Miller, D., *The Drafting of the Covenant*, New York: Putnam's, 1928.

Moore, J. B., *A Digest of International Law*, vol. ii, Washington: Government Printing Office, 1996.

Moorhouse, F., *Dark Palace*, Sydney: Vintage, 2001.

Morgenthau, H., *Ambassador Morgenthau's Story*, New York: Doubleday and Page, 1918.

Mowat, F., *A History of European Diplomacy 1815–1914*, New York: Longmans, 1922.

Nicholas, H. G., *The United Nations* (2nd edn), Oxford University Press, 1962.

Nicolson, H., *The Congress of Vienna*, San Diego: Harcourt Publishers, 1974.

Ninic, D., *The Problem of Sovereignty in the Charter and Practice of the United Nations*, The Hague: M. Nijhoff, 1970.

Northrop, F. S. C., *Ideological Differences and World Order*, New Haven: Yale University Press, 1949.

The Taming of Nations, New York: Macmillan, 1952.

'Contemporary Jurisprudence and International Law' (1956) 61 *Yale Law Journal* 636.

Note. (1905) 18 *Harvard Law Review* 274.

Nozick, R., *Anarchy, State and Utopia*, Oxford: Blackwell, 1974.

Nussbaum, A., *A Concise History of the Law of Nations* (2nd edn), New York: Macmillan, 1962.

Nys, E., *Etudes de droit international et de droit politique*, Brussels, 1896–1901.

Olney, R., 'The Development of International Law' (1907) 1 *American Journal of International Law* 419.

Onuf, N. G., *Law-Making in the Global Community*, Durham, NC: Carolina Academic Press, 1982.

Oppenheim, L., *Die Zukunft des Volkerrechts*, Leipzig, 1911.

The Future of International Law, Carnegie Endowment for International Peace, Pamphlet No. 39, 1920.

International Law (3rd edn), (ed. R. Roxburgh), London: Longmans, 1920.

International Law: A Treatise (7th edn), (ed. H. Lauterpacht), London: Longmans, 1948.

Orford, A., 'Muscular Humanitarianism: Reading the Narratives of the New Interventionism' (1999) 10:4 *European Journal of International Law* 679.

'A Radical Agenda for Collective Security Reform' (1995) *Proceedings of the Australian and New Zealand Society of International Law, Third Annual Meeting* 71.

Ott, D., *Public International Law in the Modern World*, London: Pitman, 1987.

Palmer, A., *Metternich, Councillor of Europe*, London: Weidenfeld and Nicolson, 1972.

Pearce Higgins, A., *The Hague Peace Conferences*, Cambridge University Press, 1909.

Pellet, A., 'Can a State Commit a Crime? Definitely, Yes!' (1999) 10:2 *European Journal of International Law* 433.

'The Opinions of the Badinter Arbitration Committee: A Second Breath for the Self-Determination of Peoples'; Alain Pellet, Appendix: Opinions No. 1, 2 and 3 of the Arbitration Committee of the International Conference on Yugoslavia (1993) 4 *European Journal of International Law* 178.

Peterson, G., 'The Equality of States as Dogma and Reality II. Political Inequality at the Congress of Vienna' (1945) 60 *Political Science Quarterly* 532.

Phillimore, R., *Commentaries on International Law*, Philadelphia: T. & J. Johnson, 1854.

Commentaries (3rd edn), London: Butterworths, 1879.

Phillips, W. A., *The Confederation of Europe: A Study of the European Alliance, 1813–1823, as an Experiment in the International Organization of Peace*, London and New York: Longmans Green and Co., 1920.

Picco, G., 'The UN and the Use of Force: Leave the Secretary General Out of It' (1994) 73 *Foreign Affairs* 14.

Politis, N., *The New Aspects of International Law*, Lectures Delivered at Columbia University, July 1926.

Pomerance, M., 'Self-Determination Today: The Metamorphosis of an Ideal' (1984) 19 *Israel Law Review* 310.

Potter, P., *Introduction to the Study of International Organisations*, New York: Century, 1922.

Pufendorf, S., *Two Books of the Elements of Jurisprudence*, Oxford: Carnegie Foundation, 1922.

Raman, K. V., *Introduction, Dispute Settlement Through the United Nations*, New York: Oceans Publications with UNITAR, 1977.

Ranke, L., *The Great Powers*, in *The Formative Years* (ed. T. H. von Laue), Princeton University Press, 1950.

Rawls, J., 'Law of Peoples' in S. Shute and S. Hurley (eds.), *On Human Rights*, New York: Basic Books, 1993.

A Theory of Justice, Cambridge, MA: Harvard University Press, 1971.

Collected Works (ed. S. Freeman), Cambridge, MA: Harvard University Press, 1999.

The Law of Peoples, Cambridge, MA: Harvard University Press, 1999.

Political Liberalism, New York: Columbia University Press, 1993.

Reinsch, P., *Colonial Government: An Introduction to the Study of Colonial Institutions*, London: Macmillan, 1911.

Reisman, W. M., 'Coercion and Self-Determination: Construing Charter Article 2(4)' (1984) 78 *American Journal of International Law* 642.

'Sovereignty and Human Rights in Contemporary International Law' (1990) 84 *American Journal of International Law* 866.

'Unilateral Action and the Transformations of the World Constitutive Process: The Special Problem of Humanitarian Intervention' (2000) 11:1 *European Journal of International Law* 3.

Reus-Smit, C., *The Moral Purpose of the State: Culture, Social Identity, and Institutional Rationality in International Relations*, Princeton University Press, 1999.

Richardson, J., 'Contending Liberalisms: Past and Present' (1997) 3:1 *European Journal of International Relations* 5.

Risse, T., Roppe, S. and Sikkink, K., *The Power of Human Rights*, Cambridge University Press, 1999.

Roberts, A., 'NATO's "Humanitarian War" over Kosovo' 1999 *Survival* (Autumn).

Roberts, A. and Kingsbury, B., *Presiding Over a Divided World: Changing UN Roles, 1945–1993*, Oxford: Clarendon, 1994.

Rodley, N., 'Breaking the Cycle of Impunity for Gross Violations of Human Rights: The Pinochet Case in Perspective' (2000) 69:1 *Nordic Journal of International Law* 11.

Rosenberg, J., *The Empire of Civil Society*, London: Verso, 1994.

Rosenstock, R., 'An International Criminal Responsibility of States?', In ILC, *International Law on the Eve of the Twenty-First Century – Views from the International Law Commission* (1997), 272.

Ross, A., *A Textbook on International Law*, London: Longmans, 1947.

Rousseau, J.-J., 'A Discourse on the Origin of Inequality' in *The Social Contract and Discourses*, London: Everyman, 1993.

Russell, R., *A History of the United Nations Charter: The Role of the United States 1940–1945*, Washington, DC: Brookings Institution, 1958.

Schabas, W., *Introduction to the International Criminal Court*, Oxford University Press, 2001.

Schachter, O., *International Law in Theory and Practice*, Dordrecht and Boston: Martinus Nijhoff, 1991.

Schama, S., *Citizens: A Chronicle of the French Revolution*, London: Viking, 1989.

Schelling, T., *Causes and Consequences: Perspectives of an Errant Economist*, Cambridge, MA: Harvard University Press, 1984.

Schieder, S., 'Pragmatism as a Path towards a Discursive and Open Theory of International Law' (2000) 11 *European Journal of International Law* 663.

Schmitt, C., *The Concept of the Political* (trans. G. Schwab), Chicago University Press, 1996.

Schreuer, C., 'The Waning of the Sovereign State: Towards a New Paradigm for International Law?' (1993) 4:4 *European Journal of International Law* 447.

Schucking, W., *The International Union of the Hague Conferences* (trans. Charles Fenwick), Oxford University Press, 1918.

Schwarzenberger, G., *International law and Totalitarian Lawlessness*, London: Cape, 1943.

   The League of Nations and World Order: A Treatise on the Principle of Universality in the Theory and Practice of the League of Nations, London: Constable, 1936.

   Power Politics, London: Cape, 1941.

   'Equality and Discrimination in International Economic Law' 25 *Yearbook of World Affairs* 163.

Scott, J. B. (ed.), *American Addresses at the Second Hague Peace Conference, delivered by Joseph H. Choate, General Horace Porter, James Brown Scott*, Boston; London, For the International School of Peace, Ginn and Company, 1910.

Hague Peace Conferences 1899 and 1907, A Series of Lectures before Johns Hopkins, Baltimore: The Johns Hopkins University Press, 1909.

Proceedings of the Hague Peace Conferences, Conference of 1907, vol. II, New York: Oxford University Press, 1921.

Sellers, M., 'Republican Principles in International Law' (1996) 11:3 *Connecticut Journal of International Law* 403.

Sen, A., *Inequality Reexamined*, Cambridge, MA: Harvard University Press, 1997.

Seymour, C., *The Intimate Papers of Colonel House*, London: Benn, 1926–8.

Shaw, M., *International Law* (4th edn), Cambridge, MA: Grotius, 1997.

Shklar, J., *Legalism: Law, Morals and Political Trials*, Cambridge, MA: Harvard University Press, 1986.

Simma, B., *The Charter of the United Nations: A Commentary*, Oxford University Press, 1994.

'Nato, the UN and the Use of Force: Legal Aspects' (1999) 10 *European Journal of International Law* 1.

Simons, G., *Iraq-Primus Inter Pariahs: A Crisis Chronology, 1997–98*, New York: St Martin's Press, 1999.

Simpson, A. B. W., *Human Rights and the End of Empire, Britain and the Genesis of the European Convention*, Oxford University Press, 2001.

Simpson, G. (ed.) *The Nature of International Law*, Burlington, VT: Ashgate, 2001.

'The Diffusion of Sovereignty' (1996) 32:2 *Stanford Journal of International Law* 255.

'On the Magic Mountain: Teaching Public International Law' (1999) 10:1 *European Journal of International Law* 70.

'The Situation on the International Legal Theory Front: The Power of Rules and the Rule of Power' (2000) 11:2 *European Journal of International Law* 439.

'Two Liberalisms' (2001) 12:3 *European Journal of International Law* 537.

Singer, M. and Wildavsky, A., *The Real World Order: Zones of Peace/Zones of Turmoil*, Chatham House Publishers, 1993.

Slaughter, A.-M., 'International Law in a World of Liberal States' (1995) 6 *European Journal of International Law* 503.

'The Liberal Agenda for Peace: International Relations Theory and the Future of the United Nations' (1994) 4 *Transnational Law and Contemporary Problems* 377.

Smith, B. F. (ed.), *The American Road to Nuremberg*, Stanford: Hoover Institution Press, 1982.

Smith, F. E. (Earl of Birkenhead), *International Law* (4th edn, revised and enlarged by J. Wylie), Boston: Little Brown & Co.; London: J. M. Dent & Sons Ltd, 1911.

(Earl of Birkenhead), *International Law* (5th edn, revised and enlarged by Coleman Phillipson), London and Toronto, J. M. Dent & Sons Ltd, 1911.

Smith, J. C., *The Western Idea of Law*, London: Butterworths, 1983.

Sneghaas, D., 'A Clash of Civilisations – An Idée Fixe' (1998) 35:1 *Journal of Peace Research* 127.

Sohn, L., 'Important Improvements in the Functioning of the Principal Organs of the United Nations That Can Be Made Without Charter Revision' (1991) 91 *American Journal of International Law* 652.

'Weighting of Votes in an International Assembly' (1944) 38 *American Political Science Review* 1192.

Solano, J., 'NATO's Success in Kosovo' (1999) 76:8 *Foreign Affairs* 114–20.

Sousa, N., *The Capitulatory Regime of Turkey*, Baltimore: The Johns Hopkins University Press, 1933.

Starke, J. G., *Introduction to International Law* (9th edn), London: Butterworths, 1984.

Starr, H., *Anarchy, Order and Integration*, Ann Arbor: Michigan University Press, 1997.

Steiner, H., 'Political Participation as a Human Right' (1988) 1 *Harvard Human Rights Yearbook* 77.

Stivatchis, Y., *The Enlargement of International Society: Culture versus Anarchy and Greece's Entry into International Society*, London: Longmans, 1998.

Swain, R., 'A Discussion of the Pinochet Case: Noting the Juxtaposition of International Relations and International Law Perspectives' (2000) 69:1 *Nordic Journal of International Law* 223.

Symposium 'Hans Kelsen' (1998) 9 *European Journal of International Law* 287.

Temperely, H. and Penson, L. (eds.), *Foundations of British Foreign Policy, 1792–1902*, New York: Barnes and Noble, 1966.

Tesón, F., *Humanitarian Intervention: An Enquiry into Law and Morality*, New York: Transnational Publishers, 1988.

A Philosophy of International Law, Boulder, CO: Westview, 1998.

'Collective Humanitarian Intervention' (1996) 17 *Michigan Journal of International Law* 323.

'The Kantian Theory of International Law' (1992) 92:1 *Columbia Law Review* 53.

Theunissen, H., 'Ottoman-Venetian Diplomatics: The *Ahd-names*. The Historical Background and the Development of a Category of Political-Commercial Instruments Together with an Annotated Edition of a Corpus of Relevant Documents' (1998) 1:2 *Electronic Journal of Oriental Studies* 1.

Thornberry, P., *International Law and the Rights of Minorities*, Oxford: Clarendon, 1991.

Thucydides, *The Landmark Thucydides* (ed. R. Strassler), New York: Free Press 1996.

Tiffrerer, O., *Commentary on the Rome Statute*, Baden: Nomos, 1999.

Touval, S., 'Why the UN Fails' (1994) 73 *Foreign Affairs* 44.

Trebilcock, M. and Howse, R., *The Regulation of International Trade*, New York: Routledge, 1999.

Treitschke, H. von, *Politics*, vol. II (trans. A. J. Balfour), London: Constable, 1916.

Tucker, R., *The Inequality of Nations*, New York: Basic Books, 1977.

Twiss, T., *The Law of Nations Considered as Independent Political Communities*, Oxford University Press, 1861.

Vandenberg Jr, A. H. (ed.), *The Private Papers of Senator Vandenberg*, London: Gollancz, 1953.

Vasquez, J., *The Power of Power Politics*, Cambridge University Press, 1998.

Vattel, de E., *Le droit des gens* (trans. C. G. Fenwick), Classics of International Law, Washington, 1916.

Verwey, A., 'Humanitarian Intervention under International Law' (1985) 32 *Netherlands International Law Review* 357.

de Visscher, C., *Theory and Reality in Public International Law* (3rd edn), Princeton University Press, 1968.

Walker, A., *The Science of International Law*, London: C. J. Clay & Sons, 1893.

Walker, R. B. J., *Inside/Outside: International Relations as Political Theory*, Cambridge University Press, 1993.

Wallace, R., *International Law*, London: Sweet & Maxwell, 1986.

Wallerstein, I., *After Liberalism*, New York: New Press, 1995.

Waltz, K., *Man, the State and War: A Theoretical Analysis*, New York: Columbia University Press, 1954.

Watson, A., *The Evolution of International Society*, London: Routledge, 1992.

Watson, J. S., *Theory and Reality in the International Protection of Human Rights*, New York: Transnational Publishers, 1999.

Watson, J., 'A Realistic Jurisprudence' (1980) 30 *Yearbook of World Affairs* 265.

Watts, A., 'The International Rule of Law' (1993) 36 *German Yearbook of International Law* 15.

Weber, C. and Biersteker, T. J., *State Sovereignty as Social Construct*, Cambridge and New York: Cambridge University Press, 1996.

Wedgwood, R., 'NATO's Campaign in Yugoslavia' (1999) 93:4 *American Journal of International Law* 828.
   'Unilateral Action in the UN System' (2000) 11 *European Journal of International Law* 349.

Wehberg, H., *The Problem of an International Court of Justice* (trans. C. G. Fenwick), Oxford: Clarendon, 1918.

Weil, P., 'Towards Relative Normativity in International Law?' (1983) 77:3 *American Journal of International Law* 413.

Weiler, J., Cassese, A. and Spinedi, M., *International Crimes of State: A Critical Analysis of the ILC's Draft Article 19 on State*, Berlin and New York: De Gruyter, 1989.

Wellens, K., *Resolutions and Statements of the United Nations Security Council (1946–1989): A Thematic Guide*, The Hague: Kluwer, 1990.

Wendt, A., *Social Theory of International Politics*, Cambridge and New York: Cambridge University Press, 1999.

Westlake, J., *Chapters on the Principles of International Law*, Cambridge University Press, 1894.

Collected Papers on International Law (ed. L. Oppenheim), Cambridge University Press, 1914.

International Law (1st edn), Cambridge University Press, 1904.

Weston, B., 'The Reagan Administration versus International Law' (1987) 19 *Case Western Journal of International Law* 295

Weston, B., Falk, R. and D'Amato, A., *International Law and World Order*, St. Paul, MN, West Group, 1980.

Wheaton, H., *Elements of International Law* (2nd edn), (ed. W. B. Lawrence), Cambridge University Press, 1883.

Elements of International Law (4th edn), London: Stevens and Sons Limited, 1904.

Elements of International Law (6th edn), (ed. W. B. Lawrence), Boston: Little Brown, 1855.

Elements of International Law (8th edn), London: S. Low and Son, 1866.

Wheeler, N., *Saving Strangers: Humanitarian Intervention in International Society*, Oxford University Press, 2000.

White, N. and Cryer, R., 'Unilateral Enforcement of Resolution 678: A Threat too far?' (1999) 29 *California Western International Law Journal* 243.

Wight, M., *British Colonial Constitutions 1947*, Oxford: Clarendon, 1952.

International Theory: The Three Traditions, Leicester University Press, 1991.

Systems of States, Leicester University Press (in association with the London School of Economics and Political Science), 1977.

'An Anatomy of International Thought' (1987) 13 *Review of International Studies* 221.

Wilde, R., 'From Danzig to East Timor and Beyond: The Role of International Territorial Administration' (2001) 95:3 *American Journal of International Law* 583.

Wildman, R., *Institutes of International Law*, London: W. Benning, 1849.

Wilson, G. G., *Handbook on International Law*, St Paul, MN, 1910.

Wolff, C., *Jus Gentium methodo scientifica pertractatum*, Oxford: Clarendon, 1749.

Woolsey, T., *Introduction to the Study of International Law* (5th edn), London: Sampson Low, Marston, Searle and Rivington, 1879.

Introduction to the Study of International Law, Boston and Cambridge: J. Munroe & Co, 1860.

Yasuaki, O. (ed.), *A Normative Approach to War*, Oxford: Clarendon; New York: Oxford University Press, 1993.

Zamora, S., 'Voting in International Economic Organisations' (1980) 74 *American Journal of International Law* 566.

Zappala, S., 'Do Heads of State in Office Enjoy Immunity from Jurisdiction for International Crimes? The Ghadaffi case before the French Cour de Cassation' (2001) 12:3 *European Journal of International Law* 595.

Zimmern, A., *The League of Nations 1918–1935*, London: Macmillan, 1939.

Zolo, D., *Cosmopolis: Prospects for World Government*, Cambridge: Polity Press, 1997.

Index

CAMBRIDGE STUDIES IN INTERNATIONAL AND COMPARATIVE LAW